Economy in Changing Society

Economy in Changing Society: Consumptions, Markets, Organizations and Social Policies

Edited by

Maria Nawojczyk

CAMBRIDGE SCHOLARS PUBLISHING

Economy in Changing Society:
Consumptions, Markets, Organizations and Social Policies,
Edited by Maria Nawojczyk

This book first published 2011

Cambridge Scholars Publishing

12 Back Chapman Street, Newcastle upon Tyne, NE6 2XX, UK

British Library Cataloguing in Publication Data
A catalogue record for this book is available from the British Library

ISBN (10): 1-4438-2699-5, ISBN (13): 978-1-4438-2699-0

TABLE OF CONTENTS

INTRODUCTION: ECONOMY IN CHANGING SOCIETY

MARIA NAWOJCZYK[1]

Economic arrangements are on one hand embedded in social contexts, and on the other instituted through formal and informal rules, conventions of conduct and exchange, systems of politics and regulations. However, the stress on both dimensions has changed in economic sociology over time. In Old Economic Sociology, embeddedness implies that economy is an instituted process, and the level of embeddedness changes through the processes of marketization of the economy, i.e. modernization (Polanyi 1992). On the other hand, according to New Economic Sociology, economy is embedded in ongoing concrete social networks, and the level of embeddedness changes little from one form of society to another (Granovetter 1985). Nevertheless, economic processes are increasingly international in character. Therefore, it is particularly important to focus on both their embedded and instituted nature.

Three interrelated processes are crucial in setting the frame of analysis for this book: globalisation, development of post-industrial societies, and transformation of European post-socialist countries. Within this framework the main issues will be as follows: (1) Economies in transition: reliable patterns, imitation, local adaptation, cultural embeddedness; (2) Multiplicity of markets: commodification of life, new markets in old societies; (3) Economic behavior: households, micro-enterprises, local and global influences; (4) Contemporary polities i.e. states, the European Union and global corporations. The stress will be placed on actors, relations and institutions as the driving forces of the above described processes.

The concept of economic globalisation refers, in general terms, to the problem of how the exchange of goods, information, labor, money and images comes to operate on an increasingly international scale. The sociological debate over globalisation asks the questions: what these shifts entail for the organization of social and political power, how embedded

[1] Faculty of Humanities, AGH University of Science and Technology, Krakow.

they are in local contexts, and whether these processes can be controlled or resisted (Tonkiss 2006, X). From this perspective corporations are important actors in global economy—because they operate above the level of nation state, a significant part of decision making competences are removed from the rules of public inspection and justification, thus become disintegrated from the local political systems and are not subject to principles of parliamentary democracy anymore (Beck 1997). Therefore, Urlich Beck considers consumer votes as nothing less than a tool of power (1997). Since companies are in fact obliged to cooperate with consumer power in organized consumer behavior, a social movement (which can become the counterpoint of the global capital) constantly evades social responsibility, and social corporate responsibility becomes a new research field within the analysis of globalization processes. In some analyses the corporations can be considered as citizens; citizens that are organizational in nature and embodied by their organizational entity. Therefore, the notion that in a globalized world economic actors operate in a plurality of spaces economically, juristically, ecologically, culturally is becoming ever more relevant for corporations, which are seen as crucial actors in global governance frameworks (Keohane 2008; Zadek 2008).

Corporations position themselves in the broader social networks as citizens with rights and duties in the civic, social and political domain as well as regarding economic, ecological and cultural issues in order to ensure both the legality and legitimacy of their business practices (Leisinger 2007). This brings us back to the relationship between market economy and morality which has occupied social scientists since the days of Adam Smith and Emile Durkheim. However, because the relationship of morality and the market have never been a central topic for New Economic Sociology, the moral economy is still quite a vague concept that on the one hand is comprised of concrete norms and values like justice, responsibility and equality but on the other extends to "conceptions of the good" (Sayer 2000, see "Can the Market be Moral?" 2004). On the other hand we can observe that the modern market is shifting from a mainly economic space to an area of political and moral action, a tool of regulation and social participation.New social movements, internet activism and international networks all offer new possibilities for involvement (Inglehart 1997, Norris 2002). These are the features of the process of becoming a post-industrial society. I am not going to discuss the notion of post-industrial society in detail (see e.g. Bell 1999) or the criticisms of this concept (see e.g. Theobald 1994). I would like, however, to highlight the issues connected with social transition from industrial to post-industrial society which will be covered by the chapters of this book.

Moving away from classical analysis of change to a new type of society based on the transition from manufacturing to services, and the intensification of knowledge across the spheres of work, research and innovation (Bell 1999) toward the more recent ideas regarding the role of symbolic goods in contemporary economies, I would like to point to the notion of reflexivity as a reference point to many fruitful analyses (Lash and Urry 1994). According to Scott Lash and John Urry, we are facing the process of reflexive accumulation in economic life (1994, 5). This process is reflected in economic practices in three dimensions: the function of reflexive knowledge in production; reflexive modes of consumption; and the role of non-material goods. In the new type of society, consumption moved away from the satisfaction of specific needs. Production is no longer aimed at manufacturing goods but at creating signs and images. Instead of objects, consumers were supplied with ideas, images and symbols.

Reflexive consumption is based upon customized consumer patterns, niche marketing and product diversity. Aesthetic reflexivity is particularly important in this context, as symbolic or cultural codes determine consumer choices. As consumption logic dominates over production logic, symbolic goods are placed in the center of economic activity as, for example, trademark, which accumulated additional functions from sign of authorship to proper quality to product and social distinctions. New social phenomena emerged considering non-material goods piracy and counterfeiting. Piracy breaks copyrights while counterfeiting infringes registered trademark owners' rights. Copyrights are the rights given to authors of creative works, such as movies, music, software and written works. Trademarks are used by producers to distinguish their products from competing products. Nowadays not only entrepreneurs but also whole nations (particularly economies in transition) are involved in the production and realization of counterfeiting.

The sociology of consumption previously criticised consumption on the grounds of over consumption or conspicuous consumption (Bauman 2004), but today consumption is an integral part of modern life. Links between consumption choices and the formation of individual identities are intensified. Consumption becomes a matter of ethical choices—ethical consumption is a manifest of reflexive consumption. As a social movement, ethical consumerism can also effect political culture and play an important role in public policy aimed at sustainable development. The rationality of consumption is seen to be inherent in the pattern of interaction that takes place within and between networks. Therefore, the rationality of consumption must be broadened by formulating such interaction more substantively, by drawing for example on Max Weber's (1978) notion of substantive rationality or what Karl Polanyi (1992) called the substantive meaning of the economic.

One of the most influential syntheses of a theoretical program combined with the range of concrete studies of consumption practices came from Pierre Bourdieu. He introduced the ideas of cultural and social capital into the analysis of consumption (Bourdieu 1984). His concept of habitus links institutions with culture because culture is that particular aspect of reality which defines the image of the world and the relations of particular actors towards its substantive elements. Thus, his ideas can be employed to the analysis of reflexive consumption as well as reflexive production. Bourdieu argues that the field of cultural production is shaped by two kinds of logic: the logic of the market (characteristic for the field of economic power) and the "logic of art for art's sake" (characteristic for some types of art). Individuals who follow the logic of market aim at financial rewards—high levels of financial capital, which are the results of high sales, are a measure of success. Those for whom the principle of "art for art's sake" is more important tend to look for symbolic capital recognition (e.g. from critics, other artists) and "brand loyalty" (Bourdieu 2005).

Reflexive production, in the conception of Lash and Urry, operates on two levels: aesthetic reflexivity which refers to the processing of symbolic content (here lies the common ground with Bourdieu's ideas) and cognitive reflexivity which refers to the processing of information (1994). Cognitive reflexivity is central to the technical organization of production and the regulation of work. Such cognitive labor is undertaken by both human and non-human actors, reproduced through research, design and technical expertise, and programmed into advanced manufacturing technologies (Tonkiss 2006, 113). Because of this, the ideas of reflexive work first refer to fairly advanced levels of technology and expertise but also influence more ordinary workplace settings, and the notion of life-long learning is therefore underlined in the concept of the post-industrial society. Social support for life-long learning and better health by improved means of working conditions, and the combating of popular negative stereotypes about different minority and marginalized groups of workers, should also help to promote labor force participation. However, these factors depend also on general economic development and on other issues such as: (1) cultural norms; (2) prejudices; (3) expectations; (4) individual factors like the meaning of work and leisure; (5) family responsibilities; (6) life choices within couples living together; (7) available income. These factors are particularly important for economies in transition.

Post-socialist countries have joined capitalist countries at a time when socio-economic changes have led to the formation of a flexible, global and competitive job market, a time often referred to as the "disorganised phase of capitalism" (Lash and Urry 1994). According to common post-socialist theories (Dahrendorf 1991, Nee 1989), transition can be described as a process that brings changes of institutions, economics and political systems from the socialist stage to the democratic. Following this approach, everyday life, attitudes and behavior should be regarded as a consequence of institutional transitional reforms. The clash between rapid changes in political and economic systems and changes of informal social institutions has occurred. This took place because the fall of socialism in 1989–1990 led to the end of the Central Eastern European communist economies and to the emergence of transition economies where these rapid economic institutional changes occurred.

However, post-socialist transition does not proceed in a vacuum, consisting of the replacement of one reality with another. It is a highly complex process that reformulates existing structures and creates new ones (King and Szelenyi 2005). Surprisingly, few new articles and chapters appearing within the field of economic sociology deal with the empirical process of the development and the shaping of new market agents within post-socialist conditions (see Brinton and Nee 2001; Granovetter and Swedberg 2001; Nee and Swedberg 2005). Instead, many articles, books and collections assume: (a) that market participants are somehow already 'embedded' in social and market structures, and as such ultimately shaped as market actors; and (b) that we deal with "mature entrepreneurs" who know all the (formal and informal) rules of market competition. Here the ideas of Bourdieu, who wrote: "the appearance of a new, effective agent modifies the structure of the field. Similarly adoption of a new technology or the acquisition of a greater market share modifies the relative positions and field of all species of capital held by the other firms" (Bourdieu 2005, 80), are a very good point of reference.

In this collection we present a large number of chapters devoted to actors of the transition in Central and Eastern Europe and we would like to point out to what extent our analyses can draw from the concepts present in economic sociology, as well as what we can add to them on the basis of our research findings. Taking into account the above presented conceptual approach to economy in changing society, the book has been divided into four parts, dealing respectively with consumption, markets, organizations, and social policies.

Part One, "Toward postmodern consumption?", is devoted to the issues which in particular highlight the relationship between economic behavior and cultural norms. One of these issues, which attracts growing scholarly interest, is ethical consumption. Sebastian Koos, in Chapter One, understands it as the buying or not buying of goods, for ethical, political or environmental reasons. He analyzes this kind of consumption from the perspective of moral economy. After presenting hypotheses on individual and national differences in ethical consumer behaviour he introduces the empirical strategy and tests hypotheses for a cross section of 19 European countries, using multilevel analysis. On the individual level he finds that especially education and values related to environmental care provide important explanations for ethical buying or boycotting behaviour. The micro results mostly confirm the hypotheses, but reveal some additional interesting phenomena. First, education seems to have a stronger influence than class on the probability to consume ethically. The value dimensions reveal a strong environmental frame in ethical consumption. Finally, while boycotting is clearly connected to distrust in political institutions, this is not the case for ethical buying. Nevertheless, both ethical buying and boycotting are positively linked to political interests. Differences in ethical consumption at the national level of can, to a large degree, be explained by the affluence of respective countries. Overall, it seems to be common to buy products for ethical, political or environmental reasons in the Scandinavian countries and Switzerland, whereas in Southern and Eastern Europe only a relatively small number of people report such an action. In Chapter Two, Emese Gulyas also addresses the problem of ethical consumption, but from the perspective of political consumption, as a form of social governance, examining its relevance as a way of public participation. She tries to find an answer to the question of whether the spread of ethical consumption should be imagined at the demise of classical political institutions, or as complementary to them. Ethical consumers take part in solving social problems by using market and consumer power as social adjustment mechanisms. The author concentrates on the local case of political consumption in Hungary. According to Gulyas, ethical consumers are more likely to assign importance to parliamentary election participation; nevertheless they are less likely to consider it as an efficient means for expressing opinions and representing interests. Her study is primarily based on data describing Hungarian political participatory culture, as well as an attitude survey of a representative sample. In choosing products, besides the price–value balance, the majority of the population would consider patriotism, environmental protection, fair employment, and consumer information to be important. In Hungary, over the past 15 years, willingness to join boycotts has slowly increased to 15–17% of the population.

The following two chapters in the first part deal with problems well described in the literature but bring them into a new cultural context. In Chapter Three, Masudur Rahman returns to the discussion about culturally embedded consumption, based on his study in Bangladesh. He pointed out that marginalists, with a nonembedded approach to the analysis of consumption, assume that individuals maximize economic utility with preferences that are independent of other people, social values, and of time. They maintain that the same concept of rationality applies to all societies, in temporal and spatial settings. They cannot capture a large number of choices and preferences that greatly depend on interaction with others, and that consumption goals include non-economic utility and future goals. Rahman poses a question of how social networks set goals of consumption, both at present and in the future. He focuses on various elite sub-groups in Bangladesh. Using data derived from observation and oral testimony, the author relates various aspects of luxury consumption to network norms. His findings suggest that consumption is an interactive process, expressed in individual efforts to meet network obligations. In the wider social arena, through repeated interaction, the objective structures of elite culture are developed in the form of probabilities of social domination through creation of identity, achievement of status, recognition, and competition for access to resources and power. A complex mix of network norms and cultural values sets consumption goals as immediate and ultimate. The rationality of such consumption behaviour goes beyond formal rationality in economics. It must be understood in terms of substantive rationality. In Chapter Four, Zoya Kotelnikova focuses on producers' dependency of sign-production on the Russian market. She stresses that the product no longer indicates workmanship and skills—the brand, trademark, rather than the physical product is important. Trademark has become a focus for social community formation. She applies the concept "counterfeiting" and lists some reasons for its market expansion. According to her, market for fakes falls into two categories. The first implies that consumers, unknowingly, buy counterfeited goods; they are deceived with product originality. The second implies that consumers know that they are buying counterfeited goods—the consumer is a collaborator of counterfeiters. Such counterfeited goods include: unauthorized introduction of original products into the commercial turnover; pirated goods; fashion goods; imitations; fakes of high quality; fakes which are not dangerous to consumers' health. Kotelnikova presents research findings on the counterfeited goods problem in Russia and indicates how owners of registered trademarks support the distribution of counterfeited goods. She shows that Russia is a country of counterfeit consumption but not production—in Russia social attitudes to intellectual property rights protection have changed and people have begun to understand its significance and importance. However, she points out that removal of counterfeiting from the Russian markets directly depends on its victims and how active the owners of registered trademarks are going to be in protection of their intellectual property rights.

In Part Two, "Dynamics of markets," a picture of individual and collective actors of economies in transition has been drawn. Barbara Gąciarz and Włodzimierz Pańków, in Chapter Five, discuss a sequence of actions and processes, which during the last 10 years has led to the current state of the labor market in Poland, characterized by a growing disproportion between supply and demand of a qualified labor force. They address the key problems from an institutional perspective and on a level of national economy. They propose some explanations for this specific situation and pay special attention to its predictable consequences which in the future may cause barriers for further development of the national economy and for the country's general progress of civilization, despite the high inflow of FDI (including those which come from international corporations), and considerable financial means gained from EU funding. The economy in transition in Poland, according to Gąciarz and Pańków, can be divided into new and old. New economy, unlike the old, was and still is a zone in which trade unions do not operate (in many cases due to an intentional counteracts of owners). The greater the share of new enterprises in the whole structure of the Polish economy, the stronger the pressure grows on de-regulation and de-institutionalization of industrial relations. As many studies show, the biggest nationwide trade unions, Solidarity and the OPZZ (The All Poland Alliance of Trade Unions), were "prisoners" of their own traditions. A lack of consistency in trade union activities and their hidden conformism towards political elites contribute to a gradual fall of their societal influence and authority. In Chapter Six, Maria Nawojczyk analyses a new sector of Polish economy, micro-entrepreneurship, from a sociological point of view. Based on her field research among micro and small entrepreneurs in two cities in Poland she draws a picture of emerging entrepreneurial society in a post-socialist country. She also discusses the problem to what extent the models of entrepreneurship, developed in stable capitalistic economies, can be applied to the study of this phenomenon in economies in transition. In Chapter Seven, Drago Cengic argues that the process of making of new market actors in the post-socialist context is very complex, demanding a long time period. The case he presents in this chapter, of Kutjevo winemakers in Croatia, proves that the production and "self-production" of new (mostly small and medium) entrepreneurs is intermingled with the multidimensional behaviour and attitudes of all involved stakeholders from local and central administration, the winemakers themselves to experts and foreign competitors. The following issues are especially elaborated in this chapter: pre-market habitus, entrepreneurial transformation and market behavour; market and its behavior; economic interest and the embeddedness policy within the local community; culture, habitus and the question of mutual cooperation. He concludes with the thesis that the market future of Kutjevo winemakers is mostly dependent on their future economic growth, the quality of their wines and new forms of self-organizing and mutual cooperation.

As the above presented three chapters of this part are concerned mostly with the problem of adjustment to market economy in post-socialist countries, the last analyzes the emergence of completely new actors in economies in transition. Partyk Gałuszka, in Chapter Eight, deals with netlabels—virtual record labels that distribute music primarily through digital audio formats (mainly MP3 or Ogg Vorbis) over the internet. Netlabels are different from traditional record companies, as most of them distribute music for free, often under licenses that encourage works to be shared (e.g. Creative Commons licenses), while artists usually retain copyright. He compares netlabels with regular record labels and do-it-yourself micro-independent record labels, which have been described in the literature. Gałuszka argues that, while some netlabels try to employ some elements of traditional business attitudes of the "regular" record companies, other follow the do-it-yourself ideology and try to operate in non-market ways. His analysis is based on two case studies of Polish netlabels and general discussion of relationship between the net-audio movement, listeners, artists and the music business.

Organizations are independent agents in economy as well as being the embodiment of managers as the most influential group within organizations. Their mutual relationship in structural and cultural contexts is a main thread of Part Three: "Economic organizations in transition." In Chapter Nine, Ingo Stolz makes an assessment of the degree to which corporations have the organizational skills necessary to position themselves as corporate citizens within their societal environment. Therefore, like individual citizens, corporations need the skills that enable them to act in their broader societal environment in a participatory, active and reflective way. These skills also include the capability for nurturing, developing and framing the internal creation, evaluation and verification of corporate citizenship practices. Thus, the processes of the internal creation, evaluation, and verification of citizenship practices seem considerably less developed in comparison to the skills of managing external accountability issues, such as those required by law. On the corporate level, not having these organizational skills could have financial implications, consequences for work performance and effects on organizational sustainability and organizational functioning. On the societal level, he argues that only corporations with the appropriate internal skills show the ability to define their new role within society. In Chapter Ten, Raimo Blom and Harri Melin, based on their studies of Russian managers, verify their hypothesis about social capital, networks and trust in managerial practices. They argue that theoretical concepts, like "hybrid capitalism," "nomenklatura capitalism" or "industrial feudalism" are only partially valid in a description of Russian society and therefore need modification. The authors start by stressing the significance of social capital and trust in the context of managerial practices. This leads them to the questions of informal relations and norms, and also to the significance of old practices and changes in the moral code. As they point out, the main reasons behind these kinds of practices are an insecure environment, the shadow economy and corruption. Trust is a precondition for the new upheaval of Russian manufacturing industries. In their opinion, without a serious "injection" of social capital in the Russian economy, without the restoration of trust between businessmen in social institutions, and the introduction of the Russian Federation into the WTO, the managerial practices will hamper economic development. Beata Chorągwicka and Barbara Janta show in Chapter Eleven to what extent the supranational institutions could influence the organizational outcome. They first focus on the EU Human Capital Funds that became available to new member states upon EU accession. They present the opportunities that Human Capital funds create for Small and Medium sized Enterprises (SMEs) in accession countries ("Eastern Enlargement"), and analyze the real and potential impact of the EU funds on SMEs in Poland. In this way, they present the topic from the wider European perspective and afterwards focus on the Polish case. Next, they explain the role and importance of economic utility estimations in SMEs and then they present the data and equations needed to carry out those estimations and finally apply the presented equations to a case of training program in a Polish SME. However, all calculations can be easily applied to data produced at any enterprise and in any country, so the scope of the analysis in this part of the chapter starts with a national angle and later moves towards a more global perspective.

The two remaining chapters of this part are anthropological studies of cultural embeddedness and very much empirically oriented. The main aim of Jarosław Królewski in Chapter Twelve is to show how Poles fare in the

Scottish labor market, a culture new to them, determining a specific company organization style, as well as to show the specific cultural situation, the certain changes in Polish emigrants' behavior and their attitude to work; and finally to show the basic factors that could be observed when studying national cultures and relations governing their job markets. The analysis is based on 28 in-depth interviews conducted among Polish migrants in Scotland. As a point of reference the author uses Geert Hofstede's four dimensional model of cultural differences on the individual, organizational and national level. The influence of national culture on relations within a company as well as on the entrepreneur's attitudes is analyzed by Maria Stojkow in Chapter Thirteen. In an attempt to reconstruct the way small trade companies function in Damascus, Syria, she concentrates on the analysis of Islamic mentality and presents her research findings from among the small business owners in Damascus since 2005–2007. As an area of special interest, she scrutinizes the tendency of entrepreneurs to display innovative behavior or the lack of it. She also pays attention to such elements as the analysis of classical Arab thought, particularly Islamic, regarding the question of economy and labor.

There are sensitive issues of social policy to which Part Four, "Changing economies and social policies," is devoted. The first issue of retirement policy, a current subject of discussion in the EU, is covered over two chapters. Alberto Veira and Jesus Sanchez follow the trends of early retirement in Chapter Fourteen. From their analysis it is clear that legal systems and established patterns of interaction between social partners, specific to each country, operating at national and company level, are major forces which have a great impact on retirement practices and are currently playing a decisive role in favor of greater divergence. Thus, collective agreements regarding early retirement between workers, governments and firms, do not lead to the same outcomes in each country. The authors mostly focus on Spain but place their findings in the European context. Compared to Scandinavian and English speaking countries, Spain is in a very disadvantageous position, since the percentage of Spanish men and women from 55 to 64 years of age remaining in employment is significantly lower than in those countries. A characteristic feature for Spain is that smaller firms tend to employ higher percentages of older senior workers than larger ones, especially those aged 60 to 64. Opinions, preferences and attitudes towards retirement in Polish society are the subject of Chapter Fifteen, written by Jolanta Perek-Białas and Małgorzata Rószkiewicz. In Poland, the pension reform was introduced in 1999 and has since been a topic present in mainstream public debate and seems interesting to analyze from the perspective of a combination of economics and sociology. The authors examine saving for old age and its relevant position among other needs. It seems that this need does not yet play a significant role with relation to attitude and decision about (early) retirement. Therefore, there is still an open question as to how workers in Poland could be convinced that early retirement with insufficient savings for old age will not allow them to achieve their optimistic expectations of living a good life is in retirement, expressed in surveys and presented in this chapter. Another sensitive issue, particularly in post-socialist countries, is the commercialization of health services. Elena Berdysheva, in Chapter Sixteen, refers to many recent studies regarding out-of-pocket payments which are widely distributed in medical systems in the countries of Eastern Europe, modern Russia not being an exception. In this situation, doctors are to a great extent free in making decisions about price. Thus, in the case of informal commercial services of public dentistry, she makes a relevant example for studying principles observed by price makers when setting prices. Since medicine became more market oriented the doctor patient relationships have gained some new features. According to Berdysheva, Russian doctors have lost complete power over patients as their profit now depends on money paid by them. Patients, on the contrary, have obtained the advantage to act as consumers of medical services. The mutual positions of doctor and patient have become much more equal than they were before. The main purpose of Berdysheva's research was to identify and to explore principles observed by dentists while defining the size of out-of pocket payments for each patient. She explains how doctors manage prices in order to make up for their costs and to increase their profit or how pricing is driven by values, norms, traditions, social attitudes the level of personification of doctor patient relationships, the previous experience of treatment provided by this doctor, social status of a patient may cause the variation of prices for informal dental services.

One of the effects of systemic transition in post-socialist countries is the emergence of the property market. Chapter Seventeen, by Katarzyna Królikowska, discusses homeownership as an economic institution and its social perception within transitional societies. The ownership of a property, as the key phenomenon, should be regarded not only in relation to its strict economic function, but its broader social connotations. The main thesis of the chapter is that the current ongoing changes of ownership relations in various post-socialist transition countries lead to an identical outcome: the emergence of widespread low-cost homeownership and to creation and preservation of specific attitudes to that ownership. The scope of her analysis is international and includes changes in the housing market of Central Eastern European countries during the time of transition.

Institutional and social changes in the transition period, as she points out, leads to the emergence of cheap low cost homeownership, not only in economic terms. Her research findings show that cheap ownership also influences social perception—the discount prices paid for ownership of the dwellings do not help the appreciation of the real value of the property. Therefore, people do not consider their dwelling as a marketable commodity and the relatively high levels of homeownership do not constitute real economic wealth.

To sum up these introductory remarks, in my opinion the authors of this collection analyze, based on their empirical material, very interesting socio-economic issues. These are: ethical consumption from the perspective of the moral economy and its connection to political institutions in Europe (and particularly in Hungary); the cultural context of consumption, both in the case of social networks in Bangladesh and of counterfeited goods on the Russian market; the new and old, individual and organizational actors in transition economies, for instance in Poland and Croatia; the new approach to corporations as global actors, stressing their social responsibility; the dynamics of managerial practices in the example of Russia; the influence of EU funds and policies on the Polish SMEs market; the cultural embeddedness of economic behavior, in the case of Poles working in the Scottish market and of entrepreneurs in Damascus; the retirement policy in the fast aging societies of Spain and Poland; and the emergence of the new markets, like that of health services, in Russia and that of the property market in Eastern and Central Europe.

References

Bauman, Zygmunt. *Wasted Lives. Modernity and its Outcasts*. Cambridge: Polity Press, 2004

Beck, Ulrich. *The reinvention of politics: rethinking modernity in the global social order.* Cambridge: Polity Press, 1997.

Bell, Daniel. *The Coming of Post-Industrial Society*. New York: Basic Books, 1999.

Bourdieu, Pierre. *Distinction: A Social Critique of the Judgement of Taste*. Cambridge: Harvard University Press, 1984.

Bourdieu, Pierre. "Principles of Economic Anthropology." In *The Handbook of Economic Sociology 2nd Edition*. Edited by Neil J. Smelser and Richard Swedberg. Princeton: Princeton University Press, 2005.

Brinton, Mary C., and Victor Nee. *The New Institutionalism in Sociology.* Stanford: Stanford University Press, 2001.

Can the Market be Moral? *Journal of Interdisciplinary Studies* (2004): 1/2.

Dahrendorf, Ralf. *Reflections on the Revolutions in Europe*. London: Chatto andWindus, 1991.

Granovetter, Mark. "Economic Action and Social Structure: The Problem of Embeddedness." *American Journal of Sociology* 91 (1985): 481–510.

Granovetter, Mark and Richard Swedberg. *The Sociology of Economic Life*. Cambridge, MA: Westview Press, 2001.

Inglehart, Ronald. *Modernization and Postmodernization, Cultural, Economic and Political Change in 43 Societies.* New Jersey: Princeton University Press, 1997.

Keohane, Robert O. "Complex accountability and power in global governance: Issues for global business." *Corporate Governance* 8 (4) (2008): 361–367.

King, Lawrence P. And Ivan Szelenyi. "Post-comunist Economic Systems." In *The Handbook of Economic Sociology 2nd Edition*. Edited by Neil J. Smelser and Richard Swedberg. Princeton: Princeton University Press, 2005.

Lash Scott and John Urry. *Economies of Signs & Space*. London: Sage, 1994.

Leisinger, Klaus M. *Corporate responsibility with the United Nations Global Compact*. Basel, Switzerland: Novartis, 2007.

Nee, Victor. "A theory of Market Transition: From Redistribution to Markets in State Socialism". *American Sociological Review* 54 (1989): 663–681.

Nee, Victor and Richard Swedberg. *The Economic Sociology of Capitalism.* Princeton: Princeton University Press, 2005.

Norris, Pippa. *Democratic Phoenix. Reinventing Political Activism.* Cambridge: Cambridge University Press, 2002.

Polanyi, Karl. "The Economy as Instituted Process." In *The Sociology of Economic Life*, edited by Mark Granovetter and Richard Swedberg. Boulder: Westwood, 1992.

Sayer, Andrew. "Moral Economy and Political Economy." *Studies in Political Economy* 61 (2000): 79–104.

Theobald, Robin. *Understanding Industrial Society*. New York: St. Martin's Press, 1994.

Weber, Max. *Economy and Society,* Berkeley: University of California Press, 1978.

Zadek, Simon. "Global collaborative governance: There is no alternative." *Corporate Governance* 8 (4) (2008): 374–388.

PART I

TOWARD POSTMODERN CONSUMPTION?

CHAPTER ONE

EXPLAINING ETHICAL CONSUMPTION BEHAVIOUR IN EUROPE: A COMPARATIVE ANALYSIS

SEBASTIAN KOOS[1]

Introduction

The relationship between the market-economy and morality has occupied social scientists since the days of Adam Smith and Emile Durkheim. While heated debates revolve around the issue of civilizing versus destructive effects of market economies on the moral order (Hirschman 1982), economic sociology posits a rather feeble connection between both (Fourcade and Healy 2007), starting from the assumption that economic action and markets in general are embedded in specific social contexts and structures. Hence, the relationship of morality to the market has never been a central topic for New Economic Sociology. Nevertheless, public concern and even outrage, as well as political action, have always targeted the economic system (Friedman 1999; Thompson 1971; Vogel 2004). Recent authors even proclaim a "moralization of the markets" (Stehr, Henning and Weiler 2006), meaning that producers and consumers as the main actors on markets increasingly acknowledge the moral embeddeness of economic exchange. Indeed, the sale of fair trade products and of organic food has increased enormously in Europe over the last 10 years (Krier 2005; Willer and Yussefi 2007). Labelling schemes for both kinds of products have emerged and, in their diversity and magnitude, can now hardly be overlooked. Furthermore, over the last 20 years consumers have increasingly boycotted products which do not meet certain ethical standards (Stolle, Hooghe and Micheletti 2005).

[1] Faculty of Social Sciences, University of Mannheim.

In this chapter I will investigate the phenomenon of ethical consumption, which has so far been mainly the concern of political scientists (Lamla 2006; Micheletti 2003; Micheletti, Follesdal and Stolle 2004b) and business ethicists (Koslowski and Priddat 2006), and attempt an empirical approach to the determinants of ethical consumption practices in Europe. Ethical consumption is understood as the buying (or not buying) of goods, for ethical, political or environmental reasons. Economic Sociology, by taking a sociological perspective on economic phenomenon, tends to focus more on the side of production and neglects or even ignores consumption (Zelizer 2005; Zukin and Maguire 2004). Thus ethical consumption has not been systematically analyzed in the sociology of consumption. The consumer has gained enormous power in the last century, with mass production allowing for mass consumption and a shift towards buyer markets. Sociology of consumption tends to criticise consumption on the grounds of over, or conspicuous, consumption (Veblen 1949). Contrary to this, ethical consumption acknowledges consumption as an integral part of modern life, and sets out to create a specific form of buying and using resources in a considerate way with regard to sustainability and human rights.

This kind of consumption is analyzed from the perspective of the moral economy. In the next section I present a brief theoretical background, developing a concept of a moral economy of consumption. After presenting some hypotheses on individual and country differences in ethical consumer behaviour I introduce the empirical strategy and test hypotheses for a cross section of 19 European countries using multilevel analysis. On the individual level I find that education and values concerned with environmental care are especially important explanations for ethical buying or boycotting behaviour. Country level differences in ethical consumption can to a large degree be explained by the affluence of countries. After the discussion of the results a summary concludes the chapter.

Theoretical Background

The classical approach to explaining consumption is the economic or rational choice theory. Why Consumers adopt ethical reasons in their decision to buy is not explainable within the boundaries of standard economics (Hedtke 2001, 34; Schoenheit 2007, 217). First, I will briefly lay out the core assumptions of a narrow rational choice theory and then suggest an alternative approach based on moral values. Following this I will present the hypotheses to be tested in the empirical part of the chapter.

Rationality and the Moral Economy of Consumption

The narrow model of rational choice theory is built mainly on the assumption that subjects are fully informed and able to choose among alternatives that are structured by objective tangible constraints, so to maximise their utility for given self-interested preferences (Opp 1999, 174). This understanding of action is not sufficient to explain the buying of products that are more expensive, but not necessarily of higher quality than average products, which is the case for fair trade or organic products. A heuristic is needed that incorporates moral values, and therefore I turn to the moral economy approach.

The notion of the moral economy was first introduced by Edward P. Thompson (1971) in his classic study on English villagers. Thompson used the term to explain food riots, which were not merely "riots of the belly," but turbulence due to violations of the norm of "fair price." Recently this notion has been taken up by political economists to constitute a Cultural Political Economy (Arnold 2001; Booth 1994; Sayer 2000). They perceive moral economy as the study of "how economic activities of all kinds are influenced and structured by moral dispositions and norms, and how in turn those norms may be compromised, overridden or reinforced by economic pressures" (Sayer 2006, 78). Moral Economy can be seen both as a mode of inquiry and as an object of study, and here I set out to consider it as the object of study—the moral economy of consumption. The moral economy is still a vague concept that on the one hand is comprised of concrete norms and values like justice, responsibility and equality, but on the other is extended to "conceptions of the good" (Sayer 2000, 79), and in this regard could be extended to incorporate concern for the environment. The terms moral and ethical here are used interchangeably—they signify "norms, values and dispositions regarding behaviour that effects others, and they imply certain conceptions of the good" (Sayer 2006, 79). The concept of the moral economy indicates the existence of collectively shared beliefs about the "good economy," beliefs which transcend economic action, rendering it meaningful in different ways. This does not mean that economic action is irrational but rather that there are different "forms" of rationality that have to be taken into account. "It must not be forgotten that one can in fact 'rationalize' life from a vast variety of ultimate vantage points. Moreover, one can do so in very different directions" (Weber 2002, 37). One direction often overlooked is the orientation towards the "common good."

Hypothesis

In the following section, I will first introduce hypotheses for the macro-level and then discuss micro-level predictions. As Andersen and Tobiasen note, in the consideration of belief regarding political consumption: "the most relevant questions belong to the macro level" (Andersen and Tobiasen 2004, 205). In contrast with most other studies on political consumption (Andersen and Tobiasen 2004; Shaw 2005; Stolle and Micheletti 2005; Worcester and Dawkins 2005), I use cross sectional data, allowing the testing of macro level explanations.[2] In the literature on morality, markets and political consumption, four different explanatory causes on the macro level can be distinguished. These are the influence of affluence, knowledgeability, globalisation and availability of ethical products (Lamla 2006; Micheletti, Follesdal, and Stolle 2004b; Stehr 2007; Stehr, Henning, and Weiler 2006).

The economic wealth or affluence of societies can be regarded as one of the main causes of ethical consumption. Affluence reflects the availability of resources for a given entity—if a society is characterised by scarcity then choice between different options in consumption would not be possible. Hence with increasing affluence the opportunity structure of a society changes and allows for ethical consumption. In less affluent societies where consumers are more concerned with product availability and price, the market would have less room for ethical concerns, and other forms of exchange would have to be considered in regard to a moral economy (Booth 1994; Polanyi 1992).

The globalisation argument is put forward by Beck (1997, 2000) and taken up by most of the writers on political consumption. They assume that the process of economic globalisation is creating a situation of "global ungovernability" (Micheletti, Follesdal, and Stolle 2004a, xii), that the spread and growth of multinational corporations in recent decades renders national politics less powerful. Hence with increasing globalisation people expect their government to lose power and it follows that voting in the classic sense of political participation loses its impact. People living in countries that are highly globalised tend to be ethical consumers more often then people in less globalised countries. "Just as globalization squeezes orthodox avenues for politics, through the state and organized

---

[2] For an exception to this see the paper by Stolle, Hooghe et al. (2005), who have data for three countries and the working paper by Ferrer and Fraile (2006) who work with the same data used here (European Social Survey 2002/2003) but do not consider macro variables.

labor so new ones are being prized open, in consumer power" (Scammell 2000, 352).

A second factor quite closely linked to globalisation is knowledgeability. This factor is introduced by Nico Stehr (2007) and denotes the key importance of knowledge in modern societies. Stehr defines knowledgeability as the "ability for social action," it is "the potential to set something in motion" (Stehr 2007, 248). This remains a somewhat open definition, but gains clarity with the remark that "knowledge only performs an active function in that kind of societal action procedures, where action does not follow stereotype patterns or is regulated otherwise … but where there is leeway for decisions" (Ibid., 250f). Hence ethical consumption can be regarded as creative action that requires some kind of knowledge, like a basic understanding of market principles or the potential negative consequences of market outcomes, and certain degrees of freedom to be put into motion.

Lastly, a fourth factor will be introduced that is based on a "supply side" argument—to actually buy ethically, products that have special qualities must be available. Thus, the amount of shops there are to buy ethical products from is important, and the supply of these products within countries might be an effective explanation for ethical buying. This is not the case for boycott action. These macro explanations for differences in ethical consumption might also alter the effect of micro explanations of ethical consumption, thus I will also look at how macro effects constitute an opportunity structure for micro level effects.

Turning to explanations on the micro-level, I will first introduce hypotheses for the standard socio-economic factors, before examining hypotheses regarding personal values. After considering the political dimension of ethical consumption, I conclude with hypotheses regarding the religious dimension. Since ethical consumption is expensive, in accordance with a rational choice theory I expect that people with a high income are more inclined to buy ethically. Taking class as a proxy for income, people with a higher class position will have a higher probability of buying ethical products, than people with lower class status. Since boycotts are not cost intensive I do not expect a relationship with class here.[3] Education, and as a result knowledge, is expected to be of critical relevance for boycotting or ethical buying. People with higher education are expected to be better informed and have a greater understanding of the complex interplay in economic processes and their consequences. Age is not expected to alter the probability of ethical consumption by itself,

---

[3] However class position does reflect much more than economic wealth.

however it is expected that the probability increases to a certain degree with age, since people have more resources, and decrease at a certain age, because older people may not be aware of opportunities—hence I expect an inverted U-shaped curve. In the literature on political consumption Micheletti et al. generally suggest a stronger probability for women to use this method of political participation, because other options have historically been restricted (Micheletti 2004). However, as Zukin and Maguire (2004) note, in general there has always been a gender gap in consumption. Therefore, even if there is a pluralisation of ways of living, women are still expected to have a higher probability of ethical consumption. Another determinant of ethical consumption is availability of such products, as mentioned above. Since Fair Trade shops and organic supermarkets are most often located in cities I controlled for differences between urban and rural areas, expecting city dwellers to have a higher probability for ethical buying, but not necessarily a higher propensity on boycotting.

Next, I introduce the notion of personal values or preferences. Following theory, strict Rational Choice models are expected to be insufficient to explain ethical consumption. Personal values directed towards others or the "common good" are strong motivators to boycott or buy ethically. Hence I expect that people with a strong conviction in solidarity with other human beings or a high preference to care for nature will have a higher probability for ethical consumption, and people with a strong materialistic identity will not engage in ethical consumption. Another predictor is the amount of generalized trust, one dimension of social capital—people who generally trust others are expected to be ethical consumers because they would also trust in other people to act in an ethical way. Therefore generalized trust can be regarded as a measure of reciprocity.

Lastly, I introduce some hypotheses stemming from the literature on political consumption (Micheletti 2003; Stolle and Hooghe 2004) to account for the political dimension of ethical consumption. These considerations reflect notions of sub-politics and risk society put forward by Beck (1992; 1997; 2000). If ethical consumption is a political act, respondents interested in politics should show a stronger probability for ethical consumption than people with little interest in politics (Andersen and Tobiasen 2004). Another claim argues that political consumers are "frustrated citizens, who are fed up with national institutions" (Stolle, Hooghe and Micheletti 2005, 253). Hence citizens that do not trust national political institutions are expected to show a higher degree of political consumption. This has been empirically tested by Stolle, Hooghe et al. (2005), who find a significant negative correlation between political consumption and institutional trust in a survey conducted with students of Social Sciences in three countries. Andersen and Tobiasen (2004, 241) however find a positive correlation for institutional trust and political consumerism in their study on Denmark. This may also hold true for politicians—if respondents think politicians are "corrupt" or only act in regard to their self-interest they might envision political consumption as an alternative to voting.

Finally, the religious dimension of ethical consumption should not be overlooked. Some fair trade organizations, like GEPA (the biggest fair trade company in Europe) or Max Havelaar, have a Christian background and major shareholders of GEPA are organizations of the Roman Catholic and Protestant churches.[4] Therefore I expect that church attendees have higher levels of access and knowledgeability of these organizations and products and I expect higher levels of religiosity, and especially higher levels of church attendance, to have a positive effect on ethical buying. In the next section I introduce the data and methods, before presenting the analyses for testing the presented hypotheses.

Empirical Analyses

Data, Variables and Method

The data used for analysis is the European Social Survey (ESS) of 2002/ 2003 (Jowell and Central Coordination Team 2003). The European Social Survey is a multi-country survey project administered every two years, and in 2002 the survey included 21 European countries and Israel.[5] The ESS questionnaire consists of a fixed basic part and additional separate modules, different for each survey. Overall, the 2002/2003 survey allows for a reasonable amount of operationalization of the concepts of interest, but unfortunately one of the measures for the dependent variable has not been repeated.

Ethical consumption has been operationalized by two dichotomous variables: ethical buying and the boycott of products. The respondents indicated whether in the last twelve months they either had "[d]eliberately bought certain products for political, ethical or environmental reasons" or "[b]oycotted certain products?" (European Social Survey 2003, 10). This

---

[4] Compare with www.gepa.de.

[5] The data and extensive documentation can be downloaded from the Norwegian Social Science Data Services (NSD) online: http://ess.nsd.uib.no/

provides a good way to measure ethical consumption. Both variables have been frequently used in studies on political consumption (Andersen and Tobiasen 2004; Stolle, Hooghe, and Micheletti 2005). The operationalization of the independent micro-variables can be seen in table 1 in the appendix. Information for the explanatory variables on the macro-level has been gathered from different sources. As a measure for affluence I used gross domestic product per capita in purchasing power parities—GDPpc (PPP) in constant 2000 international $ for the year 2002 provided by the Worldbank (2008). From the same data source the measure of knowledge society was obtained. I measure "knowledgeability" as the number of internet users per 100 residents. As a measure of economic globalization I used the openness of the economy, widely used to grasp globalization (Barro 2008; Brady, Beckfield, and Zhao 2007; Harrison 1996; OECD 2005). It measures openness to the economic world market as the sum of exports and imports divided by real GDP. The measure was self constructed by data from Eurostat (2008). The last independent variable on the macro level tries to measure the availability of ethical products. I used the number of shops that sell fair trade products per 100,000 residents as a measure of availability. The data was provided by The European Fair Trade Association (Krier 2001) and standardized by the author. Unfortunately, no data were available for Poland, Hungary, or Slovenia. All variables were centred (subtracting the grand mean of all variables) to allow for an easier interpretation and for introducing interaction terms (Kohler and Kreuter 2001, 223f.).

To analyse the data I used a logistical random intercept model. Multilevel models are frequently used in Cross Cultural Research (Van de Vjver, Van Hemert, and Poortinga 2008) to account for the hierarchical data structure of individuals nested within countries. These models provide for the fact that two randomly chosen individuals from the same country will be more similar than two individuals from different countries. An alternative method would be to use a standard maximum likelihood regression model with country fixed effects. However, as "standard statistical tests lean heavily on the assumption of independence of observations" (Hox 2002, 5), this assumption is clearly disproved using cross sectional data of individuals and would lead to "spuriously significant results." The best approach is therefore to estimate random intercept or multilevel models for this kind of clustered data. The model fit can be assessed by looking at the likelihood ratios of the different models. A useful feature of hierarchical modelling is that it allows for the introduction of cross level interactions, and this means it can be tested to see how macro variables alter the effect of independent micro variables on the dependent phenomenon.

Results and Discussion

First I will present country differences in ethical consumption behaviour (fig. 1.1 below) showing a huge variation between countries for both kinds of actions, ranging from 8% of the respondents that have bought ethical products in the last 12 month in Greece to 58% in Sweden. In Portugal, only 3% of the respondents report boycotting behaviour, while in Sweden and Switzerland 35% of the respondents boycotted products in the last 12 months. Overall, it seems quite common to buy products for ethical, political or environmental reasons in the Scandinavian countries and Switzerland, whereas in Southern and Eastern Europe only a few people report such actions.

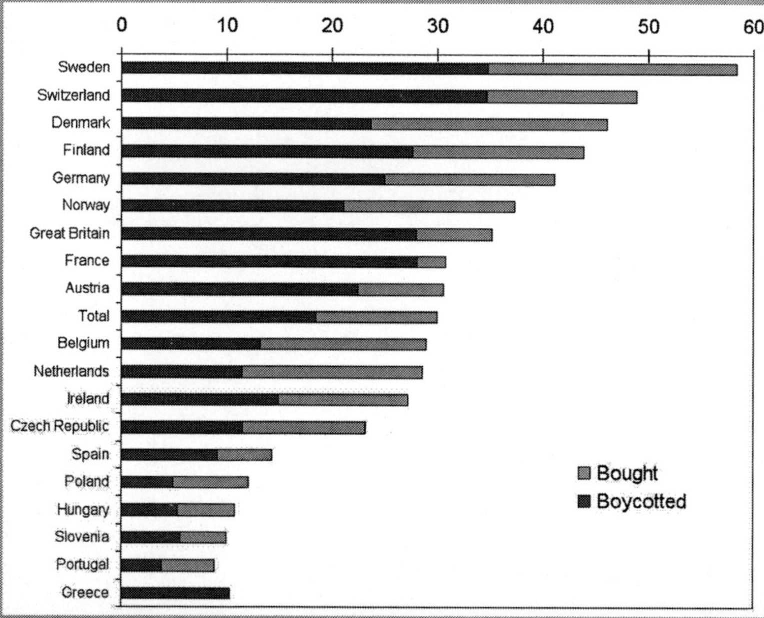

Fig. 1.1
Mean of respondents that bought or boycotted products in the last 12 months (% yes answers).
Source: ESS 2002/2003; author's own calculations.

A similar pattern can be found for boycotting behaviour. Generally, people tend to boycott less than buy for ethical reasons (except people in Greece, where only 8% report positive buying, but 10% report boycotting). Noticeably, people in France and Great Britain rank 3rd and 4th for mean boycotting behaviour (both 28%). Therefore, I find some systematic country differences that vary between both dependent variables. In the next step I will explain first individual differences and second the presented cross national variation in ethical consumption by applying a multivariate multilevel logistic regression model.

To determine whether a multilevel analysis has to be performed I estimate the conditional intraclass correlation, an indicator of how much the data is clustered, for both of the dependent concepts (Rabe-Hesketh and Skorndal 2008, 256). The conditional intraclass correlation for ethical buying is 0.17 and for boycotting is 0.11, denoting the proportion of the variance at the macro level, thus it is useful to estimate random intercept logistic models. The results of the models are given in table 2 and 3 in the appendix. The interpretation of logistic regression results is different to that for OLS. The coefficients in the tables are log odds, which denote the logarithm of the chance to boycott or buy (Kohler and Kreuter 2001, 266). For reasons of simplicity and comprehensibility of the interpretation I rely on predicted probabilities and conditional effect plots. Predicted probabilities denote the probability of a certain respondent with fixed attributes to buy or boycott products. For continuous variables this probability can be graphed, varying certain "conditions."

Based on the logistic regression results, I constructed ideal types of ethical consumers and plot them to see the differences in probability of buying or boycotting products. An ideal type means that all the variables in the model are fixed at a meaningful value (e.g. a male low-educated Swedish lower grade white collar worker etc.) and in a next step one variable by the other is varied to see how much the probability for boycotting or buying a ethical product changes regarding every hypothesis of interest (e.g. a <u>female</u> low-educated Swedish lower grade white collar worker etc.). I first construct an ideal type, who is theoretically expected to have a low probability to consume ethically, a "low-ethical consumer ideal type" (LECIT). To interpret the micro variables I fixed the macro variables to Sweden.[6] LECIT is a 47 year old male, with 12 years of schooling

---

[6] Since I estimated random intercept models the probabilities for other countries might differ to some extent, but the differences between groups will be the same. To overcome this limitation one needs to either run country wise regressions or random slope models. I have done both, but for reasons of space only report the results for the random intercept models.

(education) working as a skilled blue collar worker (class) living in a village, is not interested in politics, neither trusting nor distrusting political institutions, thinking that only some politicians care about public opinions, and goes to church only on special holidays. He is identified not as a person that cares for nature or for equal opportunities, but as someone for whom it is important to be rich. Also, he is someone that thinks you "cannot be too careful" (low general trust).

Turning now to the interpretation in fig. 1.2 below, I present the predicted probabilities of the dichotomous variables, showing conditional effect plots for some of the continuous variables.

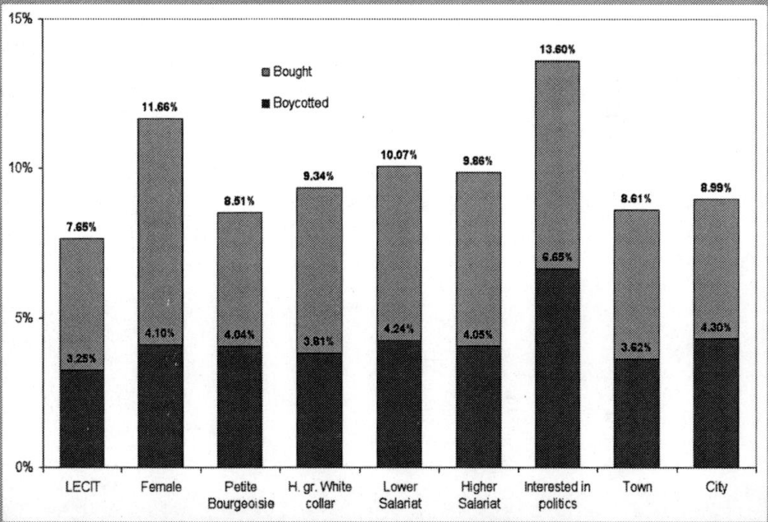

Fig. 1.2
Predicted probabilities for ideal types of buying or boycotting.
Note: "LECIT" = low ethical consumer ideal type: a 47 year old male, with 12 years of schooling (education) working as a skilled blue collar worker (class) living in a village, not interested in politics and going to church only on special holidays. He identifies not as a person that cares for nature or equal opportunities, but as someone for whom it is important to be rich. Furthermore, he is someone that thinks you cannot be too careful (low general trust). He is not interested in politics and neither trust nor distrusts political institutions and thinks that only some politicians care about public opinions.
Source: ESS 2002/2003; author's own calculations

The first hypotheses concern the effect of socio-economic factors. As proposed, women choose more often to either buy or boycott. Female respondents have a 4% higher probability to report ethical buying than male respondents (compared to the LECIT). The effect for boycotting is less pronounced. Class is a powerful explanatory concept in many regards. I find that with a higher class position the probability for ethical buying rises, however, the increase is only about 1% point per higher occupational status. Regarding boycott behaviour I did not expect a clear class difference. The multivariate results show a significant effect for class, nevertheless turning to the predicted probabilities I find that there is almost no difference between classes. Somewhat contrary to the conclusion of Ferrer and Fraile (2006), I do not find class to be a decisive factor in this kind of political action. Education, however, seems to have a great impact on both boycotting and buying. Holding all other factors at a fixed value, the effect of education years increases the probability of buying ethically from 8% to almost 50% ranging from 0 to 28 years of education, and an increase from 5% to 28% for boycotting (fig. 1.3 and 1.4 below).

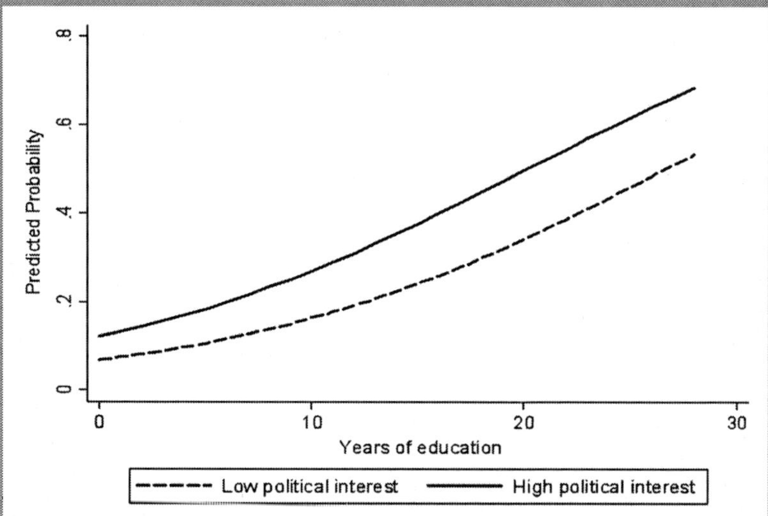

Fig. 1.3
Conditional effect of education on ethical buying.
Source: ESS 2002/2003; author's own calculations.

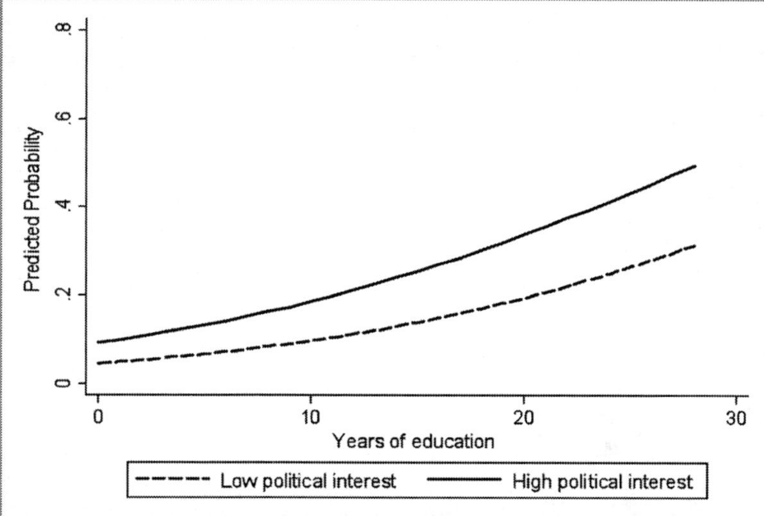

Fig. 1.4
Conditional effect of education on boycotting.
Source: ESS 2002/2003; author's own calculations.

Age was not expected to have a significant effect by itself, controlling for all other variables. However, I find an inverted u-shaped curve for the effect of age on the probability of ethical consumption, people in their thirties having the highest probability for ethical consumption. The effect of city and town versus village is significant for both boycott and ethical buying—despite being small, it points in the expected direction. People living in the city have a higher probability than people living in towns or villages to consume ethically. The effect for religious participation and ethical buying cannot be found in the model for ethical buying. People going to church, however, regularly have a significantly lower chance of boycotting products.

I will now explore the effect of individual moral preferences on ethical consumption. Comparing materialistic, solidarity and ecological personality traits, I find that all three variables have significant effects for both buying and boycotting. Looking at the predicted probabilities reveals that only respondents who reported that they care about the environment show a visible increase in their probability to consume ethically. Respondents who strongly identify as someone who cares for nature have an almost 30% higher probability to buy ethically (boycott ~ 10%) than those who do not care for nature at all. Identifying as neither a materialistic person nor as a person with strong sense of solidarity to other human beings has a clear effect on buying ethical, even though both variables are significant (fig. 1.5 and 1.6 below). This might reflect the centrality of ecological debates in European societies, compared to other issues, like international solidarity or even materialistic issues.

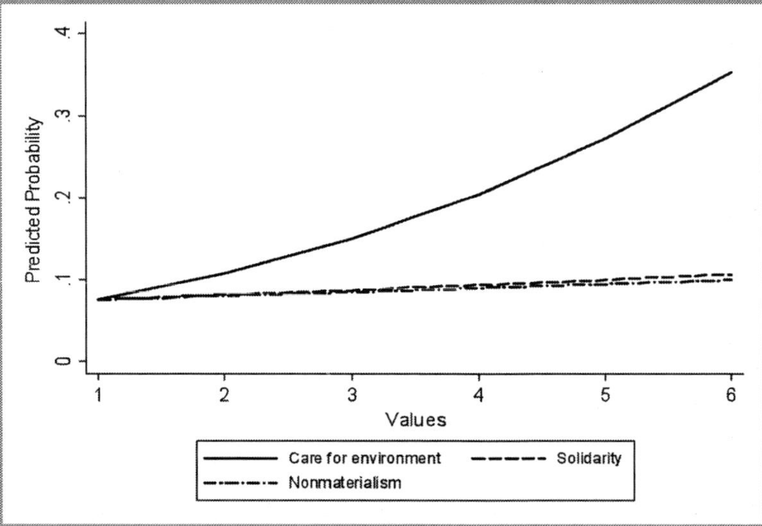

Fig. 1.5
Conditional effect of moral values on ethical buying.
Source: ESS 2002/2003; author's own calculations.

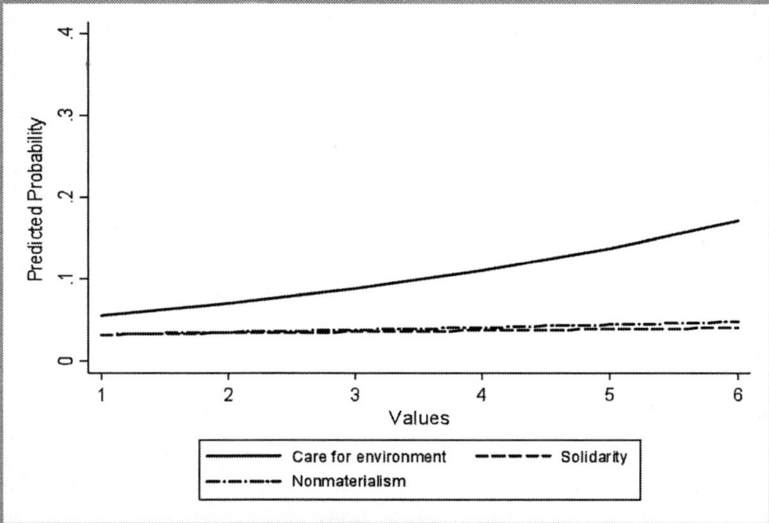

Fig. 1.6
Conditional effect of moral values on boycotting.
Source: ESS 2002/2003; author's own calculations.

There is some evidence to demonstrate that generalized trust, as a measure for social capital, has a significant effect on ethical consumption. Now I will turn to the variables suggested by the political consumption literature. Political interest has a significant positive effect for both buying and boycotting. Being interested in politics raises the probability of buying ethically by almost 6%, and of boycotting by 3%. Political interest thus almost doubles the probability of the LECIT, pointing to the political character of ethical consumption. According to my hypothesis, I expect ethical consumers to be frustrated with traditional politics. Interestingly, for ethical buying, I do not find the negative effect expected for political trust, however the more that people are convinced that politicians really care for public opinion, the higher the chance of buying ethically. Nevertheless, I find the expected effect for boycotting behaviour. Respondents reporting a higher degree of trust in the political institutions have a lower probability of boycotting products. This lends support to the hypothesis of the general political nature of ethical consumption, but reveals different political motivations for the two dependent concepts.

The micro results mostly confirm the hypotheses, but reveal some interesting information. First, education seems to have a stronger influence on the probability to consume ethically than class, the value dimensions revealing a strong environmental frame in ethical consumption. Finally, while boycotting is clearly connected to distrust in political institutions this is not the case for ethical buying. Nevertheless, both ethical buying and boycotting are positively linked to political interest.

Complementary to the micro analysis, I consider cross cultural differences. So far there have been no studies that systematically explored cross cultural differences in ethical consumption. I expect the macro effects to be of great importance in shaping the opportunity structure for ethical consumption. Globalisation is often cited as one of the driving forces of ethical consumption. I take the openness to trade of the economy as a proxy for economic globalisation which does not have a significant effect on buying ethically. However, I find a slightly significant negative effect of globalisation on boycotting behaviour. Contrary to the globalisation hypothesis, the probability of boycotting declines with increasing globalisation. Arguably, I only measure globalisation in one way and many other measures for globalisation should be tested. Also, the individual perception of globalisation might be decisive. Nevertheless, this is a widely accepted measure for economic globalisation and it gives an accurate perspective of the influence of international trade within a country.

The second explanation for ethical buying is that affluence is a driving force behind ethical consumption. This relates somewhat to the hypothesis of the civilizing force of markets. I find that affluence is a powerful predictor for ethical buying. Affluence is measured as the country average per capita income in power purchasing parities (PPP). Since ethical products (e.g. labelled products) are usually more costly than normal products, this indicator is a good measure for the opportunity structure of ethical shopping. The economic wealth of a country has a strong positive effect on the chance of buying ethically. Surprisingly, however, it is also a good predictor for boycotting behaviour. This points to the existence of other factors, such as political culture or economic history (age of market system) that I have not accounted for, and this is an area in which further research is needed.

In making decisions, knowledge is a crucial resource and therefore the level of "knowledgeability" of a society is analyzed. The country mean of people having access to the internet has a significant positive effect on ethical buying; however, I do not find it a significant influence on boycotting. Lastly, I turn to the availability of labelled products. This is only important for ethical buying. If the amount of Fair Trade shops per 100,000 citizens for the available countries is included, I do get a positive significant result. However, if the other macro variables are included the effect loses its significance.[7] So far I only include the market structure of Fair Trade products, though arguably the market for organic products might be even more important.

The macro factors presented above can be understood as contextual factors that influence the effect of individual variables. Therefore I have estimated a cross-level interaction between affluence (macro) and individual care for nature (micro). The interaction effect becomes significant for ethical shopping. In fig. 1.7 below a conditional effect plot of different GDP per capita levels and how they change the effect of caring for nature is presented.

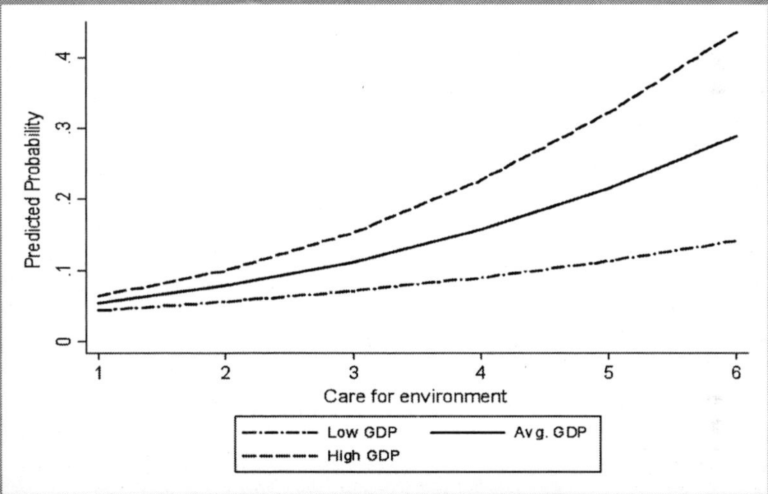

Fig. 1.7
Conditional effect plot for the cross level interaction of GDP per capita (PPP) and individual care for environment.
Source: ESS 2002/2003; author's own calculations

Respondents with a high preference for the environment will have a bigger (around 30%) probability in richer countries to act according to their conviction and buy products for ethical reasons than people in poorer countries. Hence ethical buying might increase as a country becomes

[7] Results are not reported in the tables, but can be obtained from the author.

richer and people gain the resources to act according to their moral preferences.

Conclusion

In this chapter I have begun to work towards an explanation for how people make buying decisions for ethical, political or environmental reasons. Theoretically, I draw on a notion of a moral economy of consumption, meaning that moral values and preferences enter the market place and influence people's decisions on what to buy or even to boycott. I find considerable variation in ethical consumption practices among European countries; differences which can be mostly explained by levels of affluence and knowledgeability within countries. Globalisation did not prove to be a decisive predictor for ethical consumption. However, as a recent review by Brady et al. (2007) shows, so far hardly any influences of economic globalization on civil society or politics can be shown. Perhaps a different measure for globalization should be applied, one which might better reveal political and social globalization. Other factors, like political culture or the structure of the organic market should be included in future analyses. Regarding individual level explanations I find that moral values have a strong influence on the decision to buy or boycott products. Environmental concern is a particularly good predictor for ethical consumption. Nevertheless, the effect of individual level variables depends on the societal macro structures. Affluence at the country level increases the likelihood of individuals to act according to their moral convictions. Education and, as a result, knowledge proved to be a decisive indicator of ethical consumption. Even though I find some significant class differences, these do not alter the probability of buying or boycotting as drastically as expected, especially considering the price of labelled products. Finally, ethical consumers are politically interested, but nevertheless ethical buying and boycotting have different underlying political motivations. Respondents who report engaging in boycotts have significantly lower trust in political institutions, while respondents reporting positive buying do trust the political system. Therefore further analyses of the political character of ethical consumption are needed. While an empirical analysis of ethical consumption proved to be quite fruitful, more detailed data is needed to get a more coherent idea of the moral economy of consumption in Europe

Appendix

Table 1.1. Operationalization of independent variables

Construct/Variable	Specification
Micro- Controls	
Socio-economic attributes	
Female	Gender (dummy): female=1, male =0
Age (c.)	Centered age of respondents
Age^2 (c.)	Centered squared age of respondents
Years of Education (c.)	Years of education centered
Class (EGP)	*Erickson-Goldthorpe Class Scheme. Dummy group: 1= yes; 0=no.*
Higher Salariat	Service class 1 (Large employers, higher grade professionals) (dummy)
Lower Salariat	Service Class 2 (Lower grade professionals) (dummy)
Higher grade white collar workers	Intermediate occupations (dummy)
Petite Bourgeoisie	Self employed, small employers and farmers (dummy)
Skilled blue collar workers	Lower supervisory and lower technical occupations (dummy)
Lower grade white collar workers	Lower services, sales, and clerical occupations (dummy)
Semi- and non-skilled workers	Routine occupations (dummy)
Place of residence	*Dummy group: 1= yes; 0=no.*
City	Living in a big city or suburbs (dummy)
Town	Living in a town (dummy)
Village	Living in a village or farm (dummy)
Religion	
Church attendance (c.)	Church attendance of respondent: coded 0 to 6 (0 = never; 6 = every day)
Values	
Care for Environment (c.)	Respondent self-identifies as a person who cares for nature: coded 1 to 6 (1=not like me at all; 6=very much like me)
Solidarity (c.)	Respondent self-identifies as a person for whom it is important that people are treated equally: coded 1 to 6 (1=not like me at all; 6=very much like me)

Nonmaterialism (c.)	Respondent self-identifies as a person for whom it is not important to be rich: coded 1 to 6 (1=not like me at all; 6=very much like me)
Generalized Trust (c.)	Respondent's assessment if most people can be trusted: coded 1 to 10 (10=most people can be trusted)
Interest in Politics	Respondent's interest in politics (dummy): 1=very or quite interested; 0=hardly or not at al interested)
Politicans Care for Public Opinion (c.)	Respondent's assessment if politicians care, what people like respondent think: coded 1 to 5 (1=hardly any politicians care; 5=most politicians care)
Trust in Political Institutions (c.)	Factor of respondent's trust in political institutions (parliament, legal system, police) (Eigenvalue: 2.65; all factor loadings higher than 0.75).
Macro- Controls	
GDP per capita	GDP per capita in constant 2000 US$ in 2002 per country
Openness of Economy	Proportion of Exports plus Imports of a countries GDP
Internet Users (per 100 residents)	Number of Internet user per 100 residents
Free Trade Shops (per 100.000 residents)	Number of Fair Trade Shops per 100.000 residents
Cross Level Interactions	
GDP per capita * Care for Environment	Interaction of GDP per capita with priority for environmental care

Table 1.2. Determinants of Ethical Buying

Variable	Model 1		Model 2		Model 3	
Micro-controls						
Constant	-2.222***	(-0.185)	-2.536***	(0.130)	-2.169***	(0.107)
Age (c)	0.030***	(0.005)	0.030***	(0.005)	0.030***	(0.005)
Age^2 (c)	-0.001***	(0.000)	-0.001***	(0.000)	-0.001***	(0.000)
Female	0.465***	(0.032)	0.465***	(0.032)	0.466***	(0.032)
EGP-Class (Ref.: Semi- and unskilled workers)						
Higher Salariat	0.544***	(0.065)	0.542***	(0.065)	0.541***	(0.065)
Lower Salariat	0.564***	(0.055)	0.563***	(0.055)	0.564***	(0.055)
Higher grade white collar workers	0.483***	(0.061)	0.482***	(0.061)	0.482***	(0.062)
Petite Bourgeoisie	0.384***	(0.066)	0.384***	(0.066)	0.379***	(0.067)
Skilled blue collar workers	0.264***	(0.055)	0.264***	(0.055)	0.262***	(0.055)
Lower grade white collar workers	0.256***	(0.061)	0.255***	(0.061)	0.255***	(0.062)
Years of education (c)	0.097***	(0.005)	0.098***	(0.005)	0.099***	(0.005)
Place of residence (Ref.: Village)						
City	0.179***	(0.037)	0.180***	(0.037)	0.177***	(0.037)
Town	0.127***	(0.037)	0.128***	(0.037)	0.129***	(0.037)
Religious attendance (c)	-0.001	(0.011)	-0.001	(0.011)	0.000	(0.011)
Values						
Solidarity (c)	0.073***	(0.015)	0.073***	(0.015)	0.074***	(0.015)
Care for environment (c)	0.388***	(0.017)	0.389***	(0.017)	0.371***	(0.031)
Nonmaterialism (c)	0.060***	(0.012)	0.060***	(0.012)	0.059***	(0.012)
Generalized trust (c)	0.064***	(0.007)	0.064***	(0.007)	0.064***	(0.007)

Interest in politics	0.641***	(0.032)	0.639***	(0.032)	0.643***	(0.033)
Politicians care for Public Opinion (c)	0.140***	(0.017)	0.140***	(0.017)	0.140***	(0.017)
Trust in political Institutions (c)	-0.033	(0.018)	-0.034	(0.018)	-0.036	(0.018)
Macro-controls						
Openess of Economy (c)			-0.002	(0.003)	-0.002	(0.003)
GDP per capita (PPP) (c)			0.039***	(0.012)	0.038**	(0.012)
Internet Users (per 100 residents) (c)			0.030**	(0.010)	0.030**	(0.010)
Cross-Level-Interactions						
GDP per capita * Care for Environment					0.007*	(0.003)
Variance Components						
Variance Random Intercept	0.596		0.154		0.153	
Variance Random Slope (Care for Environment)					0.011	
Log-Likelihood	-14335.213		-14322.624		-14311.302	

Note: Dependent variable: Ethical buying. Continuous variables are centered (c). Standard errors in brackets; *** p>0.001, *** p > 0.01, * p> 0.05. Source: ESS 2002/2003, own calculations. N=29,142 respondents, 19 countries.

Table 1.3. Determinants of Boycotting

Variable	Model 1		Model 2	
Micro-controls				
Constant	-2.814***	(0.192)	-3.012***	(0.142)
Age (c)	0.033***	(0.006)	0.033***	(0.006)
Age^2 (c)	-0.001***	(0.000)	-0.001***	(0.000)
Female	0.243***	(0.036)	0.243***	(0.036)
EGP-Class (Ref.: Semi- and unskilled workers)				
Higher Salariat	0.378***	(0.073)	0.378***	(0.073)
Lower Salariat	0.426***	(0.063)	0.425***	(0.063)
Higher grade white collar workers	0.315***	(0.071)	0.315***	(0.071)
Petite Bourgeoisie	0.380***	(0.075)	0.380***	(0.075)
Skilled blue collar workers	0.154*	(0.065)	0.154*	(0.065)
Lower grade white collar workers	0.204**	(0.071)	0.204**	(0.071)
Years of education (c)	0.080***	(0.006)	0.080***	(0.006)
Place of residence (Ref.: Village)				
City	0.290***	(0.041)	0.291***	(0.041)
Town	0.113**	(0.042)	0.114**	(0.042)
Religious attendance (c)	-0.049***	(0.013)	-0.049***	(0.013)
Values				
Solidarity (c)	0.046**	(0.017)	0.047**	(0.017)
Care for environment (c)	0.334***	(0.019)	0.335***	(0.019)
Nonmaterialism (c)	0.083***	(0.014)	0.083***	(0.014)
Generalized trust (c)	0.024**	(0.008)	0.023**	(0.008)

Interest in politics	0.751***	(0.038)	0.749***	(0.038)
Politicians care for Public Opinion (c)	0.021	(0.019)	0.021	(0.019)
Trust in political Institutions (c)	-0.142***	(0.021)	-0.144***	(0.021)
Macro-controls				
Openess of Economy (c)			-0.006*	(0.003)
GDP per capita (PPP) (c)			0.052***	(0.013)
Internet Users (per 100 residents) (c)			0.016	(0.010)
Cross-Level-Interactions				
Internet Users * Care for Environment				
Variance Components				
Variance Random Intercept	0.623		0.169	
Variance Random Slope (Care for Environment)				
Log-Likelihood	-11896.953		-11884.929	

Note: Dependent variable: Boycotting. Continuous variables are centered (c). Standard errors in brackets; *** p>0,001, *** p > 0,01, * p> 0,05. Source: ESS 2002/2003, own calculations. N = 29,142 respondents, 19 countries.

References

Andersen, Jorgen Goul and Mette Tobiasen. "Who Are These Political Consumers Anyway?" In *Politics, Products, and Markets.* Edited by Michele Micheletti, Andreas Follesdal, and Dietlind Stolle. Brunswick, London: Transaction Publishers, 2004.

Arnold, Thomas Clay. "Rethinking Moral Economy." *American Political Science Review* 95 (2001): 85–95.

Barro, Robert J. *Macroeconomics. A modern approach.* Madson: Thompson, South-Western, 2008.

Beck, Ullrich. *Risk Society: Towards a New Modernity.* London: Sage, 1992.

—. *The Reinvention of Politics: Rethinking Modernity in the Global Science Order.* Oxford: Polity Press, 1997.

—. *What is Globalisation?* Cambridge: Cambridge University Press, 2000.

Booth, William James. "On the Idea of the Moral Economy." *American Political Science Review* 88 (1994): 653–667.

Brady, David, Jason Beckfield, and Wei Zhao. "The Consequences of Economic Globalization for Affluent Democracies." *Annual Review of Sociology* 33 (2007): 313–334.

European Social Survey, 2002/2003. Source Questionaire (Round 1, 2002/2003): 2003.

Eurostat. "Economy and Finance." Eurostat, 2008.

Ferrer, Mariona and Marta Fraile. "Exploring the social determinants of political consumerism in Western Europe." *UAM Estudio/Working Paper* 57, 2006.

Fourcade, Marion and Kieran Healy. "Moral Views of Market Society." *Annual Review of Sociology* 33 (2007): 285–311.

Friedman, Monroe. *Consumer Boycotts: Effecting Change through the Marketplace and the Media.* New York and London: Routledge, 1999.

Harrison, Ann E. "Openness and Growth: A Time Series, Cross-Country Analysis for Developing Countries." *Journal of Development Economics* 48 (1996): 419–447.

Hedtke, Reinhold. *Konsum und Ökonomik. Grundlagen, Kritik und Perspektiven* [*Consumption and Economics. Foundations, Critics and Perspectives*]. Konstanz: UVK Verlagsgesellschaft, 2001.

Hirschman, Albert O. "Rival interpretations of market society: civilizing, destructive or feeble?" *Journal of Economic Literature* 20 (1982): 1463–84.

Hox, Joop. *Multilevel Analysis. Techniques and Applications.* New Jersey/London: Lawrence Erlbaum Associates, 2002.

Jowell, R. and European Social Survey 2002/2003 Central Coordination Team. *Technical Report.* London: Center for Comparative Social Surveys, City University, 2003.

Kohler, Ulrich and Frauke Kreuter. *Datenanalyse mit Stata* [*Data analysis with Stata*]. München: R. Oldenburg Verlag, 2001.

Koslowski, Peter and Birger P. Priddat. *Ethik des Konsums* [*The Ethic of consumption*]. München: Wilhelm Fink Verlag, 2006.

Krier, Jean Marie. *Fair Trade in Europe 2001. Facts and Figures on the Fair Trade sector in 18 European countries.* Maastricht: European Fair Trade Organization, 2001.

—. *Fair Trade in Europe 2005. Facts and Figures on the Fair Trade 25 European countries.* Maastricht: European Fair Trade Organization, 2005.

Lamla, Jörn. "Politisierter Konsum—konsumierte Politik. Kritikmuster und Engagenmantformen im kulturellen Kapitalismus" ["Politized consumption—consumed politics"]. In *Politisierter Konsum - konsumierte Politik.* Edited by Jörn Lamal and Sighard Neckel. Wiesbaden: VS Verlag, 2006.

Micheletti, Michele. *Political Virtue and Shopping. Individual, Consumerism, and Collective Action.* New York: Palgrave Macmillan, 2003.

—. "Why More Women? Issues of Gender and Political Consumption." In *Politics, Products, and Markets.* Edited by Michele Micheletti, Andreas Follesdal, and Dietlind Stolle. New Brunswick, London: Transaction Publishers, 2004.

Micheletti, Michele, Andreas Follesdal, and Dietlind Stolle. "Introduction." In *Politics, Products, and Markets.* Edited by Michele Micheletti, Andreas Follesdal, and Dietlind Stolle. New Brunswick, London: Transaction Publishers, 2004a.

Micheletti, Michele, Andreas Follesdal, and Dietlind Stolle. *Politics, Products, and Markets. Exploring Political Consumerism Past and Present.* New Brunswick, London: Transaction Publishers, 2004b.

OECD. "Measuring Globalisation." *OECD Handbook on Economic Globalisation Indicators*. Paris: OECD, 2005.

Opp, Karl-Dieter. "Contending Conceptions Of The Theory Of Rational Action." *Journal of Theoretical Politics* 11 (1999): 171–202.

Polanyi, Karl. "The Economy as Instituted Process." In *The Sociology of Economic Life*. Edited by Mark Granovetter and Richard Swedberg. Boulder: Westwood, 1992.

Rabe-Hesketh, Sophia and Anders Skorndal. *Multilevel and Longitudinal Modeling Using Stata.* Colege Station: Stata Press, 2008.

Sayer, Andrew. "Moral Economy and Political Economy." *Studies in Political Economy* 61 (2000): 79–104.
—. "Approaching Moral Economy." In *The Moralization of the Markets.* Edited by Nico Stehr, Christoph Henning and Bernd Weiler. New Brunswick: Transaction Publisher, 2006.
Scammell, Margaret. "The Internet and Civic Engagement: The Age of the Citizen Consumer." *Political Communication* 17 (2000): 351–355.
Schoenheit, Ingo. "Politischer Konsum. Ein Beitrag zum faustischen Konsumentenverhalten. [Political Consumption]." In *Ambivalenzen des Konsums und der werblichen Kommunikation.* Edited by Michael Jäckel. Wiesbaden: VS Verlag, 2007.
Shaw, Deirdre. "Modelling Consumer Decision Making in Fair Trade." In *The Ethical Consumer.* Edited by Rob Harrison, Terry Newholm, and Deirdre Shaw. London: SAGE Publications Ltd., 2005.
Stehr, Nico. *Die Moralisierung der Märkte. Eine Gesellschaftstheorie* [*The moralization of the markets. A social theory*]. Frankfurt (Main): suhrkamp, 2007.
Stehr, Nico, Christoph Henning, and Bernd Weiler. *The Moralization of the Markets.* New Brunswick: Transaction Publishers, 2006.
Stolle, Dietlind and Marc Hooghe. "Consumers as Politival Participants? Shifts in Political Action Repertoires in Western Societies." In *Politics, Products, and Markets.* Edited by Michele Micheletti, Andreas Follesdal, and Dietland Stolle. New Brunswick, London: Transaction Publisher, 2004.
Stolle, Dietlind, Marc Hooghe, and Michele Micheletti. "Politics in the Supermarket: Political Consumerism as a Form of Political Participation." *International Political Science Review* 26 (2005): 245–269.
Stolle, Dietlind and Michele Micheletti. "Warum werden Käufer zu 'politischen Verbrauchern'?" ["How do consumers become 'political consumers'?"]" *Forschungsjournal Neue Soziale Bewegungen* 18 (2005): 41–52.
Thompson, Edward P. "The Moral Economy of the English Crowd in the Eighteenth Century." *Past and Present* 50 (1971): 79–136.
Van de Vjver, Fons J. R., Dianne A. Van Hemert, and Ype H. Poortinga. *Multilevel Analysis of Individuals and Cultures.* New York: Lawrence Erlbaum Associates, 2008.
Veblen, Thorstein. *A Theory of the Leisure Class.* London: Allen & Unwin, 1949.
Vogel, David. "Tracing the American Roots of Political Consumerism Movement." In *Politics, Products, and Markets.* Edited by Michele

Micheletti, Andreas Follesdal, and Dietland Stolle. New Brunswick, London: Transaction Publishers, 2004.

Weber, Max. *The Protestant Ethic and the Spirit of Modern Capitalism.* Translated by S. Kalberg. Los Angeles: Roxbury, 2002.

Willer, Helga and Minou Yussefi. *The World of Organic Agriculture: Statistics and Emerging Trends 2007, Vol. 9.* Bonn: International Federation of Organic Agriculture Movements, 2007.

Worcester, Robert and Jenny Dawkins. "Surveying Ethical and Environmental Attitudes." In *The Ethical Consumer.* Edited by Rob Harrison, Terry Newholm, and Deirdre Shaw. London: SAGE Publications Ltd., 2005.

Worldbank. "Key Development Data & Statistics." In *Worldbank*, 2008.

Zelizer, Viviana. "Culture and Consumption." In *The Handbook of Economic Sociology.* Edited by Neil J. Smelser and Richard Swedberg. Princeton: Princeton University Press, 2005.

Zukin, Sharon and Jennifer Smith Maguire. "Consumers and Consumption." *Annual Review of Sociology* (2004): 173–197.

CHAPTER TWO

THE RELATIONSHIP BETWEEN POLITICAL AND CONSUMER ATTITUDES: EMERGING PATTERNS OF ETHICAL CONSUMERISM IN HUNGARY

EMESE GULYÁS[1]

Introduction

During the first decade of the twenty-first century around a dozen boycotts were called in Hungary; there are several ecologically and socially aware food communities directly linking consumers and producers; fair trade products appear on more and more shop shelves. All of these initiatives signal the emergence of new attitudes and values, a new type of behavior, that of "ethical consumerism."

According to latest research trends on ethical consumption introduced in this chapter, the above phenomenon may in part be a symptom of changing political and market relations. Formerly, the mostly economic relationship between market influences—consumers and producers—is now charged with political content, which in the longer term can lead to institutional changes both to the market and within politics. The wide scale spread of ethical consumption can lead to the transformation of market functions, the modern market changing from a mainly economic space to an area of moral action, a tool of regulation and social participation. As a social movement, ethical consumerism can effect political culture and play an important role in public policy aiming towards sustainable development. According to the relevant literature, as well as concrete experience, ethical consumerism is increasingly playing this role in Western-Europe,[2] and the

[1] Sociology Doctoral School, Corvinus University of Budapest.

[2] For example the terminology and the principles of fair trade, which originates from social movements of the early twentieth century, are now part of the EU

appearance locally of the movement invites the questions: what sort of values characterize this new consumer culture in Hungary; and how are these values interconnected with political participation attitudes.

The first part of this study gives an overview of the literature on ethical consumption, explicating the main research themes. In the second part, out of the interpretational possibilities, I look at ethical consumption as political consumption, as a form of social governance, examining its relevance as a way of public participation. I try to find an answer to the question of whether the spread of ethical consumption should be imagined as the demise of classical political institutions, or as complementary to them. The following part concentrates on the local appearance of political consumption in Hungary. It introduces the ethical issues that are most likely to mobilize the public, and discovers the relationship between ethical consumption and political participation attitudes. The study is primarily based on data describing Hungarian political participatory culture, as well as an attitude survey of a representative sample.

Interpretations of Ethical Consumption

Value-based attitudes and models of ethical consumption entered the realm of Anglo-American social sciences from the end of the 1960s. Since then several expressions have been used to describe the concept which today is usually termed "ethical consumption." The most often used terms are "(socially) responsible consumption," "environmentally conscious consumption," and later "sustainable consumption." Although researching value-based consumption goes back several decades, ethical consumption has no notable theories, only a variety of explanatory trends. Literature providing an interdisciplinary overview is almost entirely missing (for an exemption see Brinkmann 2004), therefore it is worth summarizing the characteristic approaches to ethical consumption. Below, based on literature review, I sketch out the main trends as stemming from a general definition of ethical consumption, as well as those which, while not dealing directly with ethical consumption, nevertheless provide a relevant framework for its interpretation.

Most studies dealing with ethical consumer behavior and consumer movements simply define ethical consumption as: "the conscious endeavor of the consumer to make their choices on the basis of their values or ethical principles." The forms of ethical consumption most often referred

legislations. For a summary see: "Communication from the Commission to the Council on 'fair trade'." (COM, 1999), 619.

to are intentional non-consumption, value-based regular shopping, boycott, positive boycott ("buycott"), usage and placement after usage, disposal. The varying approaches accentuate different aspects of consumer behavior and ethics. Surveying the literature on ethical consumption, six tendencies can be identified, but I must emphasize that the below approaches are not well crystallized theories or distinct disciplines, rather occasionally overlapping interpretational possibilities. Not all of the approaches have solid theoretical foundations, and some more theoretically oriented works do not always have a proper discursive frame for describing ethical consumer behaviors. Therefore the first part is intended as an introduction to the notion of ethical consumption rather than a critical comparative analysis of different theories.

The normative analysis of consumer behavior examines the consumer from the point of view of "ethically questionable consumer behavior," the main question being what is considered right or condemnable in a concrete consumption situation. Muncy and Vitell developed a later widely popular and internationally tested method for the examination of the ethics of consumer behavior. The consumers were asked to make ethical statements concerning various consumption situations: e.g. drinking beverages without paying in a supermarket, gaining advantages in passive ways as a result of the inadvertence of the sales-clerk etc. (Muncy and Vitell 1992,Vitell and Muncy 2005). This type of research became popular with corporate managers rather than among social scientists but, and since it is not closely related to the subject of this study, I will not introduce it in detail.

The central ideas of what might be termed the "(self) critique of consumption or consumer society" is "overconsumption," and its counterpart "sustainable consumption," based on the general notion of sustainable development—namely, that development should meet the needs of the present without compromising the ability of future generations to meet their own needs. It is often claimed that after a certain point material consumption can only be maintained at the expense of the quality of life (Singer 1996; Kasser 2003). The amount of relevant literature is immense, since this is the approach that has become embedded in governmental and international policies and in the institutional system. For example the United Nations Environmental Program has developed a "10–Year Framework of Programmes on Sustainable Consumption and Production" (the so called Marrakech process), and the issue is also central to the sustainable development strategy of the European Union, among others. Most theories, studies, and public policies assume that the present consumption rate of the Euro-Atlantic region is ecologically not sustainable, and will result in the depletion of the natural environment even on the short term. Over-excessive material consumption is not right; the citizens of the wealthiest countries have a moral obligation to transform their consumption habits for the sake of sustainability. According to certain academic studies dealing with sustainable consumption, the key to long term, lasting changes in consumption behavior is the strengthening of common values that deviate from consumerist attitudes, and the presentation of alternative lifestyles, and life-models (Brown and Cameron 2000; Barnett et al. 2005; Soper 2007).

The approaches which attempt to explain ethical consumption via expanding the notion of "consumer preference" are also in line with "rational, self-satisfying consumption models of economics." Rational consumer behavior, which measures various choices according to preference, in this case is not only influenced by price and quality, often considered the only markers. During the consumer's ordering of preference "ethical consumers are not, therefore, ignoring price and quality, but applying some additional (and sometimes prior) criteria in the decision-making process," states the preface of a representative book on ethical consumerism compiled by the founding-editor of the British magazine *Ethical Consumer* (Harrison et al. 2005, 2). Behavior which is in line with these motivations increases individual utility just as if one was following their self-interest in the strictest sense. Following pro-social motivations causes moral gratification on one hand, and can be interpreted as the manifestation of enlightened self-interest on the other. In addition there are those, for example Miller (2001), who argue that in many instances the motivations of ethical consumption can be traced back to self-interest in its narrowest sense, to selfish motivations such as better taste, health, prestige-consumption, etc.

Anthropological or anthropologically oriented sociological studies emphasize that consumption is a system of signs, a language. Following the logic of these works, we can say that ethical consumption is a "communicative process of values," and as such it is nothing more than the re-labeling of an ever-present phenomenon. Consumption was always a culturally and socially determined, value-based activity, in which the members of society express their values, beliefs, worldviews and shape the forms of their social interaction; consumer decisions are obviously value-based, but they also contribute to the a development of values (Douglas and Isherwood 1996). It is worth highlighting Douglas' theory (1996, 1997) which sees consumption as a cultural activity, in which through their consumer decisions people decide what kind of world they wish to live in; they choose certain goods because they are accepted in the desirable world, or "condemned" in the undesirable world. At the same time, detailing further the idea of "consumption as a form of identity-expression" she adds that consumers have a much clearer idea about what they are protesting against than what they would indeed identify with. She states that consumers do not want to define their identities via the products purchased, rather that consumption is the definition of what is not the consumer.

Besides ethical consumption as political consumption (see below), the most widespread interpretation of ethical consumption is that of "responsible consumption." According to commentators on responsible consumption, the consumer not only considers the satisfaction of their own needs, but reflects on their own experience as consumers. Preference-ordering is no longer only about self-interest, but the consumer estimates and evaluates the expected effects of their decisions, the interests of the "planet," of society and the environment (Webster 1975; Mohr et al. 2001; Miller 2001). For example, when consumers satisfy their mobility needs, they do not only weigh up whether the bus, the car or the bicycle is the swiftest and most comfortable way of reaching their destinations, but also what strain various transport modes place on their environment; in certain cases they subordinate their own interests to those of the community. The key-words of this approach are "pro-social behavior," "altruism" and "helping." Many scholars view assistance, helping-behavior, as the parallel of socially responsible consumption, since both stress the importance of serving other people's interest and curbing individual advantages (Anderson and Cunningham 1972; Klein et al. 2004). While there is no coherent theoretical background in social science to the ethical consumption as responsible consumption approach, there are several studies of empirical research. Using market segmentation methods, Anderson and Cunningham (1972) showed that there is a very distinct vanguard as far as social responsibility and altruistic helping is concerned, whose responsible attitude is manifest in concrete consumer decisions. Also worth highlighting is the research done by Cooper-Martin and Holbrook (1993), which compiled the behavioral prototypes of ethical consumption and distinguished the active (e.g. buying cruelty-free products, purchasing reusable bottles) and the passive (boycotts and not-buying) forms of ethical consumption. The consumers polled felt that altruist activities were right. According to conclusions of their study, ethically superior consumption experiences are active and selfless activities.

The studies interpreting ethical consumption cluster around three poles according to whether they use normative or descriptive approaches, whether they see ethical consumption as an individual action, or as both individual and collective, or as purely a collective action, and finally whether the behavior of the consumer is instrumental or expressive.

Ethical Consumption as a Form of Public Participation: Political Consumption

In recent years there has been a re-emergence in interpreting ethical consumption as political consumption, which is probably related to pluralization, i.e. the emergence and spread of new forms of political participation, as well as the negative effects of globalization (the free flow of capital) and growing power of transnational organizations (WTO, European Union), which do not provide a "direct" say for the citizens, becoming more evident. Below I will introduce the main ideas about ethical consumption as a form of public participation, as well as briefly summarizing its remarkable antecedents in sociological thought.

Scholars who interpret value-oriented consumption as political consumption stress the pressurizing nature of ethical consumption, seeing consumers not just as market players, but as political actors as well. The market is also a place for political and moral action: "market decisions reflect on the interpretations of material goods placed within a complex social and normative context" (Micheletti 2003, 3), which according to the often used "dollar vote" analogy means that through their purchasing decisions consumers participate in shaping society, just as they do through their political vote (Dickinson and Hollander 1991; Dickinson and Carsky 2005). The appreciation of the power of the consumer vote varies—certain scholars speak of the expression of political views, the shaping and influencing of social processes[3]; others are more blunt, describing ethical consumption as a regulatory process, as the curbing of the power of (global) corporations.[4] Beck (2005) for example, considers consumer votes as nothing less than a tool of power. Since companies are in fact obliged to cooperate with consumer power, he envisions a social movement which can become the counterpoint of the global capital, and which constantly evades social responsibility. In comparison to the others, when considering political consumption the instrumental nature of consumption has a central role: the aim to see changes in unwanted corporate or political practices is an important motivation for the decisions of the consumer. Based on empirical research carried out in Denmark, Andersen and Tobiasen (2004)

---

[3] Among others Dickinson and Hollander (1991), Miller (1997), Dickinson and Carsky (2005), Stolle and Hooge (2004), Andersen and Tobiasen (2004).

[4] This viewpoint is held by Smith (1990), Micheletti (2003, 2004), Beck (2005).

claim that in fact this intention to influence and to contribute to changes as well as the belief that individual consumption choices can lead to collective results is what differentiates political consumption from consumption concentrating only on the satisfaction of ones own needs. This need for change usually manifests itself in boycotts called for by various pressure-groups (Hirschman 1970; Smith 1990), though the Danish researchers also include the various consumption-oriented solidarity groups, for example the Fair Trade movements.

That ethical consumption can be interpreted as a form of public participation also has historical antecedents. The school which describes ethical consumption as political consumption has examined many cases related to consumer movements, the aims of which have been reinforced by or have been placed on the political agenda via these movements. To mention only a few of the better known ones, in the 19th century American consumers stood up for universal freedom rights when they boycotted tea and sugar products from plantations using slave-labor (Glickman 2004). In Germany, Chancellor Kohl personally supported Greenpeace in their boycott of Shell, protesting the marine sinking of a decommissioned oil-drilling tower. The success of the cooperation between NGOs, consumers, and politics strengthened the cause of environmentalism within German politics, and gave weight to German environmental concerns in the Franco-German debate on deep-sea nuclear testing (Beck 1998). The success of the struggle against apartheid in South-Africa was in large part due to the international boycott movement announced by Nelson Mandela in 1993 (Irving et al. 2005).

Based on the ethical consumption as political consumption approach, hereafter I present some middle-range theory arguments that ethical consumption can be interpreted as public participation. According to some authors, people turn to organized consumer action (for example boycotts) when this is the only remaining or the most effective means of fighting for their interests (Micheletti 2003; Harrison et al. 2005), and the increase in the significance of movements for ethical consumption goes hand in hand with a decrease in the significance of traditional politics (Miller 1997). Still, judging by the research, which describes the transformation of political culture, the spread of ethical consumption is expected rather as a form of participation complementing, not replacing, traditional political actions. If we interpret ethical consumption as a new form of participation, then we can assume that it came to be as a part of certain transformations within political culture, while at the same time it retroactively effects the institutions and the issues of politics, i.e. it is in a recursive relationship with the political systems. The question is—which features or transformational processes of the political systems have contributed to the emergence and spread of the phenomena of ethical consumption?

According to Habermas (1973), Beck (1992, 1997, 1998, 2005), Inglehart (1997), Norris (2002) and others it is a general tendency that within most of the wealthy northern countries trust in the government is declining, leading to a crisis which questions their legitimacy. This is due in part to the widely discussed decline of their efficiency, the poor regulatory performance of government, and in to changes in values. Habermas and Beck see the reasons for declining government efficiency, leading to problems of legitimacy, in the fact that governments are incapable of harmonizing political, social and economic interests. The state has to simultaneously create the conditions for a prosperous economy and soften the dysfunctional effects of capitalism, and doing so in a way that does not curtail the fundamental functions of the economy. Though the state and the government depend on the dynamics of the economy, they are more and more unable to participate in actively shaping it; the maneuvering-room of the state is economically limited. Beck and Habermas agree that the globalization of labor and capital restrict the influence of governments and nation-states. The question is, what sort of actions and reactions does the decline of legitimacy evoke on the part of citizens?

Political participation research describes Western democracies as not at all apathetic; they are increasingly active in exploring new forms of political participation, while the election turnout remains relatively stable. Interest in politics is changing both as far as its players, its issues and target-groups are concerned. However, in many cases political action is no longer directed towards traditional political institutions, states and governments, but at international corporations (see boycotts). One of the main trends of this transformation is that so called protest-politics moves from the periphery of political action to its centre. Its popularity has risen and since the 1990s has become a decisive form of political action. New social movements, internet activism and international networks all offer new possibilities for involvement (Inglehart 1997, Norris 2002), and these international tendencies are also apparent in Hungary (Kiss and Boda 2005, Angelusz and Tardos 2006, Tóka 2006).

Among the middle-range theories, Beck's theory on the transformation of political culture provides the most relevant framework for the interpretation of ethical consumerism as a form of public participation. The central idea of the theory of reflexive modernization and of sub-politics is: as a consequence of the nontransparent, non-democratic operation of the techno-economic and techno-scientific sphere, "risks become the motor of the self-politicization of modernity in industrial society; furthermore, in the risk society, the concept, place and media of politics change" (Beck 1999, 183). What are the characteristics of these changes? Beck states that in the industrial society a significant part of decision making competences are removed from the rules of public inspection and justification, and thus become disconnected from the political system and are no longer subject to principles of parliamentary democracy. The demarcation between politics and non-politics becomes dubious, and politics is limited merely to the management of the formal political system. The most significant transformations that influence social changes come from the techno-scientific sphere and do not occur through the processes of the political system, but in a non-political manner. Nevertheless their significance varies inversely with their legitimation. Certain actions acquire new political and moral dimensions, and become sub-politics, between politics and non-politics. In his earlier works, such as *Risk Society*, Beck uses the expression "sub-politics" mainly in connection with the scientific-technical-economic sphere—he later extends this notion to all kinds of groups that had previously existed as separate from politics, such as the private sphere, cities and every day life, including consumption. (Beck 1999, 183–187). Beck's latest works make more and more references to consumer movements as the role-players with one of the most potential to solve global environmental and social challenges (Journal of Consumer Culture, 2001).

Ethical consumption is public political participation, sub-politics in a Beckian sense, as a previously politically neutral action—consumption becomes charged with political content, and becomes a means for influencing politics. Ethical consumers take part in solving social problems by using market and consumer power as a social adjustment mechanism.

Ethical Consumerism and its Relation to Political Participation in Hungary

We can find several historical antecedents of ethical consumption in Hungary from the mid-nineteenth century and the early twentieth century.[5] Concerning the present state of ethical consumption there exist surveys on consumer attitudes and data on the number of boycott-calls: in Hungary,

[5] The most well-known are the Védegylet (Hungarian Association of Patriots) and the Tulip movement, both patriotic organizations, a shoemaker boycott from 1905 and a landlord boycott from 1907.

after the turn of the millennium, there was a boycott virtually every year—between 2001 and 2007 there were 16 boycotts and 4 buycotts that we know of. From among the mapped boycotts only a few managed to gain wide scale publicity and coverage from the media. Out of the examples listed below several reached the political agenda, and gained the support of politicians, with a few cases where politicians effectively assisted in finding a solution to the problem (e.g. Danone and Pepsi cases in 2001, the Matáv boycott in 2002, the boycott of Austrian products in 2007) where politicians themselves spoke out and supported the campaigns. Most of these boycotts or buycotts are related to some economic problem, but there were several environmental, animal rights or general social issues as well. Besides the number of boycotts, we know from well documented representative survey data that 15–17 percent of the population claim that during the past few years they have joined boycotts (Association of Conscious Consumers 2005, Braun & Partners 2006).

Besides the actual cases, an interesting question is—which are those causes and social issues that consumers are sensitive to, which can grow to be state-wide movements, given the proper organizational capacity behind them? Based on a 2005 survey, commissioned by the Association of Conscious Consumers, a civil society organization for ethical consumption, it is possible to draw up a list on how important different social and environmental causes are, as well as the group of potential boycotters and buycotters. The data of the survey contained 1015 representative cases for the adult population according to gender, age-group, and settlement-type. The margin of error for the statistical sample was < 3.2 % of N = 1000 persons. Delivered by the Hungarian Gallup Institute.

Table 2.1. Boycotts and buycotts in Hungary 2001–2007

Target	Initiator	Causes/Aims	Year
Pepsi	Waste Prevention Alliance (HUMUSZ) + 19 NGOs.	Pepsi pulled returnable bottles from the market, advertising disposable packaging.	2001
⊕ Returnable bottles	Return to returnables! Campaign: (HUMUSZ) + 19 NGOs.	Keeping returnable bottles on the market.	2001
Danone	“Viktor, Jano” anonym.	Against the closing of the Győri Biscuit Factory previously purchased by Danone.	2001
Matáv (Hungarian Telecommunications Company)	Private individuals, who later founded the Netért (For the Net) Association.	For recalling the “Mindenkinet (For all)” package, which did away with cheap internet access.	2002
OTP Bank	Chain email.	OTP Faktoring bought up the assets of the Budapest Chamber of Commerce and Industry; the data-use was solicitous.	2002
⊕ buying the weeklies Heti Válasz and Demokrata, and the daily Magyar Nemzet (conservative media publications)	Viktor Orbán, former Prime Minister, leader of the opposition at the time.	Getting people to buy and prescribe to certain papers in order to a have a more well balanced media.	2002
Brau-Heineken	Brau shareholders (anonym).	Heineken wished to buy up the Soproni Beer-Company through dishonest means, thus causing harm to the shareholders.	2003
Westel, Mobile phone service provider	Latinovits Zoltán Civic Circle, the readers of the weekly, Demokrata	Westel is not willing to advertise in the Demokrata.	2003

Procter & Gamble, Iams	People for the Ethical Treatment of Animals (PETA) – local implementation of a international campaign, anonym activists.	Against experimentation on animals.	2003
⊕ NGOs fighting against the creation of the Rosia Montana goldmine in Transylvania	Tibor Kocsis, director of the documentary film New Eldorado.	10% of the movie-ticket revenue offered to support of a local NGO.	2004
ESSO	Local implementation of an international campaign by Greenpeace.	Countering ESSO's systematic campaign against the Kyoto Protocol: ESSO spent millions of dollars on advertisements questioning the validity of the Kyoto process and the climate-protection institutions involved with it.	2004
MOL, Hungarian Petrol (Hungarian petrol company)	National Alliance of Transporters and the Federation of International Private Transporters.	Against high gasoline prices.	2005
Benetton	International Campaign	Against animal-mutilation during wool-production.	2005
Törley (Champagne Company)	Waste Prevention Alliance (HUMUSZ)	Against Törley terminating returnable champagne bottles.	2005
Rauch soft drinks	Chain-mail, producers.	Because they are not willing to buy Hungarian fruits, or only at a reduced price.	2006
Axe cosmetics (Unilever)	Chain-mail Nina Umniakov choreographer.	Sexist advertisements.	2006
⊕ Fradi (football team)	Gábor Borókai, editor of Heti Válasz (political weekly).	Everyone should buy season-tickets to "save" the team financially.	2006

Auchan retail group and multinational companies in general	Krisztina Morvai, civic rights-advocate.	They do not respect human rights.	2007
Insurance companies which plan to participate in the privatization of the health sector	Christian-democratic People's Party	Against privatization of health services.	2007
Sponsors of the Gay-lesbian festival	Christian-democratic People's Party	One year boycott of sponsors who support the "offensive" festival.	2007

Source: author's own research

Table 2.2. Potential boycott causes in Hungary

Negative information on corporate performance that might influence consumer decisions [1] The company...	Ratio of those who consider the information important or very important (%) (A)	Ratio of those within the previous group who would choose other products of another company even if they were more expensive (%) (B)	Potential boycotters (%) (A) x (B)
pollutes the environment	88,80	52,0	46,18
applies misleading advertisement techniques	90,00	49,1	44,19
employs child labor	75,80	54,9	41,61
outsources its production capacities from Hungary	72,80	52,7	38,37
provides humiliating working conditions	79,70	46,1	36,74
produces in sweatshops in third world countries	71,40	49,2	35,13
is involved in corruption	65,90	48,9	32,23
applies animal testing for cosmetic purposes	57,80	49,2	28,44
does not pay its subcontractors	60,70	44,3	26,89
avoids taxes	63,60	39,8	25,31

[1] Answers to the question: Which are the most important aspects of business performance that consumers should be informed about?

restricts the operation of trade unions	54,00	45,3	24,46
is involved in arms production	52,30	46,2	24,16
produces in countries under oppressive regimes	45,40	46,4	21,07
has interests in the nuclear industry	45,90	43,8	20,10
has tax reliefs from the government	53,60	30,1	16,13

Source: data from the Association of Conscious Consumers and the author's calculation

Table 2.3. Potential buycott causes in Hungary

Positive information on corporate performance that might influence consumer decisions.[2] The company…	Ratio of those who consider the information important or very important (%) (A)	Ratio of those within the previous group who would choose the products of these companies even if they were more expensive (%) (B)	Potential buycotters (%) (A) x (B)
produces in Hungary	82,15	54,22	44,52
has an environmental program	83,76	48,72	40,78
has charity activities, offers donations	71,37	51,79	36,98
supports the employment of the disadvantaged	78,27	46,37	36,31
has Hungarian owners	70,45	50,03	35,22
has above average care for employees (e.g. family friendly workplace)	75,18	43,69	32,85
supports the development of the local community	69,89	43,23	30,22

[2] Answers to the question: Which are the most important aspects of business performance that consumers should be informed about?

supports cultural activities	65,20	41,56	27,10
does not apply animal testing	59,72	42,16	25,17
regularly reports on its social and environmental performance	59,40	39,71	23,58
involves civil society organizations and local governments in its decision making processes	56,93	35,61	20,26
was awarded by civil organizations	38,25	40,81	15,59

Source: data from the Association of Conscious Consumers and the author's calculation

Besides giving an overview of the presence of ethical consumption, further analysis provides a proper starting point for the foundation of a concept of ethical consumption as a form of public participation. According to the theoretical principles found in international literature I examined the presented data with the aim of discovering the relationship between ethical consumption and political participation attitudes. It was not the aim of the study to determine the causal relations or direction of such a relationship, or to reveal the basis of consumer and political attitudes, but merely to show the existing context. Based on the survey questions concerning consumer attitudes, I developed a simplified, soft profile of the ethical consumer, following which I compared the corresponding cases with all the others in respect of political attitudes.

In the questionnaire there were questions both about negative and positive corporate issues which were the inverse of one another much of the time. For example, in making consumer choices it would be important to know if a company has environmental programs and it would be important to know if the company pollutes the environment. According to Douglas (1996) and Bourdieu (1984) protest behaviour, similar to political protest voting, plays an important role in shaping consumer identity. Therefore the development of the ethical consumer profile is based on the responses to negatively phrased questions. This is a soft method for constructing an ethical consumer profile, but provides enough cases for statistically valid analysis and conclusions. Those respondents identified as ethical consumers were those who assigned importance to the three most popular environmental, social and political issues in connection with consumer choices, namely environmental pollution, the misleading of consumers and child labor.

In the following I will concentrate on one central theme of ethical consumption as political consumption which is also widely discussed in the literature—the relationship between ethical consumerism and political participation. How do ethical consumers relate to the usage of different, classical and new political means? Is there evidence for the substituting nature of traditional and new political participation, or rather the contrary? There are references for literature to support both scenarios (Micheletti 2003, Harrison et al. 2005 and Inglehart 1997, Norris 2002).

Two hypotheses were set up to explore this theme further: Consumers who consider environmental and social issues important when talking about consumer decisions (termed as ethical consumers):

H_1: Ethical consumers are more likely to assign importance to the traditional political participation opportunities (e.g. parliamentary elections, party politics) than the majority.

Respondents were asked if they found participation in different kinds of voting important.

Table 2.4. Voting willingness among ethical consumers and the majority

Is it important to participate in the following voting?		Ethical consumer Yes	Ethical consumer No	Total	Pearson Chi-square	df	Sig.	Odds ratio	Limits of the 95%-os confidence interval
Parliamentary elections	Yes	72 91%	687 75%	759 76%	10,554	1	0,001	3,444	1,563; 7,589
	No	7 9%	230 25%	237 24%					
Local elections	Yes	68 86%	604 66%	672 68%	13,451	1	0,000	3,193	1,665; 6,126
	No	11 14%	312 34%	323 32%					
Interim parliamentary elections	Yes	49 61%	412 45%	461 46%	7,835	1	0,005	1,934	1,211; 3,088
	No	31 39%	504 55%	535 54%					
Interim local elections	Yes	53 67%	450 49%	503 51%	9,387	1	0,002	2,111	1,297; 3,435
	No	26 33%	466 51%	492 49%					
National referendums	Yes	71 90%	646 70%	717 72%	13,524	1	0,000	3,709	1,762; 0,568
	No	8 10%	270 30%	278 28%					
Local referendums	Yes	67 84%	580 63%	647 65%	13,574	1	0,000	2,995	1,629; 5,506
	No	13 16%	337 37%	349 35%					

The statistically significant results show that ethical consumers are two to three times more likely to consider participation in political elections important, especially in parliamentary elections and local elections. The most significant relationship with ethical consumer attitudes is shown with assigning importance to local elections and to referendums (both local and national).

H_2: Ethical consumers are more likely to assign importance to new, civil political participation opportunities (e.g. social movements, petitions, media campaigns) than the majority.

Openness to new civil participation was measured by a standard question in political culture and value surveys. Respondents were asked to mark the three most efficient means through which they can express their opinion and represent their interests from a short list. The results of the contingency analysis are the following.

Table 2.5. The perceptions about the efficiency of different means through which people can express their opinion and represent their interests among ethical consumers and the majority

Do you find the below means efficient for expressing opinion and representing people's interest?		Ethical consumer: Yes	Ethical consumer: No	Total	Pearson Chi-square	df	Sig.	Odds ratio	Limits of the 95%-os confidence interval
Voting for the appropriate party on the parliamentary elections	Yes	45 56%	576 69%	621 68%	6,346	1	0,012	0,556	0,350; 0,882
	No	36 44%	256 31%	292 32%					
Participation in dialogues with political parties	Yes	27 34%	253 30%	280 31%	0,383	1	0,536	1,166	0,717; 1,896
	No	53 66%	579 70%	632 69%					
Signing a petition	Yes	35 43%	351 42%	386 42%	0,032	1	0,859	1,043	0,658; 1,653
	No	46 57%	481 58%	527 58%					
Organising social forums, discussions	Yes	46 56%	371 45%	416 46%	4,037	1	0,045	1,601	1,008; 2,542
	No	35 44%	462 55%	497 54%					
Attending peaceful demonstrations	Yes	13 16%	185 23%	198 22%	1,538	1	0,215	0,679	0,366; 1,256
	No	67 84%	647 77%	714 78%					

Supporting issue oriented pressure group CSOs	Yes	11 14%	115 14%	126 14%	0,000	1	0,989	0,995	0,511; 1,937
	No	69 86%	718 86%	787 86%					
Organising media campaigns	Yes	32 40%	337 40%	369 40%	0,006	1	0,937	0,981	0,614; 1,564
	No	48 60%	496 60%	544 60%					
Joining boycotts	Yes	32 40%	245 29%	277 30%	3,843	1	0,050	1,597	0,997; 2,559
	No	48 60%	587 71%	635 70%					

According to the statistically significant results, ethical consumers are half as likely to consider parliamentary elections as an efficient means for expressing opinion and representing their interests, while are more than one and a half times more likely to find social forums and sixty percent more likely to find boycotts efficient than the majority of the respondents. The results also suggest that from the means of civic or movement politics, ethical consumers are more attached to methods closer to the institutions of direct democracy, namely boycotts and social forums as contrary to representative democracy (parliamentary elections).

The results also shed light on an interesting contradiction. Ethical consumers are more likely to assign importance to parliamentary election participation; nevertheless they are less likely to consider it as an efficient means for expressing opinions and representing interests. The contradiction might be resolved if we presume something of a "political hyperactivity" about ethical consumers—they find each political channel important independently of their efficiency. A plausible explanation might also be that ethical consumers find bearing witness for representative democratic institutions important, but are not convinced that politicians represent their interests. At this stage of the research these notions are based on presumption with no statistical evidence, and a richer database is required for further analysis. However the above data supports the concept that new social movements, such as ethical consumerism, complement but do not replace traditional, representative political participation.

Conclusions

Ethical consumption has been on the agenda of social sciences for decades, but up to the present day no dominant theories have emerged, merely various research trends. There are six major definable trends describing ethical consumption: (1) as ethically questionable consumer behavior; (2) as the (self) critique of consumption or consumer society; (3) as the extension of rational consumer behavior; (4) as a communications process of values; (5) as responsible consumption; (6) as political consumption, social governance. At the turn of the millennium, the most popular approach of ethical consumption was that of political consumption. Empirical studies point to the interrelatedness of political participation and ethical consumption attitudes, showing as a form of public participation, and ethical consumption which complements, but does not replace traditional political forms.

Ethical consumption attitudes and behavior are present in Hungary as well. In choosing products, besides the price-value balance, the majority of the population would consider patriotism, environmental protection, fair employment, and consumer-information to be important. In the past 15 years, willingness to join boycotts is slowly increasing— 15–17 percent of the population stated that they had joined boycotts in recent years. At present, the majority of Hungarian consumers are aware of their "purchasing–power," of the possibilities for enforcing their consumer interests. In line with the European rates, about 35–45% of the population belongs to the group of potential boycotters and buycotters.

According to the analyses of the ethical consumer and political participation attitudes of Hungarians, the following conclusions are presented: compared to the majority, consumers with ethical consumer attitudes:

- Were much more likely to consider participation in political elections important, and were more likely to attribute significance to the use of traditional participative forms of representative democracy
- Despite assigning them importance, they were less likely to consider participation in parliamentary elections as an efficient tool for enforcing their interests and expressing their opinions
- Were more likely to consider social forums and dialogues as an efficient tool for enforcing their interests and expressing their opinions

Thus the results of the study show that ethical consumers have a very strong commitment to the use of traditional political tools, such as participation in various types of elections, though they are much more sceptical about the efficiency of these forms. From the tools of civic or movement politics they are more attached to methods closer to the institutions of direct democracy, namely boycotts and social forums.

The above results are the first that describe political consumerism in Hungary. For a better understanding and to make conclusions on its role in shaping present political and market institutions, further research is needed.

References

Angelusz Róbert and Tardos Róbert, "Választási részvétel, 2006" ["Election turnout, 2006"]. In *Társadalmi Riport 2006* [*Social Report, 2006*]. Edited by Kolosi Tamás and Tóth István György. Budapest: TÁRKI, 2006.

Andersen, Jørgen Goul and Mette Tobiasen. "Who Are These Political Consumers Anyway? Survey Evidence from Denmark." In *Politics, Products and Markets—Exploring Political Consumerism Past and Present*. Edited by Michele Micheletti, Andreas Follesdal and Dietlind Stolle. New Jersey: Transaction Publishers, 2004.

Anderson, W. Thomas Jr. and William H. Cunningham. "The Socially Conscious Consumer." *Journal of Marketing* 36 (1972): 23–31.

Association of Conscious Consumers. *Etikus fogyasztói attitűdök Magyarországon. Kutatási Beszámoló.* [*Ethical Consumer Attitudes in Hungary. Research Report*]. Budapest: Association of Conscious Consumers, 2005.

Barnett, Clive, Philip Cafaro and Terry Newholm. "Philosophy and Ethical Consumption." In *The Ethical Consumer*. Edited by Rob Harrison, Terry Newholm and Deirdre Shaw. London: Sage Publications, 2005.

Beck, Ulrich. *Risk Society: Towards a New Modernity*. London: Sage Publications, 1992.

—. *The Reinvention of Politics: Rethinking Modernity in the Global Social Order*. Cambridge: Polity Press, 1997.

—. *Was ist Globalisierung? Irrtümer des Globalismus—Antworten auf Globalisierung* [*What is Globalization? Errors of Globalism—Answers to Globalization*]. Frankfurt am Main: Suhrkamp Verlag, 1998.

—. *Was zur Wahl steht* [*The Stake of Choice*]. Frankfurt am Main: Suhrkamp Verlag, 2005.

Braun & Partners. *Közvélemény-kutatás a vállalatok társadalmi felelősségvállalásáról—Reprezentatív felmérés arról, hogy mit tudnak és mit gondolnak az emberek a CSR-ről* [*A Public Opinion Survey about Corporate Responsibility—What People Think and Know about CSR*]. Budapest: Braun & Partners Kft., 2006.

Brinkmann, Johannes. "Looking At Consumer Behavior In A Moral Perspective." *Journal of Business Ethics* 51 (2004): 129–141.

Bourdieu, Pierre. *Distinction. A Social Critique of the Judgement of Taste.* London and New York: Routledge & Kegan Paul, 1984.

Brown, Paul M. and Linda D. Cameron. "What can be done to reduce overconsumption?" *Ecological Economics* 32 (2000): 27–41.

Cooper-Martin, Elisabeth and Morris B. Hoolbrook. "Ethical Consumption Experiences and Ethical Space." *Advances in Consumer Research* 20 (1993): 113–118.

Dickinson, Roger A. and Mary L. Carsky. "The Consumer as Economic Voter." In *The Ethical Consumer.* Edited by Rob Harrison, Terry Newholm and Deirdre Shaw. London: Sage Publications, 2005.

Dickinson, Roger and Stanley C. Hollander. "Consumer Votes." *Journal of Business Research* 22 (1991): 335–346.

Douglas, Mary. *Thought Styles: Critical Essays on Good Taste.* London: Sage Publications, 1996.

—. "In Defence of Shopping." In *The Shopping Experience.* Edited by Pasi Falk and Colin Campbell. London: Sage Publications, 1997.

Douglas, Mary and Baron Isherwood. *The World of Goods and Towards an Anthropology of Consumption.* London: Routledge, 1996.

Glickman, Lawrence. "Consommer pour réformer le capitalisme américain. Le citoyen et le consommateur au début du XXe siècle" ["Consuming for Reforming the American Capitalism. The citizen and the Consumer at the Beginning of the 20th Century"]. *Sience de la société* 62 (2004): 17–45.

Habermas, Jürgen. *Legitimationsprobleme im Spätkapitalismus* [*Legitimation Crisis*]. Franfurt am Main: Suhrkamp Verlag, 1973.

Harrison, Rob, Terry Newholm and Deirdre Shaw. "Introduction." In *The Ethical Consumer.* Edited by Rob Harrison, Terry Newholm and Deirdre Shaw. London: Sage Publications, 2005.

Hirschman, Albert O. *Exit, Voice and Loyalty: Responses to Decline in Firms, Organizations and States.* London: Harvard University Press, 1970.

Inglehart, Ronald. *Modernization and Postmodernization, Cultural, Economic and Political Change in 43 Societies.* New Jersey: Princeton University Press, 1997.

Journal of Consumer Culture. "Interview with Ulrich Beck." *Journal of Consumer Culture* 1(2) (2001): 261–277.

Kasser, Tim. *The High Price of Materialism.* Cambridge: MIT Press, 2003.

Kiss, Balázs and Boda Zsolt. *Politika az interneten* [*Politics on the Internet*]. Budapest: Századvég, 2005.

Klein, Gabrielle Jill, N. Craig Smith and Andrew John. "Why We Boycott: Consumer Motivations for Boycott Participation." *Journal of Marketing* 68 (2004): 92–109.

Micheletti, Michele. *Political Virtue and Shopping: Individuals, Consumerism and Collective Action*. New York: Palgrave Macmillan, 2003.

—. "Le consumérisme politique. Une nouvelle forme de gouvernance transnationale?" ["Political Consumption. A New Form of Transnational Governance?"] *Sience de la société* 62 (2004): 119–145.

Miller, Daniel. "Could Shopping Ever Really Matter?" In *The Shopping Experience.* Edited by Pasi Falk and Colin Campbell. London: Sage Publications, 1997.

—. *The Dialectics of Shopping.* Chicago: The University of Chicago Press, 2001.

Mohr, Lois A., Deborah J. Webb and Katherine E. Harris. "Do Consumers Expect Companies to be Socially Responsible? The Impact of Corporate Social Responsibility on Buying Behaviour." *Journal of Consumer Affairs* 35 (2001): 45–72.

Muncy, James A. and Vitell Scott J. "Consumer Ethics: An Investigation of the Ethical Beliefs of the Final Consumer." *Journal of Business Research* 24 Vol.4. (1992): 297-311.

Norris, Pippa. *Democratic Phoenix. Reinventing Political Activism.* Cambridge, Cambridge University Press, 2002.

Tóka Gábor. "Vezérek csodálói. A magyar választói magatartás nemzetközi összehasonlításban" ["Admirers of Leaders. Hungarian Voter Behaviour in an International Context"]. In *Parlamenti választás 2006. Elemzések és adatok* [*Parlametary Elections 2006. Analysis and Data*]. Edited by Gergely Karácsony. Budapest: Demokrácia Kutatások Magyarországi Központja Közhasznú Alapítvány és Budapesti Corvinus Egyetem Politikatudományi Intézet, 2006.

Singer, Peter. "Coping with Global Change: The Need for Different Values." *Journal of Human Values* 2 (1) (1996): 37–48.

Smith, N. Craig. *Morality and the Market, Consumer Pressure for Corporate Accountability.* London: Routledge, 1990.

Stolle, Dietlind and Marc Hooghe. "Consumers as Political Participants? Shifts in Political Action Repertoires in Western Societies." In *Politics, Products and markets and Exploring Political Consumerism Past and Present,* Edited by Michele Micheletti, Andreas Follesdal and Dietlind Stolle. New Jersey: Transaction Publishers, 2004.

Soper, Kate. "Re-thinking the 'good life': the citizenship dimension of consumer disaffection with consumerism." *Journal of Consumer Culture* 7 (2) (2007): 205–229.

Vitell, Scott J. and James Muncy. "The Muncy-Vitell Consumer Ethics Scale: A Modification and Applicaiton" *Journal of Business Ethics* 62 (2005): 267-275.

Webster, Frederick E. Jr: "Determining the Characteristics of the Socially Conscious Consumer." *Journal of Consumer Research* 2 (1975): 188–196.

CHAPTER THREE

WHERE DO THE BENGALI ELITE SPEND AND WHY? NETWORK INFLUENCES ON CONSUMPTION AND INVESTMENT

MASUDUR RAHMAN[1]

Introduction

Most economists assume that the preferences of individuals are determined by the basic biological needs for food, drink and shelter, and all the more so in poorer countries where families spend over half their incomes on food, and a further quarter on shelter. These economists have a non-embedded notion of consumption which implies that it is primarily an economic activity, linked to utility maximization and expressed through market demand,[2] that individual decisions regarding consumption are unfettered by others, and that goods are consumed at present, independent of past and future orientations (Becker 1998). They regard consumption as an individual end in itself and fail to see that it can be a means to achieve other ends (Frenzen, Hirsch and Zerillo 1994). Theorists within this tradition find that the same basic market principle of utility maximization exists in all societies; pre-industrial and industrial, or market and non-market, and in all temporal and spatial settings. The notion of the rational and utility maximising individual in the market is however controversial.[3]

---

[1] The Faculty of Social Sciences, Bodø University College.

[2] I am referring to a generalized marginalist perception, not to any particular theorist. Some notable exceptions are Veblen 1979, Duesenberry 1949, Leibenstein 1976, Becker 1998.

[3] The controversies are apparent in both institutional economics (Veblen) and new institutional economics (Leibenstein, Becker) as well as in sociology and anthropology (Polanyi, Coleman, Granovetter).

Becker (1998), For instance, suggests going beyond the assumption that consumption is an individual decision, and to include past experiences and social forces in the analyses of consumption.

There are theoretical arguments and practical evidences as to why consumption should be viewed as embedded in social relations: consumption is eminently social, relational, rather than private and atomic (Appadurai 1986), and individuals take the behavior of others into consideration when they state preferences (Coleman 1994; Frenzen, Hirsch and Zerillo 1994); there are connections between consumption and social ranks (Bourdieu1989); consumption behavior entails goals of status, identity etc. (Bourdieu and Passeron 1994; Lunt 1995; Miller 1995); families have large-scale consumption rituals (Douglas and Isherwood 1996); and interpersonal relations affect consumption (Granovetter and Soong 1985).

Whereas the significance of social relations are recognized, sociological perspectives on consumption frequently take social structure and culture as the shapers and determinants of the amount, content, and patterns of consumption (Frenzen, Hirsch, and Zerillo 1994). There are also disagreements within economic sociology as to how to perceive embeddedness. In the Old Economic Sociology, embeddedness implies economy as an instituted process, and the level of embeddedness changes through processes of marketization of the economy i.e. modernization (Polanyi 1957). On the other hand, according to the New Economic Sociology, economy is embedded in ongoing concrete social networks and the level of embeddedness changes little from one form of society to another (Granovetter (1991). Granovetter further asserts that individuals in non-market societies are as rational as in market societies.[4]

In this chapter the embedded nature of consumption is further examined. The rationality of consumption is seen to be inherent in the pattern of interaction that takes place within and between networks, and consumption behavior of various elite sub-groups in Bangladesh is proposed as a case in point. I have observed that they spend heavily on luxury consumption, and by using qualitative data, both interview and observation, I have tried to analyse how they perceive utility, and how structures of relations set goals of consumption.

The findings take us beyond the narrow notion of economic rationality. Individuals maximise utility but they take both social obligations and

---

[4] Market societies refer to societies in which the market is subordinated to other social institutions and social relations (Polanyi 1957), where industrialization and capitalist development have not yet reached the western standard. In this article, I use developing poor countries.

economic utility into consideration. Individuals' perceptions of obligations and utility of current consumption are extended in time beyond present goals, both economic and non-economic. The findings also put theories that rely heavily on social and cultural values under critical scrutiny. Placing too much emphasis on structures and norms, those theories pay little attention to individual agency in the creation of networks, and the use of network ties. The case in hand directs our attention to interactions between individuals and their networks that constitutes structures within which choices are made. The rationality of consumption must be broadened by formulating such interaction more substantially, and doing so I draw on Weber's (1978) notion of substantive rationality, and what Polanyi (1957) called the "substantive" meaning of economic.

In the following section, I develop my theoretical arguments for incorporating substantive rationality and the substantive meaning of economic issues into consumption goals. This is followed by an interpretation of findings from observation and interviews of consumption and investment behavior of various elite sub-groups in Dhaka, Bangladesh. I then analyse the structure of relations before concluding with a discussion on the theoretical impacts of this analysis. By highlighting the significance of norms of networks my conclusion complements the embeddedness approach to economic sociology.

The Substances of Substantive Rationality

Zukin and DiMaggio (1994) put forward four kinds of interdependence challenging the assumptions of neoclassical economics: (1) Our utility of a commodity may be a function not only of our personal welfare but the welfare of those we care about; (2) The value of specific goods or services may depend on the extent to which others consume them; (3) Individuals' ability to act may be constrained by the fact that others will respond; (4) Individuals may only be able to enhance their welfare by cooperating with others. This will require the integration of different utility functions in one way or another.

The marginalist notion of utility implies that each individual gains utility by gaining control of resources, and loses utility by giving up control of resources. Coleman (1994) claims that individuals may gain utility by giving up control over a resource— by transferring action from one to another, one can ensure a better outcome and better future utility. By meeting present obligations individuals ensure future expectations, and investment in friendship or in social capital may deliver positive results in the future. Social capital depends on properties of the social network, with certain kinds of social structures generating extensive social capital. Furthermore, the rights of individuals are also the outcome of social processes; they act rationally to further their interests by collectively establishing a rights allocation. This involves a hierarchy of actions—actions at one level of the hierarchy determine rights at the next. A commonality in values in network relations is used as a resource to realise the interests of all.

These four kinds of interdependence and Coleman's commonality of values direct our attention to what Polanyi (1957) termed as various "social arrangements" which reconcile human needs, rights and obligations. Whether individuals are striving for maximising economic utility or power, it is the "social arrangement" that makes the goal meaningful or rational. Differences in "social arrangements" generate different types of interests, which are at the root of two meanings of "economic"—"substantive" and "formal." The first refers to the interaction of human beings with their social environment. The second refers to a process of economising scarce means to make the most efficient use of what is available for particular ends—economists use only this formal meaning in their economic analyses.

For Polanyi, the ways in which the economy acquires unity and stability may display different patterns. A combination of patterns is called the transactional mode or a "form of integration." There are three main forms: (1) Reciprocity; (2) Redistribution; (3) Exchange. Social transformations are changes in forms of integration. In earlier societies, production, saving and consumption were defined by reciprocal norms. Political and religious institutions performed the redistributive transactions. The exchange mode integrates market societies in a strictly economic sense and the self-interested economic man is a product of the market.

There is little controversy on the exchange mode of transactions in market societies. There is a problem with the claim that the self-interested economic man is a unique feature of the disembedded market—the self-interested economic man exists in all societies (Weber 1978), and later studies support this (Pospisil 1963; Geertz 1979). In addition, the interaction of individuals, within a family and a community, does not eliminate economic motives. Interpersonal impacts on consumption do not mean behavior is non-rational, rationality being a question of how to make best use of one's resources (Føllesdal 1982). In Granovetter's words: "what looks to the analysts like non-rational behavior may be quite sensible when situational constraints, especially those of embeddedness, are fully appreciated" (Granovetter 1991, 506).

Granovetter claims that modern market economies are embedded in ongoing social relations, but only a fraction have become "re-embedded" after a massive process of disembedding. In most developing countries, the process of disembedding has not come very far. Economic actions in those societies emerge as "an exchange of inalienable things between persons who are in a state of reciprocal dependence" (Gregory 1982, 19, an interpretation of Mauss 1954)—the obligations of individuals to their family have important an impact on their economic activities.

The point is, it is not self-interest but socially ascribed means which people adopt to achieve economic goals that explain rationality. Weber's notions of formal and substantive rationality clarify this point further. For Weber, rationality refers to a system of reasoning and standards of orientation, involving choice of a course of action in a given situation and weighing up of means and ends. The ends may be economic, non-economic, immediate and ultimate. Such standards change with the process of social change, and different types of rationality become dominant at different stages of social change. It is in this relation that Weber distinguished between substantive and formal rationality (Weber 1978).

The notion of substantive rationality is not restricted to the straightforward attainment of goals. It is termed as social rationality characterising a total system where formal rationality is one aspect (Godelier 1967). Economic actions are not only means to an end relationships, but also means to meet other social demands. Substantive rationality of economic actions refers to the degree to which action is shaped by an orientation to ultimate values, the adequacy of actions for achieving ultimate goals, including economic welfare, quality of life etc. Goals of actions are not determined by actors themselves, but by the social environment. Thus, substantive rationality is rationality for something (Weber 1978).

Formal rationality implies that the economy as guided by certain criteria, based mainly on market principles (Weber 1978). Rationality may be thought of as formal when there is a view to expressing a situation, solving a problem or conceptualising an action by a straightforward application of calculable standards. The operation of modern Western market societies is largely based on formal rationality. In this sense, economic actions involve quantitative calculation and an accounting procedure informing a decision to ensure consistency in attaining goals—formal rationality is rationality in itself.

A high level of formal rationality is possible only under certain substantive conditions i.e. a mix of self-interest, moral sentiments etc.

People in market societies enhance their interest through rational calculation, whereas people in non-market societies are relatively more inclined to satisfy social demands whereby the economic motives may remain hidden, as ulterior motives. Affiliations and obligations to social networks guide individuals' economic actions, and economic self-interest also persists.

The attachment of the individual to society via social relations may take different forms, and social and economic transformations involve a changed form of attachment expressed in, for example, increased individualism or institution based trust. In particular, it appears in the manifestation of exchange relations (Polanyi), increased formal rationality and the extension of purposive rational action in modern market societies (Weber). Weber viewed the market in terms of exchange and the highest degree of formal rationality implying the absence of influences restricting market autonomy. Coase and Baker did so when they defined the market as an institution that facilitates exchange (Coase 1937; Baker 1990).

In many developing societies, it is the reciprocity form of interaction that shapes the base of institutions and networks, enabling the creation of a framework for the economy (the substantive meaning of the economic). Individuals' choice of means to attain their goals also depends on such a form of interaction—they use networks to interpret and adjust to social relationships and the economy (substantive rationality). The family ensures access to material resources and to create a better outcome for the old and young, which is why the most important consumption of the family is in the meeting of its obligations (Caldwell 1976). Family prestige, honor etc., may appear as obligations. This explains why duties to networks come to the fore, and which economic goals remain behind non-economic goals.

Where do They Spend?

Bangladesh is a poor country. Despite poverty there is an elite class consisting of a few political leaders, top bureaucrats and a few rich businessmen. They constitute a fraction of the total population (less than 2% of 140 million) who are concentrated to a minority in Dhaka.[5] Though small in number, with their ownership and control over vast economic resources they command a disproportionate influence on the rest of the

[5] This estimate is made according to residence in wealthy areas. Siddiqui (1990) also used this method, but the exact number is hard to ascertain. The number of the elite is increasing due to political patronisation—each change in government opens up the possibility for new groups to be included in the dominating elite.

society. Through luxury consumption they create significant social division and there has been increased inequality both in terms of life styles and access to resources.

A survey provided data on expenditures on food, accommodation, gifts, matrimonial relations, education for their children, and investments on houses, cars and consumer durables (television, stereo, fridge and video equipment). Observation and interviews served the purpose of gathering relational data to unfold interweaving relations in which consumption behavior of the elite in Dhaka is shaped. The respondents were asked: what influenced their choice of food, accommodation, education, gifts etc?

People in general perceive providing their family members with food and accommodation as their obligation, and my respondents' perceptions of obligation reconciles with this general view. Types and varieties of food express intimacy of relationships, and furthermore food symbolises and represents social and symbolic values, as an index of status and identity. Maintaining these values they regard as an obligation, an obligation which displays both a social dimension and the influence of past experiences.

Family traditions and relevant past experiences of consumption have a strong influence on choice of food—habits of the traditionally rich in present day Bangladesh replicate the old aristocracies during colonial era. Those who became wealthy more recently also have inclinations towards the past. As many of them were deprived of a decent life style, they did not want their children to experience deprivation of any kind. Therefore, they make efforts to provide their children with something extra.

Consumption of education takes place directly through the family's values and lifestyle. The choice of school is embedded in social relations over time, linking past, present and future. The dignity of the family, flowing from the consumption of schooling in the past, endowed parents with knowledge of the association between educational qualifications and future well-being, whether as a sense of personal fulfilment, for example, or a prestigious job. In order to pursue all these goals, the respondents juggle prestigious schools and house tutors.

Ownership of a house, though a family matter, has a social dimension. Neighbors have a significant influence on the choice regarding where to live, people adopting and imitating one another's way of life. Owning a luxury house in a respectable area is a way of participation in social life—they are a step closer to being recognized as a gentlemen (*bhadralok*), adding to their reputation. Social participation is not easy for those who have become wealthy more recently. They have to struggle to integrate with those who had been living there for many years and are critical of those moving into the neighborhood. Therefore, they make an extra effort to participate in social life through the practice of gift giving at social festivities.

Obligation to family members has obvious influences on the present goals of owning consumer durables. A television is an essential part of their children's everyday life. One respondent put this as follows: "I had no option. I had to buy such things. Anyway these are used by my family members. I made efforts to satisfy family needs as short-term goals of consumption." Possession of such things is further stimulated by individuals whom respondents interact with, friendship and neighborhood generating further obligations which have an extended time frame. Therefore I asked: What obligations were relevant to them and what types of expectation did they have regarding their friends and neighbors? Whether they felt maintaining a life style similar to that of neighbors was a pressure on them?

Responses directly or indirectly indicated that obligations were relevant for respondents due to social purposes and practices (as emphasized by Appadurai 1986). This form of relations has a lot to say about which obligations are relevant to them, and what are expected from those relations. Key informants provided further evidence on social participation. A performative process and their efforts to follow the trends in the life styles of the affluent in society exerted further pressure upon respondents to consume. Gift giving is a reciprocal obligatory practice and according to Levi Strauss: "the automatic laws of the cycle of reciprocity are the unconscious principle of obligation to give, the obligation to return a gift and the obligation to receive" (Strauss 1987, 43). A striking feature of gift giving among the rich people in Bangladesh is that they give expensive gold ornaments, clothes, furniture, a fridge, a stereo and in some cases a car as gifts on wedding ceremonies, as well as arranging a grandiose wedding ceremony. They follow standards set by their friends and neighbors, and breaking standards is distancing oneself from others. They are aware of a risk—violation of standard obligatory practices may result in the loss of status and prestige, and so extravagant ceremonies and gift giving are necessary in order to maintain reputation. Furthermore, precious gifts, especially gold ornaments, given to family members work as insurance. Obligations to give and receive gifts not only link them together but link the past with the present, and the present with the future, both materially and symbolically.

Respondents interact, not only with close and existing friends, but also with casual and new friends. For many respondents their initial friendship took place in schools and universities. Establishing a new relationship requires extending boundaries by fostering participation in other social settings. They initiated contacts in their neighborhood and they imitated their lifestyles, while some became members of various clubs. A good deal of their identity derived from their friends, neighbors and club membership.

Life styles of new relations and acquaintances effected to escalate respondents' consumption of durables or the interior decoration of their houses, for example—their children talked of a wide screen television or a stereo which a neighbor had just bought. There was a tendency for maintaining homogeneity of the neighborhood and friendship regarding status through possession of those durables. Similarity of status facilitates participation and interaction among friends and neighbors, and there are expectations of exchange of favor and services from such relations. Those who fall into the category of the new elite emphasise the importance of friendship in providing practical support, whether for getting one's son or daughter admitted to a school, a college or at a university, or for getting a job, for a loan request or for an import license, a good friend is a great help.

The choice regarding selection of schools must be seen as a social mechanism for reproducing families who are able to mobilise a high level of economic and social capital. Higher education, especially from well-reputed institutions, is preferable as a vehicle for social mobility. Sons and daughters who perform well at school and get a higher degree are a source of pride for their family, and friendship develops amongst parents of children who attend similar schools. Students from exclusive schools maintain networks which are used for inter-network services and favors when they enter into economic life. A recent trend is that the rich send their children abroad. Not only do they achieve a foreign degree, they also make new friends abroad, connections that facilitate getting a job or business prosperity.

The magnitude of consumption expenditures shows evidence of the respondents' financial strength by which they achieve a place in the world of others. They also occasionally exaggerate the claim of their financial strength, a sign by which they indicate that they desire reputation. By consuming luxuries they convey the message to others of who they are and who they want to be. Their lifestyles signal exclusiveness regarding family dignity and identity. They arrange frequent gala parties and give donations to different cultural organisations. They desire positive evaluation of their worth by others, i.e. recognition. Recognition stipulates the requirements of status and honor, and is also a part of the struggle for accumulation of material possessions to satisfy a set of wants, both familial and social. They know being able to earn and spend money are qualities of a man with respect and prestige. A well decorated luxury house in a posh area and membership of a club are sources of status and ways of maintaining connections. In the words of a respondent:

> A person, what he does, where he lives and how good is his office, make up important criteria in gaining popularity in a social circle. Again the club life, and aspects like this, and if you are not a member of a good club, you are not considered to be one of the richest people in the society. So staying in certain areas, visiting a certain club, dining at certain restaurants, adds value to your value in the society. And in return, you get benefits when you do business. A businessman needs a lot of things, his experience, and the right product. But contacts are more important. Personal contact in this part of the world is a price of a wider roll in business. And to gain that, you have to live your life where you are, in contact with the elite, and with the decision-makers of the country.
> (C.A. Shahrukh, a businessman and respondent. Interview in Dhaka. January 2000).

The statement illustrates how respondents perceive utilities of certain present investments, both in terms of present meaning and expected returns in future.

In short, an intertwined and complex mixture of norms of network relations, as well as economic, cultural and symbolic values, produce meanings which have an impact on the attitude of respondents towards consumption. Though complex, their consumption shows certain patterns—consumption is aimed at meeting obligations within networks, and maintaining status, and a desire for recognition. Utilities of consumption have social and time dimensions, which include social, cultural, symbolic and material values. The patterns are good illustrations of consumption as an interaction process, which takes place within network structures, though I do not draw a conclusion from this as further analysis of network structures that sustain such patterns is necessary.

Structures of Relations

Network influences on consumption give rise to a concern about how they work and what social networks mean in the ongoing process of organising economy. In the above analysis, the mechanism involves obligations to network relations. In the broader social setting, meeting social obligations ensures rights, recognition, power, and trust. The most important attribute of network relations, the foundation of network relations, is trust. Trust is a form of confidence in probable outcomes of a commitment to fulfilling the legitimate expectations of others (Gidden 1990). The main factors that produce trust in economic and social life are social relations and the obligations inherent in them (Granovetter 1985). Consumption serves to create groups of trustworthy agents and to stimulate repeated interaction among network members, the structure of network relations explaining which obligations are relevant. Structures are combinations of the forms and the content of network relations.

Relational Forms

By relational forms I mean the strength or weakness of network ties, the strength of ties referring to density and durability of a relationship. Density describes closeness, intensity and the level of links among individuals within a network, and is a measurement to summarise the overall pattern of connections (Burt 1980). Forms also include the patterns and shape of connections, vertical or horizontal relations, and the number of ties within dyads, triads and groups. When respondents see some connections as being close to others, I find the closest networks tend to be those that are composed mainly of family.

The notion of family in Bangladesh has an extended meaning. It includes grandparents, uncles, aunts, cousins and nephews, and the extended family is tied to core members in a variety of ways. They are obliged to one another, they can claim equal treatment and a favor, and they share the identity and status of the family. Kinship is a reciprocal and horizontal relation even though one family may be better off than another. My respondents are wealthy, they cannot deny the bonds of kinship—no matter what the social status of their kin is, they usually come together when there is a family gathering. Lower status of a family member may be threatening to one with higher income and status.

Friendship is a reciprocal relationship. There are close, strong and lasting friendships, or weak and distanced relationships, and also relatively casual friendships or acquaintances. The degree of density and durability of friendship may vary, and there are varied degrees of intimacy. Exchanges between friends are mostly balanced horizontally. However, especially among casual friends, there may be an expectation of returns from such relations.

Alongside these two forms there is a third category. There are temporary coalitions, both within and between networks, that fall under "cliques." These coalitions take the shape of particular configurations of interpersonal relations, for instance among the respondents, some members have core positions within a political party. They have created a circle of horizontal relations among them and with bureaucratic and business elite.

Relational Contents

Relational contents are those characteristics of relations that express specific links among network members (Knoke and Kuklinski 1982). I have observed sentimental, obligational, transactional and instrumental relations. For simplification I have narrowed these relational contents to a single typology of "social demands" and "social domination."

Social Demands

By social demands, I mean that which is expected from people by those whom they interact with. Social demands include obligations to and love and affection for family and friends, as well as cultural norms and values. My respondents are simultaneously members of various networks, the content of all forms of network relations connecting them to one another. They are connected first of all through reciprocal and informal personal relations of family and friends, then through other social acquaintances. Obligation is a major connecting link. Similarly, within a clique there is a degree of group feeling and certain obligatory norms have been established.

A general understanding of the term obligation among Bengalis implies its two interrelated meanings, *kartabya* and *daitya*. The first meaning refers to immediate tasks to be performed, such as daily expenses for the household. The second meaning refers to long-term responsibilities, for example higher education aimed at achieving social and economic competence, or establishing a matrimonial relationship with a respectable family. Both these terms are rooted in the *shastra*, a framework of social order, guiding individual actions. In traditional Bengali society, *kartabya* and *daitya* together provided a framework for overall social order and moral qualities to guide behavior according to the value system including obligations to family, kin, friends, neighbors and others, as well as observance of rituals (Maloney 1988). There are two schools in the *shastra*: the *dharmashastra* or belief with regard to what is right and righteous for the individual, and the *arthashastra* or the science of material gains containing instructions concerning material prosperity (Sen 1987). Respondents also drew a distinction between what they called *paribarik* and *shamajik* when they talked about their consumption and investment behavior. By *paribarik* they meant family affair. By *shamajik* they meant obligations to others, and social norms and values. There were mutual obligations among friends, neighbors and other social relations.

Though distinct, they are interconnected. One's perception of family obligation is influenced by how others perceive it. A rich family is socially obliged to help kin or a neighbor in need—generosity is a social obligation for wealthy families in the society. Such a mix is at the root of the notion of *shamajikata*, meaning social demands. *Shamajikata* provides the guiding principles of all activities, both within the family and in social life. In practice what happens within the family is very much influenced by *shamajikata*. The matrimonial relationship, a family affair, is also a social responsibility. What people eat, whom they eat with, how much they give to charity, for example, have implications for the dignity of the family, and in turn they help people in achieving trust. Both dignity and the level of trust depend on one's capability to meet obligations to various forms of relationships. Obligations to family include maintaining family dignity as a long-term responsibility.

The notion of dignity is rooted in and is an expression of the nature of social stratification of Bengali society. In traditional Bengal, the notions of pure and impure classified social groups. A family was socially obliged to maintain its dignity through distinctive lifestyles and consumption of exclusive items. The notion of purity defined choices of food, housing, matrimonial relationship and consumption of rituals, and was incorporated with the notions of pride and prejudice through interaction of the Bengali culture with external culture. During British colonial rule, the "gentlemen" (the educated middle class known as *bhadralok*) maintained a distinctive family life based upon, for example, consumption of exclusive commodities, food habits, schooling, charity or club life. Such a historic legacy left a strong imprint on what people perceive as social demand in present day Bengali society, in the family and social spheres.

Political alliances and cliques are dense but fragile relations, containing some aspects of obligation and the norm of reciprocity, however, characterised by particular reciprocity. Obligational relations sustain hierarchies based on gift giving and charity by the rich. In such alliances, one's position in the power circle defines his obligations to other members of a party. The core members of the alliances of political-bureaucratic-business elite create a circle of horizontal relations among themselves. They maintain direct contact and some kind of reciprocal obligatory relations—gala parties, gifts and donations are examples.

Domination

The notion of social domination includes distribution of power and economic resources, the family and the kinship system having important influence on the process. A family with a high status enjoys privileges regarding distribution of wealth, and is also a guarantee for one's power. In the case where a family's social position does not work, one can get access to power and move upwards through other connections—friends can be trusted for such a purpose.

Friendship, a reciprocal relationship, can be instrumental, and there may be an expectation of economic returns from friends. A casual friend who holds a top position in the state administration or in politics receives special attention as they represent the possibility of economic returns, and norms of particularistic reciprocity govern such a relationship. This kind of relation overlaps with cliques.

Cliques are alliances of power networks, meaning that power has a net-like structure interlinking various positions. Cliques are often used to strengthen one's position and influence within a party or an association. The main characteristics of such ties are an instrumental relationship and exchange form of interaction. The newly rich make special efforts to include themselves in the networks of the dominating elite, and amongst their aims is a new identity, as the relational content of their family has little to say about status and power. As part of such a strategy, they invest heavily in various political parties, for example making donations and financing party meetings, or giving gifts to top bureaucrats. In this way they establish matrimonial relations with families that have a higher status.

Realtional Forms, Contents, Consumption and Investments.

Relational forms	Relational contents	Consumption expenditures and investments	
Paribarik Family and kin (Close, dense, durable)	Obligational Sentimental Wedding ceremonies	Shelter, Food, Clothes, Schooling	Higher education Luxury housing, Matrimonial relations
Shamajik Friends and acquaintances (Close, dense, durable and fragile)	Obligational Sentimental Instrumental	Gift giving,	Precious gifts,
Coalitions, Cliques	Instrumental	Gala parties	Charity, Donations
(Dense but fragile)	Transactional Obligational		

People comply with network norms and *shamajikata* when the situation demands. They suppress their own interests as well as *shamajikata* when necessary for pursuing their own interests, and this is due to an ongoing tension between social demands and individual aims. Satisfaction of social demands is crucial for individual rights of access to resources, and meeting family obligations is also linked to this. Networks are resources, and also work as social capital. Respondents make investments in various social networks and accumulate social capital, which they use for pursuing their own interests, including economic opportunity, social influence, and political power.

Wider network connections mean a greater stock of social capital and the opening up of more avenues for privileged access to resources, and therefore respondents establish connections as widely as possible. They use political connections as a form of social capital in getting further access to economic resources. With similar objectives there are temporary coalitions, both within and between networks, taking the shape of various cliques. Respondents make use of cliques in their struggle for identity and access to resources. This shows the aspect of power relationships within a network, such as domination. One or more members of a network attempt to control the behavior of others by offering or withholding certain benefits, and thus a power-elite is established at the intersection of social formation; a dominant elite maintaining privileged access to resources, and struggling for identity and control over resources.

Goals of consumption and investments are connected to the content of forms of relationship. Network structures therefore have a lot to say about goals of consumption, both as short-term tasks and as long-term responsibility. Events of consumption express not just one but many relational contents, and also have cultural and symbolic meanings.

Contents of Network Relations and Consumption Goals.

Contents	Immediate short-term goals	Long-term future goals
Social demands	Obligations, Love, Affection	Status, Identity, Security Maintenance of networks
Social domination	Recognition Trust, Social capital	Power, Economic capital

Concluding Remarks

The analysis above highlights structures of relations and their influences on consumption and investment behavior. Network structures have impacts on the perception of respondents' obligations, and are also linked to broader social phenomena i.e. social demand and domination. Rationality, utility and goals of consumption practices depend further on which other transactions are involved in the entire network relationship, of which obligation is only one part. Network relations can also offer benefits. Important theoretical issues are implicit in the above analysis of network influences on consumption patterns.

The consumption patterns of various elite sub-groups highlight the embedded nature of economic actions. The patterns may be of value for a substantive critique of the formal economic approach as the market norm of exchange is not useful in elucidating people's consumption behavior in a non-market society. It is necessary to go beyond the logic of pure economic rationality and utility. The needs and choices of means to satisfy those needs are influenced by others whom people interact with—the pattern of interaction is the substance of the notion of the substantive rationality of Weber. The substance lies in their weighing up of means and ends including meeting obligations to networks, participation in social life etc., as goals of consumption, and consumption sometimes may be seen as a goal in itself. Consumption is also a means for realising future goals, which may be both non-economic (status, prestige etc.) and economic (access to material resources).

People desire luxury items in order to convey their social significance, and therefore consumption of luxuries is an important method of social participation, seen as an obligation. Fulfilment of social obligations facilitates further social participation. Obligations, status, dignity and recognition are connected to the substantive meaning of the economic, and express both social interaction and time dimensions of consumption. Satisfaction of one demand requires satisfaction of other demands. Respondents act under a kind of social pressure to make a long-term decision, their individual capacity to comply with long-term responsibilities depending on membership of many networks simultaneously. The non-family networks act as those endowed with multiple opportunities. Therefore, the timeframe of social responsibility is much wider than that of the family. Respondents direct their consumption at forming network ties with significant others, and as widely as possible. This agrees with Granovetters' notion of the strength of weak ties, or structural embeddedness. Consumption provides respondents a connection with dispersed social networks.

The patterns also call attention to an ambiguity in the notion of utility that relies heavily on social values. I also recognise a dual effect of network influences on consumption behavior. Networks constitute the structure in which luxury consumption is both stimulated and constrained. Through repeated interactions, the objective structures of elite culture have developed. My respondents felt the urge to consume certain items or invest in something as a product of the social and cultural milieu in which they were embedded. The contents of network relationships, and their interplay with cultural and symbolic meanings of consumption generated different forms of social capital for the Bengali elites under investigation, which have a reverse causality.

A final comment is to what extent my findings can be compared with other societies over time. Veblen (1899, 1934) analyzed consumption behavior of the American leisure class in the nineteenth century in terms of three kinds of impulses: animism; emulation; domination. These impulses derive from others whom one compares themselves with. Consumption patterns of the rich in many developing countries replicate these impulses. Among the affluent consumers in Asian countries, sales of the luxury car Lamborghini have grown 30% annually. In Singapore, Russian caviar and French champagnes are selling well in restaurants. The newly wealthy in China, Malaysia and India invest in luxury houses, cars, yachts and even in private jets (Wall Street Journal, Asia, March 28–30, 2008). The new middle-class in Shanghai invests in golf clubs for social reasons, playing with friends. They are also aware of when friendship does not pay: "Almost all of my investments that have failed were related to friendship" (Jia-Bin Duh, A Chinese businessman).

References

Appadurai, Arjun. "Introduction: Commodities and the Politics of Value." In *The Social Life of Things: Commodities in Cultural Perspective*. Edited by Arjun Appadurai. Cambridge: Canbridge University Press, 1986.

Baker, Wayne E. "Market Networks and Corporate Behaviour." *American Journal of Sociology* 3 (1990): 589–625.

Becker, Garry S. *Accounting for Tastes*. London: Harvard University Press, 1998.

Bourdieu, Pierre. *Distinction: A social critique of the judgement of taste*. London: Macmillan, 1989.

Bourdieu, Pierre and Jean Claude Passeron. *Reproduction in Education, Society and Culture*. London: Sage, 1994.

Burt, Ronald S. *Toward a structural Theory of Action: Network Models of Social Structure, perceptions and Action.* New York: Academic, 1980.

Caldwell, John C. "Toward a Restatement of Demographic Transition Theory." *Population and Development Review* 2 (1976): 321–366.

Coase, Ronald. "The nature of the firms." *Economica* 4 (1937): 386–405.

Coleman, James S. "A rational Choice Perspective on Economic Sociology." In *The Handbook of Economic Sociology*. Edited by Neil J. Smelser and Richard Swedberg. Princeton: Princeton University Press, 1994.

Douglas, Mary and Baron Isherwood. *The World of Goods: Towards an Anthropology of Consumption*. London: Routledge, 1996.

Frenzen, Jonathan, Paul M. Hirsch, and Philip C. Zerrillo. "Consumption, Preferences and Changing Lifestyles." In *The Handbook of Economic Sociology*. Edited by Neil J. Smelser and Richard Swedberg. Princeton: Princeton University Press, 1994.

Føllesdal, Dagfinn. "The Status of Rationality Assumptions in Interpretation and in the Explanation of Action." *Dialectica* 36 (4) (1982): 301–316.

Geertz, Clifford. "Suq: The Bazar Economy in Sefrou." In *Meaning and Order in Moroccan Society*. Edited by Clifford Geertz, Hildred Geertz and Lawrence Rosen. New York: Cambridge University Press, 1979.

Giddens, Anthony. *Capitalism and Modern Social Theory: An Analysis of the Writings of Marx, Durkheim and Max Weber*. Cambridge: Cambridge University Press, 1971.

Godelier, Maurice. "System, Structure, and Contradiction in Capital." *Capitalist socialist register*, 1967.

Gregory, Chris A. *Gifts and Commodities*. London and New York, Academic Press, 1982.

Granovetter, Mark, and Roland Soong. "Threshold models of interpersonal effects in consumer demand." *Journal of economic behaviour and organization* 7 (1986): 83–99.

Granovetter, Mark. "Economic Action and Social Structure: The Problem of Embeddedness." *American Journal of Sociology* 91 (1985): 481–510.

Knoke, David and James H. Kuklinski. "Network analysis: basic concepts." In *Markets, Hierarchies & Networks: The coordination of social life*. Edited by Grahame Thompson, Jennifer Frances, Rosalind Levcic and Jeremy Mitchell. London: Sage, 1991.

Levi-Strauss, Claude. *Introduction to the Work of Marcel Mauss*. Translated by Felicity Baker, London: Routledge & Kegan Paul, 1987.

Lunt, Peter K. and Sonia M. Livingstone. *Mass consumption and Identity*. Buckingham and Philadelphia: Open University Press, 1992.

Mauss, Marcel. *The Gift: Forms and Functions of Exchange in Archaic Society*. London: Cohen and West, 1954.

Millar, David. *Ackowledging consumption: A review of new studies*. London: Routlege, 1996.

Polanyi, Karl. et al. *Trade and Market in the Early Empires: Economics in History and Theory*. Glencoe IL.: The Free Press, 1957.

Polanyi, Karl. *The Great Transformation: the political and economic origins of our time*. Boston: Beacon Press, 1957.

Pospisil, Leopold. "Kapauku Papuan Economy." *Yale University Publications in Anthropology, no.67*. New Haven: Yale University Press, 1963.

Putnam, Robert. *Making Democracy Work: Civic and Tradition in Modern Italy*. Princeton: Princeton University Press, 1993.

Sen, Amartya. *On Ethics and Economics*. Oxford, New York: Blackwell, 1987.

Veblen, Thorsten. *The Theory of leisure Class*. Middlesex: Penguin Books, 1967.

Weber, Max. *Economy and Society*. Berkeley: University of California Press, 1978.

Zukin, Sharon and Paul DiMaggio. *Structures of capital: the social organization of the economy*. Cambridge: Cambridge University Press, 1994.

Weekend Journal: *The Wall Street Journal*. March 28–30, 2008.

CHAPTER FOUR

GOODS WITH FAKE FACES: WHY DO OWNERS OF TRADEMARKS CONTRIBUTE TO COUNTERFEITING?[1]

ZOYA KOTELNIKOVA[2]

Introduction

Historically speaking, counterfeiting has always been a problem. Egyptian artisans in 2000 B.C. copied Cretan crockery, and decorators borrowed some ornaments and designs from the islanders' works (Tsiporukha 2000). Although the history of fakes is longstanding, it has only in the last two decades emerged as a global challenge. The OECD study shows that, in the present day, counterfeited and pirated goods are being produced and consumed in virtually all economies: "In 2005 international trade in counterfeited and pirated products could have been up to USD 200 billion" (OECD 2007, 15).

In addition, national governments and intergovernmental organizations are overly concerned about the rapidly growing global problem of counterfeiting and piracy. For instance, in its economic policy agenda, the 2007 G8 summit addressed the global problem of IPR protection. The year 2004 saw the first Global Congress on Combating Counterfeiting and Piracy convened by the World Customs Organization (WCO) and Interpol, with the support of the World Intellectual Property Organization (WIPO). In 2002 Interpol created an Intellectual Property Crime Action Group.

Thus, we can propose that the 20th century promoted counterfeiting to a global challenge. This raises an interesting question for sociologists: what brought about the market expansion of counterfeited goods? There

---

[1] I am grateful to Prof. Vadim Radaev for helpful comments.

[2] Department of Economic Sociology, State University - the Higher School of Economics, Moscow.

are several different reasons: production of fakes is a profitable and low-risk business; consumers are tolerant towards this sort of infringement; whole nations engage in production and distribution of counterfeited and pirated products, and so on. But there is perhaps one more important reason: victims of counterfeiting—owners of registered trademarks—pursue a contradictory policy relating to it; that is they are not always active in the protection of their intellectual property rights. Why does this happen? Supposedly, this great proliferation of counterfeits in the consumer markets is the result of producers' dependency on sign-consumption. Therefore we aim to find an answer to this question through creating a typology of strategies of owners of trademarks in regard to counterfeiting in Russia.

The layout of the chapter is as follows. Firstly, we will focus on the producers' dependency on sign-production. Secondly, we will define the concept "counterfeiting" and list some reasons for its market expansion. Thirdly, we will present research findings on the counterfeited goods problem in Russia and indicate how individuals—owners of registered trademarks—support counterfeited goods.

Producers' Dependency on Sign Consumption

According to Baudrillard, consumption falls into two categories: essential consumption and sign consumption. The former, if it may be referred to as consumption at all, is a process of need satisfaction, while the latter is "a systematic act of the manipulation of signs" (Baudrillard 1998, 15). Contemporary consumption is supposed to have emerged in the mid-20th century, when Western society began speaking about the age of affluence and abundance. A sign-object differs from the traditional symbol as there are no ties between sign-objects and the existing material world; a sign-object is placed inside the abstract system made up by relationships among signs, and this system itself generates the meanings of signs. The consumption of an object implies that the object itself is not consumed, but rather that of the idea of a relationship between objects (Baudrillard 1998).

Kopytoff suggests that "from a cultural perspective, the production of commodities is also a cultural and cognitive process: commodities must be not only produced materially as things, but also culturally marked as being a certain kind of thing" (Kopytoff 1986, 64). However, in the new type of society, consumption has moved away from satisfaction of specific needs—production is no longer aimed at manufacturing goods but at creating signs and images. Instead of objects, consumers are supplied with ideas, images and symbols. For instance, one advertisement ends: "The answer to the question: 'What do you do at Matsushita Electric?' is 'We create people, their images, and also produce electrical products'" (Panasonic 2005).

Because the utility of objects has become less important than their symbolic significance, the trademark has turned into a business cult. Golofast confirms that "there has been no trust in objects; only firms, signs, i.e. institutionalized symbols, in particular market and stratification, deserve a confidence" (Golofast 2000). Along with the higher significance of sign-objects there have also been changes in producers' preferences and economic hierarchy. Today, a firm's economic status directly depends on how successful it is in tackling the cultural task of production. For example, in 2000 (in comparison with 1980) in Great Britain and the USA, the company balance-market value ratio was reduced by 5 times. Nowadays in England only 30% of a company's market value is included in its balance; the rest accounts for its intangible assets—know-how, patents, goodwill, author's rights, and brands as the most important asset. Thus, British Petroleum has tangible-intangible assets in the ratio of 29:71, Coca-Cola the ratio of 4:96 (Lukianova 2001).

Beside use and change-value, a product has sign-value (Baudrilliard 1998; Radaev 2005), which determines the market price of a given product. For example, metronidazole made in Russia costs 3 rubles (about $ 0.15) per unit while branded analogues have much higher price—above 1000 rubles per unit (about $30) (Danishevsky 2006). Thus, it is obvious that the trademark steers the business philosophy of companies as well as their economic success.

What Does Trademark Stand For?

The concept of trademark is as old as the world itself.[3] For example, the Greeks are known to have marked their works of art with the name of the sculptor: "The cup handles from the Ceramicus of Athens beside the maker's name often bore real trade marks as figures of Mercury staffs, oil jugs, bees, lions' heads, and the like" (Jennings 1989, 809).

Traditionally trademark served as a sign indicating authorship of a given object. First trademarks included different brands, stamps, marks,

[3] There are two similar terms in wide use: brand and trademark. Some consider them as interchangeable terms, others see them as different concepts—we stick to the former. For example, according to the American Marketing Association, "brand is a name, term, design, symbol, or any other feature that identifies one seller's good or service as distinct from those of other sellers. The legal term for brand is trademark."

and so on. Later they acquired an additional function as a guarantor of proper quality and accepted product standards. For instance, in the article based on the comparison of the second names of vases with trade data, Kruckshol assumes that second names indicate the identity of big exporters ordering a large consignment of amphorae in a given pottery (Kruckshol 1962). Using the second name, a buyer could judge the quality of wine, while first names pointed to the month and year of wine-making, i.e. the time of bottling. Rhodian branding proved to be subject to aims of goods production primarily.

Bulgakov illustrates that branding as well as market control was among the moral prerogatives of rulers (Bulgakov 2000). Branding dedicated to express the idea of justice directly connected to the fundamental concepts of the Byzantine economic legislation—just measures and fair prices. It should be noticed that at this point, one of trademark's meanings is "the recognized standard of quality," implying a generalized form of confidence of consumers in a producer's reputation.

Later the expansion of mass production and enlargement of supply of homogenous goods meant that trademark obtained one more meaning—making a differentiation. With reference to Industry Statutes (1906), Shershenevich defines trademark as a sign which a merchant is going to use in order to make his or her goods distinct from those of competitors' (Shershenevich 1908). This sign is used by a manufacturer or a seller and it should be stressed that this meaning of trademark is printed in the contemporary international law on intellectual property rights.

By the end of the 20th century, communities of handicraft secret keepers and old guilds of craftsmen who made muskets, tissues, horseshoes, vans, chests of drawers had been replaced by larger and freer consumer societies (Boorstin 1974). This resulted in a reconstruction of the sense of trademark. It now no longer indicates workmanship and skills or marks features of goods—trademark has become an implement for social community formation. As Boorstin states, it means that through and by consumption of a given brand an individual has an opportunity to join one or another consumer society. Thus the trademark is aimed at grouping people into some communities by drawing distinctions among them according to their sign-consumption.

TRADEMARK

social distinction

product differentiation

proper quality and recognized product standards

sign of authorship

Thus we can summarise that the field of trademark meanings has been expanded. As consumption logic dominated over production logic, trademark accumulated additional functions: from sign of authorship to proper quality to product and social distinctions.

What is Counterfeiting?

In general, counterfeiting means "a range of illicit activities linked with the trademark infringement" (OECD 2007). It is important to stress that trademark infringement differs from product falsification. Because counterfeiting does not deal with product features, it is concerned only with registered trademarks and the exclusive rights of owners to them. In practice, however, they overlap, and it is therefore necessary to clarify the boundaries of counterfeit in detail.

The bulk of literature devoted to counterfeiting shows a difficulty in offering a suitable definition because there are several similar types of activities commonly grouped together under one heading (see Lay and Zaichkowsky 1999; Jennings 1989; Cheung and Prendergast 2004). For example, on reviewing different works on counterfeiting, Hoe et al. divide trademark infringements into 5 categories: deceptive counterfeiting, piracy, imitations, grey market and custom-made copies (Hoe et al. 2003).

Based on the Civil Code of the Russian Federation Part 4 and interviews with experts, we suggest the following classification of fakes:

Table 4.1. Types of Fakes

	Falsification	Piracy	Counterfeiting		
			Direct copies	Imitations	Infringements of owners' exclusive rights to registered trademarks
Definition	A deliberate distortion of the information about product's original features	Unlicensed copies of works of authorship	Unauthorized use of a registered trademark		
			A spurious trademark which is identical with a registered trademark	A spurious trademark which is similar to a registered trademark (look likes, copycats)	Introduction of original products with a registered trademark into the commercial turnover without a permission from the owner of a registered trademark
Deception of consumers	+	-	+ / –	+ / –	–
Infringements of intellectual property rights of owners of registered trademarks	-	+	+	+	+
Grey market	+ / –	+	+	+ / –	+

Note: "+" – presence; "–" – absence; "+ / –" – may be / may be not.

Firstly, fakes can be defined as a distortion of product information. In this case they are referred to as *falsification*, implying that a producer or seller deceives consumers with false information concerning features of goods including quality, ingredients and durability. Falsified goods can be produced and sold on both white and grey markets. Falsification differs from counterfeiting in that it implies only a deception of buyers and not an infringement of intellectual property rights. On the contrary, counterfeiting and piracy are originally administrated by civil law protecting the interests of other economic actors, and are not concerned with the rights of consumers—piracy breaks copyright, while counterfeiting infringes the rights of registered trademark owners. Copyrights are given to authors of creative works, such as movies, music, software and written works, while trademarks are used by producers to distinguish their products from competing products. The reason why counterfeiting and piracy are under corporate law is that criminals always break the rights of other economic actors, but do not always infringe on those of the consumer—it is well known that there is a steady consumer demand for counterfeited goods.

The market for fakes therefore falls into two categories (Grossman, Shapiro 1988; OECD 2007): the first implies that consumers unknowingly buy counterfeited goods—they are deceived with product originality; the second implies that consumers know that they are buying counterfeited goods. In the second case the consumer is in collaboration with the counterfeiters. Such goods may include: unauthorized introduction of original products into the commercial turnover; pirated goods; fashion goods; imitations; fakes of high quality; fakes that are not dangerous to consumer health.

Thus, the orientation to other corporate actors (but not to consumers) forms juridical bases according to which all economic crimes concerning intellectual property rights fall under law implemented without regard to the quality of fakes and the consumer demand for them. We can assume that "counterfeiting" is a complex notion including: goods, labels, packages on which are placed a spurious trademark which is identical to a registered trademark; goods, labels, packages on which are placed a spurious trademark which is similar to a registered trademark; unauthorized introduction of geniune goods into the commercial turnover.

In contrast to direct copies, imitations look like originals—for example, "Diezel" jeans instead of Diesel—but unlike direct copies they can be produced and realized in the white market, and that they are referred to as counterfeiting has yet to be proved. For instance, there was controversy lasting for three years between Beiersdorf and BRK-Kosmetiks (Tilling 2006). The former, a German producer, owns the brand Nivea, while the latter Russian company makes cosmetics branded "Livea." After numerous hearings, The Supreme Arbitrage of Russia has finally recognized that BRK-Kosmetiks infringes on Beiersdorf's intellectual property rights.

A further type of counterfeiting is the unauthorized introduction of originals into the commercial turnover. In this case we focus on the exclusivity of intellectual property rights implying that nobody can use a registered trademark without permission from the owner. For example, counterfeiting covers a scenario in which original goods are imported at the same time as a seller who has exclusivity on that product, or the unauthorized sale of production overruns by legitimately contracted manufacturers.

The Expansion of Counterfeited Goods

The peak of popularity for trademarks coincides with the rapid growth of counterfeiting. As Fig. 4.1 below illustrates, the latter half of the 20th century saw an unprecedented increase in using trademarks in commercial circulation, despite its long history.

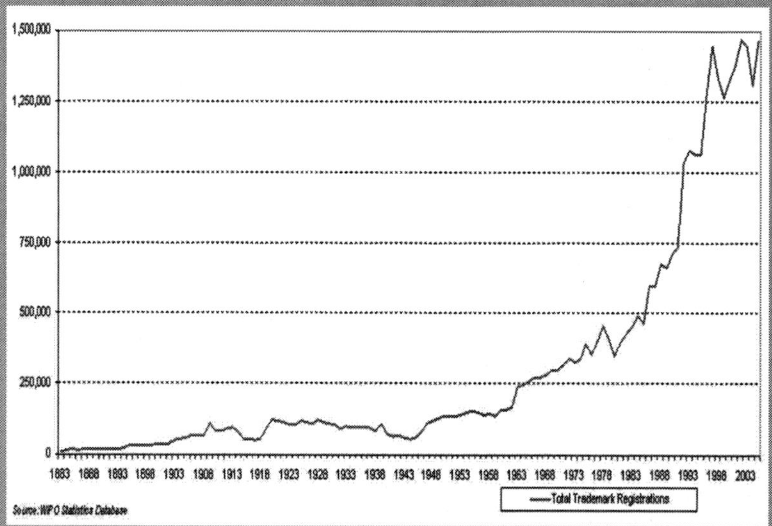

Fig. 4.1
Total amount of registered trademarks in the global economy, 1883 to 2007.
Source: WIPO statistic database.

According to the International Anticounterfeiting Coalition, in 2007 the international trade of illegal products was about $600 billion, while in 1982 it was about $5.5 billion. As a result, today counterfeited goods make up about 5–7% of total international trade (The International Anticounterfeting Coalition 2008). At the present time, not only entrepreneurs but also whole nations are involved in the production and realization of counterfeiting.

The supply of counterfeits is constantly increasing for two reasons: first, the number of trademarks used in the world economy has increased significantly; second, the counterfeit structure has changed dramatically. Nowadays counterfeiting of status goods has been replaced by counterfeiting of mass products (OECD 2007).

It was stated above that the market for fakes can be divided into two sectors—fakes bought by consumers unknowingly and fakes bought by consumers deliberately. Research shows that there are different motives as to why consumers buy counterfeited goods, in particular Cheung and Prendergast point out three incentives: price factor; status factor; and the system of distribution (Cheung & Prendegrast, 2004).

Regarding the factor of status in more detail, all goods are generally split into the following categories: essential goods and luxuries; mass goods and elite goods. Luxuries are known to settle some social issues such as identification of social boundaries and representation of distinctions between elite and mass, and the function of luxuries goes far beyond utility. Conspicuous consumption is particular to the elite as well as the masses (Veblen 1994). Simmel focuses on the concept of "seeping effect," supposing that lower layers strive to mimic higher layers (Simmel 1997) and in this way demonstrate non-existent connections to the elite. As a result, today we have the situation whereby any person can buy Dior sunglasses and Lois Vuitton bags in alleys of Italian towns, or Gucci belts in Russian metro passages.

That the counterfeiting of luxuries has been replaced by the counterfeiting of mass goods is partly the result of the actions of producers themselves, having begun to exploit status and image in the distribution of mass goods. Thus they have created an image-based social structure which is quite arbitrary to the existing social stratification, and buyers therefore do not need to be related to higher classes in any way. Producers offer a number of collective identities which consumers can easily join, and has resulted in an increase in the number of attractive objects for counterfeiters. Moreover, the promotion system, including advertising and merchandising, is subject to the one aim: to determine consumer societies and to instill loyalty to offered signs in a given consumer society. Finally, one of brand loyalty's side effects is that the brand becomes more important for consumers than the goods themselves (Boorstin 1974), this fact serving implicitly as a reason for consumers to buy counterfeited goods (Hoe et al. 2003).

All the above mentioned demonstrates some grounds to suppose that a great number of trademarks in the present day commercial turnover, and the dependency of producers on brands, create many favorable opportunities for maintaining a counterfeit supply and demand. Baudrillard confirms that a society resists unlimited consumption, and this struggle has a latent form, appearing in the same manner as unmotivated crimes, depression (asthenia, suicides, and neuroses) or collective escapes from reality (hippies and drugs) (Baudrillard 1998). Therefore we can assume that the rapid growth of counterfeiting is another unforeseen economic reaction to conspicuous waste.

Empirical Data

This chapter is based on two research projects: "The scope of counterfeited and grey imported goods in the Russian consumer markets" (2003), and "The trends in production and dissemination of counterfeited and grey imported goods in the Russian consumer markets" (2008). Both studies were carried out at the Higher School of Economics (directed by Professor Vadim Radaev) at the request of the Association of Branded Goods Manufacturers—"RusBrand"—with all global producers operating in Russia as its members. The empirical data was collected from 38 in-depth interviews with leading managers and experts.

In 2003 we interviewed 18 managers of international manufacturers, while in 2007 we interviewed 10 managers of global producers and 10 experts of other organizations, including the Federal Customs Service of Russia, the Ministry of the Interior of Russia, the Federal Service for Intellectual Property, Patents and Trademarks, different business associations, full-service law firms and security firms, all of them actively involved in combating counterfeiting.

The transnational interviewed companies are engaged in production of alcohol products, shaving items, feminine hygiene products, drugs and medicines, perfumery and cosmetics, sportswear and footwear, tobacco goods, tea, coffee, detergents, batteries and accumulators.

Counterfeiting in Russian Economy

Counterfeiting is a longstanding problem for Russia, but the scope for counterfeited goods in present day Russian markets is truly shocking; international experts state that Russia is among the countries with the largest amount of counterfeited goods. For example, Luc Devigne, Head of the Intellectual Property Unit, Directorate General for Trade and European Commission, indicated those countries which the EU had to start a bilateral dialogue with (Devigne 2007)—China, Russia, Turkey, Ukraine, Chilly, Korea, and countries of ASEAN and Mercosur. The following is an attempt to identify the key trends in counterfeiting in Russian consumer markets.

Defining a Counterfeit

Before talks began regarding Russia's possible entry into the WTO, there had been little concern about counterfeiting in Russian markets, and furthermore most people did not think that unauthorized use of trademarks was a crime. The fact of its occurrence was simply tolerated, and was not seen as a reason to pursue businessmen for criminal activity. However, the early 2000s saw changes in how the issue of counterfeiting was viewed in Russia. Global producers were the first to raise the alarm at the level of counterfeiting in Russia; they demonstrated losses in the Federal budget caused by counterfeited goods as well as those of companies. The law enforcement authorities then joined the global producers' campaign against counterfeiting. There were numerous media reports, focusing on the threat to consumer health as well as demonstrative raids and hearings. Counterfeiting began to be considered as a challenge to the Russian economy.

In addition to this, in the 2000s there was also a dramatic change in the definition of counterfeiting; at the beginning of the 21st century, the practice of law enforcement viewed it as "goods with a spurious trademark," but the concept did not encompass infringements to the owner's exclusive right to a given registered trademark (for instance, grey importation). It took about 7 years to modify the concept of counterfeiting. Today both a registered trademark and owner's sole rights to it are referred to as the objects under the protection of the law.

Scopes and Structure of Counterfeits

To determine the real scope of counterfeited goods in Russian markets is quite a difficult task. At present, all estimations we have are expert data concerning one product category or a given company and its brands, and all of these figures are differentiated and desultory. Therefore, the total amount of counterfeiting in Russian consumer markets is at present somewhat vague. The reasons for this are, firstly, that producers, marketing firms and state services do not have adequate measures and methods to help them gather correct estimates, and secondly that forgeries are often circulated in grey and black economies, and therefore they cannot be easily identified. However, it should be stated that since the mid-2000s, volumes of counterfeited goods on Russian markets have been decreasing gradually, something which is also supported by our respondents' data. For example, in 2007 the owners we interviewed gave us data according to which the total amount of counterfeited goods varied from 1% to 15% (for a given company or its brand), while in 2003 their variation made up 5–50 %.

Despite some difficulties in measuring counterfeited goods, we have some ratings drawn up by the Federal Customs Service of Russia, the Ministry of the Interior of Russia, the Federal Service for Intellectual Property, Patents and Trademark and the Federal Service for Human Rights and Well-being Protection of Russia, amongst others. Because they use different methods for defining the scope of counterfeiting, the ratings are not identical, but all of them list the same product categories which are subject to be counterfeited.

Sources of Counterfeiting

There are two key sources of counterfeiting: import and local production. The experts we interviewed confirm that Russia is a country of counterfeit consumption rather than production. Volumes of locally produced counterfeited goods are much less than those of imported ones. Largely counterfeited goods come to Russia from Eastern Europe and the Commonwealth of Independent States, but the key production sources of counterfeits for Russian markets are Asian countries, in particular China, Taiwan and Singapore. The local production of counterfeited goods involves many different types of entrepreneurs, for example leading companies of the white economy. A well-known example is Bryntsalov's case, where in the midnight shifts his factory made higher quality counterfeits of all global pharma-producers' popular brands (Bryntsalov-

A., 2007). Sometimes charities, prisons and individual entrepreneurs also turn out to be involved in production and distribution of counterfeit goods in Russia

Counterfeiting in Retail

In the 1990s, key counterfeiting trade channels were open markets and peddling (kiosks, booths and so on). Along with stronger state control under retailing, counterfeited goods circulated in open markets and peddling began to decrease. In the present day, major channels for counterfeited goods are small traditional shops located in remote city districts and on the internet.

However, it should be stated that anyone can become a victim of counterfeiting today. You can find counterfeits anywhere, even in respectable shops, but in present day Russian practice this is a cursory fact. For example, there are some tradesmen who can secretly accept a consignment of counterfeited goods which they then combine with originals and sell to consumers. Another method is high quality counterfeited goods being sold using forged documents as to their authenticity, as an examination to determine the originality of these goods is a task out of the reach of both tradesmen and the owner of a registered trademark.

In viewing key trends in counterfeiting in Russian retail markets, we can conclude that many positive changes occurred during the period 2000–2007: a growth in the understanding of the importance of intellectual property rights protection; a decrease in counterfeiting; a decrease in the amount of business involved in forgery importation and production. This is a result of the fact that state services, including the Federal Customs and Court system and Global producers, became more conscious of the counterfeiting problem. It remains, however, a problem for the Russian economy for a number of reasons, a key cause being that owners of registered trademarks pursue contradictory policies concerning counterfeiting. Moreover, the distinction of the Russian situation is that the responsibility in combating counterfeiting largely falls to the leading global producers, and the efficiency of this struggle depends on the strategies of trademark owners—they may, for example, teach customs inspectors, officials of MIR, how to make a distinction between genuine and counterfeited goods.

Brand Means a Trap For Consumers as Well as Producers

All owners whose trademarks are subject to counterfeiting fall into two categories: "fighters," those who combat counterfeiting, and "non-fighters," those who do nothing. Additionally each of these two categories can be divided into two subgroups: fighters consists of aggressive-fighters and lazy-fighters; non-fighters are made up by selfish non-fighters and discouraged non-fighters, and each subgroup is described in detail bellow. Preceding this is a fact that integrates all distinguished types of owners of registered trademarks: the implication that all of them make a considerable effort to hide information about fakes from external observers. Almost all interviews we conducted started with the same talk:

> "For a start, let's talk about the company's leading brand…"
> "For what purpose? We don't want our brands to be mentioned anywhere in regard to the theme we are talking about."
> —International company of branded consumer pharmaceutical products Lawyer, 2007

Such dialogue appears strange—we didn't talk about profit or know-how. Producers themselves initiated this research project. They are not criminals; on the contrary, they are victims of counterfeiting. And at the same time they were afraid of any, even a very small chance that anyone might know that their brands are being counterfeited. Why are the owners of registered trademarks frightened of the fact that information about fakes may become widely known? In all probability, the brand is a trap for consumers as well as producers, its popularity a key to success for both the owner and counterfeiters. Therefore, the more well known a trademark is, the more attractive it to criminals.

The greater the number of fakes there are, the more effort owners make in order to hide the information from consumers. Partly, they are threatened at breaking the market status-quo:

> I don't know a company that would have declared: "Guys, listen, here we have fakes, and you can tell them from originals this way and that. Only producers of luxuries can afford to behave in such way. I don't know any producer of washing powder or pampers who makes the information about fakes open. It is killing for any brand!
> —International company of branded food products General Director, 2003

Formerly, only large corporations were among those who could afford brand promotion, branding itself serving as a key to economic success. During this time, a corporation with a strong brand seemed to have an untouchable market position. Presently there are numerous trademarks on the market, and a greater number of methods for brand promotion as it became a relatively cheap process (D'Alessandro 2002). As a result, manufactures offer consumers practically indistinguishable brand concepts, the associated consumer loyalty becoming too fragile and breakable. Producers are currently fearful of any scandal which can shake their trademark's strength or goodwill, the amount of risk of losing a market position having rapidly increased for companies.

In addition to this, aggressive fighters carry on a struggle hidden from external observers. For example, global producers' warranty services accept counterfeited goods without informing consumers that the product is counterfeited: "...it surprised me that all counterfeited TVs were taken for warranty repair. About what does it talk?" (Official of MIR, 2007).

Types of Owners of Registered Trademarks

Fighters

Companies referred to in this category are engaged in the struggle against counterfeiting to some extent.

Table 4.2. Differences between aggressive fighters and lazy fighters

Characteristics of struggle	Aggressive fighters	Lazy fighters
Form of struggle	Permanent	Discrete
Means of struggle	Complex of means	Selected means
Orientation of struggle	Orientation to long term returns	Orientation to intermediate or short term returns
Scope of struggle	All infringements	Selected cases
Level of problem	Global / regional	Local
Reasons for fighting	Independent of the total amounts of fakes	The total amounts of fakes significantly influence company's business results

The key difference between aggressive fighters and lazy fighters is that the former carry on a permanent and integral struggle, the latter a chaotic and disorderly one. The former deliberately formulate strategies on how to remove counterfeiting from the market and use all possible means including information, juridical, political, administrative, and economic tools; the latter apply selected means to combat fakes dependent of a given case. The former pursue all criminals without exception, the latter pursue only large ones. The former combat forgery regardless of the amount of fakes, the latter begin fighting only if the volume of forgeries significantly influences their sales.

> As far as I know the European business community supposes that it is necessary to combat counterfeiting, in case if there is over 10% of fakes in retail; they think that this volume of fakes implies a start for affecting business results.
> —International company of branded sportswear General Director, 2003

That owners of trademarks follow such completely different strategies in regard to counterfeiting is explained by differences in their estimations of the cost-gain ratio. Struggling with counterfeiting implies high costs including money, time and labor. For example, expenses for product protection system development (complexity of a package, periodicity of its renewal, and development of a hologram), market monitoring and detection of infringements, assistance with legal implementation and criminal prosecutions, and so on. In weighing possible expenses against potential gains, some companies come to the conclusion that, economically, combating counterfeiting is groundless, while others see the struggle as worthy despite the very high costs involved:

> Of course you may remove counterfeiting from market at all, but it means that the company has to earn money only for this struggle. It is not expedient, and from standpoint of efficiency too.
> —International company of branded sportswear General Director, 2003

Firstly, trademark owners judge possible returns from the struggle differently because they face difficulties in measurement of losses caused by counterfeiting. An added complexity is that there is no direct and obvious relation between the total amount of counterfeited goods on the market and the company's business results, but counterfeiting is known to damage the company's brand and goodwill—fakes mainly differ from originals in the difference of quality. However, companies have no effective means to measure the losses they have. They usually estimate damage caused by counterfeiting by relying on simple calculations—multiplying volumes of counterfeited goods by the market price of originals. Indeed, owners of registered trademarks do not know what their losses are, as brand and goodwill are immeasurable assets.

> You know, counterfeiting causes damage not only to our sales but also to a brand itself. And how can we measure this damage to brand? For this we have to estimate a brand itself… Well, you can order to carry out a sociological research; try to prove that brand confidence has been so, and

> now it is less. That has resulted in reducing a brand price. You know, these all estimations are subjunctive, of course.
> —International company of branded alcohol beverages Lawyer, 2007

Secondly, fighting counterfeiting, especially in cases which do not significantly influence business results of a given company, is work for the long-term future (to prevent a possible increase in counterfeiting and to support brand and reputation). Aggressive fighters orient toward returns in the long term, lazy fighters to getting returns in the mid and short terms. The former consider that counterfeited goods cause damage that will devalue their company's image and brand in the further future.

> At first they seem to be losers; they invest money into void; there is no return at all; and I shut my eyes to counterfeiting and I'm absolutely right. As a result you may face a problem; for example, today you prefer to keep your eyes shut; and possibly there is no problem, but you don't fix this challenge at a given level, you just ignore it. And it may happen that several years after you will face a rapidly increasing problem that will affect your business results.
> —International company of branded sportswear General Director 2007

Thirdly, for a given owner counterfeiting can be a problem on different levels: global, regional or local. As a rule (but not always), if counterfeiting is a global challenge, the head office invests a lot of money into a solution for the problem, developing special programs to combat it. For example, they may keep a price balanced and control discount policies in different countries, or strictly control a distribution system. But if the problem is regional or local, responsibility for finding a solution rests on the local office manager's shoulders, and in this case we need to have faith in their responsibility and foresight.

Non-Fighters

The second group of owners consists of those who do nothing in regard to counterfeiting or protecting their trademarks and sole rights. Non-fighters also fall into two subgroups: selfish non-fighters and discouraged non-fighters. Discouraged non-fighters are companies who ignore counterfeited goods due to economic constraints. They do not have enough economic resources (money, labor, information) to combat counterfeiting, and have failed to develop a monitoring system and establish market control.

> We didn't have a systematic approach to solve a counterfeit problem, we didn't' have a deliberate strategy, we didn't have a responsible person tackled this problem; our management was not interested in solving the problem. To solve the problem we need a lot of time, labor and money resources.
> —International company of branded consumer pharmaceuticals Lawyer, 2007

The discouraged non-fighters also include those whose actions are impeded by fear. Firstly, there is fear of losing a market position—for example, controlling services may make a decision to remove goods from the market, something which often occurs in food and pharmaceutical markets. Secondly, foreign managers fear criminals involved in counterfeiting production and trade, and they are influenced by myths concerning the Russian rules of business running.

> Well, if a company is governed by foreign management, 100% foreigners, they are scared of the Russian reality. They are unrestrained fearful. As for our last General Manager, a 100% American, Russia was too far from him. It took long time to persuade him that there was nothing to be scared of.
> —International company of branded coffee Lawyer, 2007

Selfish non-fighters consist of trademark owners who try to gain from counterfeiting, considering such expansion favorable especially at the level of market penetration. Counterfeited goods help to market a brand in niches where the legitimate owner has yet to reach—in such cases counterfeiting plays the role of advertisement of a trademark. With its assistance, people may know about a commodity and brand, forming consumer preferences and developing loyalty to a given trademark. Among such owners are those who are indifferent to the Russian market:

> Well. All sorts of sunglasses produced by French and Italian firms… they said us that they were not care a straw about it – counterfeit what you want. There was no difference for us. On the contrary, it's important for us, that our trademarks were getting popular, and then we would come to markets…
> —Business Association Director, 2007

Additionally, selfish non-fighters also include those companies the local management of which is involved in a collusion with criminals. They make informal agreements with criminal businessmen and get part of the income from this illegal activity.

> …and at the same time we have the information that he goes shares with criminals; because he couldn't help noticing that and being informed about that. By the way this is one of aspects of the discussed issue: sometimes local managers are involved in the collusion. As usually said, these are Russians who tell them stories about the Russian reality – here everything goes bad, law machinery doesn't work; everybody is involved in crimes, we are alone who try to do something.
> —Official of MIR, 2007

In summary, we may conclude that the dependency of producers on sign-consumption is additionally determined by local economic and cultural contexts. Local context can take the form of an obstacle or the efforts made by an owner to protect their intellectual property rights.

Conclusion

According to Baudrillard, the consumer society is not just an abundant society, but one in which consumption emerges as a key element to the social organization. Consumption is no longer confined to the satisfaction of needs, but is increasingly connected with the manipulation of signs (Baudrillard 1998, 61).

The economic sense of the trademark has changed dramatically. Formerly a trademark represented a commodity's tie with its properties and authorship, but then obtained another function as making a distinction: initially as an external distinction between one product and others, then a social distinction between one collective identity and others.

Producers' dependency on sign-consumption is revealed, in the present day, as they engaging in creating signs and symbols rather than in manufacturing goods. The trademark has changed into a business philosophy, and a firm's economic position substantially depends on how successful it is in the formation and deployment of social identities. The dependency of producers on consumption implicitly or explicitly stimulates the expansion of counterfeiting, defined as a range of illicit activities linked to trademark infringement. Therefore, the popularity of a brand is a success for both its owner and counterfeiters. Moreover, the more producers try to instill consumer loyalty to a given brand the greater the consumer demand for counterfeiting: the brand is more important for them than the product itself.

The empirical part of the chapter focused on the attitudes of global producers of mass goods to counterfeiting in Russian consumer markets, empirical data being collected from 38 in-depth interviews with the top managers and experts in manufacturing. In the 2000s, Russia saw dramatic changes in counterfeiting, the total volume of fakes having decreased and the number of businesses involved in counterfeiting getting smaller and smaller. In Russia social attitudes to intellectual property rights protection have changed and people have begun to understand its significance and importance. However the removal of counterfeiting from the Russian market directly depends on its victims—how owners of registered trademarks are going to act in the protection of their intellectual property rights.

Using the example of global producers we can say that the dependency of producers on sign consumption blocks their activity in the protection of their rights, and sometimes causes them not to fight. Primarily, producers take considerable efforts to hide the information about fakes from consumers as a consumer's tie with collective identity offered by a given producer turns out to be illusive and imagined.

All owners of trademarks can be divided into 4 groups: aggressive fighters, lazy fighters, discouraged non-fighters and selfish non-fighters. The difference between aggressive fighters and lazy fighters is based on the fact that they estimate the efficiency of their struggle differently, which appears to be very expensive and unfavorable. In this case "unfavorable" means that owners facing difficulties in measurement of brand and goodwill cannot determine damage caused by counterfeiting and the implications resulting from its removal. Aggressive fighters think that the struggle should be a permanent one with orientation toward the long term future, thus they support their brands and reputation. Lazy fighters underestimate possible dangers to brands and prefer to react here and now. Non-fighters do nothing. Discouraged non-fighters do not have enough economic resources to struggle, or they wrongly understand the Russian business practice—for example, foreign management is influenced by a myth regarding the disregarding of law in Russia. Selfish fighters not only turn a blind eye to counterfeiting but also try to benefit from the market of fakes. Some of them consider that at the stage of market penetration counterfeited goods advertise and promote their brands, whilst others make informal agreements with criminals.

In conclusion, it can be stated that counterfeited goods emerged as a global challenge of the 20th century caused by the formation of a consumer society. The majority of social theorists turned our attention to different forms of social protest to the dominance of sign-consumption, such as collective escape from the reality, anomie, and so on. It could be stated, however, that the most obvious economic and social reaction to consumer society age is counterfeiting.

References

American Marketing Association. Resource Library: Dictionary. http://www.marketingpower.com/_layouts/Dictionary.aspx?dLetter=B (accessed April 25, 2008).

Baudrillard, Jean. *The Consumer Society: Myths and Structures*. Thousand Oaks, CA: Sage Publications, 1998.

Boorstin, Daniel. J. "Consumption Communities." In *The Americans: The Democratic Experience*. Edited by Daniel J. Boorstin. New York: Vintage Books, 1974.

Bulgakov, Valery. 2001. Vizantiiskiye Amorphnie Kleima XI veka s Monogrammoi Imeni Konstantin [Byzantine Vase Brands of the XIth Century with a Monogram of the Name of Constantin], *Morskaya Torgovlia v Severnom Prichernomorie* (*Морская торговля в Северном Причерноморье*). http://archaeology.kiev.ua/byzantine/amphorae/stamps/bulgakov1.htm (accessed April 25, 2008).

Cheung, Wah-leung, and Gerard Prendergast. *Profiling Buyers Of Pirated Products In China: The Case Of Wuhan*. BRC Working papers, Hong Kong Baptist University, 2004.

Danishevsky, Kirill. *Intellektualnaya Sobstvennost v Meditsine v Rossii* [*The Intellectual Property in Medicine in Russia*], 2004. http://www.osdm.org/modules.php?name=Smi&op=page&folder=8&contentsite=28.htm (accessed April 25, 2008).

D'Alessandro, David F. and Michele Owens. *Brand Warfare: 10 Rules For Building the Killer Brand*. USA: McGraw-Hill Companies, 2003.

Delo "Bryntsalov-A" Peredano v Sud. [The Case of Bryntsalov-A was taken into court]. 2007. *Kommersant.ru*, 09 Noyabria. http://www.kommersant.ru/doc.aspx?DocsID=823874&NodesID=6 (accessed April 25, 2008).

Devigne, Luc P. "The European Union: Coordination and Cooperation in the Enforcement of IPR." Paper presented at the Third Global Congress on Combating Counterfeiting and Piracy, Geneva, Switzerland, January 30–31, 2007.

Golofast, Valery. "Liudy i Veshchi" ["People and Objects"]. *Sociologichesky Jurnal* 1/2 (2000): 58–65.

Grossman, Gene M., and Carl Shapiro. "Foreign Counterfeiting of Status Goods." *The Quarterly Journal of Economics* 103 (1) (1988): 79–100.

Hoe, Lee, Gillian Hogg, and Susan Hart. 2003. "Fakin' It: Counterfeiting And Consumer Contradictions." In *European Advances in Consumer*

Research 6. Edited by Darach Turley and Stephen Brown, 60–67. Provo, UT: Association for Consumer Research.

Jennings, Jonathan S. "Trademark Counterfeiting: An Unpunished Crime." *The Journal of Criminal Law and Criminology* 80 (3) (1989): 805–841.

Kompania OVeKon. *Istoria Torgovoy Marki "Panasonic"* [*History of the Trademark "Panasonic"*]. http://www.ovecon.ru/PanasonicHistory.php (accessed April 25, 2008).

Kopytoff, Igor. "The Cultural Biography of Things: Commoditization as Process." In *The Social Life of Things: Commodities in Cultural Perspective.* Edited by Arjun Appadurai. Cambridge: Cambridge University Press, 1986.

Kruckshol, Yury. "O Znachenii Vtoykh Imen Rodosskih Amorphnikh Kleim" ["Of Significance of the Second Names of Rhodian vases' brands"]. *Drevni Mir. Sbornik Statei Akademiku V.V. Struve,* M. Izdatelstvo Vostochnoi Literaturi. Tsitirovana Retsenzia N. B. Beregovskoi na Ukaz. Soch, 1962. http://annals.xlegio.ru/books/recstruv.htm (accessed April 25, 2008).

Lai, Kay K., and Judith L. Zaichkowsky. "Brand imitation: Do the Chinese have different views?" *Asia Pacific Journal of Management* 16 (2) (1999): 179–192.

Lukianova, Evgenia. "Neuchtennie Milliardy" ["Unaccounted Billions"]. *Expert 10* (270), 12 Marta, 2001. http://www.aclub.ru/page.php?pageId=14&matterId=351 (accessed April 25, 2008).

OECD. The Economic Impact of Counterfeiting and Piracy: The Executive Summary, 2007. http://www.oecd.org/dataoecd/13/12/38707619.pdf (accessed April 25, 2008).

Radaev, Vadim. *Ekonomicheskaya Sociologia* [*Economic Sociology*]. M.: SU-HSE, 2005.

Shershenevich, Gabriel. "Kurs Torgovogo Prava" ["Textbook of Commercial Law"]. T. II. Tovar (Goods). *Torgovie Sdelki* [*Trade Transactions*], 60. Tovarny Znak M. Bashmakov, 1908. http://download.nchti.ru/libr/books/Right/ClassicOfRussianCivilistic/Elib/896.html

Simmel, Georg. "The Philosophy of Fashion." In *Simmel on Culture: Selected Writings*. Edited by David P. Frisby, Mike Featherstone. London: Sage Publication Ltd, 1997.

The International Anticounterfeting Coalition. "About Counterfeiting: Get Real – The Truth About Counterfeiting."

http://www.iacc.org/counterfeiting/counterfeiting.php (accessed April 25, 2008).

Tilling, Ekaterina. "Nivea Pobedila Livea" ["Nivea won a battle against Livea"]. *Vedomosti* 131 (1658): 19 July 2006. http://www.arbitr.ru/as/vas/smi/2391.html (accessed April 25, 2008).

Tsiporukha, Mikhail. "Morekhody Krita, Epochi Argonaphtov i Troyanskoy Voiny" ["The Cretan Seafarers in the age of Argonauts and Trojan War"]. *History* 27 (2007). http://his.1september.ru/articlef.php?ID=200002701 (accessed April 25, 2008)

Veblen, Thorstein. *The Theory of the Leisure Class*. London: Penguin Classic, 1994.

World Intellectual Property Organization: Trademark Registrations by Office since 1883. http://www.wipo.int/ipstats/en/statistics/marks/registrations/office.html (accessed April 25, 2008).

PART II:

DYNAMICS OF MARKETS

CHAPTER FIVE

FROM DISEQUILIBRIUM BETWEEN SOCIAL PARTNERS TOWARD DISTURBANCES ON THE LABOR MARKET

BARBARA GĄCIARZ[1]
AND WŁODZIMIERZ PAŃKÓW[2]

Industrial Relations in Poland on the Threshold of the 21st Century

This chapter will discuss a sequence of actions and processes which, during the last 10 years, has led to the current state of the labor market in Poland, characterized by a growing disproportion between supply and demand of a qualified labor force. Some explanations for this situation are proposed and attention given to predicting its consequences, which in the future may cause barriers for the further development of the national economy and for the country's general progress, despite the high inflow of FDI (including those from international corporations), and considerable financial means gained from EU funds. Key problems will be considered from an institutional perspective and on the level of the national economy, while references to evidence that can be drawn from the empirical studies related to specific industrial branches or regional (local) markets will not be avoided.

The aforementioned process which commenced 10 years ago began after an election victory of the Solidarity Election Action (AWS) in 1997, subsequently taking over the government by its coalition with the Freedom Union (UW). These events took place when strong and constantly growing disequilibrium between key social partners had occurred, i.e. overtly manifested domination of capital over work exerted crucial impact to the

[1] Faculty of Humanities, AGH University of Science and Technology, Krakow.
[2] Institute of Philosophy and Sociology, Polish Academy of Science, Warsaw.

contents and general character of industrial relations in Poland. This meant, on the one hand, that an influence of Polish (as well as foreign) employers' associations had arisen, and on the other that an increasing erosion of the trade unions was taking place.[3] This tendency has been reinforced strongly by a direct involvement in politics of all nationwide trade union organizations, in particular when the elite activists decided to take part in a parliamentary election and had effectively gained a noteworthy number of seats in the Sejm (lower chamber of the Parliament).

A key nationwide trade union, Solidarity, revealed (not for the first time) its dualistic, imminently contradictory identity by its involvement in the implementation of the package of four social reforms developed by Jerzy Buzek's government.[4] But, first and foremost, the most harmful choice for labor force interests made by trade union representatives in the government was the backing given to a very tough monetary policy founded on giving priority to anti-inflation measures, termed the strategy of "cooling economy." Obviously, this kind of policy did not have a lot in common with the protection of employee's interests, due especially to the fact that it slowed down the relative prosperity the Polish economy had enjoyed in the preceding years, GDP growth amounting to over 6% per year. The implementation of the above mentioned reforms caused *inter alia* the emergence of the following processes:

- Recession (GDP growth was a little higher than zero over the course of three years)
- Increase of unemployment, which in three years had reached a rate of 20%
- Deterioration of labor conditions and industrial relations within the vast majority of Polish companies (the range of this phenomenon has been revealed by a European Survey carried out between 2004 and 2005)
- Further deepening of an imbalance between positions and strengths of influence held by employers compared with

[3] For a more detailed description of this process see Gardawski, J., Gąciarz, B., Mokrzyszewski, A., Pańków, W., *Rozpad bastionu? Związki zawodowe w gospodarce prywatyzowanej* [*The fall of a fortress? Trade unions in privatized economy*], (Warszawa. Instytut Spraw Publicznych [Institute of Public Affairs], 1999).

[4] Mr. J. Buzek's Government (1997–2001) implemented four major reforms, which concerned the pension system, the health care system, education and decentralization of public administration and the new territorial division of the country.

employees, both at the level of nationwide organizations and at the level of individual branches and enterprises

- Escalating economic immigration of Polish employees to the EU countries (enabled by the liberalization of labor markets in the consecutive Member States; according to estimations presented by several European statistical institutions the number of Polish immigrants amounted to 1.5–2 million people by 2005)
- Further dropping of the level of vocational activity in Poland; at the turn of the century the rate of vocational activity was already very low, only just exceeding 50%

The polish economy at the beginning of the 21st century demonstrated all the symptoms of a crisis. The then governing political forces decided to implement all remedies typical for a neoliberal economic paradigm, which on the one hand proved to have a very limited effectiveness in reversing negative economic trends, while on the other strengthening at least two socio-political processes that defined features of political and social relations for almost a whole decade, i.e. the rise of populism (both left and right wing) on the political scene and expansion of paternalism in the area of industrial relations.[5]

However, alterations within the framework of industrial relations in Poland were not of such a spectacular character as the democratic transformation of the political system, the establishment of the rule of law or restoration of the free market economy and private entrepreneurship, but they were closely related to these major changes. Their influence on the individual and collective behavior of employees should not be underestimated, and comes into focus if one tries to understand the patterns of work relations at different levels of social organization (factory, company, branch, national economy). In general terms, the situation within this area could be described as a rejection of the worker's participation as a regulative framework for industrial relations, both on institutional and informal levels of relations. Institutions of worker's participation (so-called Employees' Councils) were set up in the 1980s in all state-owned enterprises as a part of reformative efforts targeted at

[5] D. Ost proposes a novel theory about the role of anger in politics to explain the rise of populism, authoritarian attitudes, xenophobia and nationalism, why such voices matter, and how they profoundly affect political outcomes. For his comprehensive analysis of these phenomena based on broad evidence drawn from historical, sociological and political studies see Ost, D., *The Defeat of Solidarity: Anger and Politics in Postcommunist Europe*, (Cornell University Press, 2005).

improving effectiveness of management and making the economy more independent from political interferences.[6] Their role in the public sector had been confirmed by law on state-owned enterprises and their privatization at the beginning of the 1990s.[7] The participation of workers proved to be a laboratory for development of entrepreneurship and rational management practices, and primarily in accustomizing all social actors in companies to negotiations and a consensual approach to problem solving. Therefore Employees' Councils (especially the hundreds of members who gained practical managerial experience thanks to involvement with its activities) played an important role in successful privatization of many enterprises, particularly in the case of small and medium size public companies.[8]

But privatization and neoliberal economic policy was steered by a very old-fashioned vision of capitalism, of roles of entrepreneurs and workers and a model of relations between them in companies, which relied on such ideological concepts like "sacred property right" or "only concrete owners

---

[6] See: Gąciarz, B., "Employee Self-Management in the 1980's," in *The Protracted Death - Agony of Real Socialism. Political Mechanisms of Societal Life in Poland in the 1980's*, edited by Hausner, J., Klementewicz, T., (Warszawa, Wydawnictwo ISP PAN, Publishing House of the Institute of Political Studies, Polish Academy of Science, 1992).

[7] The Law of July 13th 1990 (called the privatization law) provided the framework for transforming more than 8,000 state enterprises into private firms. The framework appeared to reflect both the conviction that privatization should proceed swiftly and include minimal state involvement, but also the possibility for workers to shape the process. Of the various privatization methods, the one considered the fastest and most effective way of transferring ownership rights in Poland was "direct" privatization. The majority of firms privatized through this method were transformed into employee–owned companies. In this process, the state firm was "liquidated," i.e. legally it ceased to exist as a state enterprise, and its assets were transferred to a newly formed private company made up of the majority of the workforce of the former state enterprise. Direct privatization had been generally seen as "success story" on the map of privatization in Poland. According to the Ministry of Treasury Report (2000) 1,727 out of total 4,957 transformed state enterprises were privatized through direct privatization (1,216 resulted in employee-ownership).

For more details see: Jarosz, M., ed., *Direct Privatization. Investors, Managers, Employees*, (Warszawa: Wydawnictwo ISP PAN, 1999); Blaszczyk, B., Woodward, R., eds., *Privatization and Company Restructuring in Poland*, (Warsaw: Center for Social and Economic Research, 1999).

[8] See: Gąciarz, B., Pańków, W. "Effective Strategies in Direct Privatization," In *Direct Privatization. Investors, Managers, Employees*, edited by Jarosz, M., (Warszawa: Wydawnictwo ISP PAN, 1999), 137–151.

guarantee rational economy," or "protection of interests of owners as prerequisite of any development." This persuasive language was consequently imposed onto all public discourse and excluded the possibility of the formulation of any alternative versions of socio-economic reforms. For nearly all journalists, representatives of think tanks and consulting companies, and politicians of the dominant political parties this simplified version of capitalist enterprise, rooted in the 19th century, became the only one they knew and would accept. In these circumstances it was inevitable that industrial relations evolved towards a model we called "enlightened paternalism."[9] This specific model of industrial relations has been reconstructed from broad empirical evidence collected during the course of several extensive studies devoted to privatization, the functioning of worker's participation and trade unions in Polish enterprises. It should be stated that this construct is an ideal type, in the Weberian sense of the term, and therefore it should not be treated as an exact description of the realm of any concrete enterprise. But it is worthwhile to use it as a tool for analysis of social relationships in real workplaces. It comprises such elements as:

- Employers' hegemony—employer has a free hand to define conditions of work, including the form of a labor contract, remuneration, and discrete power for promotions as well as hiring people; obviously, legal constraints have to be taking into account, but a standard practice is to evade legally binding commitments by informal arrangements related to salaries, some additional privileges but also duties of workers (e.g. compulsory non-paid overtime)
- Atomization of employees, i.e. exclusion of any kind of collective negotiations between employer and employees; only individual agreements between both parties are acceptable; employees adapt themselves to this situation by developing individualistic strategies for protecting their own interests and reaching a better status—their essential feature is what we term "forced cooperativeness"
- Employers offer some security for employees, but only at their discretion and dependent on personal obedience and loyalty to

[9] See: Gąciarz, B., Pańków, W., "Industrial relations in Poland: from social partnership to enlightened paternalism," In *Poland into the new millennium*, edited by Blazyca, G., Rapacki, R., (Cheltenham; Northampton. Edward Elgar Economies and Societies in Transition, 2001), 72–90.

the owner or manager; key concerns refer to building a good social climate stimulated by satisfaction related to technical and organizational working conditions, respect to individual workers and their opinion on different aspects of production processes
- Informal social relations between workers and managerial staff (mainly middle-range managers and line supervisors) take over key regulative roles in a domain of labor; these informal networks are built upon a high personal authority of superiors and confidence given to them by workers[10]

In fact, the appearance and wide circulation of this pattern of industrial relations was a significant but secondary phenomenon to a broader process of structural transformation in the Polish economy, i.e. the emergence of a new economy, consisting of newly established private enterprises (a significant amount of them were "greenfield" investments), extending the number of branches or joint ventures of foreign companies, a large number of SMEs (mostly in the 3rd sector), and a growing number of freelancers. The new economy, unlike the previous, was (and still is) a zone in which trade unions did not occur, in many cases due to an intentional counteraction by owners.

The former economy zone was a domain in which trade unions played an important role, however their output was ambiguous and, to some extent, surprising. As many studies had shown the biggest nationwide trade unions—Solidarity and the OPZZ (The All Poland Alliance of Trade Unions)—were "prisoners" of their own traditions. Contemporary Solidarity is a successor of the legendary social movement that had arisen after a wave of strikes in August 1980 and for a whole decade led the fight against the communist regime. Thus, Solidarity cultivates an image of a firm and uncompromising organization that always opposes those who are currently governing and movements for the rights of workers. It once made far-reaching claims and applied tough methods such as long-lasting strikes and street demonstrations, often leading to riots. One cannot pass over the serious losses of Solidarity's reputation as an advocate of worker's interests, since it abandoned the original values and principles of the social movement expressed in the concept of workers' democratic control or self-management of the means of production, and supported

---

[10] See: *Opinie o związkach zawodowych. Komunikat z badań.* [*Opinions on trade unions. Research report*]. BS/52/99, (Warszawa: Centrum Badania Opinii Spolecznej [Public Opinion Research Center], 1999).

"shock therapy," a radical neoliberal policy promoted by the Vice Prime Minister, Leszek Balcerowicz at the end of 1989. This involvement of Solidarity with transformation processes was termed "an umbrella stretched over reforms." Irrespective of the historical rationale of such a choice made by the leadership of Solidarity, it has instigated a truly paradoxical outcome: a decline of labor, i.e. the erosion of workers' powers and actual loss of its influence on the further development of the country. This process had—and still has—a decisive role in the rise of privatized economy and established a version of capitalism in Poland.

Since the OPZZ was founded in the early 80s under the control of the communist regime, it has never played as much of a powerful and influential role in the main political and socio-economic changes as Solidarity. But, in terms of number of members, the scale of activity (in particular on a level of enterprise and some branches) and an ability to negotiate with the government, the OPZZ in the late 90s displayed considerable strength. Notwithstanding its potential, the OPZZ maintained rather passive positions with regards to key challenging socio-economic questions, and confined itself to taking a defensive stand on such important matters like privatization, employment and other social policies. The OPZZ leaders have limited their own activity to defending the narrowly defined social privileges of employees, which were mostly inherited from the times of real socialism, and to looking after minor but concrete problems related strictly to workplaces (e.g. guarding whether work safety provisions are observed, or whether special supplements and allowances for some categories of workers are paid). This type of strategy did not allow the OPZZ to play a more decisive role in the transformation processes, the more so because its leaders behaved in a manner that could be characterized as "clientelism"—they bargained for some minor wage privileges and social safeguards with their political "patrons" and paid them with support or at least neutrality regarding great, systemic questions. An interesting side-effect of this strategy was that the OPZZ was almost imperceptible for workers on the level of enterprise. This phenomenon was identified during a series of interviews carried out in hundreds of enterprises between 1997–2001, in which the vast majority of workers stated that they did not notice any activity by the OPZZ in their plants. These statements stood in contrast to reports presented by top managers and politicians, who emphasized that they had good relations and frequent contact with activists of that particular organization.

A lack of consistency in the activities of trade unions and hidden conformism towards the political elite contributed very much to a gradual decline in their influence and authority. Both nationwide unions have been perceived as being strongly involved in politics, in the struggle for power between political parties, and have been labeled with the inclination to generate conflict and to push up its stake, not always in the interests of the employees.[11] In Poland, a specific model of trade unionism has emerged called "conflicting pluralism,"[12] the key element of which is the existence within most companies of at least two competing trade unions, neither of which was able to prevail over the other or genuinely represent the workforce as a whole. The chief drawback of this model is that it makes it difficult, if not almost impossible, for the unions to successfully struggle for workers' interests: they fail to represent the interests of the whole company workforce, as they have to focus on their own "clientele."

Those are general reasons why so many employees are reluctant to accept the great trade unions in the role of mediator in negotiations with employers. One of the most visible effects of such an attitude is decreasing membership in trade unions and a general lack of young people amongst their members.[13] Hence, recently we have heard many announcements made by noteworthy trade unionists that the time has come to rethink the role and strategy of their organizations, and they have encouraged a new formula for its activity. If one considers the logic of their evolution over the last twenty years it should be of no surprise that key proposals put forward so far have been directed toward professionalization of trade union activities and improving managerial skills of leaders, for example.

In this context it is justified to affirm that although Polish trade unions have for a long time been regarded as powerful institutions, they have in

---

[11] In analysis presented by one of the well-known experts on trade unions matters we read: "Both main trade union organizations were for a long time directly entangled in politics. They did not act as trade union pressure groups on politicians but themselves constituted an integral part of competing political parties or, in the case of NSZZ Solidarność, were transformed into political parties. NSZZ Solidarność has been seen as representing the right wing of the political scene and OPZZ the left wing. Whether or not these perceived orientations are correct, what matters is that they have been clearly distinguished by workers and that they have confirmed and reinforced political divisions among workers." Gardawski, J., *Problems facing the trade union movement analyzed*, (EIRO On-line, N° 08, 2003). www.eurofound.europa.eu (accessed October 3, 2010).

[12] Gardawski, J. *Problems facing the trade union movement analyzed.*

[13] According to the survey carried out by the CBOS in 2003 only 14.3% of employees were affiliated to any trade union. There were no trade union cells in 60% of enterprises. See: Gardawski, J., *Związki zawodowe: liczebność, sklad, postawy. Komunikat z badań.* [*Trade Unions: number of members, composition, attitudes. Research report*], BS/55/2003, (Warszawa: Centrum Badania Opinii Spolecznej [Public Opinion Research Center], 2003).

fact become imperceptibly weak and ineffective. Apart from a decreasing number of members, a lack of means to mobilize workers is especially destructive to the capacity of trade unions to undertake effective action.

All of these phenomena facilitated changes in the general framework of employer–employee relations. The share of new enterprises in the whole structure of Polish economy became greater the stronger the pressure on de-regulation grew, along with the de-institutionalization of industrial relations. In addition, the deteriorating power of trade unions in the old economy (comprising state and privatized, and former state enterprises) facilitated both tendencies. De-institutionalization means first of all a diminishing range of collective labor agreements, which are in fact applied in no more than 1/3 of enterprises, mainly in traditional heavy industry branches in which large-scale factories are the dominating form of production organization (e.g. coal mining, steel and metal industry), and in the public sector (e.g. special regulations for teachers). Other aspects of this process will be highlighted below when we consider the issue of distortions in a functioning of social dialogue. De-regulation pressure focuses mainly on efforts to ease the restrictive character of the Labor Code, especially its provisions for regulating the hiring of employees and employers' liabilities in entering into a long-term employment agreement.

Both the aforementioned tendencies are characterized by a variable dynamism that throughout last ten years has been particularly high, mainly due to the cumulating effects of internal changes and influence exerted by the European integration process (at the stage of negotiations on membership as well as after the accession to the EU). In the following we present a description of the differentiated stages of evolution of industrial relations and the labor market in Poland from 1998 to 2008.

Changes on the Labor Market and its Outcomes

1st Stage: 1998–2002. Soaring Unemployment and Shrinking Social Dialogue[14]

In the late 1990s, Polish economy had been confronted with the after-effects of global financial crisis caused by the "bubble-burst" in East-Asia and the collapse of the Russian currency which exerted a damaging effect on the prosperity of Eastern European countries. These factors presented a serious threat to the prospects of further growth of GPD in Poland, but an answer to that challenge was a choice between alternative economic strategies, generally characterized as neoliberal (based mostly on monetarism) and interventionist (based on post-Keynesian theories). Following the parliamentary elections in 1997, the new government recognized an inflation and depreciation of Polish currency as key dangers for the national economy, and it became clear that a profound shift in economic strategy was inevitable. High interest rates imposed by the National Bank of Poland and a set of other anti-inflation measures had effectively "cooled" the Polish economy. However, macroeconomic stability had been retained, despite many controversies regarding the measures and methods applied for evaluation, and the complex socio-economic effects of the policy which may not be unequivocally appreciated. Reasons for this criticism are clear if we compile a list of negative social phenomena, outcomes of the economic policy implemented by the then ruling Cabinet of Ministers:

- An increase in the unemployment rate of 19% (in absolute numbers that meant an exclusion from labor market of around 1 million new unemployed; the total number of unemployed reached 3 million)
- The expansion of the grey economy (evasion of taxation, illegal work, hiding of corporate and personal incomes, smuggling, deception of social benefits) that diminished budgetary revenues

[14] This subparagraph contains a short summary of analysis presented in an earlier published monograph: Gąciarz, B., Pańków, W., *Dialog spoleczny po polsku – fikcja czy szansa* [*Social dialogue in Polish style – fiction or opportunity*], (Warszawa. Instytut Spraw Publicznych [Institute of Public Affairs], 2001); and the article: Gąciarz, B., Pańków, W., "Consensual democracy and the political market in Poland," in *La Pologne dans l`Europe. Une integration achevee?*, ed. Dupont, B., (Special Issue: CAHIERS Lillois d'Economie et de Sociologie, Universite de Lille: I. L`Harmatan, 2005), 213–237.

- The "creeping" crisis of the whole system of public services, with the exemption of the service provided by local governments since the decentralization of public administration in the early 1990s, suffered by permanent under-financing and mismanagement; it triggered common frustrations due to mounting obstacles in access to services and poor quality, and caused the proliferation of corruption to an extent intolerable for most of society (thus the fight against corruption became an organizing concern of politics for several years)
- The expansion of populism and the variety of radical political movements, which fully exploited the frustration spreading across almost all social classes to discredit all political and social elites and to undermine credibility of all public institutions; anti-establishment opposition appeared and was quickly consolidated, whose *raison d'être* was to deny all accomplished outcomes of transformation and its general direction[15]

These processes all impinged on the condition of social dialogue in Poland, not only because negotiations between employers and employees are always exposed to positive or negative consequences of an economic policy conducted by government, but first and foremost because an institutional framework of this dialogue in Poland has very peculiar traits. Unlike the equivalent type of negotiations held in many European countries and at the level of European Communities, where representatives of two parties, usually trade unions and business associations, sit around the table, in the case of Poland there are three parties involved. The third is governmental which on the one hand plays the role of mediator between trade unions and representatives of employers, and on the other either bears direct responsibility for implementation of agreements or fulfils a function of guarantee with regard to any deals made by the other partners. This mechanism is reflected in the name of the central body responsible for holding negotiations: The Tripartite Commission (henceforth: the TC).[16] The construction of this body makes it very vulnerable to political

[15] A serious indicator of its rising power was a referendum on accession to the EU. Despite high rates of support for European integration in public opinion polls, all anti-establshment parties were able to provide very aggressive and stimulating campaigns against the European choice and to put the final result of the vote at risk.

[16] This specific attachment to the governmental power structures was even increased a couple years ago, when according to the Law on the Tripartite

interference and manipulation, and above all exposes any agreement to a dependency on the willingness of the government. These shortcomings of the TC date back to the early 1990s when the first body to hold tripartite negotiations was appointed under the auspices of the Minister of Labour and Social Policy in 1993, and was intended as a remedy to waves of strikes affecting Polish economy and an uncontrollable combination of wage and other claims orchestrated by competing trade unions on all levels of activity. At that time, the government was an absolutely indispensable part of this body, since the state-owned enterprises were still a dominating influence in the economy, and the state was itself the biggest employer with a large amount of salaries under strict state control. To impose order on the relationships between trade unions, private and public employers and the government was an imperative for everybody who bore the responsibility for the future of the Polish economy and was supposed to endeavour to avoid bankruptcy of the state and the vast majority of enterprises. It should be stated that it was successful, since the involvement of trade unions in permanent negotiations contributed to reducing tensions within branch structures and in individual enterprises. A more peaceful climate prevailed in mutual relations between all institutions involved in the economic processes, but since this time some profound changes occurred that essentially modified the structure of economy and the mechanisms of its functioning, the most important being the following:

- At present, the private sector dominates the Polish economy both in terms of its share in the GDP and its rate of employment
- The state withdrew from the control of salaries in the private sector and limited such control over the public sector
- The scope of common negotiating areas between the government, trade unions and business associations shrank at a remarkable rate; a great part of current negotiations makes up macroeconomic agenda that coincides with competences of other representative bodies, primarily all of the parliament
- The representativeness of trade unions and of several business associations is very dubious, which has a discouraging impact

Commission for Social and Economic Affairs and provincial commission on social dialogue (2001), 16 regional bodies have been established and affiliated to one of the Voievoda's offices (representatives of the Council of Ministers to the province).

on the government's willingness to make any far-reaching commitments

Unfortunately for the quality of social dialogue in Poland, when the time came to establish its legal framework an anachronous solution had been chosen, well-known from the recent past but of limited functionality to contemporary requirements. If we link this fact with the previously outlined outcomes of neoliberal policy, we may explain the reasons for the recent atrophy or weakening of social dialogue in Poland. Our argumentation will be based on the empirical studies conducted between 2000–2002, mainly interviewing those who participated in the activity of social dialogue bodies. If we look at the main features of social dialogue as our respondents perceived them, particularly respondents representing social partners and political groups, the following were mentioned:

- Politicisation
- Instrumentalisation of the legal rules of social dialogue (inclination to abuse any ambiguity and loophole
- Poor institutionalisation of social dialogue
- Dependence on personalities of participating leaders (personalisation or personification of social dialogue)
- Fragmentation of the social dialogue
- Focus on expressive functions (mutual legitimisation) instead on matters of substance or focus on only the "soft" forms of dialogue
- Ideologization, i.e. reference mainly to symbols and values exclusively, such as selection, particularly by the government, of one's "own" or privileged partners, narrowing down the dialogue to secondary problems, underdevelopment or complete absence of so-called intellectual-expert resources for the participants of social dialogue and of social partners in particular

The data we collected allowed us to point to the following factors blocking, or producing atrophy of, social dialogue:

(1) Globalisation and integration of the Polish economy with world economy, especially with European Union economy, which actually diminished the scope of issues that would be subject to a decision of the TC

(2) Necessary (according to some) voluntarism of the state authorities in the process of realisation of the systemic and sector reforms
(3) Subordination of the trade union elite to the political leadership of the main competing political parties
(4) The immaturity and organisational underdevelopment of employment agencies and their competition for participation in social dialogue
(5) The fact that participants of the so-called autonomous dialogue are focused on mutual legitimisation of their partners
(6) The tendency to move the social dialogue "down," to the provincial, economic sector or plant level, meaning actual marginalization
(7) The priorities of the government, and particularly the Ministry of Labour, concerning "partial" dialogue at the expense of the development of institutional dialogue structures
(8) Petrifaction of the non-representative "initial" institutional structures of social dialogue
(9) The feeling that corporatism is threatening parliamentary democracy
(10) Mutual prejudice and stereotyping harboured by the potential participants of social dialogue
(11) The pre-election clinch which developed between the major trade union organisations and political groups

Due to the specific circumstances that occurred at the turn of the century, an attempt to develop genuine and efficient social dialogue was unsuccessful. Two key reasons for failure were: the anachronous format of established institutional framework and a gradual loss of interest in this type of dialogue by the government and by business milieu, caused in both cases by deep structural changes in an economy.

2nd Stage: 2002–2004. Towards Further Strengthening of Employers' Position and Deterioration of Work Conditions [17]

The following years brought a further strengthening of the tendencies outlined above. The most conspicuous feature of the labor market was instability of employment: Poland led in statistics of people who were

---

[17] This subparagraph is based on conclusions drawn up from the article summarizing part of the results of the European Social Survey: Gąciarz, B., Pańków, W., "Praca w Polsce na tle innych krajów europejskich" ["Labor in Poland against a background of other European countries"], in *W środku Europy? Wyniku europejskiego sondażu spolecznego* [*In the middle of Europe? Results of the European Social Survey*], eds. Domański, H., Ostrowska, A., Sztabiński, P. B., (Warszawa: Wydawnictwo: IFiS PAN, 2006).

permanently jobless or were searching for work for a long time (over 3 months) with a rate of 35.7%. Additionally, it has to be noted that amongst jobless people over 65% qualified for the category of structurally unemployed (they were jobless over 12 months). It was not an isolated trait of that situation but part of a wider syndrome, which comprises such phenomena as:

- A high rate of subjective feeling regarding uncertainty of work—over half of employees declared a lack of certainty that they would be working in the upcoming months
- The low level of salaries; officially paid wages were for most families only a half of incomes necessary for maintenance
- A relatively high share of social benefits and pensions in the total incomes of families
- The growing amount of short-term employment contracts
- An increasing number of employees getting early retirement

These symptoms showed the growing domination of employers over employees, and that the latter did not dispense any effective means to oppose this state of affairs. As much research had declared, the employers fully exploited this to their own advantage. They not only kept salaries at a very low level and forced employees to work overtime without extra payment, but they often violated fundamental rights of workers, e.g. salaries were paid irregularly or not paid for several months, or they arbitrarily changed conditions of work and payment. In this context it is not surprisingly that Poles actively searched for work abroad. As the ESS showed, over 7% of Poles took up work abroad at some stage in the 10 years preceding the survey being conducted—only Spaniards, Greeks and Luxembourgers were more active in this regard. Taking into account that at the time Poles did not have free access to the labor market in the EU countries, this indicates their determination in finding a solution for their own living problems abroad and a relatively high potential of mobility and resourcefulness, which could not find appropriate domestic conditions to benefit from.

In general terms, these years saw a continuation of tendencies well-known from preceding periods, in particular:

- Further shrinking of rates of unionization among all branches of economy
- Fading of worker participation both in institutional and practical terms

- Growth of paternalistic and autocratic styles of management in enterprises

The ESS disclosed another interesting aspect of social climate in Polish enterprises—a low level of solidarity amongst employees. Their reluctance to join trade unions and to act collectively vis-à-vis their employer is supplemented by a low sense of commitment in support of companions at workplace. Only a few workers declared that they might count on the aid of their colleagues if they were to get into trouble, e.g. by falling into debt. This is a striking indicator of a lack of confidence amongst people, which is possibly a key source of preference for individualistic strategies of resolving living problems so popular amongst Poles.

For the sake of completing this analysis it should be stated that the institutional social dialogue had gone into a phase of stagnation, i.e. either meetings of relevant bodies had not been convened, or its agenda consisted of minor issues.

3rd Stage: 2004 –2007. Economic Immigration and Improving Status of Employees

Undoubtedly, accession to the EU posed a turning point for the evolution of the labor market in Poland. Since then, the main factor steering the process is the mass economic immigration of Poles to the EU countries. However, from the very beginning only the UK, Ireland and Sweden abolished any limitations in access to their labor markets for Poles—1.5–2 million (numbers differ depending on sources) left their homeland and took a job abroad. The dominating, economic explanation for this phenomenon reduces decisions made by immigrants to pure commercial motivations. In our opinion this is incorrect, and even if immigrants themselves express such opinions there are more complex reasons for such a spectacular wave of migration. The pressure to migrate from Poland derives from many economic, social and psychological reasons, a (not comprehensive) list of which is compiled below:

- Economic factors related to employee status: low salaries and total incomes of families, low living standards, shallow labor market (small number of offers of work, inadequacy of jobs with regard to qualifications of workforce)
- Macroeconomic factors: domination of traditional industrial branches, relatively weak SME sector; underdevelopment of

service sector; underdeveloped infrastructure; poor competitiveness of Polish enterprises

- Social factors: model of industrial relations, e.g. instability of employment, overregulation of employment agreements, lack of flexible forms of employment; growing inequalities between social classes and regions; barrier to access of high quality education and other public services
- Psychological factors: employers' patterns of behavior (autocratic and non-cooperative), lack of mutual confidence between employees and employers; low level of respect for labor[18]

Mass immigration has profoundly changed relations between supply and demand on the labor market—employers are confronted with a workforce deficit, especially troublesome for those searching for qualified workers, engineers and other technical specialists. The most important consequence of this new situation has been a serious increase in salaries. The balance of power on the labor market has shifted significantly towards employees. All these processes have gradually activated a self-regulation mechanism in the labor market, and has brought about the growth of more effective pressure by different social and vocational groups on employers in order to get an increase in salaries. Nonetheless, it so far has not triggered a significant growth in the rate of vocational activity. At the same time, there are some indications as to the effects exerted by these phenomena on economic processes, in particular on the increase of consumption prices and general inflation

So far, key benefits gained by employees are related only to their incomes. They have not yet made use of their new standing to initiate deep structural changes in the framework of industrial relations, and it should be stated that there are no indicators that this will happen in the near future. It may mean that improvement of the status of employees will be of only a temporary nature and will fade if general economic conditions worsen.

---

[18] Interesting results has been recently disclosed from research conducted amongst Polish immigrants who returned to their homeland in recent years. A remarkable number of them declared that the fair, just and friendly employers' attitudes was one of the most satisfactory aspects of their work abroad. See: Frelak, J., B. Roguska, *Powroty do Polski. Wyniki badań* [*Returns to Poland. Report*], (Warszawa: ISP, 2008).

Beyond 2007–Ambiguous Perspectives for Social Dialogue

On the basis of the evidence and the discussion above we have to conclude that the Solidarity-led governments that came to power in 1990 developed concepts contradictory to its original ideas and interests. Solidarity advanced the development of private property relations and ceased to represent the democratic principle of self-management. This ideological transformation worked itself out in the privatization procedures, which initially granted substantial participatory rights to workers, but also led to the destruction of Workers' Councils, and over time to the erosion of workers' shareholding status. At present, workers have lost the institutional means to exercise control in the privatized economy, and do not appear to have created alternative institutions in their place. The ideas such as those underlying workers' struggles for genuine and substantive democracy in the workplace had been effectively limited by the social conditions within which they developed. The institutions of social dialogue established in the meantime do not prove effective in balancing interests of private entrepreneurs and workers. They do not deliver any decisive stimulus for improvement of general industrial relations in Poland and to set up a more reasonable employment policy. The most visible consequence of such a development is the serious disequilibrium of the labor market which is mostly regulated by spontaneous mechanisms. Establishment of a more useful institutional framework for the labor market and industrial relations is still to be achieved by the Polish authorities and civil society organizations.

References

Blaszczyk, Barbara and Richard Woodward. *Privatization and Company Restructuring in Poland*. Warsaw: Center for Social and Economic Research, 1999.

Frelak, Joanna and Beata Roguska. *Powroty do Polski. Wyniki badań*. [*Returns to Poland. Report*]. Warszawa: ISP, 2008.

Gardawski, Juliusz , Barbara Gąciarz, Andrzej Mokrzyszewski, and Włodzimierz Pańków. *Rozpad bastionu? Związki zawodowe w gospodarce prywatyzowanej* [*The fall of a fortress? Trade unions in privatized economy*]. Warszawa. Instytut Spraw Publicznych, 1999.

Gąciarz, Barbara. "Employee Self-Management in the 1980's." In *The Protracted Death—Agony of Real Socialism. Political Mechanisms of Societal Life in Poland in the 1980's.* Edited by Jerzy Hausner and Tadeusz Klementewicz. Warszawa. Wydawnictwo ISP PAN, 1992.

Gąciarz, Barbara and Włodzimierz Pańków. "Effective Strategies in Direct Privatization." In *Direct Privatization. Investors, Managers, Employees.* Edited by Maria Jarosz. Warszawa: Wydawnictwo ISP PAN. 1999.

—. "Industrial Relations in Poland: From Social Partnership to Enlightened Paternalism." In *Poland into the New Millennium.* Edited by George Blazyca and Ryszard Rapacki. Cheltenham; Northampton. Edward Elgar Economies and Societies in Transition, 2001.

—. *Dialog Spoleczny Po Polsku – Fikcja Czy Szansa* [*Social Dialogue In Polish Style – Fiction Or Opportunity*]. Warszawa, Instytut Spraw Publicznych, 2001.

—. "Consensual Democracy and the Political Market in Poland." In *La Pologne dans l'Europe. Une integration achevee?* Edited by Bernard Dupont. Special Issue: CAHIERS Lillois d'Economie et de Sociologie, Universite de Lille: I. L'Harmatan, 2005.

—. "Praca w Polsce na tle innych krajów Europejskich" ["Labor in Poland against a background of other European countries"]. In *W środku Europy? Wyniku europejskiego sondażu spolecznego.* [*In the middle of Europe? Results of the European Social Survey*]. Edited by Henryk Domański, Anna Ostrowska and Paweł B. Sztabiński. Warszawa: Wydawnictwo: IFiS PAN, 2006.

Jarosz, Maria. *Direct Privatization. Investors, Managers, Employees.* Warszawa: Wydawnictwo ISP PAN, 1999.

Ost, David. *The Defeat of Solidarity: Anger and Politics in Postcommunist Europe*. Ithaca: Cornell University Press, 2005.

CHAPTER SIX

"WORMS"[1] OF POLISH ECONOMIC TRANSITION[2]

MARIA NAWOJCZYK[3]

Introduction

Initiative, action, innovation, and entrepreneurship have always been recognized as the constitutive elements of a capitalist market. Yet, despite the emphasis on its role in economic development, entrepreneurship was, for a long time, overlooked by mainstream discussions in the social sciences. As the "spirit of capitalism," it has risen above the concepts of economists, the theorists of organization and management, sociologists, and social psychologists, but has not made itself manifest in the fundamental content and ideas of these specific fields.

In all of these above mentioned disciplines the dominance of discourse at the macro level has hampered a focus on phenomena belonging to the micro-analysis level. This does not mean that entrepreneurship has been completely ignored, but that it has been handled strictly within the borders of various disciplines without forming any coherent theory or even systematic definitions. Therefore, once entrepreneurial activity found itself at the center of scholarly attention at the end of the 20th century, the

---

[1] I am borrowing this term from a typology of entrepreneurs made by Akos Rona-Tas (2001). His typology differentiates between two types of entrepreneurs: the first, who have the potential for economic growth (the caterpillar), and the second, who's activity substitutes the employment relations in over-regulated labor market (the worm). I will refer to it later in this article in more details.

[2] This article is based on the field research I conducted among small entrepreneurs in Poland. As a result I published the book in Polish (Nawojczyk 2009) and this text is a kind of summary of this project. Some of these findings I published also in EEQ (Nawojczyk 2008).

[3] Faculty of Humanities, AGH University of Science and Technology, Krakow.

discussion on this subject was weighed down by imprecision or ambiguity, or a lack of definition, methodological principles, or accurate theoretical references. Therefore a significant portion of my book (Nawojczyk 2009) is devoted precisely to the presentation and categorization of the scholarly achievements made thus far in the study of entrepreneurship. In this chapter I will refer only to ideas which I found important as a background to my research study (more information in the next chapter).

Nevertheless, since the moment when entrepreneurship began to attract my professional interest and I commenced analysis of the literature dedicated to this topic, I have sensed an incompatibility between the focus of my empirical curiosity and many of its theoretical models. Scholars hypothesizing on this subject constantly and consistently stress such characteristics as innovation, creativity, and effectiveness in action (Morris 1998). However, with reference to persons described as being entrepreneurial, social scientists mention such personality traits as achievement motivation and an internal locus of control, as well as a penchant for calculated risk-taking, tolerance for ambiguity, alertness to chances appearing on the market, and persistence (McClelland 1987). The results of these inquiries clearly refer to those societies which are building an economy based upon free market principles along an evolutionary path. In my opinion, such an image does not reflect the impulsive entrepreneurial activity of the first stage of the Polish transformation at the end of the 1980s and in the 1990s.

Entrepreneurship in Economy in Transition

Small businesses constitute the most dynamic element of growth in the emerging markets of the Central and Eastern European (CEE) region in the last decade of the 20th century (Hull 1999). In the post-socialist countries, the small-firm sector has an important structural function. Small firms are regarded as institutions which improve the flexibility of the economy as a whole, particularly in terms of innovation and the necessary adaptation to the rapid changes of supply and demand (Brezinski and Fritsch 1996). Moreover, the birth and death of enterprises may contribute considerably to the structural change that allows a national economy to be competitive in the world market. Small and new enterprises also perform an important political task in creating a pluralistic society. The right to establish an enterprise whenever, in whatever field, and wherever, constitutes a shift toward democratization and decentralization of economic power.

Poland is among the leaders in the CEE region in sustained economic growth and in attracting Western European investors and partners. The economic liberalization program embodied in the Balcerowicz Plan (1989–1990) laid the groundwork which made successful private sector development possible in Poland. However, a clear weakness in Polish entrepreneurship is its heavy concentration in the service sector, with little activity in manufacturing, caused by low barriers to entry into small commerce or trade, into self-employment or "into survival entrepreneurship."

Taking into consideration the influence of entrepreneurship on economic development, the disproportion between small businesses and entrepreneurial ventures is clearly evident. For this reason, too, in economic models of entrepreneurship an accent is placed on such indicators as pure uncertainty (type A), pure innovation (type B), uncertainty plus innovative knowledge (type C), and perception of possibilities and adaptation to them (type D) (Hébert and Link 1982). The most popular among these is type B (the Schumpeterian type entrepreneur) and type D (the Kirznian type entrepreneur).[4]

The systemic transformation from a centralized to a market economy generated especially advantageous conditions for Kirznerian type entrepreneurship in its opening phase. Nonetheless, the tempo of the changes in subsequent stages, as well as the dynamics of the economic development was linked more to the appearance of Schumpeterian type entrepreneurship. Judging by economic development indicators, Poland is dealing with both these types. However, among the (almost 100) businessmen I studied, perhaps only one-tenth of them could be classified as Kirznerian, while not one could be classified as Schumpeterian. Therefore, with respect to solely economic concepts, it would be difficult to term the persons interviewed by me "entrepreneurs."

The problem is that, in the long term, economic growth is assisted only by Schumpeterian entrepreneurs, the type missing from Poland. Thus there is a need to teach potential candidates the basics of what constitutes a business and how it should be run.[5]

Who are the Polish Entrepreneurs?

Based on forty five in-depth interviews conducted during the summer of 2002 and fifty interviews conducted in winter 2005/2006 in Poland

---

[4] The Kirznian-type entrepreneurship is also described as "low-level" entrepreneurship because it transfers resources from low to high productivity uses in the new opportunities of the market economy, while Schumpeterian type entrepreneurship, as a "high-level" entrepreneurship, is an innovative, driving force for economic development.

[5] There are numerous EU training programs devoted to education of SMEs.

among self-employed owners of small businesses, I would like to discuss these small business owners as being "the essence of capitalism." Regarding their educational background and work experience, as well as their understanding of the role of market economy, I will argue that their decisions to be self-employed are a survival strategy rather than an embodiment of entrepreneurial attitudes.

Their primary importance in transforming the economy is social rather than economic in nature. Most of them will not contribute to the growing and strengthening of a market economy, but they will contribute to changing the attitudes of individuals seeking support from the state toward being independent and self-reliant. This is perhaps the first step in creating a pro-market environment capable of socializing the next generation of Schumpeterian entrepreneurs.

The field research in 2002 was conducted in a medium sized town (of about 200,000 inhabitants) with an unemployment rate close to the national average of 18%. In this city, there used to be a number of big state-owned companies which went bankrupt, but there are also examples of a successful transformation of ownership from state to private hands in the case of several medium size firms. The interviews were held among the owners of micro or small scale businesses in one shopping street in one district of the town, just outside the downtown section. The population of this district is mixed in terms of economic status and includes unemployed, retired, and wealthy people. In this shopping street, at the length of three blocks, over one hundred businesses are located. Forty five randomly selected shopkeepers and owners of permanent stands on the Farmers' Market were interviewed.

The second field research in 2005 was carried out in a similar city landscape concerning urban settings but in a much larger city (about 750,000 inhabitants). The differences between the two places in the number of inhabitants, the unemployment rate (in the larger city it was 7% in 2005) and in the general economic situation of the country (in 2002 a period of stagnation, in 2005 economic recovery) influenced the job market conditions in both cases.

Most crucial in this world are the interactions taking place within this market rather than with its environs, including agencies of the global market and governments. Competition strategies are of a local dimension—local patterns of behavior emerge and economic awareness is incorporated as part of everyday practice. Social factors often take on greater meaning than economic ones in conducting business activity. Precisely such a perspective on entrepreneurship—from an ecological and geographical clustering approach—yields new analytical possibilities (Thornton 1999).

My analysis of the materials collected during this project serves not only as a description of a key part of our economic and social life, but also as an exemplification of the difficulties encountered in applying theoretical concepts to field research.

If, as proposed by some, we consider the creation of a new discipline (i.e. entrepreneurship studies) with a narrow understanding limited solely to inventive and dynamic undertakings based upon applied knowledge, then the phenomenon I have studied is not entrepreneurship at all (Acs and Audretch 2003). From the point of view of socio-professional structures, what label should be applied to this group I have studied?

The first problem with which one must deal is the issue of branding, and what would be the most accurate name for the people involved in such activity. The existing literature differentiates entrepreneurial ventures from small businesses (Morris 1998), the latter being status quo oriented, with a deep involvement on the part of family members and a blurred interaction between personal and professional activities. The structure is more informal with a small and steady number of employees; the focus is present-oriented with a preference for low-risk/low-return investments. This description fits many of the companies investigated. Yet from this perspective are small-business owners the entrepreneurs? After all, "small entrepreneurs" is not a term that exists in the literature. Hence we return to the initial dilemma. Are the business owners of my study actually the entrepreneurs? And if so, then what is the analytical use of differentiating such an internally varied socio-professional category?

The Cognitive Approach to Entrepreneurship

It seems to me that psychology and sociology have more to offer here. If we treat entrepreneurship as a stance of actively shaping one's life (particularly with regards to one's career), then we could look at my interviewees from a fresh perspective. Under circumstances of extreme uncertainty (such as those experienced in the first stage of the transformation), these entrepreneurs decided to take control of and shape their own fate in contrast to many of their compatriots who are still demonstrating an attitude of claims and demands. Entrepreneurs demonstrated such responsibility with respect to their entire family, lightening the load of the national budget and social institutions. Furthermore, they were extraordinarily persistent in this. Through their actions they continue to form a socializing milieu which facilitates future entrepreneurial endeavors—their children will likely display more of a tendency to fulfill this social role than the children of other career options.

Greater, too, will be the chances for the appearance of the Schumpeterian type, since an upbringing which accentuates responsibility, the facing of challenges, and risk-taking wholly facilitates such an evolution.

The social circles upon which these entrepreneurs bear influence encompass not only their own families, but also the local market. It is on this market that patterns of business behavior are shaped, including norms regulating relationships among entrepreneurs as competitors, as well as between entrepreneurs and their customers. A tangle of social and cognitive biases—necessary for the exploitation of new business opportunities—becomes entwined. To analyze these relations I employed a model proposed by Donna Maria De Carolis and Patrick Saparito (see fig. 6.1 below) which simultaneously examines both social capital and cognition providing an understanding of exploitation of an entrepreneurial opportunity.

These cognitive biases include:

- Over-confidence—the excessive optimism expressed my interviewees
- An illusion of control—taking charge of nearly all aspects of the business (with perhaps the exception of financial accounting)
- Lack of representativity—a comparison of one's situation to that of only a handful of the closest competitors

All of these qualities seem to manifest themselves in my sample group. The social circumstances associated with the model are:

- Strong social ties which, among the respondents in my study, encompassed the family, workers, customers, cooperators, and competitors
- Shared codes and language such as a specific attitude towards work and clients
- Trust which, in the case of my interviewees, was limited solely to their informal social systems
- Structural holes[6]

[6] The structural hole exists when different clusters of interconnected actors are only sparsely tied to one another. As a consequence, any individual who is on the position between those clusters can capitalize the flow of information and benefit from it.

The last two conditions are, however, not met in the case of my research study group.

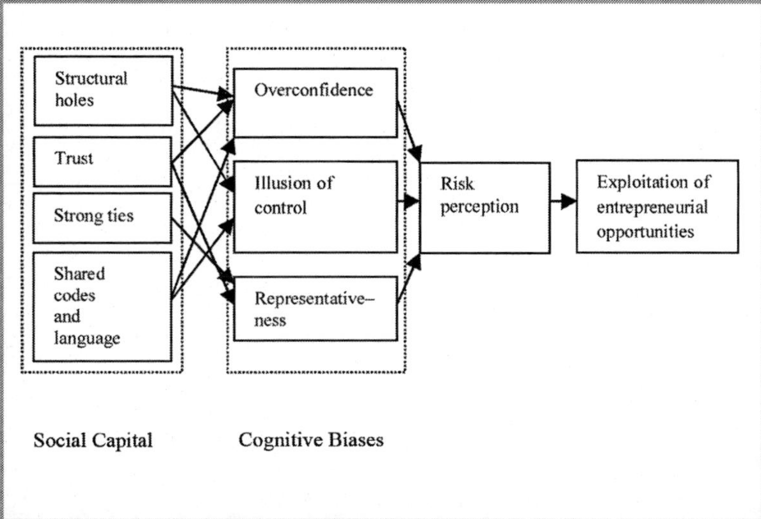

Fig. 6.1
Social Capital, Cognitive Biases and Exploitation of Entrepreneurial Opportunities.
Source: De Carolis and Saparito 2006, 43.

The level of trust in various social relations in Poland is particularly low and also pertains to business relations. Still, trust in these interactions in Poland is built on the basis of personal experience and is much easier to establish in face-to-face contact than in impersonal dealings with institutions (Nawojczyk 2007). This is why the level of trust was high within the social network of the entrepreneurs studied here, but low with regards to institutions of the broader environment. A situation in which very strong ties appear within a network does not facilitate the creation of structural holes which stimulate entrepreneurial activity (Granovetter 1974). The weakness of these two social factors is perceived as the reason behind the description of the attitude and behavior in Poland as more a matter of resourcefulness than entrepreneurship.

The strength of social ties in both cities—Toruń and Kraków—hampers the stimulation of entrepreneurial activity and is, in my opinion, a consequence of the spatial concentration of the companies. While it is true that such a concentration is capable of encouraging entrepreneurialism (Sorenson and Audia 2000), this is only possible if mechanisms exist for the transfer and transformation of knowledge in the process of its commercialization. In order for this condition to be fulfilled, there would have to be many more knowledge-based businesses concentrated in the area and facilitating the specialization of the given local environment.

The Structural and Institutional Mechanisms of Entrepreneurship

The over-representation of the trade sector hinders the formation of locally determined models of entrepreneurial activity (Saxenian 1994); for instance, values and norms regulating Toruń and Kraków companies basically do not differ. Only the general context of the macro-economic situation varies: stagnation during the course of the research in Toruń (2002) contrasting with the animated energy noted in Kraków (2005) yielded differences in some aspects of the analyzed entrepreneurial activity. Here we find a mechanism of reproduction and the imitation of structures (Di Maggio and Powel 1991), because the institutionalization of the transformational changes was determined by actions taken at the macro-economic and macro-social level. The flow of reactions from the micro to the macro sphere was blocked or at least rather clogged.

For this reason, the analytical model proposed by Martin Ruef and Michael Lounsbury (see fig. 6.2 below) could not be appropriately applied to the cases of entrepreneurship studied here. This model is perfect for analysis of the context of entrepreneurship—both the material and cognitive-institutional dimensions—by stressing economic and institutional conditions, financial and human capital, community structure and culture, as well as the identity of organizational form and the structure of a company's population. All of these themes have been undertaken in my research project. Significantly more difficult was the analysis of the effects of entrepreneurial activity—starting from the shaping of an entrepreneurial identity, through the building of a venture culture, and closing with institutional changes. These processes ran a different course in transformational economies than in the already stabilized market economies.

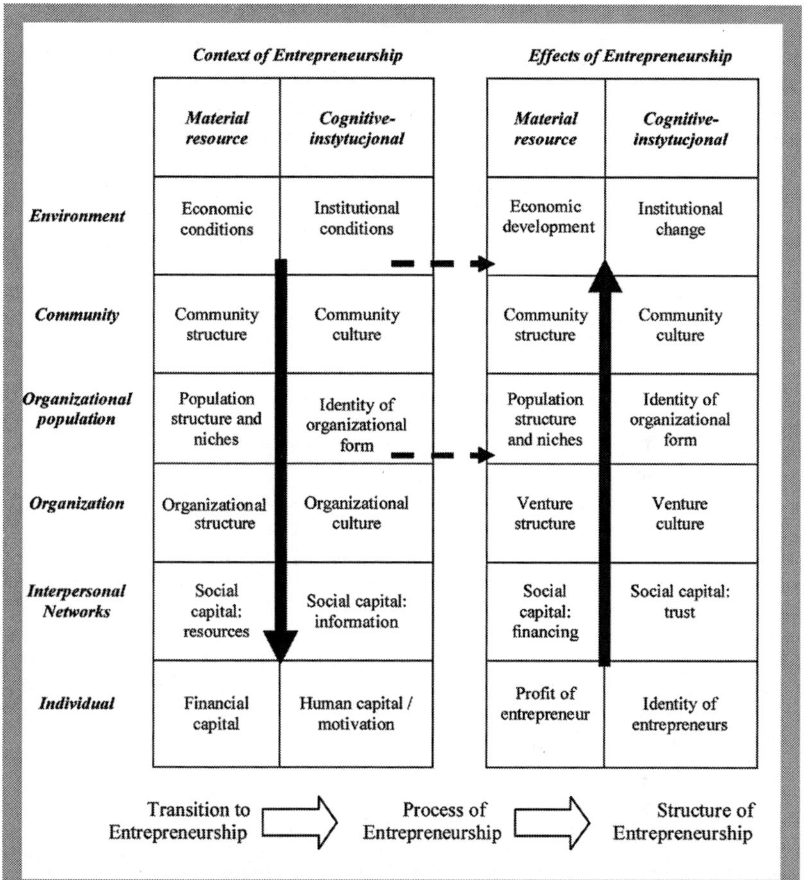

Fig. 6.2
A Multilevel Framework for the Sociology of Entrepreneurship.
Source: Ruef and Lounsbury 2007, 19.

In the latter type of economy, persons who decide to establish a business do so in certain cycles of their lives; this means that they are prepared to play a particular, chosen social role. In the former type, a decision to undertake such an endeavor was, to a great extent, spontaneous and often compelled by external dynamics. Therefore, the building of an entrepreneurial identity under such circumstances comprises a longer and more burdensome process. Playing the role of an entrepreneur in developed economies is facilitated by organizations and clubs representing the interests of specific social and professional circles, and it is precisely these agencies which influence institutional change in accordance with the needs and desires of the group. In countries undergoing transformation, such organizations were only just surfacing and encompassed a group of entrepreneurs who worked on a scale broader than those persons I interviewed. There is more of a tendency towards consolidation of interests among opportunity-driven rather than needs-based entrepreneurs. The proportion of the second of these is much greater in a transformation economy than in a stable market economy. Moreover, if the business owners are of the "worm" type, as Akos Rona-Tas described them in his typology (see table 6.1 below), then they are condemned to only imitate and are incapable of building an organizational and cultural resource base.

Table 6.1. A Typology of Entrepreneurs in Transition Economies

	The caterpillar	The worm
Main actor	Entrepreneur	Self-employed
Main unit	Enterprise with its own space	Household
Main goal	Accumulation	Survival/consumption
Main resource	Smart combination of factors of production	Labor
Genesis	Pull	Push
Strategy	Innovative, initiative, (prospector)	Defensive, reactive, imitative
Commitment	High, full-time	Low or intermittent, part-time
Contracts	Formal, legal	Informal
Employment	Employs others	Employs only self, family, good friends
Legal form	Incorporated, limited liability	Sole proprietorship, unlimited liability
Market	Anywhere, potentially even abroad	Local
Business relationships	Supplier, subcontractor to big businesses	No substantive relations
Source of profit	Market opportunities	Self-exploitation
Business cycle	Expansion in up cycle	Expansion in down cycle
Taxes	Major source of tax revenue	Often tax evading
Policy intervention	Access to credit	Training
Growth	Likely to grow when successful	Keeps its size small even if successful

Source: Rona-Tas 2001, 62

The majority of analyzed business owners shared most of characteristics of the worm. But being a worm also has advantages as well as disadvantages, of the type often not seen from an economical point of view. Worms are also the carriers of some positive changes—their understanding of the importance of customers results in changing attitudes toward these customers. In the socialist economy, a customer was a "disturbing element" in any shop, now he/she has a different position. The interviewed shopkeepers are not only aware of the importance of the presence of customers, but also of the importance of their purchasing power. This leads to a better understanding of the cyclical functioning of a market economy and to making an effort to win the loyalty of customers. The ownership of a business is a value in itself—the owners enjoy their independence and they are proud that they are able to support themselves and their families. Their self-confidence is increased, even though some of them (15%) would be willing to return to a job as a full-time employee, preferably in a public sector. Nevertheless, the experience of private economic activity for millions of people (regardless of whether they continue their businesses) could be profitable for the process of building a market economy in Poland. Their individual strategies of survival include some pathologies, but this is part of the painful journey from a socialist, communitarian society toward a more entrepreneurial market-oriented one.

Cultural Environment

The results of my research study clearly demonstrate that Polish culture still does not support or sustain entrepreneurship. At the beginning of the transformation period the dominant features of Polish culture, according to Norman Davies (1982), appeared as a patchwork of four subcultures: peasant, literary, Catholic and communist, all of them with strong anti-entrepreneurial traces (Nawojczyk and Walton 2004). For example the peasant culture was rooted in the feudal way of life and was most visible in ancient sayings. From the peasant viewpoint, wealth could be accumulated only through the deprivation of others, or as a common Polish saying goes: "When the rich become richer, the poor become poorest." Wealth is also associated with immorality and contrasted against the strong moral character of the peasant, and it is commonly said, "As wealth grows, virtue diminishes" (Marmuszewski 2003, 103). Thus a negative stereotype of the business person remains deeply rooted. This stereotype is founded on an antipathy towards rich people. My respondents, however, are not among the wealthy. Their living standard is perhaps higher when compared to that of the overwhelming majority of their clients (in both cities there are relatively large elderly and student populations while Toruń also has a high number of unemployed), but they certainly cannot be counted among the affluent.

Yet another factor in this negative stereotype is their non-observance of the law. The Public Opinion Research Center survey on Polish attitudes toward wealth was conducted twice in 1992 and again in 1999, and gives a clear picture of changes in public perception (Derczyński 1999, 8). When asked in 1992 how the rich gained their wealth, 52 percent of respondents attributed those successes to cheating, breaking or bending the law, or direct thievery, but by 1999 that number fell to 34 percent, though it remained the most popular answer. However, it is true that many of my respondents have bent or broken labor laws, but perhaps all it would take would be some simple legal regulations regarding the establishment and running of a family business in order to eliminate such phenomena. Certainly this would be advantageous for the shaping of informal norms regulating the venture culture. Such informal norms continue to be shaped on the basis of behavior which my respondents describe as "common sense." The greater the degree that their solutions stand in contradiction to formal, legal norms, the smaller the chance that law-abiding attitudes and behavior will be worked out.

The stereotype of the "evil employer" was completely abolished in the group studied. Their employees are hired on permanent contracts, are usually long-term relationships lasting sometimes even a couple of decades. The employers investigated follow the letter of the law with regards to salary limits (albeit, in most cases, at the lowest possible level), vacations, maternity and childcare leaves, even future entitlements (e.g. retirement) for their employees. The final component of this negative stereotype was incompetence, a charge also found to be untrue.

In the stereotypical image of the entrepreneur there are also positive traits such as diligence, courtesy, and courage. In the above mentioned surveys of the public's perception of the characteristics that lead to wealth accumulation (Derczyński 1999), in 1992 the predominant stress was upon negative factors, but by 1999 the heaviest stress was placed upon positive factors. Courageous risk-taking shifted from 38 to 46 percent and became the predominant choice. Industriousness came to be seen as the second most important factor, rising dramatically from 26 percent in 1992 to 41 percent in 1999. The number of respondents attributing wealth accumulation to individual abilities also rose, from 29 to 39 percent. However, when it comes to courage, one could say, at least with respect to my respondents, that they displayed this attribute in the very act of establishing their business. In that case, will the stereotype of the entrepreneur yield to change? Likely yes, but the internal diversification within this socio-economic category known as entrepreneurship does not favor such a makeover.

Conclusions

The nature of entrepreneurship could be analyzed as a process of creation in literature most frequently associated with creation of wealth, enterprise, innovation, change, employment, value, or growth (Morris 1998). This constitutes a broad framework. If we add to these contexts a variety of descriptions of entrepreneurs as those who assume the risk associated with uncertainty, suppliers of financial capital, innovators, decision makers, industrial leaders, coordinators economic resources, proprietors of an enterprise, employers, or those who allocate resources to alternative uses (Hébert and Link 1982), the picture of the scope of research becomes multidimensional and hard to define.

Therefore, in my opinion, it is thus worth conducting research on entrepreneurship in the context of such local markets. These could be, for example, the newly-founded "incubators of entrepreneurship," or centers of innovation, or also, looking at this geographically, city centers or small towns as hubs radiating out to the surroundings. Such a line of investigation could help the drawing of a map of the pluses and minuses of these local markets; this, in turn, would permit appropriate institutional changes, leading to the reinforcement of desired patterns and to the elimination of illicit or harmful practices. It is also worth referring the results of such research to the broader context in order to understand their economic circumstances and cultural roots.

References

Acs, Zoltan J. and David B. Audretsch . *Handbook of Entrepreneurship Research.* Boston-Dordrecht-London: Kulwer Academic Publishers, 2003.

Brezinski, Horst and Michael Fritsch. *The Economic Impact of New Firms in Post-Socialist Countries.* Cheltenham, Brookfield: Edward Elgar, 1996.

Davies, Norman. *God's Playground: A History of Poland.* New York: Columbia University Press, 1982.

De Carolis, Donna Marie and Patrick Saparito. "Social capital, cognition, and entrepreneurial opportunities: A theoretical framework." *Entrepreneurship Theory and Practice* 30 (2006): 41–56.

Derczyński, Włodzimierz. "Opinie o bagactwie i ludziach bogatych" ["Opinions on Wealth and Wealthy People"]. CBOS BS/2084, 1999.

DiMaggio, Paul J. and Walter W. Powell. "Introduction." In *The New Institutionalism in Organizational Analysis.* Edited by Walter W. Powell and Paul J. DiMaggio. Chicago IL: University of Chicago Press, 1991.

Granovetter, Mark S. *Getting a Job: A study of Contacts and Careers.* Cambridge MA: Harvard University Press, 1974.

Hébert, Robert F. and Albert N. Link. *The Entrepreneur.* New York: Praeger, 1982.

Hull, Galen Spencer. *Small Businesses Trickling Up in Central and Eastern Europe.* New York, London: Garland Publishing, 1999.

Marmuszewski, Stanislaw. "Potoczna percepcja biedy i bogactwa a rozwój Kapitalizmu" ["Everyday perceptions of poverty and wealth in the development of capitalism"]. In *Bieda i bogactwo w kulturze polskiej i świadomości* [*Poverty and Wealth in Polish Culture and Consciousness*]. Edited by Grażyna Skąpska. Kraków: Universitas, 2003.

McClleland, David. "Characteristics of successful entrepreneurs." *Journal of CreativeBehavior* 21 (1987): 219–233.

Morris, Michael H. *Entrepreneurial Intensity.* Westport, London: Quorum Books, 1998.

Nawojczyk, Maria and Shane Walton. "Polish perspectives on the morality of capital Accumulation." *Journal Of Interdisciplinary Studies* XVI, 1/2 (2004): 111–132.

Nawojczyk, Maria. "Zaufanie w kontaktach biznesowych i spoleczeństwach partykularnych i uniwersalistycznych" ["Trust in business relations in particularistic and universalistic societies"]. In *Kultura i gospodarka,* edited by Janusz Mucha, Maria Nawojczyk and Grażyna Woroniecka. Tychy: Śląskie Wydawnictwa Naukowe. 2007.

—. "Emerging Entrepreneurial Society: a Case Study of Self-Employed Owners of Small Businesses in Poland." *East European Quarterly* XLII (2008): 191–205

—. *Przedsiębiorczość. O trudnościach w aplikacji teorii* [*Entrepreneuship. On the difficulties of the theory application*]. Kraków: Nomos, 2009.

Rona-Tas, Akos. "The worm and the caterpillars: the small private sector in the Czech Republic, Hungary and Slovakia." In *The New Entrepreneurs of Europe and Asia: Patterns of Business Development in Russia, Eastern Europe and China.* Edited by Victoria E. Bonnell and Thomas B. Gold. Armonk, NY: M.E. Sharpe, 2001.

Ruef, Martin and Michael Lounsbury. *The Sociology of Entrepreneurship.* Amsterdam: Elsevier, 2007.

Saxenian, AnnaLee. *Regional Advantage: Culture and Competition in Silicon Valley and Rout 128.* Cambridge MA: Harvard University Press, 1994.

Sorenson, Olav and Pino G. Audia. "The social structure of entrepreneurial activity: geographic concentration of footwear production in the United States." *American Journal of Sociology* 106 (2000): 424–462.

Thornton, Patricia H. "The sociology of entrepreneurship." *Annual Review of Sociology* 25 (1999): 19–46.

CHAPTER SEVEN

HABITUS, MARKET AND KUTJEVO WINEMAKERS: A CASE STUDY

DRAGO ČENGIĆ[1]

Theoretical Approach and Key Concepts

> Each human society, from the "most primitive ones" till the "most modern ones" has some "magic word," the word people are ready to swear for. In Croatia, as in almost all of transition countries, that word is—market.
> (Županov 1995, 79)

The recent history of post-socialist European countries (from 1990 to 2004) has confirmed Županov's words. Although all post-socialist countries started new institutional changes within their economic and political systems (from ownership changes to political competition within a multiparty system) under the ideological labels of a return to a Western type of democracy, real changes within social structure were realized through the program of adaptation of society to "market economy." And, as economic sociology reminds us, market is a key phenomenon and institution in capitalist economy (Swedberg 2006, 104–130).

However, few papers within economic sociology deal with the empirical process of the development and shaping of new market agents within post-socialist conditions (Callon 1998; Štulhofer 2000; Brinton, Nee 2001; Granovetter, Swedberg, 2001; Nee, Swedberg, 2005; Swedberg 2006). Instead, they assume: (a) that market participants are somehow already "embedded" in social and market structures, and as such are ultimately shaped as market actors; (b) that we deal with "mature entrepreneurs" who know all (formal and informal) rules of market competition.

[1] Institute of Social Sciences Ivo Pilar, Zagreb.

Yet, from the sociological point of view, the market in emerging economies is always (when viewed from the individual agent's perspective) only a partially known and defined structure. It is a structure which has been mostly recognized by the parallel process of discovering one's personal managing abilities and market and economic opportunities (see also the concept of market and competition of the new Austrian school's authors: Swedberg 2006, 111–112; Radaev 2008, 2). Furthermore, for the recent analyses of post-socialist entrepreneurs some of Bourdieu's key concepts are very useful, such as the ideas of habitus and market as economic field (Bourdieu 1984). According to Wacquant (2006, 6), Bourdieu under "habitus designates the system of durable and transposable dispositions through which we perceive, judge, and act in the world." The importance is that habitus, as the mediation between past influences and present stimuli is "also a principle of both social continuity and discontinuity: continuity because it stores social forces into the individual organism and transports them across time and space; discontinuity because it can be modified through the acquisition of new dispositions and because it can trigger innovation whenever it encounters a social setting discrepant with the setting from which it issues" (Wacquant 2006, 7).

With regard to Bourdieu's understanding of economic field, it has at least two meanings. The field is "a structured space of positions, a forcefield that imposes its specific determinations upon all those who enter it" (Wacquant 2006, 8). At the same time, the economic field is "an arena of struggle through which agents and institutions seek to preserve or overturn the existing distribution of capital: it is a battlefield wherein the bases of identity and hierarchy are endlesslessly disputed over" (Wacquant 2006, 8). Swedberg thinks that with such a concept of economic field Bourdieu emphasized dependency of the market on the larger power relations, giving an impetus for a structuralist perspective in modern research of market and market structures (Swedberg 2006, 126–128).

Finally, the concept of habitus links institutions with culture since culture is the particular aspects of reality which define the image of world and the relations of particular actors towards its substantive elements. This image, enabling each of us to accept certain codes, values, aspirations and institutions, liberates the actor of the need to continually re-consider the separate fragments of a situation when they make a decision. In other words, being bound to rationality is not only a specific feature of the individual, it is "embedded into culture by which the individual is encompassed and into which he is integrated" (Franičević 1995, 163; for another concept of culture, see Swidler 1986, 273–286). In this research we assume that there is an anti-market habitus in present day Kutjevo winemakers, mostly characterized by their love of the local wine Grassevina and the small, family led production of wine during socialism. Also, we assume that the new institutional frame (emerging from the introduction of capitalism in Croatia) enabled their transformation into small entrepreneurs and confronted them with the local and European wine market—as an economic field they have to confirm themselves as new market agents.

Aim, Goals and Methodology

The aim of this chapter is to show, in the case of Kutjevo winemakers, that social production and "self-production" of market actors in post-socialist conditions is a long-term and complex process, that it covers the complex (economic and social) behavior of those involved, that their behavior is determined socially and culturally as well as by market process, and—at least in Croatian conditions—additionally determined by the factor of "time contraction" due to the possible entering of Croatia into the EU within the next few years. We'll show that Kutjevo winemakers display in their business behavior not only a typical quest for new sources of economic opportunities and profit but also a multiplex "models of exchange" between them and the local environment (be it communal or political). Through these models they defend not only their economic interests but offer at the same time possible developmental programs aimed at the local community itself.

With regard to our working hypothesis we assume that the business behavior of Kutjevo start-up winemakers is determined with several (soft) factors: their (personal, family, economic) habitus in the pre-market economic period (before 1990); their attitudes towards private entrepreneurship and winemaking during the early 1990s; the present economic power of their family wine cellars; the structure of competition in the domestic market and the structure of the larger (mostly European) economic field to which their production and selling of wines belong. These factors also have a strong impact on the different forms of their non-market oriented behavior, manifested clearly through their relationships with local economic and political structure.

Due to these assumptions, this chapter has the following goals: (a) to identify key features of the pre-market habitus of Kutjevo winemakers and the process of their transformation into new (start-up) entrepreneurs within new political and institutional conditions after 1990; (b) to identify key aspects of their market and non-market behaviour, with regard to the competition, local community and local political structure; (c) to identify the position of their "personal economic gains" within the overall structure of their actions towards local community and local political elite; (d) to identify to what extent the international "wine culture" influences the Kutjevo winemakers practice of grape growing and wine production; (e) to consider the wider "economic field" determining market moves on the international and local wine market, especially the impact of the present process of Croatia's accession to the EU. At the end of the study, we will draw conclusions regarding the business future of Kutjevo winemakers and make comparisons with winemakers in Hungary and Bulgaria.

Our data originates from the project DIOSCURI, carried out between 2004 and 2007 in several European countries, and from desk research regarding the wine production in Croatia and abroad. It was gathered through 18 semi-standardized in depth interviews (in 2005 and 2006), which were transcripted and analyzed. We interviewed 11 winemakers from Kutjevo and larger Požega area, 2 scientists cooperating with the most successful among them, 1 representative of the government, and 4 of Istria's winemakers in an attempt to gain an additional view to broader problems regarding grape growing and winemaking in Croatia.

Among those interviewed were 15 males and 3 females with an average age of 51. The majority were owners of small wine family farms or enterprises established during the 1990s, the families small in size (3 or 4 members), most of them employing between 10–14 workers, the Kutjevo joint stock company (a former socialist *agro-kombinat*) as a big business system employing 880 workers on long-term basis. Due to the seasonal nature of the work, all also employ some temporary workers. Regarding education, 8 of our respondent have at least a university education; the others finished some higher education or have some type of secondary education. All original names of our respondents have been changed in this chapter (Čengić 2007).

Some Notes about Požega–Slavonia County and the Kutjevo Wine Cellar

Požega–Slavonia county is situated in the North East of Croatia, and covers around 1.815,24 square kilometres representing some 3.21% of the total land area of Croatia.

The county has the smallest number of companies in Croatia after the Ličko-senjska county. The main part of the county's economy is trade and retail, followed by the processing industry, services and real estate. In general, as evaluated by different experts, the economy of the county is not strong. It is characterised by low per capita GDP, high unemployment, a small number of firms and a very low entrepreneurship rate (see opinions of ROP's experts in: PSC, 2005). The county's GDP per capita (in 2003) was some 6,427 EUR, which is only three-quarters of the average of the whole of Croatia for that year and less than a third of the average per capita GDP in Europe (the 25 members of the EU). In 1981 there were some 100,000 inhabitants living in the county.

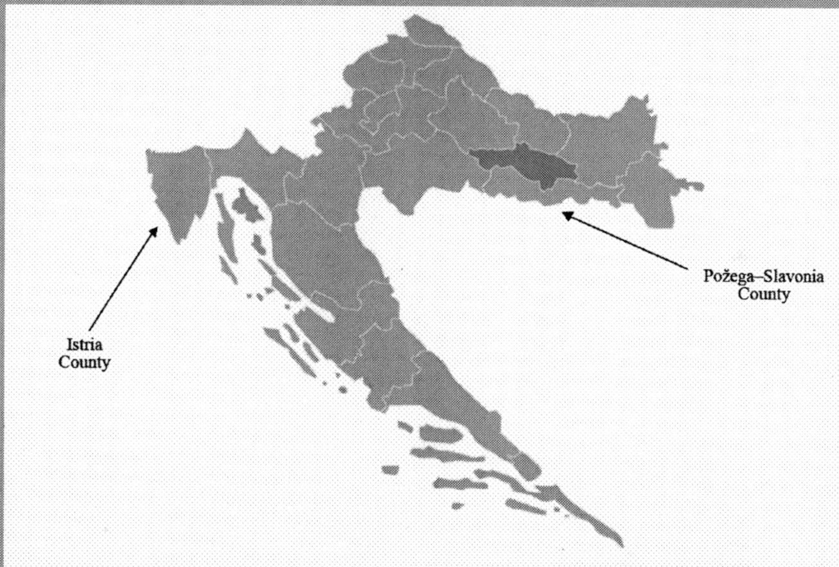

Fig. 7.1
Position of Požega–Slavonia County Within Croatia.
Source: http://www.hgk.hr

Table 7.1. Industrial wineries by wine districts in Croatia at the end of the 1990s

	Wine district and name of company	*Location of winery*	*Installed processing capacity (tons of grapes per year)*		
TOTAL INSTALLED CAPACITY					**151 790**
1	**Danube Region (4)**			**20 800**	
	Ilocki Podrumi, d.d.	Ilok	4 000		
	Vupik, d.d.	Vukovar	3 000		
	Belje, d.d.	Knezevi Vinogradi	7 800		
	IPK Osijek	Erdut	6 000		
2	**Slavonija Region (8)**			**20 750**	
	Enjingi Ivan	***Kutjevo***	***160***		
	Kutjevo, d.d.	***Kutjevo***	***11 000***		
	Krauthaker, Vlado	***Kutjevo***	***150***		
	Feravino, d.o.o.	Fericanci	2 120		
	Biskupijski Ordinariat	Dakovo	170		
	Dakovacka Vina	Dakovo	3 650		
	Vinarija Daruvar, d.o.o.	Daruvar	2 500		
	PP Orahovica, d.d.	Orahovica	1 000		
3	**Moslavina Region (1)**			**4 200**	
	Moslavacko Vinogorje, d.o.o	Voloder	4 200		
4	**Prigorje-Bilogora Region (2)**			**2 720**	
	Krizevacki Vinogradi, d.o.o	Krizevci	2 500		
	Viagro, d.d.	Slatina	220		
5	**Kupa River Region (0)**			**0**	
6	**Plesivica Region (2)**			**10 600**	
	Mladina, d.d.	Jastrebarsko	10 000		
	P.Z. Vrbnik	Vrbnik	600		
7	**Zagorje-Medimurje Region (2)**			**10 960**	
	Varazdinka, d.o.o.	Varazdin	8 700		
	Agromedimurje, d.d.	Cakovec	2 260		
8	**Istria Region (4)**			**17 480**	
	Agrolaguna, d.d.	Porec	4 500		
	Cattunar Franco	Brtonigla	2 580		
	Family Ravalico	Brtonigla	200		
	Istravinoexport	Rijeka	10 200		
				18 500	

9	**North Dalmatia Region (2)**			
	Vinarija Benkovac, d.o.o.	Benkovac	5 000	
	Vinoplod-Vinarija, d.d.	Sibenik	13 500	
10	**Dalmatinska Zagora Region (1)**			**19 390**
	Imota, d.d.	Imotski	19 390	
11	**Middle and Southern Dalmatia Region (10)**			**26 390**
	Dubrovacki Podrum	Dubrovnik	2 000	
	Poljoprivreda Blato	Blato	2 200	
	PZ Cara	Cara	1 500	
	PZ Dingac	Potomje	6 000	
	PZ Jedinstvo	Smokvica	2 030	
	PZ Kuna-1898	Kuna	880	
	PZ Stovis	Ston	1 310	
	Dalmacijavino	Split	6 000	
	Plancic	Vrbanj	110	
	PZ Vis, d.d.	Vis	4 360	

Source*:* Sellschopp, Par, and Haynes, 2000, 16.

In 1991 there were 99,344 inhabitants; the 2001 census records a population of 85,831. The continuing decline in total population is due to a rural–urban drift, particularly to the larger towns beyond the boundaries of the county and the 1991–1995 war (comp. PSC, 2005).

Those inhabitants related to this study live in or are related to the small municipality of Kutjevo, named by the same small town (for the position of Kutjevo d.d., Mr. Enjingi and Mr. Krauthaker in Croatian wine production at the end of the 1990s, see Table 1 above; Sellschopp, Par, Haynes 2000, 16). In fact, all of them are deeply linked with the historical wine cellar in Kutjevo, because Kutjevo is not only a name, it is a symbol of the wine culture of the continental region of Croatia. The wine cellar itself, together with Kutjevo castle and the nearby church, represent the unique historical character of the area, and the long history of viticulture and winemaking in Kutjevo. Some historians dealing with Croatian viticulture showed that grape growing and winemaking began developing in this territory during the Roman empire (Potrebica 1982, 3–56; Turković 1982, 5–43). The Romans were delighted with the enormous capacities offered for agricultural production and called it *Vallis Aurea*—The Golden Valley. The whole Požega-Slavonian county is well known under that name in Croatia even today.

Due to communist rule from the end of World War II, Kutjevo real estates were transformed into state property. Later, a large agro-kombinat was established here (PIK Kutjevo), which continued the activities in grape cultivation, winemaking and in all other types of agricultural production. After several attempts of privatization and re-nationalization during the 1990s, in 2004 PIK Kutjevo gained a new owner—"Božjakovina dd", an enterprise controlled by Enver Moralić, a well known businessman operating today in several businesses all over Europe.

Pre-Market Habitus, Start-Up Entrepreneurs and Market Strategies

There are certain common experiences which all Kutjevo winemakers share: lack of private initiative within viticulture and poor quality wine under socialism; the economic and social crisis during the first half of the 1990s; the new economic opportunities which appeared in independent Croatia. For the majority of them, it was not easy to start as new entrepreneurs from the bottom. When analyzing personal, professional and family backgrounds of our interviewees, we discovered three types of new Kutjevo winemakers: (a) those who entered into new winemaking businesses when leaving the Kutjevo wine cellar before 1995 (for example: Mr. Vlakraut); (b) those who established family farms when new opportunities appeared (the largest group), having a long family tradition in small scale grape growing during socialism, for example selling grapes to PIK Kutjevo or making wine only for the family; (c) those who have been a winemaking family for a long time, producing bottled wines by the late 1980s under socialism, as in the case of the famous winemaker Mr. Iven Sr.

New economic opportunities for small family farms, which were formally established with the introduction of new capitalist institutions in Croatia after the breakdown of Yugoslavia, were seen by most of the Kutjevo winemakers as a chance for a new economic start. The War and overall economic and social crisis at the beginning of the 1990s sped up some decisions about their own business in wine production. One of the most successful of the new winemakers in the Kutjevo region, Mr. Vlakraut, who worked for a years as enology expert in Kutjevo, also took a chance at that time:

> We started our own wine production in 1992, at that time I was still the main expert for wine-making in Kutjevo wine-cellar. The wages were poor at that time there and I started to plant the wine grapes by my own. They

> told me that it is not allowed to work in Kutjevo wine cellar and to have my own wine. After some time I said to them "OK, thanks!" I am going to have a business of my own. I worked for Kutjevo for a year more, and then in 1994 I left Kutjevo wine-cellar for real.
> (Dioscuri Documentation, Institut Pilar 2007)

However, all Kutjevo winemakers share the admiration for the Kutjevo winemaking tradition, for grassevina (graševina) as a type of grape and a wine, and for the new market opportunities the production of grassevina offers. Simply put, grassevina is for them a near mythical wine, and has to a large extent (together with family wine production tradition and pro-entrepreneurial attitudes) shaped the past and present habitus of Kutjevo winemakers. Grassevina came from "somewhere in Europe" and became a legend. Grassevina is as highly appreciated in Slavonia as malmsey/malvasia in Istria (see Table 7.2 below).

Table 7.2. Production of grassevina and other wine sorts in Croatia in 2006.

All Croatia		*Continental Croatia*	
1. grassevina	27%	1. grassevina	55%
2. malvazija istarska	11%	2. Rhine riesling	7%
3. plavac mali	9%	3. frankovka	5%
4. other sorts	53%	4. other sorts	33%

Source: Gašparec–Skočić, Hruškar, and Banić 2007, 5.

Mr. Ivap, the present enology expert in Kutjevo, also well known as the producer of internationally awarded Kutjevo wines during the last 7–8 years, explained this mystery:

> When Mr. Turković and his family came in Kutjevo long time ago, at the end of 19th century, he made a lot of positive things using grassevina as main grapes and principal wine. He proved that grassevina is the best when cultivated in this region—in almost world relations! Well, that is why we pretend to call it "our genuine wine sort." At the same time, it would be nice that we protect it in the world as our original sort… now some actions were initiated in order to prove that this wine sort has all characteristics of our authentic wine sort!…
>
> And when talking about the taste, the content of wine, that is what I am talking about: if you want to have top quality wines, you must have some

characteristics the grapes has to fulfill. You can not to make top quality wine from some grapes which can give you only table wine! Grassevina is so good sort (represents up to 75% of our assortment), like some other that we have, due to the fact that from grassevina you can get a series of different wines: quality wines, top quality wines, predicate wines, and archive vines! Grassevina meets all these categories of wine.
(Dioscuri Documentation, Institut Pilar 2007)

Now small winemakers have a very difficult task: to persuade the foreign customers that Croatia is becoming "a wine country," producing also quality wines which can satisfy the taste of real "wine-lovers" and specific markets. For the number of producers see table 7.3 below.

Table 7.3. Wine market turn-over in Požega-Slavonia County 2000-2006 (in hl)

Year	Total number of producers	Wine market turn-over (hl)	Enterprises	Family farms/ small wine-makers
2000	25	35.850	2	23
2001	25	33.280	1	24
2002	21	38.660	1	20
2003	23	46.860	1	22
2004	27	37.430	1	26
2005	31	57.580	1	30

Source: Gašparec–Skočić, Hruškar, and Banić 2007, 8.

According to our evidence, the strategies made for finding new (domestic or foreign) markets are multidimensional. First, the Kutjevo wine cellar, as a big wine producer, uses the strategy of a wine leader in the domestic market and of a big exporter of quality wines in specialized European markets. Kutjevo is now exporting almost 1/3 of its yearly production of different types of wines. The best among small and medium wine producers are trying at the same time to conquer specific segments of internal and foreign markets. For example, Mr. Vlakraut exports for about 22% of its wine production: 7% to Bosnia and Herzegovina; 5% to Austria; 5% to Switzerland, then into Germany and Russia. He described the fundamental experience from foreign markets:

> We are increasing our export share every years but it is hard, it takes a time! Customers on foreign markets demand the wines with prices corresponding to their quality. You have exactly to know the quality and price, you have exactly to know how we stand in relation to particular market, for example the market in Netherland; there is a strong competitive pressure from the wine producers coming all over the world. Every country, for example Switzerland, is extremely demanding, ask for the highest quality to be present there.
>
> That is the most important questions: now we fight to sell something in foreign markets. Yet, if somebody would ask us to deliver there a huge amount of bottled wines, we could not deliver such a quantity! It is one thing to sell your own wine to the restaurants and other customers abroad, and quite another is when you make business with a wholesalers, who would ask for huge quantities of wine, expecting the highest quality and law prices! I think no one from small wine producers working here is ready for such a business. We still need a lot of time. We now are working on American market, to make something, and I really afraid of that moment. We can plant new vineyards here, we can expand our cooperation with sub-contractors but I do not dare to expand on new markets without finding the concrete customer.
>
> (Dioscuri Documentation, Institut Pilar 2007)

Small Kutjevo wine producers, as well as Istria's winemakers, use a "find a customer on your door-step strategy"—the idea is to sell products at family restaurants or hotels in the area of residence. After such efforts, a new situation has emerged: there are more and more customers every year, both in Croatia and foreign countries.

Among many new questions which have emerged, there are those which determine the future of all small winemaking family farms in this territory. These questions are: (a) how to sustain the high quality of wine produced in this area; (b) how to provide the quantity of wine required to meet foreign market demands; (c) how to strenghten the business power of small producers; (d) what types of wine should be produced in order to hold good positions in domestic and foreign markets within the next ten years?

Economic Interests and Social Action in Local Community

Although the members of the scientific community and county government think all local winemakers have a respectable status within the local political and power structure, the opinions of the winemakers themselves do not support such a viewpoint. Nevertheless, we discovered that the present status that the local winemakers have within the official local political structure is due not only to the quality of their wines, but also due to the political engagement the most distinguished among them have practiced in the last ten years. For example, Mr. Vlakraut and Mr. Iven Sr. were for some time members of the county's assembly and in some other official bodies. This helped them to represent (and defend) some general winemakers' interests within local political structure.

In the meantime, the growth processes they initiated within their vineyards and wine cellars became more complex, and they are now also occupied with management, governance and production activities. Yet, the protection of their "latent corporative interests" and their lack of economic power needed for competing on the European market, pushes them once again towards the local political structure. As they know that the municipality structure is financially weak, their demands are directed towards the county and national government. Namely, some of them think that they should act as "a lobby or pressure group" and ask for more from the county government, at least the same type of support which was given (in a proportionally richer county) to Istria's winemakers. The others, like Mr. Iven Sr., want the state to act as a "technical agent" which will help them to grow by preparing more arable land for new vineyards. The problem is whether the national and county governments are the right places of addresses for the local winemakers: namely, Mrs. Kuba explained that new arable land is a resource the county has nothing to do with:

> There is still some state land of different arable degrees but all decisions regarding that land should be made by towns and municipalities! The county has nothing with it. That is one big problem and that's why people are not planting new vineyards more! The available land ready for new plantings is also today more expensive than few years ago; people do understand that wine growing is a branch with possible high income! There is an another problem here, too: the majority of arable land is very small, with no symmetrical shapes; then, it is doubtful whether the land is registered in state cadastre, etc. I think that here only Kutjevo wine cellar and Mr. E. have all land properly registered in state cadastre!
> (Dioscuri Documentation, Institut Pilar 2007)

This creates a vicious circle—the most important decisions about new land available for wine production should be made by towns and municipalities which are financially weak and subdued by different political and economic networks. As the overall practice shows, local political structure, when offering the arable land for public tenders, often offer the existing land (mostly owned by former *agro-kombinats*). Such practice produces new tensions among potential agricultural producers on a local level but also the tensions between small winemakers and the big Kutjevo wine cellar, and more importantly, we see no feasible way to resolve this situation in the short run.

Culture, Habitus and the Question of Mutual Cooperation

Culture has different meanings for different agents. In this chapter we understand culture as set of symbols, stories, knowledge, rituals and other information the market actors use as a tool kit for the business and social world (Swidler 1986, 273–286). Almost all of the interviewed winemakers' knowledge and information needed for grape cultivation and winemaking was gathered in famous Western wine producing countries, the foremost among them being France. After France, the most appreciated "wine countries" are Italy (the "learning country" especially for Istria's winemakers), Austria, Germany, Spain, USA (California), Chile and Australia.

What are the outcomes of this fascination with famous Western wine making countries? First of all, they have realized that it is one thing to know the trends in modern wine making but quite another one to apply new methods of grape cultivation and wine making at home. One young wine maker (Mr. Iven Jr.) recalled that the application of every form of "imported" knowledge is contingent by its nature, and that we have to differentiate between "Western techniques" in grape growing from the real "technologies" in winemaking:

> You can read a lot about the grape growing and winemaking, many technologies are already described. However, no one can tell you what specifically you have to make in a particular year when it comes to the particular grape sorts or wines. So, you learn every year also. Besides, the grape-growing area is always the specific synthesis of subjective and objective elements.
> (Dioscuri Documentation, Institut Pilar 2007)

Some winemakers argued that particular types of homegrown grape types require careful treatment as part of more traditional winemaking techniques. Yet no one from the small winemakers group stated that they cannot learn something from Western winemakers. Only the representative from the big Kutjevo wine cellar told us that there is no need for information and knowledge transfer form the "Western winemaking countries." Also, frequent communication with Western winemakers demonstrated to local winemakers how important it is to invest all available resources into the maintenance of the quality of the wine. What is new for them is that the wine quality has also to be checked by market demand. One of the most wellknown among Kutjevo small winemakers, Mr. Vlakraut, engaged local sub-contractors for the care of grapes and wine quality, and he is not the only one doing it this way.

Yet, we still have no definite answers; except with regard to machines imported for grape cultivation and some winemaking procedures, out of everything seen in the west what has really been applied to the vineyards of small Kutjevo wine producers? It is difficult to differentiate which knowledge and technology procedures are "foreign," and which are locally made. This is hard to pinpoint even within the science of viticulture, as Prof. Rubi explained to us. What is certain is that the Western experience is important with regard to new information regarding market tendencies, new insights regarding the quality of wines, and new technology and current marketing innovations.

As the competition among winemakers in the local and Croatian market increases, so too does the pressure for more effective ways of managing and governing their own family farms, wine cellars and small enterprises linked with them. Yet, some professionalization of particular management duties among the winemakers is more expected than it is realized—"people do not want to cooperate," said Mr. Vlakraut. Some of the interviewed winemakers augmented the evident aversion of local producers to stronger cooperation with more structural reasons. For example, Mr. Ketoz thinks such an aversion towards stronger mutual cooperation occurs mostly due to the fact that in Kutjevo they have "the first generation of independent winemakers." This generation is attempting to shorten the evident development gap in relation to Western wine producers by building everything in their wine cellars, starting from scratch. They have no time or inclination towards mutual cooperation but a strong desire to grow as fast as they can.

We think that the main problem here is in regard to the non defined form of such cooperation among wine makers. Does cooperation assume stronger professionalization within the existing association of winemakers, or would it be better to organize themselves into a new cooperative? On the other hand, some concrete measures towards new organizational forms enabling mutual (oriented locally, nationally, and to foreign countries) cooperation have been postponed due to a change in focus of the Kutjevo wine cellar management. Now under new ownership, Kutjevo have made plans to concentrate itself on the core business, and to follow only its business and marketing goals. Due to this new situation it is doubtful whether the new Kutjevo wine cellar owner and management will want to cooperate with small winemakers regarding a common agenda. So the main problem of better mutual cooperation between small winemakers themselves, and between them and the Kutjevo wine cellar, we found to be still unresolved. They share a feeling that they have to unite somehow, however, we saw no idea about who will play a new and desired role, that of a responsible person who will lead small winemakers into new forms of mutual business and social cooperation.

Economic Field, International Integration and Time as Development Resource

There are also some stakeholders interested in the growth of winemakers not belonging directly to their local community such as viticulture and winemaking experts who, due to scientific reasons, were eager to see new economic development options in that region. Two of them cooperated closely with Mr. Vlakraut and Mr. Iven Sr. in recent years. Prof. Rubi gave us some evidence regarding the latest development of the viticulture sector in Croatia in a broader time span. First, he thinks that the economic decline of Croatian small viticulture has halted. Second, there is not enough time to develop all potential and resources that the agricultural sector has due to the possibility of Croatia's entering the EU in 2010. He confirmed also that only genuine types of wine will have a promising future on European markets.

With regard to the future membership of Croatia in the EU, there is a widespread feeling among Kutjevo winemakers that many of them are not ready for the competition present on the European market. Yet, as the EU membership for Croatia became more tangible as a real political and economic option, winemakers started to attack the local and national political elite for not defending the economic interests of particular agricultural/production groups. For now this is isolated criticism, without organized political action.

One of the most well known of Istria's winemakers, Mr. Mativ, thinks that within the EU those who are very strong in production and marketing will survive, and those producing low quality wines will fail. According to him, the best strategy for Croatian winemakers to follow is that of producing and exporting the genuine, autochtonous types of wine. This idea is common, shared by Kutjevo winemakers and researchers in that region. There is also one important and common idea shared by all, that of a common presentation of Croatian winemakers in European markets. This is another variation on the Kutjevo winemakers' call for local and national unity when entering the foreign (mostly European) markets.

Conclusions

Contrary to some abstract discussions about the types of rational behavior in an entrepreneurial context, with this chapter we wanted to show, using Bourdieu's concepts of market, habitus and economic field, that the building of market agents in post-socialist capitalism (in Croatia) is a very demanding and multidimensional process, requiring a long time period. This case shows, according to our insight, that we have to differentiate between narrow and profit oriented behavior of entrepreneurs from their larger economic interests; the latter can be for a longer period congruent with the economic and development interests of the respective local community.

Similarly to other research of this type (O'Connor 2002, 36–54), personal stories (statetements on the establishment of the wine cellars or enterprises, visionary stories) and generic stories (remarks on market strategies and strategic moves) are dominant in winemakers' thought. According to the key structural attributes (sociodemographic charasteristics, education profile, wine production tradition, available production and storage capacities), they belong to the first generation of serious wine producers in this region. Although they are trying to follow the key tendencies in the grape growing and production of wine present in Western Europe, they are still in an early stage of economic growth. They have to invest a lot of financial resources in the winemaking infrastructure in order to sustain the required quality of grapes and wine.

That is why their market strategies (in Croatia and in Europe) are multidimensional, oriented to the battle with short-term and long-term challenges, with the shortage of capital, the lack of support by the relevant stakeholders (mainly the state) and to the new networking needed for the defence of their economic interests. Even though they are local in character, these strategies are part of those already noted among the new Eastern European entrepreneurs (Estrin, Meyer, Bytchkova 2006).

Comparing our insights with similar research of famous "wine regions" in Hungary and Bulgaria (Kovacs 2007; Ditchev 2007), we can draw out some interesting comparisons. First, due to the low consumption power of the local population in Bulgaria, Bulgarian wines are largely exported, mainly to the Russian market. In Croatia and Hungary, domestic markets absorbed the majority of the newly produced quality wines during recent years. That is why different market strategies of the leading winemakers in Croatia and Hungary are mostly oriented to satisfying market niches in domestic markets and not to competing with foreign wine producers. Second, in all three countries fragmented vineyard ownership structure slows down the emergence of new vineyards. Yet, Croatian wine producers still have several years (before Croatia enters the EU) for the enlargement of vineyard stock within the country.

In relation to the Hungarian Villany wine region, Kutjevo winemakers (mostly because of the Kutjevo joint stock company) own and use a larger grape growing area. However, when comparing their growth stage and financial help given by different European funds with their Hungarian counterparts, they are lagging about ten years behind Hungarian winemakers in terms of develeopment. The process of "self-westernization" (Kovacs 2007) among the five biggest winemakers in neighbouring Villanyi, mainly due to some socio-cultural and ethnic factors, started during the early 1980s, while a similar process of "self-westernization" took place among Kutjevo winemakers in the early 1990s and it is still unfinished.

We saw that Kutjevo winemakers are very critical towards the local and national political elite (mainly because of the problems with arable land for new vineyards and "incompetent negotiatiors" with the EU administration). However, trying to protect their particular interests and the development of wine tourism within the local community, the best among them participated in the local political structure for some years in the 1990s. Here we identified a similar phenomenon such as that in Villanyi: there the key winemakers from the "big five" took over the responsibility for the development of the whole region through all available (formal and informal) channels of power (Kovacs 2007). Yet, Kutjevo winemakers do not have such a capacity and will to enter all political bodies into the whole county, and restrict themselves to their municipality and some important political positions within representative county structure.

With regard to the larger "economic field," this analysis shows that the main actors of this story (when compared with well known world wine countries) are still outside the large wine markets ruled by reknowned wine producers and wholesalers. Being outside the laws of large markets, they belong to "an exotic world of wines" which is deeply rooted in local landscapes and local conditions—those who love such an exotic world will probably also love its wine. However, stronger competition among the winemakers themselves as well as Croatia's accession talks with the EU's administration produced the overall attitude that the encounter with European wine market is inevitable, and time is a restricted resource for such an encounter.

Time is needed for the improved growth of small winemakers in all of Croatia, and that is why winemakers and viticulture scientists warn the state and other stakeholders that they have to find the proper solutions for the most important problems linked with their desired economic growth in next few years. Small winemakers believe that their economic plans should also fit with the larger projects for the redesigning of the entire local community: the new situation calls for making new brands of genuine wines, reinvention of local wine landscapes and tradition, local communities and the public image of the whole country, as has already been done in the Hungarian Villanyi region.

The question is, however, which type of actors such a comprehensive developmental strategy, based on the exchange of winemakers with the larger environment, should include? In the case of Villanyi, family, ethnic and socio-cultural closeness of the key winemakers helped in supressing mutual competition while at the same time improving mutual cooperation for the benefit of the larger actors' and community's economic and social needs (Kovacs 2007). In the case of Kutjevo, new challenges demand new types of local and national politicians, as well as new developmental agents from other social strata. They should act as "social connectors" who will link the interests of winemakers with new strategies of rural and urban development on local and national levels.

If Kutjevo winemakers are left alone, their mid-term future depends mostly on two factors: (a) should they grow fast enough to transform themselves into big/bigger wine producers in European proportions; and (b) if "doomed" to stay small, whether they will be able to cooperate with each other, in order to achieve better positions in regional/larger markets. The question of cooperative business strategies is culturaly and socially dependent. The most important question is: who will organize and finance the leaders of the needed cooperative behavior?

References

Brinton, Mary C., and Victor Nee. *The New Institutionalism in Sociology.* Stanford: Stanford University Press, 2001.

Bourdieu, Pierre. *Distinction: A Social Critique of the Judgement of Taste.* Boston: Harvard University Press (Reprint), 1984.

Callon, Michael. *The Laws of the Markets.* Oxford, Malden: Blackwell Publishers, The Sociological Review, 1998.

Čengić, Drago. "Wine Producers in Golden Valley—Between Local Culture and European Market. A Case Study." *Documentation of Institute Pilar* 2007; or: http://www.dioscuriproject.net, 2008.

Estrin, Saul, Klaus E. Meyer, and Maria Bytchkova. "Entrepreneurship in Transition Economies." In *The Oxford Handbook of Entrepreneurship.*

Edited by Mark Cason, Anuradha Basu, Bernard Yeung, and Nigel Wadeson. Oxford: Oxford University Press, 2006.

Ditchev, Ivaylo. Wine Production Between the Local and the Global. The Case of Brestowitza, *Project DIOSCURI.Research Report 2007* http://www.dioscuriproject.net (accessed October 12, 2008).

Franičević Vojmir. "Problemi s racionalnim ekonomskim čovjekom: prema institucionalističkoj rekonstrukciji ekonomske teorije" ["Problems with Rational Man. Towards Institutional Reconstruction of Economic Theory"]. *Revija za sociologiju* 26 (3–4) (1995): 151–168.

Gašparec–Skočić, Ljiljana, Miodrag Hruškar, and Blaženka Banić. *Graševina Vinogorja Kutjevo u brojkama* (Grassevina in Kutjevo Region). Presentation within "First Grassevina Fair," Kutjevo, May 26, 2007.

Granovetter, Mark. "Economic Action and Social Structure: The Problem of Embeddedness." *American Journal of Sociology* 91 (3) (1985): 481–510.

—. "The Economic Sociology of Firms and Entrepreneurs." In *Entrepreneurship. The Social Science View.* Edited by Richard Swedberg. Oxford, New York: Oxford University Press, 2000.

Granovetter, Mark and Richard Swedberg. *The Sociology of Economic Life*. Cambridge, MA: Westview Press, 2001.

Kovacs, Eva. "A Small Miracle in the Lack of Foreign Investors: The Villany Wine and Westernized Local Knowledge." *Project DIOSCURI.Research Report 2007.* http://www.dioscuriproject.net (accessed October 12, 2008).

Nee, Victor and Richard Swedberg. *The Economic Sociology of Capitalism*. Princeton: Princeton University Press, 2005.

O'Connor, Ellen. Storied Business: Typology, Intertextuality, and Traffic in Entrepreneurial Narrative. *The Journal of Business Communication* 39 (2002): 36–54.

Potrebica, Filip. *Povijest vinogradarstva i podrumarstva u Požeško dolini (History of Viticulture and Wine-Cellars in Požega Valley).* Kutjevo: PPK Kutjevo, 1982.

Radaev, Vadim. "Economic Struggle and Social Ties: The Structure of Compétititive Relationships in the New Russian Retail Market." Paper presented at the conference Economy in Society: Actors, Relations, Institutions, Interim Conference of the Research Network of Economic Sociology, ESSA, Krakow, Poland, 2-4 july, 2008.

Sellschopp, Jork, Vjekoslav Par, and Jos Haynes. "Competitiveness in Agriculture and EU Accession, The Wine Sector Competitiveness Report. The Commodity Studies." Wiltshire: Landell Mills Consortium—

Prepared for Ministry of Agriculture and Forestry of Republic of Croatia, 2000.

Smelser, Neil J. and Richard Swedberg. *The Handbook of Economic Sociology*. Princeton, New York: Princeton University Press, Russel Sage Foundation, 1994.

Swedberg, Richard. *Entrepreneurship. The Social Science View*. Oxford, New York: Oxford University Press, 2000.

—. *Načela ekonomske sociologije (Principles of Economic Sociology)*. Zagreb: Mate, 2006.

Swidler, Ann. "Culture in Action: Symbols and Strategies." *American Sociological Review* 51 (1986): 273–286.

Štulhofer, Aleksandar. *Nevidljiva ruka tranzicije. Ogledi iz ekonomske sociologije [Invisible Hand of Transition. Essays in Economic Sociology]*. Zagreb: HSD, Zavod za sociologiju Filozofskog fakulteta u Zagrebu, 2000.

Turković, Zdenko. *Sto godina vinogradarstva Hrvatske (Hundred Years of Viticulture in Croatia)*. Zagreb: Savez poljoprivrednih inženjera i tehničara Hrvatske, 1982.

Wacquant, Loic. Pierre Bourdieu, at: http://sociology.berkely-edu/faculty/ wacquant_pdf/ (accessed October 22, 2008).

Županov, Josip. 1995. *Poslije potopa (After the Flood)*. Zagreb: Nakladni zavod Globus.

Požega-Slavonia County. 2005. *Regional Operational Plan (ROP),* Požega. at: www.pszupanija.hr (accessed November 2006).

CHAPTER EIGHT

NETLABEL: INDEPENDENT NON-PROFIT MICRO-ENTERPRISE OR JUST ANOTHER PLAYER IN THE MUSIC INDUSTRY?

PATRYK GAŁUSZKA[1]

Introduction

Production, distribution and consumption of music has changed dramatically over the last few years. The growing number of internet users combined with the development of methods of sound compression (e.g. the mp3 file) has led to significant reorganization of the entire music industry, and these processes are considered to be the main reason for the falling sales of physical product. Technological and social changes, however, have not only influenced the profits of record companies but have also led to the emergence of new agents on the music market. According to the concepts of Pierre Bourdieu, the music industry can be treated as a field, part of larger field of cultural production. Bourdieu wrote that "the appearance of a new, effective agent modifies the structure of the field. Similarly adoption of a new technology or the acquisition of a greater market share modifies the relative positions and field of all species of capital held by the other firms" (Bourdieu 2005, 80).

This chapter discusses the emergence of netlabels (also often called virtual record labels) which may be seen as new agents, having the capabilities of changing the structure of the music industry field. In the theoretical section, this chapter presents selected concepts used to analyze record labels as actors responsible for music production and distribution and compares netlabels with traditional record labels. In the empirical section, two case studies of netlabels based in Poland are presented. I concentrate my analysis on netlabels based in one country, but it must be

[1] Institute of Economics, University of Lodz.

emphasized that the operation of virtual record labels is not limited to Poland, as their music is promoted and distributed around the world.

Record Labels and Conflict Between Commercial and Creative

Record labels are organizations which "employ artists to make recordings that they hope to market in some way to the public. They usually sign the artist to a recording contract promising to pay the artist a royalty for recordings sold in return for the artist's promise to record exclusively for that particular label" (Hull 2004, 22). Since the advent of sound recording in the late 19th century, record labels have been engaged in financing production, distribution and promotion of physical recordings—shellac 78 rpm discs, vinyl LPs, cassette tapes, compact discs, etc.

In traditional recording business models,[2] costs of releasing a record were high, which meant that artists were generally unable to self-finance it. Furthermore, building a distribution channel was difficult and expensive, so artists needed the help of record labels to develop their careers. The fact that physical records had to be distributed (moved from a record plant to retail stores), guaranteed the recording industry a position of an intermediary between artists and listeners (Jones 2002, 222). This has led to questions regarding the nature of the relationship between record labels and artists, creativity and commerce or, in other words, art and money. Let us have a closer look at the scientific views of this relationship.

One of the most influential concepts was developed in the 1940s by Adorno and Horkheimer, who argued that popular music is produced for the purpose of profit maximization according to rationalized organizational procedures by the "culture industry" (Negus 1996, 37). The character of music production was in their opinion similar to that of production of other consumer goods, e.g. cars (having an "assembly-line character"). According to Adorno, this mode of production results in similarity in most if not all popular music songs. In fact, the whole structure of popular music is standardized, even where an attempt is made to circumvent standardization (Adorno 1989, 25–26).

[2] There are many definitions of the term "business model." In this text I am using this term in its most basic sense: "a business model is the method of doing business by which a company can sustain itself—that is, generate revenue. The business model spells-out how a company makes money by specifying where it is positioned in the value chain" (Rappa 2008).

This highly pessimistic view of music production was later shared by other researchers, for example Chapple and Garofalo, who argued that "concentration of ownership amongst a few major companies who control access to the means of recording and reproducing pop music enables capitalist corporations to 'colonize leisure'" (Negus 1995, 318). Consequently, commerce corrupts art, which inevitably leads to deterioration in the quality of musical products.

This concept was further developed by scholars who argued that the music industry cannot be treated as a whole because there are significant differences between big and small record labels, a distinction based not only on size but also on ability to distribute products. The biggest companies, which control their own distribution networks, are called major record companies, while those which are smaller and use external independent distributors are called independent record labels (Passman 2000, 83–86). According to this concept, independent record labels are less bureaucratic and more creative than majors and have better abilities at finding and releasing interesting music. In other words, conflict between commerce and creativity is much stronger in major record companies than in independent labels. While this was not always true—some small companies in the 1960s and 1970s were "even more exploitative of their musicians than were the major corporations" (Hesmondhalgh 1999, 35)—there are also examples of successful and fair cooperation between artists and small record labels, starting from the late 1970s. Such cooperation took place within, for example, punk subcultures of the late 1970s and early 1980s, which tried to provide an alternative to the music business by emphasizing do-it-yourself music production, releasing records via a network of independent labels, performing basement shows in residential homes rather than at traditional venues, avoiding corporate sponsorship, and creating self-published fanzines, amongst others (Hesmondhalgh 1999; Triggs 2006; Moore 2007). Although such attempts were successful, the do-it-yourself (DIY) movement faced cost barriers which prevented it from becoming truly global (in fact, there were many independent DIY scenes in various countries, with only a limited chance for international cooperation).

In many cases, however, if independent record labels are successful they "begin to pose a threat to the market dominance and degree of control of music making enjoyed by the big corporations" (Negus 1996, 42). Major record companies may in these situations buy smaller companies out, or form some kind of joint venture with them. The small labels which are unable to organize independent distribution of their products are often forced to sign distribution deals with majors and share their profits with them. While romanticizing the tension between "good/creative" independents and "commercial/exploitative" majors is a part of popular music mythology, many scholars argue that the differences between small and large record companies are overestimated. Garofalo notes that, while in the 1960s independent record labels may have really challenged the big companies, later "their larger function became providing research and development for majors" (Garofalo 1999, 338). Tschmuck gives other examples describing how major record labels, afraid to sign hip-hop artists in the 1980s, signed exclusive distribution deals with smaller record labels in order to profit from a booming market without taking a risk (Tschmuck 2006, 157; other examples provided by Lee 1995 and Hesmondhalgh 1998 and 1999).

Another concept contrasts the ideas of the culture industry and tension between major and independent record labels. It argues that how the production of popular music is organized is irrelevant, as "the creative possibilities are realised in the acts of 'consumption'" (Negus 1995, 320). Consequently, "whilst record companies might control the way music is produced, they are unable to control the way it is used or the meanings invested in its texts and technologies by audiences" (Ibid., 320–321). Lewis argues that if we want to understand the phenomenon of popular music, we should concentrate on a special group of music listeners—the fans. They create communities which have their own collective identities built around appreciation of a particular music style or artist. These groups have significant influence on how the public—the rest of listeners, the media, etc.—perceive such artists (Lewis 1992, 1–9).

The concepts presented above are examples of very extensive research of the contexts in which popular music is produced and consumed. While some concepts emphasize the role of industry, others concentrate on consumers. Although I find these ideas interesting, there are two reasons why they may not be entirely adequate for analyzing netlabels. First, concepts which concentrate on industry (e.g. Adorno's "the culture industry") do not pay enough attention to new contexts in which cultural production has taken place since new technologies, as well as new ideas in the field of intellectual property (Creative Commons licenses), have enabled a wide distribution of the work of amateur and semi-professional musicians. Second, concepts which pay attention mostly to the act of consumption of popular music (e.g. analyses based on sub-cultural theories), may be based on too radical a separation of the commercial and creative spheres. Paying attention to consumption of popular music should not ignore the struggles which take place between various types of record labels.

That is why, in my analysis of netlabels, I would like to turn to Pierre Bourdieu's concept of field of cultural production. Bourdieu argues that the field of cultural production is shaped by two kinds of logic: the logic of the market (characteristic for the field of economic power) and the logic of "art for art's sake" (characteristic for some types of art). Individuals who follow the logic of market aim at financial rewards—high levels of financial capital, which are the results of high sales, are a measure of success. Those for whom the principle of "art for art's sake" is more important, tend to look for symbolic capital—recognition (e.g. from critics, other artists) and "brand loyalty" (Bourdieu 1996; Bourdieu 2005, 76).

Two recent studies which used Bourdieu's concept of field to analyze small scale cultural (music) production have been published. In the first, Robert Strachan analyzed micro-independent record labels based in the UK. These labels are usually run by one or two individuals—music fans—who undertake all necessary tasks to release records commercially. Strachan argues that although these labels "are engaged with a similar set of practices: the sale, promotion and distributions of recordings" (Strachan 2007, 247), their owners employ a do-it-yourself discourse to position themselves against the "music industry" (Ibid., 250). Being owner of the label turns out to be closely related with being a fan—labels are a "direct extension of their fandom" (Ibid., 254). That is why running a label in this case is not a commercial activity (although such labels may earn some money), but rather a hobby related to the individual's identity and taste. What is especially important for such small scale cultural producers is recognition from the peer group, listeners and artists. It is certainly a reward for the effort of running a micro-scale independent label, which is hardly ever profitable. As Strachan argues: "[t]he worth of a release is rationalized primarily through its value as a successful artistic artefact and how well it is received by label owner's peer group rather than how financially successful it may be" (Ibid., 257). It bears a resemblance to Bourdieu's "production for producers," which means that in rejecting the market "cultural producers … are left pretty much to talk to each other" (Hesmondhalgh 2006, 214).

The second study was Ryan Moore's analysis of do-it-yourself music production in the San Diego region. Local small record labels are usually started by "musicians who have no other outlet for releasing their music" and "proceed to record and distribute the music of other bands they know in the local scene" (Moore 2007, 458). The main reason for which small independent record labels are started is "love for the music and the desire to see it distributed" (Ibid., 458). While this reason is certainly important, it should be seen in a wider context of local music scenes, which are built as a result of the interaction of labels, artists, fans, owners of performance venues and others. Such scenes provide an organizational framework for small scale cultural production, which is developed despite "minimal commercial success" (Ibid., 452). The success here is not measured by money earned (although some earnings are necessary to survive), but by acquiring symbolic capital—for example releasing independent records, which are appreciated by listeners and other people involved in local music scene (Ibid., 468). As Moore notes, small scale cultural producers "are motivated to produce culture without any notion of success or capital, but simply to get themselves heard, be part of the scene, have fun and make friends" (Ibid., 468).

Before we try to look for potential similarities between small scale cultural producers described by Strachan and Moore and netlabels, I would like to try to define netlabels and explain their economic environment.

Mp3, the Internet and Music Market

As I mentioned earlier, all aspects of the music business have been changing dramatically since the late 1990s with the growing popularity of mp3 files and the internet. One of the consequences of these changes is the development of new business models. Some of these business models call for direct interaction between artists and listeners, which is now possible due to low costs of music promotion and distribution via the internet. Therefore, the music industry's role of intermediary between artists and listeners should be re-examined. Before I present the selected results of my research, which may give some insight into changing relations between record labels, artists and listeners, I would like to briefly introduce the economic background of these changes.

In the traditional recording business model, costs of producing the physical product (e.g. compact discs) were high. Apart from the obvious costs of manufacturing and packaging, record labels had to take into account costs of overestimating the demand for each of the records released. That is why record labels were very careful not to end up with huge amounts of records manufactured but not sold (Lathrop and Pettigrew 1999, 94). Since digital files can be copied and transported over the internet at costs close to zero, the structure of the costs of record labels changes (Burkart and McCourt 2006, 50). Consequently, the internet may increase market competition by reducing entry barriers (especially for small labels) as well as levels of industry concentration (Fox 2004, 204–205). In the long run it should influence also prices of music products.

Although changes in music industry distribution channels are a logical consequence of the growing popularization of digital files, they are taking place relatively slowly. Distribution for many years has been a cornerstone of all marketing programs of most of the record labels. In pre-internet times, organizing a distribution chain was a complicated process and only a few record companies could build their own distribution networks. That is why the ability to distribute their own records has been a fundamental aspect of maintaining market dominance of big record companies in the 20th century. As mentioned earlier, smaller companies, which were not able to distribute their own records independently, had to sign distribution deals with major companies and share their profits with them. Development of digital music distribution through the internet may increase market competition by reducing entry barriers. It means that now almost anybody, a small label, an individual artist or even the listener can become an internet distributor of music. These changes may be especially harmful to major record companies, as they may not only lose their dominant position in production, but also in distribution of smaller companies' products. Fox argues that technological changes may help independent record labels "diminish major labels' historical hegemony over traditional distribution methods" (Fox 2004, 205). In the next part of this chapter I will show, however, that although netlabels are becoming part of a new, independent alternative to the traditional music industry distribution network, the scale of their operation is currently too small to threaten the music market giants.

The internet has also changed almost all aspects of music promotion. In the traditional recording business model, record labels struggled for radio airplay, a near–essential promotion tool in the 20th century (Lathrop and Pettigrew 1999, 161). It was based on an assumption that consumers will not buy a record if they do not hear at last one or two tracks first. Today radio airplay is still important, but there are other ways of making sure that listeners know the music before buying, for example MySpace, YouTube, Last.fm and record labels' websites.

All these changes have been taking place simultaneously in the last few years, which led to a growing awareness of the fact that the traditional music business model was perhaps not the most beneficial for a significant number of record labels, and definitely not for most artists (Future of Music Coalition 2001; McLeod 2005). It is estimated that in the traditional music business model only one out of nine records released is a commercial success and only a small percentage of recording artists sell enough records to get royalties from record companies (Passman 2000; Hesmondghalgh 2002, 20-21).

This is why in the last few years both researchers and music business practitioners have been looking for new business models, which would better correspond to changes in the technological and social environment. Fox proposed 3 new business models: broadcasting model; pay-per-track or album model; and artist to consumer model (Fox 2004), along with other proposals (Vaccaro and Cohn 2004; Eriksson et al. 2006; Swatman, Krueger and van der Beek 2006). My aim is not to discuss all proposals in this text, as only some of them consider the possibility of distributing music outside of traditional music industry contexts. I will concentrate on one innovative business model successfully implemented by netlabels.

What are Netlabels?

Netlabels are a reasonably new phenomenon and have not yet been widely described in the relevant literature. Michels defines netlabels as "non-commercial platforms, on which music is offered for free download on the Internet" (Michels 2009, 64). This definition is specified by Phlow, the biggest Internet magazine devoted to free music, which claims that:

> A Netlabel is a Netlabel if…
> …it is a platform for online distribution of quality music.
> …it allows to download music free.
> …there is more than one artist on the label.
> …there are more than two releases online.
> …the music is encoded with at least 128kbps.
> (Phlow 2010)

The simplest definition of netlabels is therefore as platforms for online distribution and promotion of music released under Creative Commons licenses. Let us try to specify this definition by employing music business terminology to compare netlabels with traditional record labels. Comparing netlabels to major record labels is arguably pointless, as the differences in the scale of their cultural production, market power and impact on music industry are too big. However, we can try to use the definition of netlabels presented above to compare them with traditional independent record labels.

Table 8.1. Comparison between traditional record labels and netlabels.

Characteristic features	Traditional record labels	Netlabels
aims	commercial	mostly non commercial
relationships with artists	contractual	mostly non contractual
character of relationship	exclusive	non exclusive (artists are free to leave anytime)
copyright	record label controls copyright	artists retain copyright
product	tangible records and music files	mostly music files
attitudes to filesharing	negative	positive
promotion	in traditional media and the internet	in the internet, mostly guerilla marketing
costs of distribution	high in case of physical records, close to zero in case of digital files	no costs of distribution

Source: author's own research.

As we can see, there are fundamental differences between traditional record labels and netlabels, and in my opinion we can compare record labels with netlabels only if we assume that the latter are profit-oriented.

I would like to present a brief profile of Magnatune, one of a few netlabels which are known for implementing a profitable business model. Magnatune, as of October 2008, cooperates with 262 artists, which have recorded 590 albums (8162 songs) representing various music genres, mostly classical (25.59%), electronica (14.91%), rock (13.38%) and world (11.35%). Magnatune distributes music under Creative Commons licenses, which means it is free for non-commercial usage. Listeners can stream tracks from the netlabel's website, buy digital files or order CDs. Prices are flexible—a downloadable album costs from $5 to $18, with the buyer determining the exact price. It is worth noting that this is a very innovative approach to music pricing. Magnatune earns money also by sub-licensing music for commercial purposes, priced from $150 to $5,000, depending on the length and type of use. Aside from that, the netlabel hopes to enter the merchandising market and one day sell "posters, clothing, mugs with artist's likeness" (http://www.magnatune.com/info/model). Profits from these sources are split between artists and the label on a 50/50 basis. Although numbers may vary on case by case basis, "fan purchases make up about half a musician's income, with the remainder coming from commercial licensing fees" (Holloway 2008, 1).

Although currently Magnatune does not earn a lot of money, its business model seems reasonable. The label has become self-sustaining and earns money for some of its artists. Three of them are provided with an income of $10,000 per year and further 30 an income of $3,000 per year (Ibid., 2). What makes the netlabel's costs low are efficient forms of music distribution (costs of streaming are low) and Creative Commons licenses (which reduces the need for paying lawyers).

It must be emphasized that Magnatune is much bigger than most netlabels and probably one of only a few which claim to be profitable. What makes Magnatune similar to other netlabels is its relationship with communities of listeners, communicating via blogs, discussion forums, email lists, MySpace and Second Life. Magnatune also has a close relationship with community music remixing site ccMixter, where it has run several remix contests (Ibid., 11). As we can see, Creative Commons licenses are a tool which encourage close cooperation with DJs, amateur music producers and listeners.

I have briefly presented information regarding Magnatune as it corresponds well with the empirical part of this chapter, which presents two short case studies of Polish netlabels. As we can see below, one of them is not far from Magnatune's approach to market, while the other has a more non-profit orientation, reminiscent of the micro-independent record labels described by Strachan.

Netlabels: Two Examples from Poland

The two short case studies presented below are based on in-depth interviews conducted with founders of netlabels in 2006 and 2007 and an analysis of netlabels' repertoire and websites. Both netlabels are based in Warsaw, Poland and both distribute music in the form of digital files under Creative Commons licenses, so according to the definition cited earlier they can be treated as netlabels.

The first netlabel—Afterbeat—was started at the beginning of 2005 by three colleagues. The idea of establishing a netlabel was born when one of the founders stumbled upon music distributed in the internet under Creative Commons licenses. It helped them realize that owing to the new technologies and legal solutions, releasing and distributing music was much easier than in the past. Therefore, we can say that there were two reasons for starting a netlabel: (1) its founders were passionate about music; (2) institutional conditions for dealing with music distribution and promotion have changed. In other words, they always wanted to deal with music in more professional way but before "the internet era" and popularization of Creative Commons licenses it was much more complicated and would require full time engagement. Since the conditions have changed, they can run their own netlabel without having to quit their jobs and face the economic risk of running a regular record label.

Afterbeat specializes in reggae and dub music. A clearly defined profile of the netlabel can be explained with the fact that its founders are fans of this kind of music. Just as in the case of micro-independent record labels analyzed by Strachan, Afterbeat can be described as a direct extension of founders' fandom. This may explain why earning money was not a motivation to start the netlabel.

According to my respondent, releasing music on netlabels is, from an artist's point of view, much better than distributing selected tracks via internet portals or the artist's own website.[3] A netlabel, even though it releases music for free, has a certain brand recognition, which guarantees the high value of distributed music. Founders of Afterbeat are determined to release only high quality music—they receive a significant number of demo records, but decline most of them due to unsatisfactory quality, which is why during more than three years of operation they have released only ten records. All the releases can be downloaded per track or in the form of a full release zipped and accompanied with CD cover. The cover can be printed by the listener if he or she wants to burn a CD-R and have "a regular" CD. Although Afterbeat distributes only digital files, it consequently releases them as digital albums or EPs. It could easily distribute even single tracks, but prefers to stick to traditional concepts of the album, EP and single.

Afterbeat has strong ties with reggaenet.pl, which is a Polish portal dedicated to reggae music. Reggaenet.pl is small but active community of Polish fans of reggae music, of which the founders of Afterbeat are also members. Herein are examples of cooperation between the netlabel and portal: the netlabels' releases are promoted and discussed on reggenet.pl forums and aired in affiliated internet radio station. The community of reggae fans is not limited to virtual reality—reggae sound systems (live DJ performances) are regularly organized in big Polish cities, during summer

[3] Please note that when the interview was conducted social networking sites (e.g. MySpace) were not popular.

there are a few reggae festivals, vinyl records distributors[4] sell records to die-hard reggae fans, etc. As the community of Polish reggae fans is small but active and well organized, anything that is distributed by the netlabel is very likely to be listened to and discussed by a significant number of people. Links between Afterbeat, reggaenet.pl and other non-virtual enterprises are a reason to believe that recognition from peer group, listeners and artists (that is possibility of having high levels of symbolic capital) have also been an important motivation to run a netlabel. Since it is essential that a netlabel has a good reputation (high levels of symbolic capital), its founders must very carefully choose the music which is released by Afterbeat. That is why my respondent emphasized strict criteria for selection of the music they release, which results in the high quality that netlabels offer.

According to my interviewee, Afterbeat will not become a regular profit-oriented enterprise. Its founders have regular jobs and cannot engage in the running of a regular record company. Apart from this, even if they could organize a company (for example together with reggaenet.pl, vinyl distributors and internet radio station), which would deal with all the promotional and management aspects of artists' careers, they would like to continue free music distribution.

Summing up, Afterbeat seems to have more in commons with small scale cultural producers described by Strachan and Moore than with traditional record labels. Afterbeat specializes in a niche music genre, which has a small but active community of listeners. The founders of the netlabel engage themselves in practices which are characteristic of fans rather than the music business and they do not receive (and do not look for) financial rewards, but have the chance of acquiring symbolic capital. There is also at least one significant difference between small scale cultural producers described by Strachan and Moore and Afterbeat—the level of financial engagement in their activities. It is a logical consequence of different economic constraints of cultural production in the non-virtual world (Strachan's and Moore's research) and in the virtual reality (where netlabels operate). Running a netlabel is much cheaper and most probably requires less effort than running any record label which releases traditional records (even a "small scale independent" one).

The second netlabel—9lives—was started at the beginning of 2006 by group of three friends who had worked for 9 years in the music industry (as producers, organizers of concerts, etc.). What is important is that they

[4] However it must be emphasized that Afterbeat does not release vinyl records, so this cooperation does not have business character.

had some experience of working with traditional record companies (both majors and independents), which led them to believe that in Poland an artist does not have much chance of earning money by releasing records, unless he or she is very famous. They decided to start a netlabel when they realized that the Polish implementation of Creative Commons licenses protects artists' rights in a satisfactory way and that they provide an institutional framework for virtual record labels.

There were two main motivations to start a netlabel: (1) helping artists to release their works; (2) belief that it is possible to create a business model based on free music distribution, which would become a vehicle for music promotion and bring income from various sources—concerts, management, selling rights to use music in commercials, films, etc. My interviewee emphasized that such a business model is based on rational assumptions, as in Poland the majority of young people do not buy records anyway.

As of October 2008, 9lives distributes 7 full releases (6 albums, 1 bootleg), 4 shorter releases (EPs and singles) and a few individual tracks. Apart from distributing free music released under Creative Commons licenses, 9lives also plans to release traditional CDs, which would be sold to upper market segments. My interviewee claimed that he believed that compact discs would be bought for at least the next ten years, provided they are released in high quality, nice looking digipak-style packaging. It is worth noting that my respondent does not follow the do-it-yourself ethics and believes that purely non commercial enterprises are not the future of the music business. The founders of 9lives consider music the most important thing in their lives and they would like to be able to concentrate only on their label one day. Although they have now full time jobs, they invest their savings into the development of their label, for example in building their own recording studio. They are also ready to invest in the production of music videos for their acts, and have some prior experience in this field.

According to my interviewee, 9lives does not want to specialize in any specific music genre—they want to release interesting music which has the potential to reach a wide audience. Consequently, they are aware of the need to promote in mainstream media, although developing contacts in such media is difficult. It is worth noting that communicating with the listeners via traditional media—radio and television—seems to be more important than building ties with any specific virtual community. There is no such community organized on the netlabel's website—although there is an internet forum, it is not very active and there are just a few posts. This should change by May 2008 as the owners of 9lives announced that they will begin work on a big internet service based on Web 2.0 mechanisms. It is probably an attempt to further professionalize the netlabel and refine their business model.

As we can see, there are significant differences between the reasons for which Afterbeat and 9lives were started. My interviewee from Afterbeat did not use economic language (e.g. the term "business model") and gave non-business reasons for starting the netlabel. Founders of Afterbeat had no earlier music business experience and they treat running a netlabel as a hobby, which gives them personal satisfaction and peer recognition. Afterbeat specializes in a strictly defined niche and has close ties to a small but active community, which provides opportunities for acquiring and using symbolic capital. 9lives is based on quite different assumptions. Although it does not sell records, it certainly tries to implement a well planned business model. My interviewee from 9lives used economic language and demonstrated a good knowledge of the music business in Poland. The founders of 9lives have previous music business experience and declare that they would like to run a regular record label one day. Although at the time of writing 9lives was still a regular netlabel, the owners declared that they had been re-organizing it. My interviewee emphasized the difference between 9lives, which they want to reach a wide market, and other netlabels which specialize in very narrow niches. Summing up, despite the fact that 9lives distributes music for free under Creative Commons licenses, its approach towards music is reminiscent in some respects to traditional record labels. We should not however forget that the fact that 9lives deals with "free music" places it far from traditional music business. My respondent emphasized that many artists and representatives of collecting societies are opposed to the idea of "free music" and did not understand how Creative Commons licenses may help change the music business. That is why 9lives should not be compared with traditional record labels or most of the niche-oriented netlabels— it would be more profitable to look for similarities between 9lives and Magnatune, which is one of the first netlabels that implemented a new, imaginative business model.

Finally, despite all these differences, my respondents seem to agree on one issue—they claim that there is not enough understanding of the ideas of Creative Commons and free culture among the public, especially the traditional media and artists. Both netlabels appreciate the new intellectual property ideas and wish that netlabels in Poland were as dynamic as in some other countries.

Conclusions

The birth of netlabels is a consequence of the introduction of new technologies and legal solutions which enable free music distribution. Although netlabels do not compete directly with the mainstream music business at present, their appearance should make us rethink the relationship between artists and the industry. In this chapter I have described two ways of thinking about netlabels: (1) as organizations similar to traditional record labels which try to develop new business models based on employing free music distribution of music published under Creative Commons licenses; (2) as organizations which are similar to micro-independent record labels, which follow the "do-it-yourself" ideology and try to operate in non-market ways. Whichever way of thinking of netlabels is followed, there are reasons to believe that the appearance of netlabels changes the relationship between the commercial and the creative, which was so carefully analyzed by scholars in the case of traditional record labels. This assumption is based on the different nature of relationships between artists, listeners and netlabels. These differences are of both an economic and social character. Although it is difficult to make generalizations based on only two examples presented in this chapter, I would argue that: (1) we should consider thinking about netlabels as completely new players on the music market; (2) we should assume that there are various types of netlabels, which have different ideas about art and commerce. It means that despite similarities between netlabels and some other actors present on the music market (especially micro-independent record labels described by Strachan), more research is necessary to determine to what extent the relationships between netlabels, artists and listeners are similar to that of the traditional music industry. Finally, we must not forget that some netlabels (e.g. Magnatune and 9lives) try to implement new business models, which may turn out to be profitable. If that happens, some traditional record labels may also consider free music distribution and this would mean that netlabels are indeed new and effective agents which are capable of modifying the structure of the music industry field.

References

Adorno, Theodore. *Introduction to the Sociology of Music*. New York: Continuum, 1989.

Bourdieu, Pierre. *The rules of art: genesis and structure of the literary field*. Stanford: Stanford University Press, 1996.

—. "Principles of Economic Anthropology." In *The Handbook of Economic Sociology 2nd Edition*. Edited by Neil J. Smelser and Richard Swedberg. Princeton: Princeton University Press, 2005.

Burkart Patrick and Tom McCourt. *Digital Music Wars. Ownership and Control of the Celestial Jukebox*. Lanham, Boulder, New York, Toronto, Oxford: Rowman & Litterfield Publishers Inc., 2006.

Eriksson Lars-Eric, Olle Findahl, Håkan Selg and Roger Wallis. *New embryonicbusiness models and value chains*, KTH Royal Institute of Technology, 2005. http://w1.nada.kth.se/media/Research/MusicLessons/Reports/ (accessed October 23, 2008).

Fox, Mark. "E-commerce Business Models for the Music Industry." *Popular Music and Society* vol. 27 (2) (2004): 201–220.

Future of Music Coalition. *Major Label Contract Clause Critique*, 2001. http://www.futureofmusic.org/images/FMCcontractcrit.pdf (accessed October 23, 2008).

Garofalo, Reebee. "From Music Publishing to MP3: Music and Industry in the Twentieth Century." *American Music* vol. 17 (3) (1999): 318–354.

Hesmondhalgh, David. "The British dance music industry: a case study of independent cultural production." *British Journal of Sociology* vol. 49 (2) (1998): 234–251.

—. "Indie: the institutional politics and aesthetics of a popular music genre." *Cultural Studies* 13 (1) (1999): 34–61.

—. *The Cultural Industries*. London, Thousand Oaks, New Delhi: Sage Publications, 2002.

—. "Bourdieu, the media and cultural production." *Media, Culture & Society* vol. 28 (2) (2006): 211–231.

Holloway, Michael. *Magnatune: the open record label*. 2008. http://blogs.magnatune.com/buckman/Magnatune.pdf (accessed October 15, 2008).

Hull, Geoffrey P. *The Recording Industry*. New York, London: Routledge, 2004.

Jones, Steve. "Music that Moves: Popular Music, Distribution and Network Technologies." *Cultural Studies* vol. 16 (2) (2002): 213–232.

Lathrop, Tad and Jim Pettigrew. *This Business of Music Marketing and Promotion*. New York: Billboard Books, 1999.

Lee, Stephen. "Independent Record Companies and Conflicting Models of Industrial Practice." The *Journal of Media Economics* 8 (4) (1995): 47–61.

Lewis, Lisa. *The Adoring Audience: Fan Culture and Popular Media*. London, New York: Routledge, 1992.

McLeod, Kembrew. "MP3s Are Killing Home Taping: The Rise of Internet Distribution and Its Challenge to the Major Label Music Monopoly." *Popular Music and Society* 28 (4) (2005): 521–531.

Michels, Antina. *Netlabels—Soziale Netze On- und Offline*. Berlin: Netaudio Berlin, 2009.

Moore, Ryan. "Friends Don't Let Friends Listen to Corporate Rock. Punk as a Field of Cultural Production." *Journal of Contemporary Ethnography* vol. 36 (4) (2007): 438– 474.

Negus, Keith. "Where the mystical meets the market: creativity and commerce in the production of popular music." *The Sociological Review* vol. 43 (2) (1995): 316–341.

—. *Popular Music in Theory. An Introduction*. Middletown: Wesleyan University Press, 1996.

Passman, Donald S. *All You Need to Know About the Music Business*. New York, London, Toronto, Sydney, Tokyo, Singapore: Simon & Schuster, 2000.

Phlow. *Our Netlabel Definition*. 2010. http://phlow.de/netlabels/index.php/Main_Page (accessed May 1, 2010).

Rappa, Michael. *Business Models on the Web*. 2008. http://digitalenterprise.org/models/models.pdf (accessed October 24, 2008).

Strachan, Robert. "Micro-independent record labels in the UK." *European Journal of Cultural Studies* vol. 10 (2) (2007): 245–265.

Swatman, Paula M. C., Cornelia Krueger and Kornelia van der Beek. "The changing digital content landscape. An evaluation of e-business model development in European online news and music." *Internet Research* vol. 16 (1) (2006): 53–80.

Triggs, Teal. "Scissors and Glue: Punk Fanzines and Creation of a DIY Aesthetics." *Journal of Design History* vol. 19 (1) (2006): 69–83.

Tschmuck, Peter. *Creativity and Innovation in the Music Industry*. Dordrecht: Springer, 2006.

Vaccaro, Valerie L. and Deborah Y. Cohn. "The Evolution of Business Models and Marketing Strategies in Music Industry." *International Journal on Media Management* 6 (1) (2004): 46–58.

PART III

ECONOMIC ORGANIZATIONS IN TRANSITION

CHAPTER NINE

CORPORATE CITIZENS: A LACK OF ORGANIZATIONAL SKILLS–EXAMPLES, CONSEQUENCES AND ANTECEDENTS

INGO STOLZ[1]

Introduction

The goals of this chapter are threefold: first, an assessment will be made of the degree to which corporations have the organizational skills necessary to position themselves as corporate citizens within their societal environment; second, consequences will be highlighted that might emerge if the level of organizational skills remains unchanged; third, antecedents will be discussed that bring about the level of organizational skills that have been identified in the first step.

This analysis was triggered by the title of the 2008 interim conference of the Research Network of Economic Sociology of the European Sociological Association in Krakow, Poland: "Economy in society—actors, relations, institutions." Provoked by this title, the author of this chapter set out to inquire of the behavioural acts of and within corporations that engender not only the corporation as an organizational entity in itself, but also establish a corporation as an actor and citizen within society on both a national and transnational level.

This analysis is based on the proposition that a corporation can be considered as a citizen—a citizen that is organizational in nature and is embodied by its organizational entity. On the one hand, this proposition rests on the observation generally made that the "political functions have gradually shifted to the corporate sphere" (Matten, Crane, and Chapple

[1] Department of Organizational Leadership, Policy, and Development, University of Minnesota.

2004, 109) and that business paradigms are omnipresent as models of governance on all levels (Aronowitz and Giroux 2000), impacting institutions and actors well beyond corporate governance structures. Therefore, the notion that in a globalized world "we act in a plurality of spaces—economically, juristically, ecologically, culturally—that are closely interleaving each other" (Armanet 2008) is becoming ever more relevant for corporations, which are seen as crucial actors in global governance frameworks (Maerki 2008; Zadek 2008; Keohane 2008). On the other hand, the proposition that corporations can be considered as citizens is based on the impact corporations have on "how we think about and valorize particular notions of citizenship" (Crane and Matten 2008, 32). Thus, the unstated assumption identified by Crane & Matten—"that corporations and citizenship are ontologically autonomous concepts, that citizenship is in some way independent from the values, actions, and impacts of corporations" (2008, 31)—is challenged: research has begun to show the role of corporations as "educational institutions for national development" (Hanson 2006, 625).

Taking these considerations regarding corporate citizenship into account, it is not surprising that studies have continuously shown that there is a positive relationship between the internationalization of trade and the growing adoption of corporate social responsibility policies by corporations (Chambers et al. 2003; Frynas 2006; Antal and Sobczak 2007; Amaeshi et al. 2006; Ahmad 2006; Newell and Muro 2006; Paul et al. 2006). By adopting these policies, corporations are reacting to two challenges: on the one hand, they position themselves in the broader social network as citizens with rights and duties in the civic, social and political domain as well as regarding economic, ecological and cultural issues in order to ensure both the legality and legitimacy of their business practices (Leisinger 2003, 2007). On the other hand, they start to find and establish new strategic mechanisms that allow them to manage the growing influence that environmental pressures have on daily business practices; consequences of the increasing access to information on an transnational level and the growing permeability of organizational structures (Post 2002). Therefore, an understanding of corporate citizenship is brought forward in this chapter that is defined as the:

> … process of identifying, analyzing, and responding to the company's social, political, and economic responsibilities as defined through law and public policy, stakeholder expectations, and voluntary acts flowing from corporate values and business strategies. Corporate citizenship involves actual results (what corporations DO) and the processes through which they are achieved (HOW they do it) (Post 2000, 29)

Based on this understanding of corporate citizenship, it is proposed that only corporations with the appropriate organizational skills show the commitment, willingness and ability to assume the responsibilities and duties of a corporate citizen within their societal environment and to react to environmental pressures in a way that enables both organizational innovation and sustainability. It is first the purpose of this chapter to identify these necessary organizational skills. Evidence will then be provided to show that too few corporations have such skills, with both the consequences and the antecedents of this condition discussed. The chapter will conclude by describing the goals and objectives affiliated with addressing the lack of these organizational skills.

Organizational Skills for Corporate Citizens

Practicing corporate citizenship necessitates both external and internal behavioural citizenship strategies. Corporations need the ability to act as citizens within their increasingly complex societal environment, and at the same time skills for nurturing, developing and framing coherent corporate citizenship practices within the organizational setting. Therefore, organizational skills for a corporate citizen consist of two further sub-sets of skills.

First, corporations have to have the skills for proactive, participatory and vigilant consideration of outside pressures and collective responsibilities in order to connect the notions of private and public work inside the organizational setting (Post 2002), to operationalize the relationship with and impacts on stakeholders and the societal environment (Waddock 2004), to find systematic approaches of internal learning—which are continuously influenced by external experiences (Logsdon and Wood 2002)—and to understand the causes and consequences of business activities (Post 2002). Therefore, like individual citizens, corporations have to have the skills that enable them to act in their broader societal environment in a participatory, active and reflective way. However, corporations being an accumulation of diverse individuals themselves, for the coherent entity of a corporate citizen to come into being equally involves a second skill-set: the skills of nurturing and developing processes of involvement and deliberation of internal stakeholders in order to support the internal creation, evaluation and verification of corporate citizenship practices. These skills refer to the organizational ability of providing a context in which individuals and networks can engage in these processes of creation, evaluation and verification, thus linking knowledge of the larger social system with internal expertise. Further, this also refers to the organizational capability to frame these processes by continuously encoding organizational routines towards coherent citizenship behaviours.

Organizational skills to practice corporate citizenship therefore first entail the ability to be proactive in a participatory and reflective way as an organizational entity within the (external) societal context. Second, they also include the capability for nurturing, developing and framing the internal creation, evaluation and verification of corporate citizenship practices. It will be shown in the next section that it is the second skill-set in particular that too few corporations have.

A lack of organizational skills on behalf of corporations

It has been stated in the research literature that there is a disconnect between the intention of corporations to adopt corporate citizenship practices and their ability to strategically manage these intentions on an organizational level (Porter 2008). Polterauer (2004) was able to show that even though patterns of involvement in congruity with internal practices and processes of corporate citizenship as stated above existed within German corporations, they were most often attributed to the skills of individual employees, vanishing when these employees left the company. She therefore found internal corporate citizenship processes not organizational in nature—framed by strategic and managerial frameworks—but rather affixed to individual expertise. This individual expertise remained volatile because it did not become enmeshed in the organizational texture. Similarly, Welford (2005) found the efforts of nurturing and developing the corporate citizenship component least developed when assessing corporate social responsibility policies in corporations in 15 countries in Europe, North America and Asia. Thus, the processes of the internal creation, evaluation, and verification of citizenship practices seem considerably less developed in comparison to the skills of managing external accountability issues, like those required by law. The study of Glazebrook (2005) gives a rationale of this lack of organizational skills regarding the internal processes to bring about and evaluate citizenship practices in comparison to the organizational skills that purely manage external accountability issues. He found processes of involvement, internal deliberation, creation, evaluation and verification not applied by the organization as a whole in his initial analysis of *BP Australia*, and could only locate those skills in centralized and isolated offices—i.e. in the Public Relations offices. With Pinkston & Carroll's (1994) findings, this observation can be generalized from *BP Australia* to the US. In their study with equal focus, the authors also found the same patterns of centralization of narrowly defined and refined quantities of organizational skills in most corporations in the United States.

Accounts like this have to be considered problematic, because it is not the whole organization that absorbs the external pressures exerted on the organization, but rather centralized expertise in the form of centralized offices. This centralized expertise might indeed suffice for dealing with issues of external accountability and image in the short-term. However, this centralized expertise can not necessarily create a reflection of the complex interrelationships the organization is actually engaged in with its environment. Experiences that are made and knowledge that is created based on the complex organization–environment interactions that are actually occurring are therefore in danger of being lost for the organization as a whole in the long-term, mainly because there are no organizational structures in place that would feed back this information and knowledge to the centre of expertise officially dealing with these interrelationships. It is the purpose of the next section to discuss the consequences that might emerge if this lack of organizational skills is not addressed.

Possible consequences of not addressing the lack of organizational skills

The implications of not addressing the lack of organizational skills to process corporate citizenship practices can be found on the corporate as well as on the societal level. On the corporate level, not having these organizational skills could have financial implications, consequences for work performance and effects on organizational sustainability and organizational functioning. On the societal level, it will be argued that only corporations with the appropriate internal skills show the ability to define their new role within society.

Several consequences for not investing in corporate citizenship practices can be identified for corporations. First, financial consequences become apparent. Recent research has clearly established a positive relationship between the social and financial performance of corporations. Most notably, Van Beurden & Gössling (2008) conclude that "there is indeed clear empirical evidence for a positive correlation between corporate social and financial performance," based on their meta-analysis of 34 research articles published about this relationship from 1991 to 2007. Fussler (2004) states that "existing managerial dedication to responsible excellence" is most likely the reason for the fact that the 76 corporations that signed the United National Global Compact and are part of the Dow Jones Sustainability Index outperformed those belonging to the Morgan

Stanley Capital Index in the time-period from 2001 and 2004. Similarly, Lougee & Wallace (2008) saw corporations in the Domini 400—an index developed for investors that are socially conscious—outperform those of the S&P 500 in the time frame from 1990 to 2006. To explain this phenomenon of enhanced business performances, Vidaver-Cohen & Altman (2000) suggest that new levels of expertise could become developed inside the organizational setting by acknowledging and managing complex organization–environment interrelationships, while Brown & Dacin (1997) point to enhanced procedures of product evaluation.

Not having the skills to practice corporate citizenship can also have consequences on work performance. It has been shown that practicing corporate citizenship increases employee satisfaction (Weiser and Zadek 2000), employee commitment (Maignan, Ferrell, and Hult 1999) and the overall work climate (Gordon, Anderson, and Bruning 1992), which again leads to enhanced financial performance (Weiser and Zadek 2000). Furthermore, organizational sustainability and organizational functioning can be impacted by the lack of organizational skills needed to practice corporate citizenship. Practicing corporate citizenship proactively on all organizational levels reduces the risks of operating in an increasingly complex global environment by enhancing receptivity to environmental changes (Waddock and Smith 2000; Pirsch, Gupta, and Grau 2007).

Implications of a lack of organizational skills necessary to practice corporate citizenship can also be found on the societal level. One consequence is that corporations fail to react to pressing issues emerging in their environment. Lougee & Wallace (2008) analyzed 500 firms regarding their investment in corporate social responsibility issues using the KLD Research & Analytics database. They found that corporations indeed increased their investment in a broad range of issues of community involvement, environment, diversity, human rights, governance and employee relations. Nevertheless, the authors found the average (net) strength regarding those issues decreasing overall in the time frame from 1991 to 2006. They attribute this to the growing number of concerns that are raised by external stakeholders and that are expected to be addressed by corporations. Corporations do not seem able to keep up with this growing list of concerns that they are asked to respond to in one way or the other. This apparent inability to continuously respond to current concerns might exist since it is not the organization as a whole that is in charge of scanning the complexities of the environment in order to continuously create, evaluate and verify corporate citizenship practices. Centralized offices might not be able to identify all issues vital to consider in organization–environment interrelationships. As a result, the increase in investments is countered by an even greater increase in concerns. This happens even though Lougee and Wallace also show—by using a regression analysis—that the financial gains are greater for corporations if concerns are continuously addressed as soon as they are raised than investing in and further strengthening only those programs regarding responsibility issues that already exist. Corporations being able to address these concerns in time therefore "could well be consistent with long-run value maximization" (Lougee and Wallace 2008, p.106). Thus—if this argument is taken for granted—a triple bottom line approach (Elkington 1994) that enhances the social, environmental as well as financial bottom line might very well be feasible. The next section will now look for reasons why corporations nevertheless show a lack of organizational skills necessary to practice corporate citizenship.

Antecedents for the lack of organizational skills

The causes leading to too few corporations having the necessary organizational skills to practice and process corporate citizenship internally can be found on the organizational as well as individual level, but also outside of corporations on a general conceptual level.

The first set of causes can be found inside corporations on the level of organizational structure and organizational culture. It has been emphasized that organizational structures regarding corporate citizenship are most often solely refined in a way to enable centralized offices to manage the interrelationships with external stakeholders that are predefined as most vital. However—beyond these isolated offices—structures and acculturated customs are actually inhibiting the nurturing, developing and framing of corporate citizenship practices. Employees as a whole are most often solely addressed through explicitly and definitively stated rules as outlined in corporate citizenship or corporate social responsibility policies, standardizing and formalizing desired internal citizenship behaviours in order "to protect organisations from their employees" (Fisher 2001, 148) and to promote routinized compliance (Kjonstad and Willmott 1995). Therefore, the intention of those policies is often to control actions of stakeholders within the organizational setting—not seldom combined with punitive semantics—ultimately leading to "a loss of personal ethical responsibility on part of the employees" (Fisher 2001, 154). This tendency has been broadly found in corporations in Europe, North America and Asia (Bondy, Matten, and Moon 2004; Fisher 2001; Kjonstad and Willmott 1995), leading to a state in which employees become acculturated to these practices regarding corporate citizenship, leaving those practices unquestioned (Glazebrook 2005).

Causes can also be found on the individual level inside corporations. Grit (2004) showed the unease of managers when dealing with moral issues because of a perceived threat to organizational harmony and efficiency. Bird & Waters (1989) found—in congruency with Fisher's (2001) findings—that managers feared for their personal image if they do so, worrying about being questioned in their integrity and in their expertise. They feel threatened when having to manage these complex and often ambiguous moral patterns that are involved in the notion of corporate citizenship (Bird and Waters 1989; Herzig and Jimmieson 2006). This again can be explained by their general lack of expertise in matters of citizenship involvement (Grit 2004), mostly not considered or taught in business schools (Zlotkowski 2004). This leaves them inexperienced in translating corporate citizenship ideas into internal organizational practice (Epstein and Roy 2001). On the other hand, employees most often do not support a further embedding of corporate citizenship practices within their every day business procedures, as they experience the topic of corporate citizenship as being handled in a restrictive and uni-dimensional way with the goal of ensuring compliance. As a consequence, they feel questioned in their integrity by being asked to do "things right rather than doing the right thing" (Fisher 2001, 149); which then again does not bring about their intrinsic motivation "to develop their own values so that they can grapple with difficult moral dilemmas" themselves (Fisher 2001, 148).

However, even if organizational and individual expertise regarding corporate citizenship practices could be assumed, managers still lack an appropriate rationale for implementing these kinds of practices. This lack directly hints to a conceptual void regarding the true scope and meaning of the corporate stake in citizenship, in itself still quite a controversial issue (Néron and Norman 2008; Crane and Matten 2008; Jones and Haigh 2007; van Oosterhout 2005, 2008). This void did neither prevent that corporate social responsibility is considered as a central component of business practice by executives (The Center for Corporate Citizenship at Boston College 2005), nor did it prevent investments in this realm (Lougee and Wallace 2008). However, this void might be a crucial antecedent of the fact that strategic implications of internal corporate citizenship practices have not been addressed, because the true complexities of organization–environment interrelationships in the realm of citizenship have not been sufficiently studied yet. It is the purpose of the concluding section to now highlight main goals and objectives of an intensified discussion about these strategic implications.

Conclusion

Goals, objectives and stakeholders of addressing the lack of organizational skills

The two main goals of discussing and addressing the problem that too few corporations have the organizational skills necessary to practice corporate citizenship are: first, establishing corporations as creative, reflective and collaborative corporate citizens that are able to continuously evaluate their stake in social cohesion and contemporary citizenship. Second, using the potential inherent in the first goal to increase efficiency and quality of corporate business practices in order to ensure organizational sustainability and economic growth.

Achieving these two goals includes the following objectives: First, adaptation of organizational structures to allow for the proactive creation, evaluation and verification of corporate citizenship practices within the organizational setting. This structural change would most often imply a change in organizational culture, and therefore has to be considered a long-term process (Cummings and Worley 2005). To trigger this kind of change, the according willingness and awareness of top executives is first needed. Innovative corporations were able to show that committed engagement in favor of corporate citizenship on the part of senior management can indeed jump-start according structural and cultural change (Leisinger 2003).

Second, both managers and employees will need to become familiar with the skill-sets that better enable them to continuously nurture, develop and frame the necessary internal processes. This objective of familiarization—even though also long-term in nature—can be achieved faster than structural and cultural change and should be considered a prerequisite for these more profound change dynamics. Organizational members at large are addressed by this objective, from top executives and mid-level managers to employees in general. As shown above, top executives and mid-level managers particularly will raise issues of economic profitability and organizational efficiency, but also questions of personal integrity. Employees on the other hand will raise the issues of trust and motivation.

Third, an appropriate rationale for internal corporate citizenship practices will need to be established. Stakeholders included in achieving this objective are researchers in the field of Corporate Citizenship and Corporate Social Responsibility, with the interdisciplinary influences of fields such as Human Resource Development, Organization Development, Education, Business Administration, Political Science, Knowledge Management, Organization Science and Business Ethics. Research would be needed that analyzes the impact of corporate practices on understandings of citizenship. Based on this understanding, the effects of strategic interventions that have the goal of enhancing the triple bottom line need to be studied. Also, frameworks have to be established that capture the new intra-organizational processes and procedures that emerge if an organization has this objective of enhancing its triple bottom line.

It has been the purpose of this chapter to assess the organizational skills that corporations currently have at their disposal for practicing corporate citizenship in the organizational setting. It has been shown that too few organizations have these organizational skills necessary. Consequences of this lack for corporations themselves as well as for society at large have been highlighted. In addition, antecedents that lead to this lack have been described. In order to develop the organizational skills necessary to practice corporate citizenship, organizational structures as well as inter and intra-personal skills have to be addressed. Further, appropriate frameworks have to be established that allow organizations and its employees to invest in strategic advancements of corporate citizenship practices.

References

Ahmad, S. Jaseem. From principles to practice. *Journal of Corporate Citizenship* 24 (2006): 115–129.

Amaeshi, Kenneth M., Bongo C. Adi, Chris Ogbechie, and Olufemi O. Amao. "Corporate social responsibility in Nigeria." *Journal of Corporate Citizenship* 24 (2006): 83–99.

Antal, Ariane Berthoin, and Andre Sobczak. "Corporate social responsibility in France: A mix of national traditions and international influences." *Business and Society* 46 (2007): 9–32.

Armanet, François. "Les débats de l'obs - Interview avec Daniel Bensaïd, professeur de philosophie à l'université de Paris-VIII." *Le Nouvel Observateur*, January 24, 2008.

Aronowitz, Stanley, and Henry A. Giroux. "The corporate university and the politics of education." *The Educational Forum* 64 (4) (2000): 332–339.

Bird, Frederick B., and James A. Waters. "The moral muteness of managers." *California Management Review* 32 (1) (1989): 73–88.

Bondy, Krista, Dirk Matten, and Jeremy Moon. "The adoption of voluntary codes of conduct in MNCs: A three-country comparative study." *Business & Society Review* 109 (4) (2004): 449–477.

Brown, Tom J., and Peter A. Dacin. "The company and the product: Corporate association and consumer product responses." *Journal of Marketing* 61 (1) (1997): 68–84.

Chambers, Eleanor W., Wendy Chapple, Jeremy Moon, and Michael Sullivan. *CSR in Asia: A seven country study of CSR website reporting.* Nottingham, UK: International Centre for Corporate Social Responsibility, 2003.

Crane, Andrew, and Dirk Matten. Incorporating the corporation in citizenship: A response to Néron and Norman. *Business Ethics Quarterly* 18 (1) (2008): 27–33.

Cummings, Thomas G., and Chrisopher G. Worley. *Organisation Development and Change*. Mason, OH: South-Western, 2005.

Elkington, John. "Towards the sustainable corporation: Win-win-win business strategies for sustainable development." *California Management Review* 36 (2) (1994): 90–100.

Epstein, Marc J., and Marie-Josee Roy. "Sustainability in action: Identifying and measuring the key performance drivers." *Long Range Planning* 34 (5) (2001): 585–604.

Fisher, Colin. "Managers' perception of ethical codes: Dialectics and dynamics." *Business Ethics: A European Review* 10 (2) (2001): 145–156.

Frynas, Jedrzej George. "Corporate social responsibility in emerging economies." *Journal of Corporate Citizenship* 24 (2006): 16–19.

Fussler, Claude. "Responsible excellence pays!" *Journal of Corporate Citizenship* 16 (2004): 33–44.

Glazebrook, Mark. "The social construction of corporate citizenship." *Journal of Corporate Citizenship* 17 (2005): 53–67.

Gordon, William I, Carolyn M. Anderson, and Stephen D. Bruning. "Employee perceptions of corporate partnership: An affective-moral quid pro quo." *Employee Responsibilities and Rights Journal* 5 (1) (1992): 75–85.

Grit, Kor. "Corporate citizenship: How to strengthen the social responsibility of managers?" *Journal of Business Ethics* 53 (1-2) (2004): 97–106.

Hanson, Mark. "Transnational corporations as educational institutions for national development: The contrasting cases of Mexico and South Korea." *Comparative Education Review* 50 (4) (2006): 625–650.

Herzig, Sharyn E., and Nerina L. Jimmieson. Middle managers' uncertainty management during organizational change. *Leadership and Organization Development Journal* 27 (4) (2006): 628–645.

Jones, Marc T., and Matthew Haigh. The transnational corporation and new corporate citizenship theory. *Journal of Corporate Citizenship* 27 (2007): 51–69.

Keohane, Robert O. "Complex accountability and power in global governance: Issues for global business." *Corporate Governance* 8 (4) (2008): 361–367.

Kjonstad, Bjørn, and Hugh Willmott. "Business ethics: Restrictive or empowering?" *Journal of Business Ethics* 14 (6) (1995): 445–464.

Leisinger, Klaus M. "Opportunities and risks of the United Nations Global Compact." *The Journal of Corporate Citizenship* 11 (2003): 113–131.

—. *Corporate responsibility with the United Nations Global Compact.* Basel, Switzerland: Novartis, 2007.

Logsdon, Jeanne M., and Donna J. Wood. "Business citizenship: From domestic to global level of analysis." *Business Ethics Quarterly* 12 (2) (2002): 155–187.

Lougee, Barbara, and James Wallace. "The corporate social responsibility (CSR) trend." *Journal of Applied Corporate Finance* 20 (1) (2008): 96–108.

Maerki, Hans Ulrich. "The globally integrated enterprise and its role in global governance." *Corporate Governance* 8 (4) (2008): 368–374.

Maignan, Isabelle, O. C. Ferrell, and G. Tomas M. Hult. "Corporate citizenship: Cultural antecedents and business benefits." *Journal of the Academy of Marketing Science* 27 (4) (1999): 455–469.

Matten, Dirk, Andrew Crane, and Wendy Chapple. "Behind the mask: Revealing the true face of corporate citizenship." *Journal of Business Ethics* 45 (1-2) (2004): 109–120.

Néron, Pierre-Yves, and Wayne Norman. "Citizenship, Inc." *Business Ethics Quarterly* 18 (1) (2008): 1–26.

Newell, Peter, and Ana Muro. "Corporate social and environmental responsibility in Argentina." *Journal of Corporate Citizenship* 24 (2006): 49–68.

Paul, Karen, Elisa Cobas, Raul Ceron, Mattias Frithiof, Angel Maass, Ivan Navarro, Lina Palmer, Loretta Serrano, and Lori Zalka Deaton. "Corporate social reporting in Mexico." *Journal of Corporate Citizenship* 22 (2006): 67–80.

Pinkston, Tammie S., and Archie Carroll, B. "Corporate citizenship perspectives and foreign direct investment in the U.S." *Journal of Business Ethics* 13 (3) (1994): 157–169.

Pirsch, Julie, Shruti Gupta, and Stacy Landreth Grau. "A framework for understanding corporate social responsibility programs as a continuum: An exploratory study." *Journal of Business Ethics* 70 (2) (2007): 125–140.

Poltauer, Judith. Gesellschaftliche "Integration durch Corporate Citizenship?" ["Social integration through corporate citizenship?"] *Diskussionspapiere zum Nonprofit-Sektor* 24 (2004): 1–34.

Porter, Terry B. "Managerial applications of corporate social responsibility and systems thinking for achieving sustainability outcomes." *Systems Research and Behavioral Science* 25 (3) (2008): 397–411.

Post, James E. "Moving from geographic to virtual communities: Global corporate citizenship in a dot.com world." *Business & Society Review* 105 (1) (2000): 27–46.

—. Global corporate citizenship: Principles to live and work by. *Business Ethics Quarterly* 12 (2) (2002): 143–153.

The Center for Corporate Citizenship at Boston College. "The state of corporate citizenship in the U.S.: Business perspectives in 2005." Boston, MA: The Center for Corporate Citizenship at Boston College, 2005.

Van Beurden, Pieter, and Tobias Gössling. "The worth of values: A literature review on the relation between corporate social and financial performance." *Journal of Business Ethics* 82 (2) (2008): 407–424.

Van Oosterhout, J (Hans). "Corporate citizenship: An idea whose time has not yet come." *Academy of Management Review* 30 (4) (2005): 677–681.

—. "Transcending the confines of economic and political organization?" *Business Ethics Quarterly* 18 (1) (2008): 35–42.

Vidaver-Cohen, Deborah, and Barbara W. Altman. "Corporate citizenship in the new millennium: Foundation for an architecture of excellence." *Business & Society Review* 105 (1) (2000): 145–168.

Waddock, Sandra. "Parallel universes: Companies, academics, and the progress of corporate citizenship." *Business & Society Review* 109 (1) (2004): 5–42.

Waddock, Sandra, and Neil Smith. "Relationships: The real challenge of corporate global citizenship." *Business & Society Review* 105 (1) (2000): 47–62.

Weiser, John, and Simon Zadek. *Conversation with disbelievers: Persuading companies to increase corporate involvement.* Edited by T. F. Foundation. New York, NY: The Ford Foundation, 2000.

Welford, Richard. "Corporate social responsibility in Europe, North America and Asia." *Journal of Corporate Citizenship* 17 (2005): 33–52.

Zadek, Simon. "Global collaborative governance: There is no alternative." *Corporate Governance* 8 (4) (2008): 374–388.

Zlotkowski, Edward. "Opportunity for all: Linking service-learning and business education." *Journal of Business Ethics* 15 (1) (2004): 5–19.

CHAPTER TEN

MANAGERIAL CHANGE IN RUSSIAN FIRMS

RAIMO BLOM AND HARRI MELIN[1]

Introduction

Sociological studies (e.g. Clarke 1995; Clarke 2006; Melin 2003; Kosonen 1999) have shown that institutional and organizational configurations have been very sustainable in Russia. Although the Soviet Union collapsed more than a decade ago, only a few firms state that they have introduced major organizational innovations. On the other hand we have witnessed rapid and profound changes in the operations and managerial practices of several Russian corporations—in certain branches of economy, Russian firms are among the biggest actors at the global level. Gazprom, Lukoil, Rusal and Severstal are all global brands and actors, and surely follow the most modern managerial and organizational patterns.

Our general framework in the studies of Russian managers has been to question social capital, networks and trust, enquiries critical in the Russian context. Theoretical concepts, such as "hybrid capitalism" (Lane 2006), "nomenklatura capitalism" (Eyel, Szelenyi and Townsley 1997) or "industrial feudalism" (Ericson 2000) are only partially valid in describing Russian society and therefore require modification. We may start from the significance of social capital and trust in the context of managerial practices which leads to questions of informal relations and norms, and also to the significance of old practices and changes in the moral code.

Russian studies suggest that the behavior managers and workers continue to replicate and uphold is connected with non-market norms and exchange relations. The studies of Russian company directors (Sil 2001, 226) refer to a persistent tendency to ignore the formally described rules, usually in favor of informal ethical norms. On the other hand they emphasize personal loyalty, solidarity, paternalistic benevolence and trust

[1] Department of Social Research, University of Tampere.

among and between business partners. There is some evidence showing that business action operating on the basis of informal ethical rules and social networks is better than activities relying on market-driven logic and formal contracts (Kharkhordin and Gerber 1994; Sil 2001, 227).

Ledeneva (1998 and 2006) gives a different interpretation to the above mentioned views, arguing that the reason for informal practices is in the dysfunction of legislation and formal practices. The unwritten laws are necessary simply because the legal administration does not work. The main reasons for this kind of practice are an insecure environment, the shadow economy and corruption.

The nature of Russian capitalism is in many respects mysterious for most foreign observers. During the last decade maybe the most widely used formulation has been that of hybrid capitalism (Lane 2006), meaning that Russian capitalism shares elements from different formations and different practices. Many researchers also state that the Soviet legacy is still functioning. There are a lot of enterprises which have very strong community ties, and which are aimed at reproducing the factory and the community (Melin 2005). Blurring local politics and business is more the rule rather than exception in many regions. In most cases, Russian firms try benefit from cheap raw materials and cheap labor instead of investing into R&D or new facilities. Finally managerial practices have changed only slowly—practices of "one man management" still exist, hierarchical structures are rigid, and modern managerial strategies appear an unobtainable ideal.

During this decade Russian economy has grown rapidly (Karhunen et al. 2008, 11). Annual growth of the GNP is at over 5%, and foreign direct investments have been at a high level for many years. The ruble has become stronger against the USD and Euro. Average monthly wages are almost ten times higher than they were in the year 2000. At the same time unemployment has decreased from 10% to less than 6%. We may say that Russia has reached a high level of macro-economic stability, which guarantees relatively good protection from financial crises. In addition, the political environment has become more stable under Putin´s presidency.

While we can see several positive developments, Russian society also faces many problems. Institutional development has been very slow while major political and legal institutions are still very weak. The only exception is the presidency and president´s administration. Corruption is a severe problem, Russia being one of the most corrupted in the World (Ibid., 63). It is estimated that about 2% of firm's expenses are needed for corruption. Corruption limits the quality of investments and reduces the expansion of urgently needed growth of high–tech companies. This is in close connection with weak intellectual property rights.

At present there is a global financial and general economic crisis. It is has, and has already had, clear negative influences on Russian economy. The decreasing oil-prices, support for the banks and other financial organizations, and the decreasing value of shares in stock market are indicators of these effects.

In the Soviet Union, manufacturing firms were not independent economic units, but were part of branch ministries. The firms operated in a system called "soft budget constraint" (Kornai 1959), with all financial resources being given to the firms by respective ministries. The plan told them what to produce, how much to produce and to whom to distribute the final products. The management was based on the idea of "one man management." This meant that the director had, at least in principle, large power resources at their disposal, with managers not having to think about marketing or innovations. In principle all such premises were given in advance. At the same time managers were also active in the local community, having party duties as well as positions in local municipal administrations (Melin 1996).

Since 1991 managerial work and managerial strategies have been changing (Blom et al. 2004), with most of the manufacturing enterprises being privatized. They are operating in market conditions, meaning that they have to earn the money themselves. All these changes mean that management must refocus their strategies, and in the following we analyze the changes in this respect.

We consider corporate managers as important actors in social change, assuming that their decisions have an impact on several institutions. Therefore the scope of our analysis is regional: we look at Russia from the perspective of St Petersburg, and although our data is regional, we believe that the results comment on the situation throughout Russia.

Our empirical analyses are based on two surveys of face to face interviews. The first was conducted in the year 1999 (N=922) and the second in the year 2004 (N=633). In both surveys the sample covered top managers of big enterprises in the St Petersburg region. The surveys were carries out by ourselves and sociologists from the St Petersburg state university of finance and economics (PhD Irina Sarno and Professor Alfred Sarno).

Organizational Management in Industrial Firms

Given the situation of suppressed general activity of managers, their rather low activity in developing the organization does not come as much of a surprise. Only three firms out of 100 were fully active in the introduction of organizational innovations.

Table 10.1. Managerial practices applied

Managerial practices applied	1999	2004
Success through organizational innovations	2.04*	2.60
Success through getting quality of management higher	2.28	2.52
Reduction of managerial layouts	2.26	2.82
Weighted mean estimation	2.19	2.65

Mean rank (standard 1 to 5 scale used), here and in further tables

Another 8% of firms reported that they have made substantial use of these innovations. During the interviews, the respondents estimated the intensity in the efforts of their firm to improve the quality of management, and assessed their own activity. In this sense they appeared to be relatively self-critical. Only 5% of managers have given themselves the maximum estimation: that is to say that, in their opinion, the quality of management in their firms had been increasing to maximum level. Almost 12% of managers have given themselves a positive, but, nevertheless, not the highest estimation—the gain in the quality of management in their firms was substantial.

Some bewilderment is caused, perhaps, by the rather low activity of management to reduce the levels of hierarchy in the managerial structure. Only 5% of firms indicated that they have carried out such practices fully, with wvery fifth firm saying that they have done it substantially. Such bewilderment is connected to the fact that one of the main motivations of participation of the personnel of Russian enterprises in radical economic reform was the reduction of excessive administrative personnel and the reduction of levels of hierarchy in managerial structures. Besides this, crises persistently demanded the dismissal of superfluous workers. It would seem that the reduction of managerial layouts fits such intentions very well.

Human resource management was traditionally the most vigorous activity for the heads of the Russian firms. It may be possible to say that in the Russian culture of industrial production prior to the beginning of radical economic reforms, the greatest attention was paid to this form of activity. To some extent the principle was that it was not so much that the personnel was involved for the sake of development of industrial production, but that manufacture was organized so that the population could receive workplaces and receive means for its own development. The data of the following 4 tables allow us to see the real activity of management concerning the personnel, such as it was four years ago.

In our study 4 directions of managerial activities in relation to human resource management have been considered:

- Increase of manageability (the possibility of managing the personnel) and maintenance of the control over the activity of the personnel
- Increase in the level of self-organizing among the personnel
- Maintenance of the identification of the personnel within a firm
- Increase in the qualifications of the personnel

Let us consider them one by one. Management in Russian industry still has the greatest focus in managing the general activities of personnel. In 2004, the situation remained practically unchanged when compared with that at the end of 1990s.

Table 10.2. Human resource management

Managerial practices applied	1999	2004
Regular evaluation of employee's performance	2.88	2.91
Wage system is result oriented system	3.30	3.28
Usage of flexible work day, work week system	2.40	2.57
Usage of group (team) work methods	2.57	2.71
Weighted mean estimation	2.63	2.86

In addition, the greatest effort has been maintained to achieve as high a quality of management of the personnel as possible. In 1999 23% of firms fully applied the system of paying the workers on the basis of the result of their work. Another 28% of firms substantially applied this system. It demonstrates the prevailing emphasis of, in particular, the material stimulation of workers in Russian firms. Such a practice shows the refusal of modern managers to stimulate the activity of workers by qualifications and the social importance of their work, factors which were declared to be the most important prior to the beginning of the radical economic reforms.

In a sense this is also proved to be true by the data of the activity of using the system of a regular estimation of individual sense of duty among workers. Only 11% apply this system fully while 32% applied it substantially. In a more favorable situation, it would be possible to assume that those other firms where the control of individual sense of duty of workers was not used or they simply did not require such control and estimation. Their personnel identified with the firm, and had a high level of responsibility and self-organization. In conditions of economic depression the absence of the control and the absence of the estimation of individual sense of duty is caused by a more prosaic reason: managers do not have the time and strength for it.

Thus, the essential reason for the application of team work methods is due to the fact that the group accepts responsibility for the control of an individual sense of duty for each worker. Application of the "flexible duration of the working day, work week system" acts only as an indirect attribute of control and the management of workers. If careful control over the activity of workers is not the custom then the use of a system of a flexible working day leads to the disorganization of manufacture.

Compared with the period prior to the beginning of radical economic reforms the attitude of the Russian managers to the self-organizing of personnel has changed (table 10.3 below). In fact team work was widely practiced during the Soviet era as well, however the basic concept was not a team but a brigade (Andreyenkova 1985). This direction of managerial activity appeared to be the indisputable last choice, and no activity examined in the year 1999 has so low average estimation—1.11. The estimation is the closest to item 1 on the scale—"not used at all." The situation is also practically the same in the year 2004.

Before the reforms, self-organizing of the collectives was declared as the main task of society and personnel management (Andreyenkova 1985). Examples of such forms of self-organizing were the Council of Employees or the Council of the Work Collective. In the middle of the 1980s a special law was accepted and introduced to practice; it underlined the self-value of the labor collective as a social self-organizing organism. In 1994 the Committee on Labor and Social Support of the State Duma of the Russian Federation tried to achieve acceptance of the new version of the law "about a labor collective." As a reminder of this campaign, in the year 1999 only 4% of firms, according to managers, fully used the practice of supporting self-organizing of the personnel, and another 6% applied it substantially. All these firms, without exception, are large machine-building enterprises, which in maintained some former traditions.

Table 10.3. Increase of self-organization of the personnel

Managerial practices applied	1999	2004
Organization of quality circles, effective in Japan	0.91	1.02
Organization of collective organs like Council of Employees, Council of Work Collective, etc.	1.28	1.30
Participation of employees in programs like LOM-program, program of Democratic Dialogue	0.77	0.71
Organization and support of trade unions in a firm	1.60	1.77
Support of tripartite practice—making agreements among three parties (employers—trade unions—state), mutual consultation and collaboration	1.04	1.23
Weighted mean estimation	1.11	1.20

During the Soviet era, trade unions were part of the official power structures—there were no enterprises in which there were no trade unions. The modern position sharply differs from that preceding the reform. According to our research in the year 1999, only 9% of firms had the support of trade unions fully, while another 8% had this support substantially. Trade Unions are very weak in Contemporary Russia (Ashwin and Clarke 2003), and this is reflected in our results. Managers in 27% of firms considered trade-union organization to be unnecessary within the firm, and even more so is their relation to the practice of tripartite, considered unnecessary from the point of view of every third manager.

A different picture can be drawn out from next table (table 10.4 below) concerning the activity of managers regarding the maintenance of the identification of the personnel within the firm. This activity also has essentially decreased in comparison with the recent past and, it seems, has found a relevant and rather stable position. Parameters for the years 1999 and 2004 are practically identical.

Table 10.4. Integration of the personnel within the firm

Managerial practices applied	1999	2004
Improving of individual reflecting by employees—improvement of understanding and acquiring his own role in his firm, understanding his possible strategies in this firm.	2.60	2.82
Improving of structural reflecting by employees—improving their understanding of different departments' roles in gaining the firm's success as a whole.	2.26	2.70
Regular investigations of the level of satisfaction of employees and their degree of motivation	2.06	1.96
Spending week-ends together with personnel, special holidays for staff, managers and employees.	2.88	2.58
Systematic collecting of innovative ideas from employees.	2.34	2.23
Weighted mean estimation.	2.46	2.47

However, maintenance of the identification of the personnel obviously does not take last place in the managerial arsenal. The most popular way to achieve this is the traditional practice of spending weekends together with personnel and special holidays for staff, managers and employees. In the year 1999 some 15% of firms fully practiced such occasions of rest, while 17% of firms were using this practice substantially.

One question in our questionnaire that is of special interest from the point of view of the present chapter is: to what extent the managers were able to increase the individual reflexivity of workers in order to develop the understanding of each worker concerning his own role in the organization. This means the development of their understanding regarding the possible strategies and ways for him to exist in the organization. Such a reflection can become a favorable base for the most effective motivation of workers—it motivates by granting a more favorable role to them within a firm (Buzanovskii, Gorelov and Krasovskii 1999). In Russian managerial culture this originates from the well-known requirement of the historic figure, Commander Suvorov. According to him, each soldier in the army has to know his own maneuver. In modern Russian management science, this requirement is interpreted as expedient to raise the level of subjectivity of the personnel as a whole, and of each worker separately. The better the competence of workers, the better knowledge they have about their role in the firm as a whole, and so the more effective the activity of the firm as a whole.

In the year 1999 more than one in ten firms were fully active in raising the subjectivity level of personnel and of each worker separately, while 21% of firms were substantially active in this direction. So that the understanding of the workers of their role in the firm can be effective, it is important that they understand the roles and functions of the various divisions of the firm well enough. This is about increasing the structural reflection of workers to enhance their understanding regarding the role of various divisions of the organization to function successfully as a whole.

Our results indicate that Russian managers do not put this approach into practice so actively. In the year 1999 only 8% of firms are fully active in applying the given principle, while 15% substantially apply it. It is typical that, during interrogation, interviewers came across cases of active rejection of this practice by managers. A rather categorical opinion was expressed: for management, it is detrimental to give information on the functioning of various divisions to ordinary workers: it encourages excessive curiosity and distracts from the execution of direct duties. However, statistically, these managers do not form a large group, with only 12% of firms placed in this category.

Regular gathering of innovative suggestions from personnel is useful, not only because of its direct purpose when any suggestion introduced increases the profit of the firm. From the point of view of many managers this practice raises feelings of workers' participation. As such, 4% of firms fully apply such a practice, and one fifth apply it substantially.

In spite of rapid economic growth during past few years, Russian firms still consider that they are in crisis. Most prominently this crisis can be seen in table 10.5 below. It analyses the activity of managers in improving the professional skills of personnel. Unfortunately, parameters of the activity appeared to be rather low for both years (1999 and 2004).

Table 10.5. In firm training

Managerial practices applied	1999	2004
Active usage of systems of distant learning for the employees	1.39	1.68
Training of employees abroad	1.52	1.38
Gaining success by hiring Western managers	0.93	0.89
Constant increase of competence of each worker in the process of everyday life of the firm	3.05	2.98
Weighted mean estimation	1.69	1.72

There are no managers who do not know that the better the qualifications of the personnel, the better the efficiency of the firm. However during the time of deep recession in the economy any effort to improve the professional skills of the personnel is perceived as an unacceptable luxury. Clearly, attracting western managers is a very expensive process for Russian firms. In the year 1999 only 1% of firms fully carried this out and 4% did so substantially, and all firms engaged in this activity were under foreign ownership.

It is also an expensive action to send employees abroad for training. Only 3% of firms allowed themselves to do this fully. In addition, the Russian firms hardly use inexpensive remote systems of training employees, some 4% of firms using these systems fully, and the same amount substantially. Therefore, the most popular system of training in conditions of crisis appears to be the increase in the competence of each worker (an exchange of experience) directly during the working day in the organization. 18% of firms fully employed this kind of training, and 24% of firms applied it substantially.

Public relations

Social trust is very important in business activities (Halpern 2005; Blom-Mamia 2006). In Russia, trust plays a key role in business relations, however there is very low confidence towards major social institutions. At the same time, when regarding infrastructural support and support of administrative structures, material resources do not act as a unique resource which can appear in deficiency. Trust and readiness to cooperate can appear to be an even more important and limited resource. We tend to state that during the years 1999–2000 this resource appeared critically scarce as a way of restructuring and beginning development of the Russian industry. So, in particular VTSIOM, carrying out gauging of dynamics of trust to various structures of the Russian society, has received in November–December of the year 1999, the data from which, we present only the part concerning managers. In table 10.6 below there are answers from the heads of firms of various branches of economy to a direct question: "In what measure are the following subjects reliable?"

Table 10.6. Trust towards important social Institutions in 1999 (%)

Subjects of the Russian state and society	Quite reliable	Not quite reliable	Not reliabl e at all	Difficult to answer
The president of Russia	3.1	20.2	69.3	7.3
The government of Russia	11.1	42.2	35.1	11.5
Regional, republican authorities	13.5	47.0	20.2	19.4
City authorities	17.0	48.8	22.8	11.4
Political parties	6.2	35.5	38.4	19.9
Militia, court, Office of Public Prosecutor	7.0	36.0	52.5	4.4
Trade unions	13.6	32.7	37.3	16.4

The data was completed with the distribution of answers by corporate managers to the following question: "Would you personally support protest action demanding resignation of the president?" 69% of those questioned have answered "yes" and "most likely yes," 23% have answered "no" and "most likely no," and for 8% it was difficult to answer. All of this indicates that managers feel a deep mistrust towards the basic structures of the state and society. Keeping this in mind, it is natural that they are not inclined to cooperate with them, that they are adjusted to survival alone, and that they show tendency to the greater autonomy. In such a situation it is difficult to expect the somewhat effective realization of the industrial policy at the state or regional level, even if it has been declared by the state.

In the year 1999 there were still fresh memories of the collapse of the financial pyramid of GKO, which was naturally perceived by businessmen as a realization of the economic initiative of the state as an embodiment of the credit of trust to the government of the Russian Federation. During the interviews of experts in the year 1999, the majority of managers declared that from their point of view there is no state, nor regional industrial policies. It is however obvious enough that in conditions of low trust among business towards social and state institutions even rational industrial politics could not be maintained and realized by political subjects.

Positive changes occurred at the beginning of 2000. The appearance of the new President in the political arena of the country, and rearrangements in the administrative and economic elites has essentially changed the situation. Our research in the year 2004 has also revealed favorable changes, and an essential growth of trust towards the basic subjects of the state and society. In the 2004 survey, the level of trust has been analyzed by two indirect parameters, helping the respondent to make his estimation of trust towards other subjects more justified.

The first parameter shows either a positive or negative reflection according to the respondent's perception of the subject. The second parameter indicates the internal readiness to support the subject, towards which this person estimates a degree of his own trust. In fact, the trust of the person towards a subject is usually revealed in these aspects: in their perception, the person creates a positive image of the subject and simultaneously creates an internal readiness to support them. On the basis of the two empirically registered attributes mentioned above, the integrated parameter—a degree of trust of managers towards various subjects of the state and a society—has been constructed. Results of this measurement in the year 2004 are shown in table 10.7 below.

Table 10.7. Trust towards important social Institutions in 2004 (%)

Subjects of the Russian state and society	Quite reliable	Not quite reliable	Not reliable at all	Difficult to answer
The President	70.2	8.2	13.4	8.1
The Government	48.9	26.8	22.1	2.2
City authorities	33.2	35.7	22.2	8.9
Parties: "Edinstvo" ("Unity"), "Fatherland—all Russia" ("Otechestvo-Vsja Rossia").	34.2	7.9	39.5	18.4
Army	44.5	22.3	28.8	4.3
Court	32.4	29.7	19.1	18.7
Office of Public Prosecutor	35.2	24.2	35.1	5.4
Trade unions	17.8	20.1	51.1	11.1

The data shows that changes taking place in Russian society clearly have a positive character. The economic and industrial policies offered by the government have a good chance to be supported and realized, since proprietors and corporate managers trust the government. For example, in his recent speech the President declared to the Federal Assembly that the Russian economy should become innovational. This declaration can be perceived seriously by businessmen and business circles. In our opinion, the empirically revealed increase of trust to public subjects and activization of managerial strategies, although rather weak at present, are connected functionally—they are conditioned and initiated by each other. There is a chance of overcoming the long-drawn-out crisis, and the question now is: how big is this chance, and whether such an increase of trust is sufficient enough for the breakthrough required by the international market.

Conclusions

To begin our conclusions we can ask what are the key factors required by firms to achieve success, and what is the role of social responsibility in this? This question is especially important for modern Russia, where the reformation of economic and social life is continuing still. If those firms are successful, and whose managers have a high social responsibility, the economic and social life of such a country can be estimated as constructive and favorable. This is also characteristic of the development of international economic relations. Was it possible for the Russian Federation to achieve such a good situation by the middle of the present decade? In fact, for a long time rigid market egoism and evasion from taxes was, alas, a rather popular style for many Russian companies. Thus, it is clear that this style in many respects has been dictated by the rigid crisis phenomena. This was accompanied by the process of social transformation, when the most categorical criterion—chances of a survival—acted as a dominating criterion in the success of businesses.

In other words, it seems that some years ago there was a successful opportunity for researchers to observe the start of a positive process, when corporate managers in North Western Russia gradually began to change former irresponsible attitudes towards subjects of their social environment. At a very early stage, certainly, structures providing development of the international market continued with an obvious deficiency of a responsible attitude. But today additional opportunities of compensation for such a deficiency, for example the practice of construction of regional innovational systems generated in economically advanced countries, have also appeared.

Growing economic productivity as a result of this kind of practice appears to be an effective catalyst for Russian managers, and may also lead towards better working structures of international markets. Innovational networks can appear in a new role of useful intermediaries among mutually advantageous Russian and foreign partners. In fact, the need to form effective innovational systems creates an additional interest of Russian regions in foreign experience, in a diverse spectrum of foreign partners. High-grade modern innovational networks predetermine expansion of communication with foreign sources of know-how, foreign suppliers and consumers. This is visible from the already growing interest of successful Russian firms in structures of the international market and in innovational centers.

It is still too early to say that managers in the St Petersburg region have already fully undertaken this many-sided social responsibility, being rather weak and fragmentary at present. In fact, the echo of the crisis phenomena in economy and social life has not quite yet dissipated. Regarding all weakness of the social responsibility of managers, this responsibility however already really arises and develops. It is possible to ascertain that as time passes, evasion from taxes and ignoring the interests of other subjects of economic and social environment will be regarded as negative indicators of the success of a firm. According to the Russian business community, and in public opinion, a successful firm is coming to be associated with the fact that its managers show a growing social responsibility. This should concern subjects in the close environment, i.e. those with whom, already now or in immediate future, functional contact is expected to take place.

The development of modern knowledge economy urgently demands development of innovation systems and activization of innovational management (Blom et al. 1999; Groth 1999; Hakala 2003; May 2002). Of the same importance is the sharp increase of human potential of firms and national economies as a whole. Unfortunately, these two directions of managerial strategies appeared to be at a rather low level during the period of the study.

In connection with this, the hostility in recent discussions between the Russian economists and businesses concerning the introduction of the Russian Federation into the WTO becomes clearer. The introduction of the change without any relevant stage of preparation could act as the second wave of shock therapy for the economic life of the country and its industry. Without doubt, the majority of economists are inclined to recommend this solution. However, we are inclined to think that this is the way which has the greatest possibility for Russian industry to begin a move towards perspectives and stop the road to stagnation.

In addition, we believe that a good starting point for positive change in industries, in fact a key condition for it, is the maintenance of adequate institutional support. That is the support that will overcome a credibility gap prevailing in the country and which will provide a qualitatively new "breakthrough" in the level of trust. For example, the Russian economy shows that the raising of human capital and strengthening of trust acts as the most important condition for the survival in global society, forming one of the major types of capital without investments. Trust is a precondition for the new upheaval of Russian manufacturing industries. In our opinion, without a serious injection of social capital in the Russian economy, and without the restoration of trust of businessmen in social institutions, and the introduction of the Russian Federation into the WTO will introduce another shock to its industries, much like the one which took place at the beginning of the 1990s.

Certainly, Russia is facing serious problems in this respect. One very difficult question concerns the sources of possible investment—in what direction and to what degree can the internal resources of the country be mobilized, and to what degree can these investments come from abroad? How can a country with rich natural resources ask for substantial help from the international community? These are important questions, but questions for which modern information society likely has sufficient resources for.

References

Andreyenkova, Nina. "The Development of Collective Forms of Labour Organization in the URSS." In *Working Life in Transition*. Edited by Antti Kasvio and Erkki Kaukonen. Department of Sociology and Social Psychology, Research Reports 8, Tampere, 1985.

Ashwin, Sarah and Simon Clarke. *Russian Trade Unions and Industrial Relations in Transition*. Basinstoke: Palgrave, 2003.

Blom Raimo. *Mikä Suomessa muuttui? Sosiologinen Kuva 1990-luvusta* [*What Changed in the Finnish Society? A Sociological Image of the 1990s*]. Helsinki:Gaudeamus, 1999.

Blom, Raimo and Tero Mamia. "Sociological perspective on economic performance and employee well-being." In *HRM—Between Performance and Employees*. Edited by SinikkaVanhala and Merja Kolehmainen. Helsinki: Helsinki School of Economics, B–75, 2006.

Blom Raimo, Harri Melin, Alfred Sarno, and Irina Sarno. "Management and Development of Innovations in Russian Economy: the Example of Industrial Enterprises of St Petersburg." *Universe of Russia* Vol.8 (2) (2004): 134–159

Buzanovskii Sergey, Nikolai Gorelov and Juri Krasovskii. *Crisis and Labor: Re-structurization of Enterprises*. University of Economics and Finance: St Petersburg, 1999.

Buzanovskii Sergey, Nikolai Gorelov and Anatoli Titkov. *Anti-crises Management: Re-structurazation and Re-ingeneering of the Personnel.* OOO Valeri SPD: St Petersburg, 1999.

Castells, Manuel. *The Information Age: Economy, Society and Culture.* Vol. 1. The Rise of the Network Society. Second edition. Oxford: Blackwell, 2000.

Clarke, Simon. *Management and Industry in Russia.* Aldershot: Avebury, 1995.

Clarke, Simon. *The Development of Capitalism in Russia.* London: Routledge, 2006.

Ericsson, Richard E. "The Post-Soviet Russian economic system: an industrial feudalism?" *BOFIT Online 8*, Bank of Finland Institute of Economies in Transition, 2000.

Eyal, Gil, Ivan Szelenyi and Caroline Townsly. *Making Capitalism Without Capitalists. Class Formation and Elite Struggles in Post-Communist Central Europe*. London: Verso, 1998.

Fedotova Valentin. "Russia in a Global and in an Internal World." *Universe of Russia* (4) (2000): 3–33.

Groth, Lars. *Future Organizational Design. The Scope for IT-based Enterprise*. Chichester: John Wiley & Sons, 1999.

Hakala, Johanna, Erkki Kaukonen, Mika Nieminen and Oili-Helena Ylijoki. *Yliopisto tieteen kehdosta projektimyllyksi?* [*University From the Cradle of Science to Project Machine?*]. Helsinki: Gaudeamus, 2003. (. In Finnish)

Halpern, David. *Social Capital*. Cambridge: Polity Press, 2005.

Inozemtsev Vladislav. *"Catching up" The Limits of Rapid Economic Development*. New Jersey: Transaction Publishers, 2000.

Karhunen, Päivi et al. *Suomalaisyritysten Strategiat Venäjän Muuttuvassa Liiketoimintaympäristössä* [*The Business Strategies of Finnish firms in the Turbulent Russian Business Environment*]. Helsinki: Helsinki School of Economics B-84, 2008.

Kharhordin, Oleg and Theodor Gerber. Russian directors business ethic: A Study of Industrial Enterprises in St Petersburg 1991, *Europa-Asia Studies* 46 (7) (2004): 1075–1107.

Kornai, Janos. *Over-centralization in Economic Administration*. London: Oxford University Press, 1959.

Kosonen Riitta. *The Russian Market Economy in the Making: Institutions, Networks and Regulation of Post-socialism. Russia: More different than most*. Helsinki: Kikimora publications, 1999.

Lane, David and Martin Myant. *Varieties of Capitalism in Post-Communist Countries*. London: Palgrave, 2006.

Ledeneva, Alena. *Russia's Economy of Favors: Blat, Networking and Informal Exchange*. Cambridge: Cambridge University Press, 1998.

—. *How Russia Really Works*. Icthaca: Cornell University Press, 2006.

May, Christopher. *The Information Society. A Skeptical View.* Cambridge: Polity Press, 2002.

Melin, Harri. Suunnitelman varjossa, *Acta Universitatis Tamperensis* [*In the shadow of plan*]. Ser. A. Vol 489,Tampere, 1996.

—. *Social Structure, Public Space and Civil Society in Karelia.* Helsinki: Kikimora Publications, 2005.

Sil, Rudra. "Privatization, Labor Politics, and Firm in Post-Soviet Russia: Non-market Norms, Market Institutions, and the Soviet Legacy." In *The Politics of Labor in a Global Age: Continuity and Change in Late-industrialising and Post-Socialist Economies.* Edited by Christopher Carland and Rudra Sil. Oxford: Oxford University Press, 2001.

CHAPTER ELEVEN

TRANSLATING HUMAN RESOURCES INTERVENTIONS INTO BUSINESS PROFIT IN SMALL AND MEDIUM-SIZED ENTERPRISES

BEATA CHORĄGWICKA AND BARBARA JANTA[1]

The recent EU enlargement created a new economic, political and institutional context in Europe, and many new opportunities in the new member state countries of Central and Eastern Europe. Yet, the new social reality also posed many challenges.

The objectives of this chapter are twofold. The first part focuses on the EU Human Capital Funds that have become available to the new member states upon EU accession. We present the opportunities that Human Capital funds create for Small and Medium-Sized Enterprises (SMEs) in accession countries, and analyse the real and potential impact of the EU funds in Poland. Therefore, in the initial part we present the topic from the wider European perspective and following this focus on the Polish context.

The second part of the chapter explains the role and importance of economic utility estimations in SMEs. We present the data and equations needed to carry out those estimations and apply them to a case of a training programme in a Polish SME. However, all calculations can easily be applied to data produced at any enterprise and in any country, and therefore the scope of the analysis in this part of the chapter starts with a national angle and later moves towards more global perspective.

[1] Barbara Janta, an associate analyst with RAND Europe, independently conducted this research while studying at Cambridge University. Beata Chorągwicka belongs to the department of Social and Basic Psychology and Methodology, University of Santiago de Compostela.

The significance of SMEs in the EU

Small and medium enterprises (SMEs) are the dominant form of business unit in the EU. In Europe, the definition of SMEs is based on two components—company size and annual turnover—meaning that three types of SMEs are normally distinguished: (1) micro enterprises employing up to 10 employees; (2) small enterprises having fewer than 50 employees and an annual turnover of less than €10million; (3) medium enterprises with up to 250 employees, and an annual turnover of €50million (European Commission 2003).

The importance of SMEs results from the fact that they constitute the most common form of enterprise in the EU countries. In total, there are 23 million SMEs in the EU representing 99% of all EU businesses. SMEs in Europe employ more than 74 million people and account for over two thirds of total employment. This demonstrates the great importance of SMEs in the EU, although their contribution to the labor market varies significantly between countries. In 2004, SMEs accounted for 81.2% of all persons employed in Italy, but only slightly more than 50% in Slovakia and in the United Kingdom. In Poland, SMEs provide employment for more than 70% of all workers (Eurostat 2008).

SMEs are potentially more dynamic than big enterprises, especially in the area of job creation. However, they are also more vulnerable to external factors, often lacking access to capital and to funding sources.

EU accession—opportunities and challenges for SMEs

EU accession created new opportunities for SMEs in the new member state countries, although entering the single market was also seen as a risk for some companies. In the matrix below we present the SWAT analysis identifying strengths, weaknesses, opportunities and threats for SMEs in the new member states, focusing on the aspect of human capital.

In the case of Poland, EU accession imposed greater requirements in a form of legal regulations and administrative bureaucracy, while one single European market brought the increase of competition among the SMEs. It placed an additional burden on many enterprises and pressed SMEs for flexibility and mobility in their activities. Yet, many Polish SMEs had limited business experience, very little knowledge about EU Structural Funds available in Poland, and a low level of economic/market knowledge and skills which made it difficult for them to gain from the new opportunities for business development created by the EU Structural Funds. It can indicate that enterprises did not explore and use all opportunities for education and training for entrepreneurship (Blajer and Zielenkiewicz n.d.).

Table 11. 1. SWAT analysis

Strengths	Weaknesses
High adaptability of enterprises to meet the pressure of the markets	Limited business experience and low level of economic/market knowledge and skills
Ability to change the profile of activity	Limited knowledge about available EU structural funds
Opportunities	**Threats**
Access to EU Structural Funds	Too many legal regulations and administrative bureaucracy
Education and training for entrepreneurship	Requirements with new (increased) quality standards

Source: Adapted from Blajer, A. and M. Zielenkiewicz.[2]

Human capital training and development programmes

EU accession facilitated an additional stream of funding available for SMEs in the new member states. Under the accession arrangements, the new member states were granted access to European Social Funds (ESF) the overall aim of which was to increase competitiveness of the companies. ESF consists of several streams, with the Human Capital Fund being the main source of financing for the human capital training and development programmes. The objectives for the Human Capital Fund are fivefold: (1) to promote active labor market policies and human capital enhancement; (2) to develop adaptation potential in enterprises and for workers; (3) to reduce social exclusion; (4) to increase the level of education in society; (5) to promote effective management mechanisms in public administration. In order to get access to these financial resources, employers have to meet some general criteria. In addition, these funds can only be allocated for specific business activity. In Poland, employers can only be subsidised for three types of activities: (1) cost associated with

[2] Akcesja Polski do Unii Europejskiej—szanse i zagrożenia dla malych i średnich przedsiębiorstw [Polish EU accession—opportunities and threats for small and medium-sized enterprises]. Available from:
www.ae.krakow.pl/~ekte/ konf/blajer.doc (accessed June 2008).

creation of new jobs; (2) employees' training and development costs; (3) consultancy services.

Below we present the general principles for the allocation of the Human Capital Funds. These conditions are regulated by the European Commission (2001) and are subject to Commission legal acts. These funds are designed to help develop economic activities of SMEs and facilitate their growth.

Creation of new jobs (EC 2204/2002)

Employers can access financial assistance when creating new jobs and when recruiting and employing disabled workers. In order to qualify, employers need to make sure that the new position created with the help of EC funds is kept for at least 24 months in micro and small enterprises, and 36 months in medium enterprises. The financial assistance covers the employee salary costs and additional social insurance costs. The level of assistance varies and depends on the enterprise's size and the region in which it is located, and can be in a range from 30% up to 70% of the total cost of the new employee, with the remaining costs covered by employers. When recruiting disabled workers, the length of employment cannot be shorter than 12 months and employer is normally subsidised up to 60% of the total cost of recruitment and new job creation.

Employees' training and development costs (EC 68/2001)

Financial assistance is an instrument aimed at encouraging employers to invest in the human capital of employees that is, in turn, seen as a mechanism that reduces the possibility of becoming unemployed. European funds can be used for 2 types of training and development programmes: general and specific. General training involves tuition which is not applicable only or principally to the employee's present or future position in the assisted firm, but which provides qualifications that are largely transferable to other firms or fields of work and thereby substantially improve the employability of the individual. Specific training involves tuition directly and principally applicable to the employee's present or future position in the assisted firm and provides qualifications which are not, or only to a limited extent, transferable to other firms or fields of work. Specific training mainly benefits the enterprise. The financial assistance for the specific training cannot exceed 35% of costs in medium enterprises and 45% for micro and small enterprises. In the case of general training, a maximum of 80% of costs can be reimbursed from European funds.

Consultancy services (EC 70/2001)

Under the Regulation, SMEs may be granted aid for consultancy and other services (such services do not constitute a permanent or regular activity and are not connected with the enterprise's ordinary running costs) and other activities (such as participation in trade fairs and shows) for up to 50% of the costs.

Real impact of the EU funds in Poland

Poland is one of the largest beneficiaries of the ESFs. Overall, Polish allocation of the Human Capital Programmes for the years 2004–2013 was more than 11 billion PLN (about €3.1 billion). Early analysis of the impact of the funds on the situation in Poland indicates that they boosted national economy and facilitated many positive social and economic changes in the labor market.

There are two main direct outcomes that can be linked to the EU Human Capital Funds. First of all, it is estimated that due to financial support from the funds, about one million workers could participate in some form of training and development activity. In this way, funds helped to create a more dynamic workforce, better equipped with the skills required in the labor market. The second outcome that can be directly related to EU funds is the creation of new jobs. It is estimated that about 320,000 new positions were created between 2004 and 2007 as a result of the financial assistance available through the funds. Three quarters of these jobs are permanent positions (Wykorzystanie funduszy europejskich 2008).

On a macro level, EU Capital Funds can be associated with many positive outcomes for Polish economy. It is estimated that the 3% increase in employment between 2006 and 2007 can be partly explained by the uptake in the EU funds. In 2006 the number of the working population increased by 167,000 people and in 2007 that figure doubled. Furthermore, EU funds also had an impact on the level of reported unemployment in Poland. At the end of 2007, the unemployment level was at 11.4% compared with 14.8% at the end of 2006, with the most positive changes observed in the decreasing rates of unemployment among the youngest workers (below 24 years of age). The above described changes can be partly associated with the financial assistance received from the EU.

European Community funds are seen as facilitators of the positive changes in the Polish labor market and therefore Polish economy (Wykorzystanie funduszy europejskich 2008).

Investment in human capital as a key priority

As we can see in the above, EU funds brought about many positive changes in the labor market in Poland, mostly through investment in human capital. We argue that further gains are possible, mainly if more funds are available for training and development programmes. Our reasoning is based on the analysis of the Eurostat data on the average spending on life-long training in Europe.[3] As we can see in Figure 11.1, there is a growing trend in the allocation of financial resources towards education and training in the 15 EU countries. A gradual increase in the proportion of the working age population that received education and training can be also observed in Poland. However, while there were 8% of people on average in education and training in 2001 in the 15 EU countries, and nearly 11% of workers in 2007, there were only about 4% of trained people in 2001 in Poland and it rose to only 5% in 2007.

Although education and training is only one of the many factors that can potentially stimulate positive changes in the labor markets, their role cannot be underestimated. As we show in the later part of this chapter, broadening access to education can further improve employment relations, and have a positive impact on workers' job satisfaction and performance.

[3] Life-long training is a variable used by Eurostat to describe the percentage of the adult population that received education and training in the last decade.

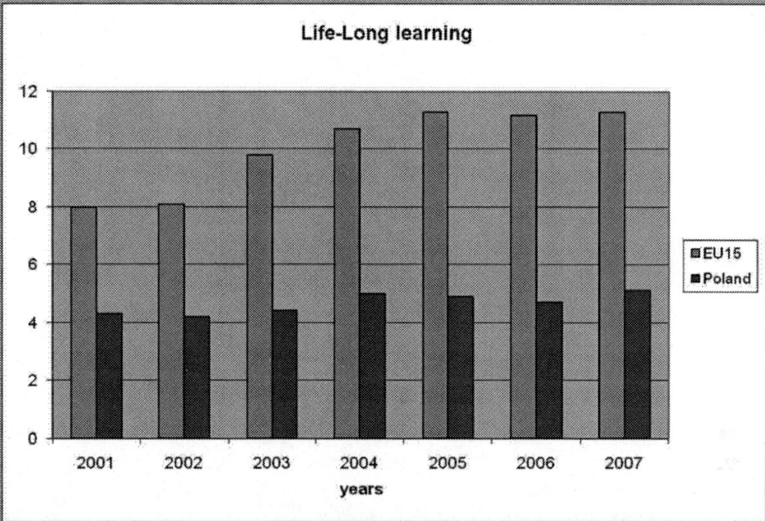

Fig. 11.1
Life long learning in the 15 EU countries and Poland.
Source: Eurostat

Ways to address the barriers to increase the uptake of EU funds in Poland

As we can observe, there was a real impact of the EU funds on the Polish labor market, with further opportunities for growth and development still arising. In order to fully utilise these opportunities, some challenges should be addressed. These challenges can be grouped into two main categories.

The first group relate to the relative lack of information about the available programmes and complicated and often changing application requirements as well as verification procedures. These challenges are subject to government policies and provision of information through campaigns promoting EU funds that should be developed to grant access to the funds more efficiently.

The second factor explaining the medium uptake of EU funds among SMEs in Poland is associated with limited business knowledge about the benefits deriving from investment in human capital. Below we present some business models and simulations that can be used by HR specialists to show the potential financial gain from the selection processes, training and education programmes in SMEs.

Value of employees' performance

Peter Drucker stated, "If you can't measure it, you can't manage it." However, the vast majority of modern enterprises do not know the exact financial value that each employee brings into their business. They may be able to say which employee's performance is better in relation to other members of staff but what does it exactly mean to be "better" or "worse"? Is it possible to calculate precisely the amount of money that each employee contributes to the company? Yes, in fact it is possible—Brogden (1949) and Cronbach and Gleser (1965) demonstrated that there is a relation between validity of a predictor, e.g. a selection method, and job performance, and it is possible to calculate and present that relationship in a monetary value (euros, dollars, pounds, etc.). This procedure is called economic utility analysis and is normally defined as an estimation of financial profit that an organization receives when using a particular method or training. It could be also an estimation of financial loss in cases where an organization does not use this procedure (Salgado 2007).

So far, the economic utility estimations were carried out in large enterprises, whereas their use in SMEs was very limited. In this chapter we would like to demonstrate that it is feasible and uncomplicated to calculate economic utility of two principal human resources interventions such as selection process and training, and that these calculations could be carried out in any company, regardless of its size.

Validity coefficient

First of all, in order to present the necessary equations that are used to calculate the economic utility, we explain the data that is required to calculate the benefits coming from any human resources intervention. In order to know if a selection program is profitable for a particular organization, first we must know the validity coefficient. It is a crucial element because the selection's utility increases together with its validity. A validity coefficient is quite easy to calculate if we know employees' score in the predictor (test, interview, assessment, etc.) and in the criterion (which is normally the performance evaluation). However, if we do not have this data, meta-analytic estimations may be used. The examples of meta-analytical validity estimations for the most commonly used selection procedures are (Salgado, Moscoso, and Lado 2002):

PREDICTOR	VALIDITY
General mental ability (intelligence)	.62
Job knowledge	.45
Situational judgement	.56
Conscientiousness	.28
Emotional stability	.19
Agreeableness	.16
Extraversion	.10
Openness	.09
Integrity	.42
Service orientation	.50
Behavioural Interview	.44
Conventional Interview	.33
Assessment Centre	.37
Biodata	.48
References	.26
Age	-.01
Experience	.18
Grade Point Average	.32
Graphology	.02

Cohen's delta

For training, the validity of the procedure must be substituted by an increment in employees' performance valuations after the training. This estimation is Cohen's delta and is defined as:

$d = (Ye-Yc)/\sigma$
Where:
d = Cohen's delta (effect size)
Ye = mean performance of trained group
Yc = mean performance of untrained group
σ = typical error

Delta estimation is easy if the company collects the data from employees' performance evaluation. However, if it is not the case, we may use the average validity coefficient calculated for training in meta-analytic study of Guzzo, Jette, and Katzel (1985), which is .39. In other words, an average growth in the productivity of employees who participated in the training is in a range of 39% or so of a significant impact. Then we need to transform this data into Cohen's delta [equation: $d = 2r/\sqrt{(1-r^2)}$], and we obtain the d = .85.

Standard deviation of the employees' performance

Secondly, we need to know the standard deviation of the employees' performance in monetary value. The greater the difference between particular employees, the greater the utility. This means, that if there is a big difference in the value of employees' contributions when different levels of performance are compared, the standard deviation is greater and it increases the economic utility. On the contrary, when the level of employees' performance is similar, the potential benefits from training or the selection process will not be significant.

There are many methods to estimate SDy empirically, however the necessary data may be not available for SMEs. On such an occasion, we may use the proportional rule developed by Hunter and Schmidt (1982). These authors reviewed empirical studies providing estimates of SDy and concluded that the average for SDy falls in a range of 40%-70% of average salary. So if we want to have a reserved estimation of SDy value, we may simply use the 40% of the average salary data.

Mean candidates' score

Thirdly, to calculate the selection method utility, we need to know the mean score of selected candidates in the predictor. This needs to be expressed in standard score (z-score).

Intervetion cost

The next variable we need is the intervention cost; that is the cost of a selection method application or the training cost. The smaller this cost is, the greater the utility of the intervention.

Selection/training rate

Finally, we also need the selection rate, which is the proportion of accepted candidates to the total number of applicants. In case of calculating trainings benefits, we substitute this index by a training rate, meaning the proportion of trained employees from the total of workers who should be or could be trained.

Economic utility equations

For the selection processes all these variables combine into the equation:

$U = (r \times SDy \times M) - (C/SR)$
Where:
U = utility of selection procedure
r = validity of the selection instrument
SDy = standard deviation expressed in monetary value (40% of average salary)
M = mean candidates score expressed in standard score
C = selection cost
SR = selection ratio

This equation estimates the annual utility per employee. However, usually more than one person is employed, and furthermore, these workers may stay in the organization longer than just one year. If we want to know the economic utility of our procedure for a particular number of employees and for the time they remain in the same job, we would need to add to the previous formula the data about number of employees selected and the average time they stay in the enterprise. In this case the equation used would be changed in the following way:

$U = (r \times SDy \times M \times N \times Y) - (C \times N/SR)$
Where:
N = number of selected candidates
Y = an average tenure

For the training procedures, the presented equations should be modified in order to include Cohen's delta instead of validity, and training ratio instead of selection ratio. Furthermore, if we want to calculate the utility for a particular period of time, we must know how long the effects of the training will last (normally to be estimated by specialists). After adding this data, the previous equation would be changed as follows:

$U = (d \times SDy) - (C/TR)$
Where:
U = economic utility for the single worker and within one year period
d = effect size (.39 if cannot be estimated empirically)
SDy = standard deviation expressed in monetary value
C = training costs
TR = training ratio (proportion of trained candidates)

Similarly, if we want to calculate the utility for the specified number of trained workers and for the time the effects of the training will remain; we would modify the previous formula in the following way:

$U = (d \times SDy \times N \times Y) - (C \times N/TR)$
Where:
N = number of trained employees
Y = duration of the effects of training (to be estimated by specialists)

Training programmes in SMEs

Both selection processes and training programs are expensive inversions for companies of all sizes, however in this chapter we would like to focus mainly on training which used to be voluntary action of the enterprises' owners, while selection processes are often the result of a simple necessity to cover vacancies. Moreover, in SMEs it may be particularly important to estimate potential advantages of training programs as the financial resources are limited and risky decisions cannot be made. On the other hand, the SMEs' owners need to be aware that, although training is an expensive inversion, it is also the basic requirement for modern enterprise operation. The factors that explain why training is important are: (1) training directly affects the employees' performance; (2) training has an important impact on enterprises' productivity; (3) training is necessary if the satisfaction of clients and users is to be achieved; (4) training is the way to adapt to volatility of the modern economical environment, where new skills and abilities are in constant demand (Salgado 2001).

In order to emphasize the economic effects of human resources interventions, we carry out some simulations applied to different scenarios of training programs, where the previously presented equations of Brogden, Cronbach and Gleser are used:

$U = (d \times SDy) - (C/TR)$
$U = (d \times SDy \times N \times Y) - (C \times N/TR)$

We use the following initial data based on Polish SMEs' reality, but which could be easily changed to be applied to any other country or setting if needed:

Effect size (d) = .39 (meta-analytically estimated)
Average Polish salary (year 2007) = 797 € × 12 months = 9,558 € (2,691.03 PLN ×12)
SDy in monetary value = 40% of an average Polish salary per year (3,823 €)
Training cost in Poland (C) = 103 € (350 PLN), 295 € (1,000 PLN), 417 € (1,500 PLN)
Number of participants (N) = 5, 10, 15, 20
Training Ratio (TR) = 1:2 (0.5); 1:4 (0.25); 1:5 (0.2)
Training effects' duration (Y) = 2, 3 and 5 years

In Table 11.2 below, six out of 108 possible simulations based on the foregoing data are displayed. In all of the 108 carried simulations, training was found to be beneficial for the enterprise. In six exemplary cases (chosen randomly) the financial profit varies from 1,153.62 € to 3,032.62 € for an individual worker and per year, and from 78,391 € to even 225,196.62 € for a group of workers and estimated duration of training effects. Having in mind that these benefits may be achieved even when total number of workers is relatively small (even 10 persons), these results seem to be of considerable impact for SMEs.

Table 11.2: Utility estimations

Training cost	1	2	3	4	5
103 €	15	3	0.5	3,032.62 €	142,648 €
103 €	5	5	0.2	2,723.62 €	78,391 €
295 €	5	2	0.5	2,648.62 €	29,436.22 €
295 €	15	5	0.25	2,058.62 €	225,196.62 €
417 €	20	3	0.5	2,404.62 €	177,637 €
417 €	20	2	0.2	1,153.62 €	87,845 €

Note: Column headings are as follows: (1) number of training participants; (2) training effects duration; (3) training ratio; (4) individual result per year; (5) group result for an estimated duration of training effects.

Conclusions

Traditionally, human resources interventions applied in the SMEs were considered costly interventions with no guarantee of a positive result for the enterprise. In this chapter we demonstrate arguments that the application of some HR interventions can be effective and cost-efficient due to the financial assistance offered via the EU structural funds for human capital development. The potential benefits of education programmes have been already recognized by the EU and it has established some programmes to activate development of human capital in Europe. The role of HR professionals is now to translate potential benefits of human resources interventions to the entrepreneurs so they can understand that the financial resources spent on new, often more efficient selection methods or training programs are actually an investment that in the long run help to generate even higher profits.

References

Blajer, Anna and Małgorzata Zielenkiewicz. *Akcesja Polski Do Unii Europejskiej—Szanse I Zagrożenia Dla Malych I Średnich Przedsiębiorstw* [*Polish EU Accession—Opportunities and Threats for Small and Medium-Sized Enterprises*]. www.ae.krakow.pl/~ekte/konf/blajer.doc (accessed June 2008).

Brogden, Hubert E. "When testing pays off." *Personnel Psychology* 2 (1949): 171–183.

Commission Regulation (EC) No 70/2001 of 12 January 2001 on the application of Articles 87 and 88 of the EC Treaty to state aid to small and medium-sized enterprises.

Cronbach, Lee J. and Goldine C. Gleser. *Psychological tests and personnel decisions*. Oxford, England: U. Illinois Press, 1965.

European Commission. Commission Regulation (EC) No 70/2001 of 12 January 2001 on the application of Articles 87 and 88 of the EC Treaty to state aid to small and medium-sized enterprises, 2001.

—. Recommendation 2003/361/EC: 2003. SME Definition, available from: http://ec.europa.eu/enterprise/enterprise_policy/sme_definition/ index_en.htm (accessed July 2008).

Eurostat. 2008. http://epp.eurostat.ec.europa.eu (accessed July 2008).

Guzzo, Richard A., Richard D. Jette, and Raymond A. Katzell. "The effects of psychologically based intervention programs on worker productivity: A meta-analysis." *Personnel Psychology* 38 (2) (1985): 275–291.

Hunter, John E., and Frank L. Schmidt. "Fitting people to jobs: The impact of personnel selection on national productivity. In Human Performance and Productivity: Human Capacity Assessment." Edited by Marvin D. Dunnette and Edwin A. Fleishman. Hillsdale, NJ: Erlbaum, 1982.

Salgado, Jesús F. *La importancia de la formación en el entorno actual. Curso de verano: Las claves de la competitividad en la empresa* [*The importance of training in present environment. Summer course: The keys for the competitiveness in the enterprise*]. Photocopy, Department of Psychology, University of Santiago de Compostela, Spain, 2001.

—. "Análisis de utilidad económica de la Entrevista Conductual Estructurada en la selección de personal de la administración general del País Vasco" ["Utility analysis of the Structured Behavioral Interview within the selection of personnel for the general administration of the Basque Country"]. *Revista de Psicología del Trabajo y de las Organizaciones* 23 (1) (2007): 139–154.

Salgado, Jesús. F., Silvia Moscoso, and Mario Lado. "Reclutamiento y selección" ["Recruitment and selection"]. In *Dirección estratégica de personas: evidencias y perspectivas para el siglo XXI* [*Strategic persons managment: evidences and perspectives for the 21st Century*]. Edited by Jaime Bonache and Angel Cabrera. Madrid: Financial Times Prentice Hall, D.L., 2006.

Świrska-Czalbowska, Karolina. "Wykorzystanie funduszy strukturalnych dla sektora malych i średnich przedsiębiorstw w Polsce po akcesji do Unii Europejskiej" ["The use of structural funds in small and medium sized enterprises sector in Poland after the EU accession"]. *Studia i Materialy—Wydzial Zarządzania* [*Studies and Data—Warsaw University Management Department*] UW, 1 (2007): 90–96.

Urząd Komitetu Integracji Europejskiej. *Wplyw akcesji Polski do Unii Europejskiej na sektor Malych i Średnich Przedsiębiorstw* [*Effect of Poland's EU accession on hte sector of small and mendium-sided enterprises*]. Warszawa, 2003.

Wykorzystanie. Funduszy Europejskich [Use of Structural Funds] 2008. Available from http://www.funduszestrukturalne.gov.pl (accessed June 2008).

Further Reading

http://ec.europa.eu
http://www.efs.gov.pl
http://eur-lex.europa.eu/
http://www.mrr.gov.pl/
www.nig.org.pl

CHAPTER TWELVE

THE POLES IN THE SCOTTISH LABOR MARKET: THE INFLUENCE OF CULTURE OF ORGANIZATION ON THE PSYCHOSOCIAL CONDITIONING OF WORK ATTITUDE

JAROSŁAW KRÓLEWSKI[1]

Introduction

The contemporary world of work is a multidimensional phenomenon. On the one hand, it is dominated by norms and rules characteristic of the values brought by waves of global changes, the escalation of the world's cosmopolitism and post-materialistic values; on the other hand, it is still the world of conservative models, whose tradition remains embedded in national culture. Work in the 21st century is one of the basic spheres of functioning for a human being. It is also a way of living, as well as a challenge faced every day by people all over the world.

The 1st May 2004 was one of the most significant days in Polish history following the collapse of socialism. On this day, Poland officially joined the European Union, a consequence being a wave of emigration to the open job markets within other EU countries.[2] Emigration abroad was connected irrevocably with the new roles face by the Polish on the levels of both micro and macro-structural existence. The idiosyncrasy of work attitudes of Poles in the conditions of cultural and organizational change has become a peculiar, though difficult to capture, area of study (Nowicka 1999). An expert on intercultural management, Geert Hofstede, proved in a number of his articles how crucial, despite being continuously underestimated, the role that "software of the mind" has in the process of

---

[1] Faculty of Humanities, AGH University of Science and Technology, Krakow.

[2] For more information on work migration of Poles after 2004 see Duszczyk 2006; Duszczyk and Wiśniewski 2007; Main Statistic Office 2007.

conceptualizing the culture in organizations and international corporations (Hofstede and Hofstede 2005). Analysis of the term "culture of organization" as a kind of mechanism uniting the organizational structures of today's companies is particularly important due to rapidly spreading globalization, and due to of the liberalization international markets.

The relevance of taking into consideration the organization culture as the characteristic factor shaping "the system of unwritten norms, values and resulting from them patterns of behavior" (Wiernek 2000, 24) of a given company stems from the presentation of Polish emigrants' multi-dimensional profiles, basing on the qualities constituting the culture of organization.

A couple of words on the research methodology

Materials used in this chapter were taken from empirical studies based on expanded and partially standardized interviews among 28 respondents. They were also grounded on the application of closed questions, introducing to the study the elements of quantity analysis. However, I would like to stress that the quantity research conducted did not enable the creation of a reliable generalization, which could reflect the national qualities and attitudes of the Polish workers abroad. The presented results are valid only to this particular group of people, but I hope to point out interesting issues connected to this phenomenon. Research was based on a non-probabilistic choice of sample. The validity of applying this approach was caused by the wish to observe the phenomena and connections which are often bypassed in extensive survey studies conducted on the basis of quantity methods of data analysis.

Two types of non-probabilistic choice of sample were applied to the study. The first was "snowball sampling," which makes it possible to conduct 28 extended interviews in a short time. While snowball sampling is appropriate from the quantity point of view in recruitment of the respondents, the second type is called "purposeful selection" (Babbie 2004, 205). This step was essential because it enabled taking into consideration the cases which in the first selections could have been omitted. The application of the two selection methods allowed for the speedy collection of differentiated empirical material, reflecting in detail the intricate dimension of the investigated phenomena and relations.

The research included 28 Polish respondents living in Perth, Tayside, Scotland. According to the official data of the Town Council of Perth and Kinross, the town is said to have the 7th largest population of Polish emigrants in Scotland.[3] The respondents did not form a homogeneous group, neither as far as metrical data such as sex, age, and accommodation is taken into consideration, nor from the perspective of quality variables (schooling). This diversity enabled the multidimensional presentation of the analyzed topic.

The culture of organization as the factor shaping the worker's awareness

In a time of globalization, when professional mobility is constantly growing, when the liberalization of European markets continues, supported by EU legislation, the world is referred to as a place without boundaries; as, metaphorically speaking, a "global village" (McLuhan 2001). Everyone, regardless of his or her nationality, denomination and culture acquired in the socialization process, can function freely. The main aim of the research conducted is to show how Poles prosper in the Scottish labor market, in a culture unfamiliar to them, determining a specific company organization style; as well as to show the specific cultural situation, the certain type of changes in Polish emigrants' behaviors, their attitude to work; and finally to show the basic factors we can observe when studying national cultures and relations governing their job markets. The research presents the point of view of the 28 respondents. Each of them has their own opinions about working abroad, as well as generally understood principles of the labor market, and life in a different culture. Perhaps predictably, the majority of Poles working in the Scottish market or in big Scottish companies are manual workers. This dependence is reflected in the general situation of the Poles on the British job market, where most of them occupy a low-status professional position. However, regardless of the position in the job market, Polish immigrants have a significant influence on both the Scottish companies as well as on Britain's cultural panorama.

Migration is a phenomenon which ought to be studied by a multidimensional analysis (Lee 1966; Massey et al. 1993). Apart from the economic and political factors which are often the grounds for most of the decisions for going abroad, there are also the cultural aspects, which are present during the adaptation to new environmental conditions.

The notion of culture has been conceptualized throughout the centuries in various more or less condensed and compatible ways. According to

[3] For more information see *Scotland Needs Migrants to Boost Economy and Population,* www.workpermit.com, March 19, 2007.

Antonina Kłoskowska, culture is a relatively "integrated sum comprising the people's behaviors following certain models shared by a given community, formed and acquired in the course of interaction; and containing the products of the above mentioned behaviors" (Kłoskowska 1980, 40). The firms and companies which established patterns, norms and rules which are the ground for their functioning, have created a characteristic system, which is nowadays referred to as the culture of organization.

As can be seen in the foreign job market analysis, cultural relativism is a term which is equally important. It accounts for certain mechanisms of the company's functioning: "The multiplicity of cultures, often substantially different, causes that people raised in one culture and treating the patterns governing this culture as a natural norm, when in touch with other culture, are prone to regard its behavior patterns as awkward, and even condemnable" (Szacka 2003, 83). For the sake of improvement of relations, both the foreign companies and migrants should be characterized by the so-called "cultural world-view relativism," which assumes that all cultures are equal. Owing to such an attitude, the companies can function correctly, and also raises their work effectiveness. However, not all the companies follow this principle.

Coming back to the phenomenon of "culture of organization" introduced to sociological analysis only recently, I would like to explain and highlight the significance of this term for companies active at present. Along with the development of the organization culture area of study, new and more precise definitions appeared. The first attempt at explaining the term was made by Elliott Jacques in 1951. He defined "the organization culture of a company as a habitual and traditional way of thinking and working, shared to some degree by all the workmates, which is has to be acquired by the new members in order for them to be accepted" (Jacques 1951, 251). This definition gave grounds for further study, developing rapidly in the 1980s and continues in the present day. When searching for motives behind this rising interest in the culture of organization, three major issues should be presented as they reflect precisely the core changes of the world in the second half of the 20th century.

The first important signal, confirming the speed of transformations in the area of world organizations, was observed in Japan, whose companies are often associated with low quality goods and services achieved in a short time leading to success on an international level. Another sign of changes was the fall of "Great Britain as the world's industrial leader" (Wiernek 2000, 8), which became the symbol for change in the world economy. The last motive analyzed here is the fact that companies entered a phase of intensified globalization and liberalization of world markets, stimulated by the development of the internet and computer technologies and the resultant heavy competition, which requires constant modification to maintain effectiveness for the internal situation of a company. These and many other reasons for the raising interest in organization culture have led to the creation of new theories and tendencies presented by management experts.

According to one of the most popular definitions, "we can treat the organization culture as a certain programming of a person's mind" (Hofstede and Hofstede 2005). Geert Hofstede highlights in his book *Cultures and Organizations* that "the organization cultures are something different than national cultures, because of the fact that being a member of a given organization is to some extend a matter of choice ... and one can always, at least theoretically, renounce this membership" (Hofstede and Hofstede 2005, 48). It is an essential approach, as it demonstrates how important it is for contemporary firms and organizations to create such an organizational atmosphere which would allow for high results and work effectiveness, and which would make a given organization a place the workers like to identify themselves with.

How should the organization culture be studied to show its most important qualities? Does it appear in all firms and companies? What influence does the national culture and socialization have on organization culture? It is difficult to give a simple straightforward answer if we treat the notion of organization culture as an entity determined only by the inside of a company or a firm. It is also crucial to investigate organization culture on a wider background, see it as an independent variable that is as a phenomenon emerging from the outside of an organization. It is also to be remembered "that it is an independent and autonomous form of expression of human and collective awareness" (Konecki and Tobera 2002, 113).

From the methodological point of view, it is very difficult to isolate all the organization culture elements of a given company, as it is a completely subconscious entity. The integrated model of organization culture has been used in a study series based on both qualitative and quantitative research, enabling the multilevel presentation of the topic.

organization culture

=

organization surrounding

+

collective awareness

+

internal environment of an organization

Fig. 12.1
The integrated model of culture of organization.

The characteristic features of culture of organization in Great Britain according to the views of respondents.

For the appropriate analysis of data from the extended interviews it is important to show a wider context of the analysis, namely the general characteristics of qualities of both countries analyzed. The national culture has a substantial influence on organization culture forming in a company or firm. Great Britain is currently one of the most developed European countries. It is also a country which consequently introduced elements of neoliberal doctrine. Nowadays the level of employment in Great Britain reaches 70%[4] and is one of the highest in Europe. It is a sign of a very good economic situation, as well as a mark of the well functioning British market. Poland is a country influenced initially by the communist system, and then by the process of systemic transformation. It is a country which is still acquiring the bases of liberalism both in economy and in worldview.

The firms and organizations on the Polish market, which are not part of bigger international corporations, try to follow the standards popular in developed countries. Poland, as any other country, has its own rich national culture, values and norms transmitted from one generation to another. This makes its organization culture particular from others. According to the integrated model of organization culture, each country on

[4] See http://epp.eurostat.ec.europa.eu

the basis of its own specific culture creates the grounds for the functioning of different types of organizations.

The cultures of Poland and Great Britain, based on the analysis of secondary data, can be ascribed to two different groups. Poland, together with Russia and Romania, is ascribed to the so-called "polichronic culture of non-persistent expressiveness," a group characterized by ambiguous law and cultural contradictions. Great Britain, together with, for example, Germany or the Netherlands, belongs to "moderate cultures" where recommendation and accepted social hierarchy are essential (Misiak 2004, 8). The study proves that Poles themselves can see the difference, which in a marked way divides those job markets: "It seems to me that all is easier here, faster, more approachable. People are more … maybe not open, but more easy-going. In Poland when you go to work, you're always tensed that you're not going to make it, or you get angry because a guy couldn't do something, or didn't have time … Here, if you come, it's OK. If you stay longer, even better. Everyone minds their own business. Everyone knows how much they work, how long is his lunch break. Everyone deserves everything. These are the differences."

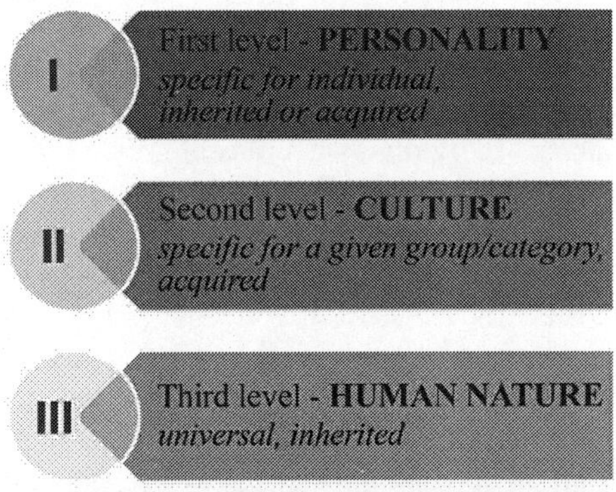

Fig. 12.2
Three levels of a man's mind programming.
Source: Hostfede and Hofstede 2005.

Depending on our birthplace, the place where we grow up and live, our minds are programmed to particular actions, behaviors appropriate to a given situation (Hofstede and Hofstede 2005). The environment in which we exist determines the way of thinking and reacting to the events in our life. According to the study by Geert Hofstede, a man functions within so-called culture layers. These layers have a direct influence on the way our mind is "culturally programmed."

Similarly, Czerska pointed out three levels of analysis: universal, characteristic to all people; collective, common to particular social groups, nations; and individual, concerning the qualities of an individual (Czerska 2003, 9). I will apply these levels of analysis for each cultural dimension characteristic for the national culture according Hofstede.

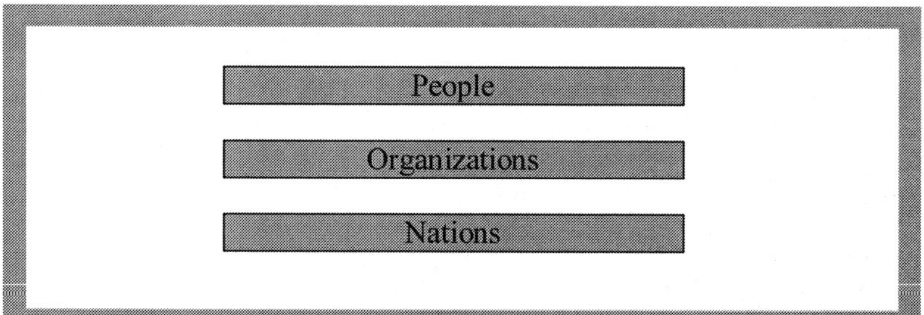

Fig. 12.3
Three levels of data analysis within the group of the respondents.

I will apply these levels of analysis for each cultural dimension characteristic for the national culture according Hofstede: power distance; uncertainty avoidance; individualism; masculinity. Based on variable indicators I have constructed the measure of these dimensions for my respondents. Each of these four were analyzed regarding Polish and Scottish work experience of interviewed people. In the presentation below I will use national characteristics offered by Hofstede as a point of reference. The comparison between the indicator for Poland and for Polish experience of my respondents will serve as a discussion to what extent my respondents are representative of national culture. The indicators for Great Britain in comparison to Scottish experience of my respondents will show in what directions the influences of the new cultural setting follow.

Power distance

One of the most important dimensions presented is the "power distance." It describes the range of expectations and acceptation for the unequal distribution of power, expressed by less influential (subordinate) members of an institution or organization (Hofstede and Hofstede 2005). When organizations are considered, it is the distance between the workers and their superiors, understood as a system of borders which make this division even deeper. In Hofstede's studies the relative value of the distance of power is measured by Power Distance Index (PDI). Its value is described on a scale from 0 to 100, and it shows the level of distance of power in particular countries of the world. In both studies, those of Hofstede, and that which is analyzed in this chapter, the distance was evaluated from the subordinates' perspective.

PDI in Hofstede's research for Poland and Great Britain was 68 and 35 respectively. According to the research of the Scottish market, L-PDI for the Polish emigrants describing their work situation in their homeland was 0.68, and overseas 0.48 (in 0 to 1 scale).

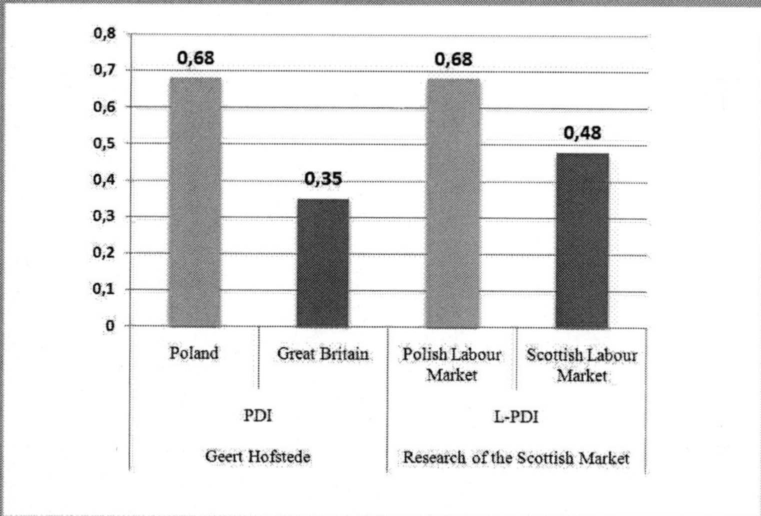

Fig. 12.4
Power distance: the analysis of dimension

The interviews show that the group of respondents tested are people for whom the distance of power characteristic to the Polish market is higher than its Scottish counterpart. When analyzing the distance of power dimension, the indexes were interpreted within three levels of analysis mentioned above. On the individual level this difference can be accounted for in the fact that the majority of respondents were people with secondary education (19/28), with short working life experience gained in the Polish and Scottish markets. Those people, when starting their professional career on the Polish market, where higher education and work experience are crucial to work position, due to their poor practical knowledge, as well as education, are often not taken into consideration in their company's decisions. The period during which their professional position stabilizes, and after which they can influence the company's decisions, is relatively long. Those people, when entering the Scottish market, where skills play the most decisive role, and the management style is more flexible, more often participate in the life of the organization than when working in Poland.

This can be seen first of all in the second level of the analysis, which is the organization. According to the research conducted, in the respondents' views the Scottish companies are characterized in most cases by casual informal relations between the superiors and the subordinates. As far as the distance of power in Polish organizations is concerned, the model of centralized structures continues to dominate. The authorities play a significant role, and the differences in payments are relatively large, which influences the analysis of this dimension as well as the L-PDI characterizing the Polish and the Scottish job market, in the eyes of the examined respondents.

The last element with a decisive influence on the marked difference between the two indexes discussed for the investigated group are the national factors within which the socialization of the respondents had taken place. One of the main reasons which may have impact on the level of the distance of power in the societies described is, according to Geert Hofstede, the political systems which shape national cultures. He claims that revolutionary change and an unstable governing system causes the increase of the distance of power index. Polish democracy is a very young system, and still impeded as the process of political transformation, traumatic for many Poles, has embedded the conception that those who have power are usually rich, and those who have worked to achieve their current financial position are in most cases criminals, or cheaters: "communism strengthened the opinion that a rich man is a bloodsucker, an exceptionally destructive person."[5] Therefore, the political factors have great influence on the way Polish society is described—it is still a divided organism. The Polish continue to find it difficult to place themselves on the political spectrum between two extremities: liberal and multi-conservative. According to Hofstede, it is right-wing governing, present in Poland, that raises the level of L-PDI. On one hand, Polish society

[5] Skąpska Grażyna, *Poverty and Wealth in Polish Culture and Awareness,* 2003: http://wyborcza.pl/1,75517,1594586.html, (accessed June 10, 2008).

considers itself poor and often demands the introduction of the progress tax[6]; on the other, it supports the lineal tax with which they could save money. Such disharmony is seen also in the other areas of respondents' life, who say that more liberal views in Scottish society influence the L-PDI level in Scottish organizations, which is relatively speaking higher than in the case of Polish market.

When comparing Hofstede's results with the results of the study of Polish emigrants on the Scottish market, the only significant difference is the higher value of L-PDI with respect to PDI for Scotland. Hofstede's study, treated as the background for the analysis of a specific group of the tested respondents, establishes the main tendencies, enumerated by the Dutch scientist. The respondents' opinions on the Scottish and Polish market reflect to a great extend Hofstede's results. The higher value of L-PDI (0.48) for Scotland in comparison to Great Britain (0.35) is caused by the fact that the evaluation of Scottish companies was made by the Poles themselves. Their views on Scotland are therefore filtered through their Polish perception of these phenomena

Individualism – Collectivism

Another very important dimension of national cultures is placing a given society on the scale of individualism and collectivism (IDV). According to Hofstede, individualism is characteristic of societies in which relations between the individuals are lax and everyone is focused on themselves and their nearest family, whereas collectivism is usually associated with the societies in which people live in strong, coherent groups. These groups protect them throughout life, and their members reciprocate with unquestionable loyalty (Hofstede and Hofstede 2005). The individualism criterion put forward by Hofstede is to a great extent characterized as an attitude suggesting self-interest, praising equality, and respect and independence of an individual. Sometimes it also reveals a high level of hedonism.

Individualistic society is usually connected with liberal economy and with the significant role of an individual in the job market. Cultures with low IDV are societies for which the collective awareness is the basis of existence. It can be seen through public opinion on interpersonal relations and active participation in public life, which is also the ground of functioning, as well as a reflection of an individual's position in the

---

[6] http://biznes.interia.pl/news/polacy-to-komunisci,1089036 (accessed June 10, 2008).

society. Considering the above mentioned elements of the individualism–collectivism dimension, it seems that it is easy to place both British and Polish society on the spectrum mentioned. In practice, however, it is not so obvious and indisputable.

According to Hofstede's research, the values of IDV for Poland and Great Britain are respectively 60 and 89. In my research, the values of L-IDV were 0.44 and 0.54 for the opinions of the respective countries.

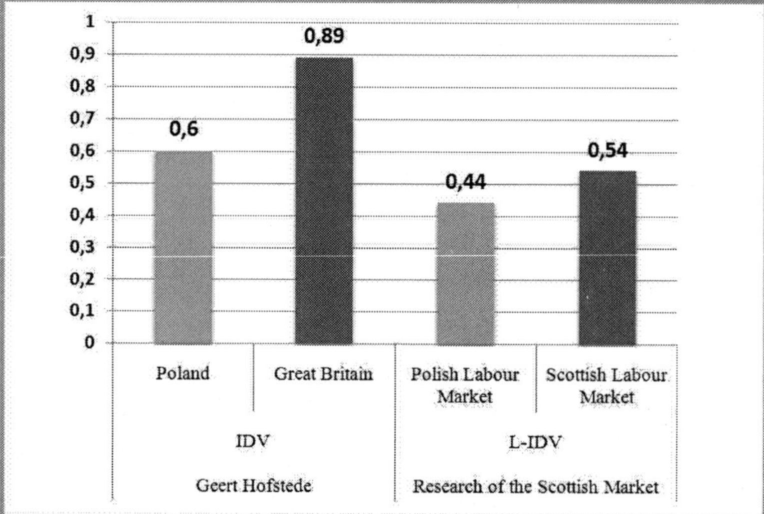

Fig. 12.5
Individualism–collectivism: analysis of the dimension.

It is easy to spot the difference between the two studies as far as the level of individualism in both countries is concerned. In Hofstede's analysis the difference was markedly higher in the case of Poland and Great Britain. This difference also appears in the studies conducted, and it concerns the Polish and the Scottish market. Why then did the Scottish market, in the eyes of the examined respondents, receive an L-IDV not much higher (0.1) than the Polish market?

For the correct analysis of this dimension a question has to be asked: are the Poles a strictly individualistic orientated nation? The reasons for determining Polish society in this way are to be investigated in the methodological approach to study on the level of individualism in the particular countries, and Hofstede's studies are often questioned in this dimension. What comes as a surprise, first of all, is the relatively high level of individualism in Polish society. The factors weakening individualism are the remnants of the socialist mentality and Catholicism as the dominating religion. The project GLOBE investigates the cultural programming of minds, and has been correlated with Hofstede's 100 degrees scale. It shows that the level of individualism in Poland is 35.29 in respect to work individualism, and 21.15 in respect to family individualism.[7] These indexes markedly differ from the IDV proposed by Hofstede.

As far as the Hofstede's individualism–collectivism dimension is concerned, is it possible that the factors for Polish society were estimated in a wrong way? Definitely not—they simply describe Polish society from another perspective, because Hofstede in his research disregarded the societal qualities concerning consolidation, national solidarity and the relations of small social groups, and focused on independence and identification with organization, which were the most important elements to him.

The differences accounting for the low (0.54) level of individualism among the respondents of the Scottish market were searched for on the three main levels of dimensions analysis presented. It appeared that most significant for the discussed dimension was national conditioning, which determines to a large degree the psychological profile (personality) of the examined respondents, whereas the organizational factors characteristic to given companies have actually a secondary influence on the perception of the individualism–collectivism dimension with respect to the Scottish market.

When analyzing the opinions of Polish workers on the Scottish market, a theory can be advanced: despite the high level of individualism (IDV), characteristic to the British market, that the importance of liberal values clashed with a collectivistic approach of the examined Polish workers does not have a significant influence on Polish attitudes within this dimension. It appears that the national values formed in the socialization process are very durable, and despite a minimal rise (0.1) with respect to a factor characterizing the situation of the examined people on the Polish market (0.44) did not undergo substantial changes after emigration to Scottish market.

We can therefore see that within the analyzed dimension, referring first of all to psychosocial qualities and values, the Scottish market, in a minimal way, modifies the psychological profile of the examined

---

[7] "Cultural Influences on Leadership and Organisations: Project GLOBE, Boston 1998," from Żakowska Magdalena, *Polish Dilemmas of an Asocial Collectivist,* 2006; http://www.racjonalista.pl/kk.php/s,4615/k,2 (accessed June 10, 2008).

respondents, oriented on the collectivistic values during the socialization process in Polish society—the significance of an organization is not the leading element.

To sum up this dimension of the analysis, the Polish attitudes and values based on the conducted research can be described as characteristic to the balanced type, where collective values and individualistic values are interwoven.

Masculinity

One of the dimensions of national cultures most difficult to describe and study analyzed in the research was that referring to the oldest dichotomous divisions of the world: the gender division. Hofstede calls it the masculinity–femininity dimension. During the research of IBM companies, two factors which significantly differentiated the national cultures were distinguished as male and female.

It was proven that men are more attached to such vales as earnings and promotion, whereas the relations with the superiors are more important to women. The information available on Hofstede's website[8] says that the masculinity index (MAS) for Poland and Great Britain are respectively 64 and 66 (in the 1-to-100 scale). They are high and do not differ much, which means that both Poland and Great Britain belong to the group of countries in which the social roles connected with gender are clearly defined, which consequently means that men are to be assertive, strict, and success oriented, whereas women are expected to be modest, caring and feminine (Hofstede and Hofstede 2005).

The study conducted on the group of Polish emigrants on the Scottish market did not confirm in a direct way the masculine characteristics of Polish society. Among the 40 answers to questions on the masculinity–femininity dimension for the Polish market, only 17 people revealed the tendency to choose scalled masculine factors. The masculinity index (L-MAS) for the Polish market was 0.43, and for the Scottish market 0.38. It is the first dimension in which my studies and Hofstede's studies markedly differ, both in the values of the indexes and in the reversed relation between the two analyzed markets. Polish emigrants, according to the research of the Scottish market, can in most cases be characterized as a society with a low level of masculine features. After re-analyzing the data

[8] http://www.geert-hofstede.com (accessed June 6, 2008).

collected in both a quantitative and qualitative way, the results become clearer than in the initial analyses.[9]

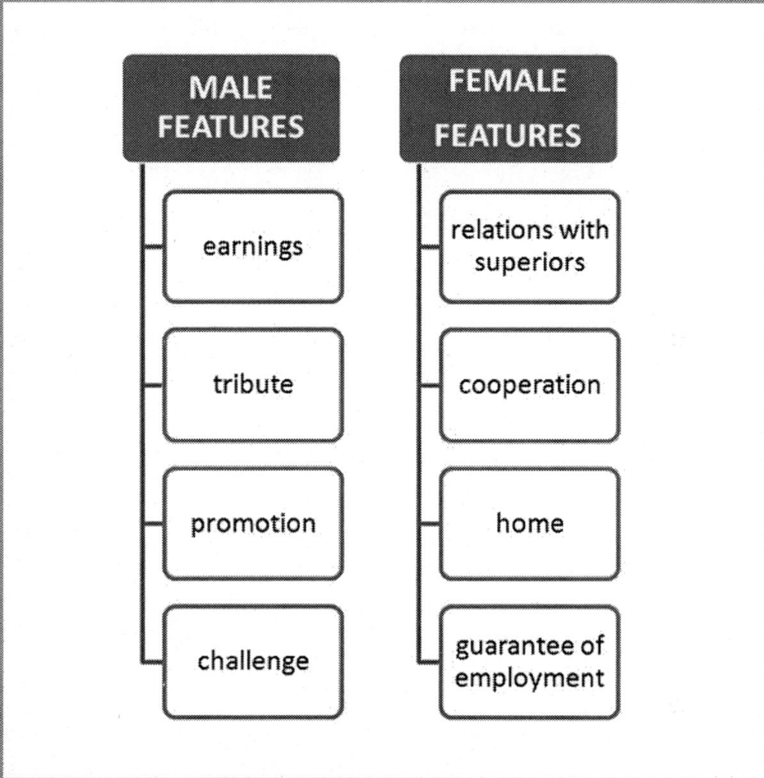

Fig. 12.6
Male and female features of national cultures.

Most of the people examined are people working in the Scottish market as unqualified workers, whose professional ambitions have been stopped in favor of everyday work, which does not provide them with great chances of development. These reasons caused, in the opinion of the Poles interviewed, such values as work security and cooperation in a given working environment to become for them the most important. This

[9] Based on: Hofstede Geert and Gert Jan Hofstede, *Cultures And Organizations: Software For The Mind*, (New York: McGraw-Hill, 2005), 115–162.

approach compensated, to some degree, the lack of work and professional development, which the examined group experienced in the Polish job market: "I would say that what has made the biggest impression on me here is that the work is actually there. When you go to an agency and you have some qualifications, they will simply find you this work. Maybe not straight away on the position that you would like, but in the area, in such a department where you would enjoy working," says one of Polish emigrants.

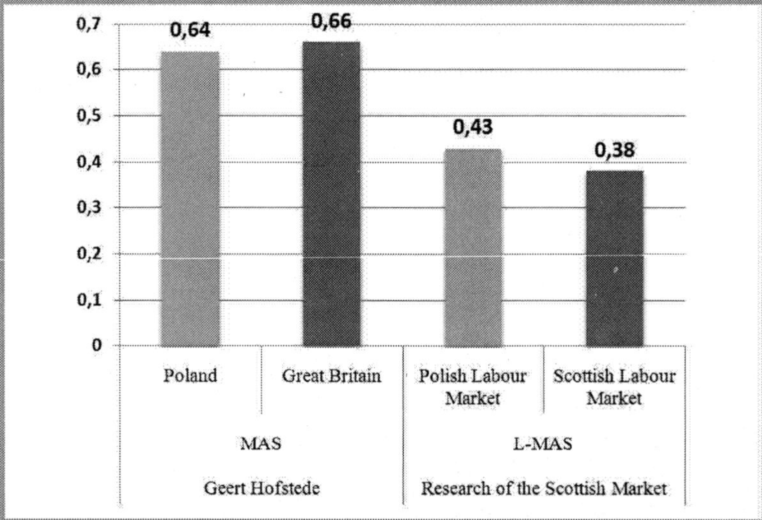

Fig. 12.7
Masculinity–Femininity: analysis of the table

As we can see on the basis of the above analyses, the differences in the indexes presented are to be located not only between national or organizational factors. The radical change of attitude to work in this characteristic of feminine societies was caused by the change in the psychological component of the individual's attitudes, for whom the lack of possibility to realize the above mentioned needs on the Polish job market lead to the fact that values concerning them have become more important while working in Scotland.

Uncertainty avoidance

The final stage of the national culture analysis, with Hofstede's study as background, was the discussion of the last dimension of Uncertainty Avoidance, measured by the Uncertainty Avoidance Index (UAI). The value of this index is measured first of all by: "stress connected with the feeling of danger, unawareness, the feeling of lost and life insecurity … higher readiness for aggression, fight, taking risk."[10] The basic assumption which should be taken into consideration at the very beginning is the fact that Polish emigrants are characterized by a feeling of insecurity regarding their work situation. This was the main ad hoc hypothesis put forward, from which it was possible to assume that the studies conducted in the Scottish market would confirm this hypothesis. Hofstede's indexes for Poland and Great Britain are respectively 93 and 35. In this research, however, they are 0.63 and 0.59.

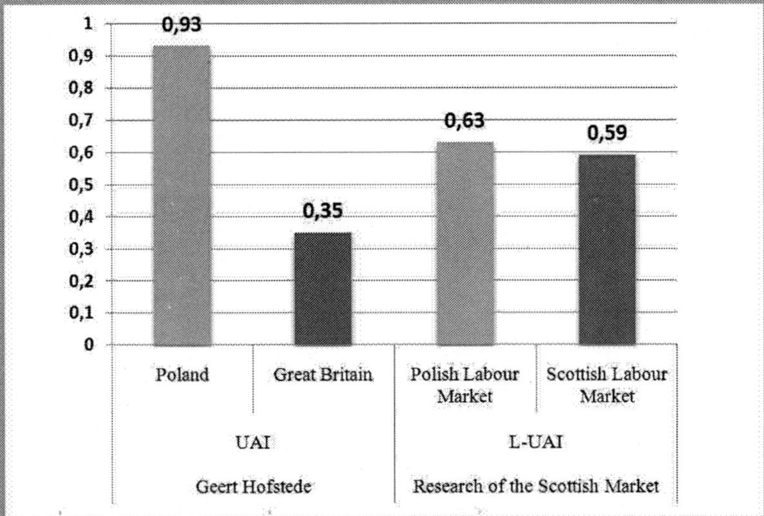

Fig. 12.8
Uncertainty avoidance: analysis of the dimension.

[10] Magdalena Żakowska, "Organization Culture of Polish Business According to Culture Programming Criteria by G.Hofstede," in *Culture and Economy,* edited by Janusz Mucha, Maria Nawojczyk and Grażyna Woroniecka, (Tychy: Śląskie Wydawnictwo Naukowe, 2004).

Such distribution of values shows that the organization culture in Great Britain, and to be more precise in Scotland, influences a minimal degree on the level of uncertainty among the Polish workers by lowering it with respect to the values estimated for the Polish job market. Both indexes do not show a great disproportion in comparison with Hofstede's study. The reason why the two indexes do not differ so much (0.4) is the fact that the examined group of respondents were equipped with certain personality features, specific for emigrants, characterized by a greater inclination to taking risks, which in most cases brought positive outcomes, the consequence of a slight decrease in the level of uncertainty among Polish workers on the Scottish job market. The difference between L-UAI estimated for the Polish market according to the examined people's opinion and UAI can be explained by the national qualities of Polish society representatives, who often combine "fatalism and disbelief in their capacities with the trust in wise and well-wishing providence."[11] What decides a high or low level of uncertainty avoidance is the configuration of personality features, often dependent on the basic national qualities acquired during socialization.

To sum up the analyses I conducted within the four basic dimensions, it can be stated that apart from the national and organizational factors which obviously heavily influence worker awareness, there are also personality features which in many cases come to be decisive as far as adopted attitudes to work are concerned. Apart from a purely analytical aspect, the interpretation conducted was to prove the fact that despite the number of essential frameworks and indexes, which in various ways define worker attitudes within different national cultures, as well as the understanding of the cultures themselves, it is indispensable to approach the quantitative studies with a hint of suspicion. The truth is that the decisive role in such an analysis is played by changeable situations, such as the time of the study, the group examined or even social moods depending on many economic or social aspects. Nevertheless, the studies of national cultures on the organization level raise many interesting questions and touch on many socio-cultural problems, which are crucial for the understanding of contemporary societies evolution.

11 Ibid., 86

Conclusion

Globalization causes the contemporary world to head for a widely understood universalism, providing us with the possibility to cross borders, which was not possible a few decades ago. Disregarding the ideological judgments of this process, it is worth highlighting that it is a phenomenon which determines significantly the workers' ways of thinking in the 21st century.

The basic question analyzed in this chapter was the way in which the Poles find themselves in a foreign country, and how the norms and values of Scottish society influenced their attitudes to work. The analysis of the collected data on the basis of results received has raised the greatest controversies, because the factors analyzed due to too small a number did not give data which would enable generalization of the results. Nevertheless, on the basis of the interviews supported by the limited quantitative data analysis, an image of a Polish emigrant can be drawn who every day functions in a society much more liberal than Poland, but who does not forget about the collectivistic values and ideals acquired during socialism. This is a person who appreciates work stability and work atmosphere, typically feminine qualities if we consider Hofstede's analysis.

The Scottish work market, when compared to Poland, is characterized by a lower index of the distance of power, which is reflected in the soft type of company management, which is characterized by more informal relations between the workers and their superiors. It is also worth underlining that it mostly concerns qualified groups of workers, because among other workers this dependence is not confirmed in the conducted research. Moreover, in many Scottish companies, the old model of management could be observed, which negatively influences the work effectiveness and relations in the eyes of respondents. As far as Scottish national culture is concerned, its influence alters a company's organizational character in only a moderate way. These companies are inclined to appreciate not only economic but also cultural values of the foreign workers.

In this analysis it was also essential to answer the question: why should we investigate the organization cultures and worker attitudes in foreign job markets? In the contemporary world, where people are much more divided, but have so much in common, it is important to notice certain relations which appear on the borders of cultures, and in the future will determine changes in the job markets as well as more profound changes, concerning for instance the worldview matters or the discussed programming of minds.

Currently, the modeling of work attitude of workers functioning abroad is influenced mostly by organizational and personality conditioning, which depends mostly on work atmosphere, directly connected with the group of reference, which shapes inter-worker relations. More importantly, work attitudes are influenced by the management system of a company, which in different cases may be based on a consultation or limitation model of worker participation in the company decision-making process. All the above factors are connected with the reasons for Polish emigration to the Scottish job market. They established the aims for the examined workers and the goals they would like to follow. They determined in advance the way of perceiving reality, which was consequently connected with their personality features acquired during socialism in their homeland.

Work is one of the most significant features of human life, thanks to which people can discover their weaknesses, identify their skills and influence one anothers' lives. It is to be remembered, however, that the relation of an individual to work is not a one-sided relation, and that there is interaction between the two. A question can be asked: how can work, as a sphere of life partly designed by people, influence them? The answer is very simple: it is national cultures that, in a greater that suspected way, shapes in the present day the formation of norms and rules governing organizations, and consequently have an impact on attitudes to work of people living in them.

References

Babbie, Earl. *The Practice of Social Research,* Belmont CA: Thomson/Wadswoth, 2004.

Cultural Influences on Leadership and Organisations: Project GLOBE, Boston 1998, From: Żakowska Magdalena. 2006. *Polish Dilemmas of an Asocial Collectivist,* http://www.racjonalista.pl/kk.php/s,4615/k,2 (accessed June 12, 2008).

Czerska, Małgorzata. *Zmiana kulturowa w organizacji. Wyzwania dla współczesnego menedżera* [*Cultural Change in Organization.* Challenges for a Contemporary Manager]. Warszawa: DIFIN, 2003.

Duszczyk, Maciej. *Emigrować i wracać. Migracje zarobkowe Polaków po 1 maja 2004r.* [To Emigrate and to Come Back. Migrations of the Poles after 1st May 2004]. Warszawa: Instytut Spraw Publicznych, 2006.
http://www.isp.org.pl/files/25728396201963370011631563O2.pdf (accessed June 12, 2008).

Duszczyk, Maciej, Wiśniewski Jakub. *Analiza społeczno-demograficzna migracji zarobkowej Polaków do państw EOG po 1 maja 2004 roku* [*Socio-demographic Analysis of Money Migrations of Poles to EEA after 1st May 2004*]. Warszawa: Instytut Spraw Publicznych, 2007. http://www.msz.gov.pl/files/docs/DKiP/ekspertyza-isp-finalny%2024%2004%2007.pdf (accessed June 12, 2008).

Main Statistics Office. *Information on the size and directions of the immigration from Poland from 2004 to 2006*. 2007. http://www.stat.gov.pl/gus/45_3583_PLK_HTML.htm (accessed June 12, 2008).

Hofstede, Geert and Gert Jan Hofstede. *Cultures And Organizations: Software For The Mind*. New York: McGraw-Hill, 2005.

Jacques, Elliot. *The changing Culture of a Factory*. Londyn: Tavistock, 1951.

Kłoskowska, Antonina. *Kultura masowa. Krytyka i obrona*. [*Mass culture. Criticism and Defence*]. Warszawa: Wydawnictwo Naukowe PWN, 1980.

Konecki Krzysztof and Piotr Tobera. *Szkice z socjologii zarządzania*. [*Drafts from Sociology of Management*]. Łódź: Wydawnictwo Uniwersytetu Łódzkiego, 2002.

Lee, Everett S. "A Theory of Migration." *Demography* 3(1) (1966): 47–57.

Massey, Douglas, Joaquin Arango, Graeme Hugo, Kouaouci, Ali Pellegrino Adela, Edward Taylor. *Theories of international migration: review and appraisal, Population and Development Review*. New York: Population Council, 1993.

McLuhan, Marshall. "The Gutenberg Galaxy." In *Essential McLuhan*. Edited by Eric McLuhan and Frank Zingrone. New York: Basic Books, 1995.

Misiak, Władysław, *Narodowe cechy kultury organizacyjnej w biznesie* [*National Qualities of the Organization Culture in Business*]. Warszawa: Wydawnictwo Uniwersytetu Warszawskiego, 2004.

Nowicka, Magdalena. "A Competition Society? The Attitudes to Work in Poland and in European Union Countries." *European Studies* 4 (1999): 51–73.

Skąpska Grażyna. *Bieda i bogactwo w polskiej kulturze i świadomości* [*Poverty and Wealth in Polish Culture and Awareness*]. 2003. http://wyborcza.pl/1,75517,1594586.html (accessed June 10, 2008).

Szacka Barbara. *Wstęp do socjologii* [*Introduction to Sociology*]. Warszawa: Oficyna Naukowa, 2003.

Wiernek Bogusław. *Kultura Organizacyjna Przedsiębiorstwa* [*Organizational Culture of Enterprise*]. Kraków: Oficyna Wydawnicza TEXT, 2000.

Żakowska Magdalena. "Kultura organizacyjna polskiego biznesu wedlug kryteriów zaprogramowania kulturowego Geerta Hofstede" ["Organization Culture of Polish Business According to Culture Programming Criteria by G.Hofstede"]. In *Kultura i gospodarka*. Edited by Janusz Mucha, Maria Nawojczyk, and Grażyna Woroniecka. Tychy: Ślaskie Wydawnictwo Naukowe, 2007.

CHAPTER THIRTEEN

THE IMPACT OF CULTURE ON THE FUNCTIONING PROCESS OF SMALL ARAB COMPANIES

MARIA STOJKOW[1]

Introduction

At present, with political transformation in the Middle East and the growing interest in the economic cooperation with this region on the part of western countries, the detailed analysis of factors which determine the functioning of enterprises seems particularly important. Differences in the ways in which enterprises function are due to many factors. Economic factors, such as the level of economic development or market conditioning play an important role, as well as factors such as the political and legal system. However, it must not be forgotten that the way in which an economic activity is run is influenced by the specific cultural pattern concerning this sphere of human activity. Not all societies consider the categories of rationality, effectiveness and rate of action equally essential in the running of a business. In the social system, all of these factors influence one another, conditioning the specific entrepreneurship and business culture; it is thanks to them that entrepreneurs take action which they regard as rational and which helps them run their own economic activity in the best way possible.

Societies understand the notion of running a business in various ways. This is often influenced by numerous factors, in particular the cultural and political. The basis of this chapter is a pattern reconstruction of the Arab organizational culture, based on analysis of research data from Damascus, which will be used as its empirical illustration. In an attempt to reconstruct the way small trade companies function in Damascus, I will concentrate on

[1] Faculty of Humanities, AGH University of Science and Technology, Krakow.

the analysis of the Islamic state of mind and the research carried out with small business owners in Damascus between 2005 to 2007. The research was conducted by means of in-depth interviews and a survey. During both stages of the research, non-probability sampling was applied. The first was the snowball method, which depends on the random selection of respondents who are identified by those previously questioned (Babbie 2006). While the snowball method ensured respondents were questioned in a quantative respect, the other method of sampling was also applied, the so-called purposive sampling.

The influence of national culture on relations within a company as well as on the entrepreneur attitude will also be analysed. An area of special interest will be the tendency of entrepreneurs to display innovative behaviour, or lack of it. Attention will also be paid to such elements as analysis of classical Arab thought, particularly Islamic, regarding the question of economy and labor.

Islamic Economic Philosophy

Every social system provides its members with its own formula for ideal life and society. Every economic perspective, being a subsystem of beliefs, works out its own criteria of maximization, explaining, among other things, how to achieve the state of a society established on the basis of superior principles. The decisions and acts of both consumer and producer are a function of what they desire to maximize. Different perceptions of what should be maximized, e.g. profit, utility, social justice, equality or a "place in heaven," as well as the issue of whose satisfaction should be maximized—the individual, the collective or God—all require a wide set of mechanisms, social and economical institutions and social behaviors. The sum of such fundamental elements determines economical philosophy. The way economical systems function is influenced by this normative set of values and beliefs (Nomani and Rahnema 1994, 21).

Analyzing the evolution of business in the Arabic world, Władysław Misiak distinguishes three periods: the first is tribal; the second is linked with the appearance of the Prophet Muhammad, and what followed with a phase of forming new rules in trade, manufacturing and economy; the third a period of modernization, which is mainly connected with the growth of countries producing and exporting petroleum (Misiak 2004, 129). This period is tightly linked with the modernization of the Arabic area, though realized to a different extent in economic, technological and infrastructural perspective. The way present day businessmen and merchants function not only in Syria but in the whole of the Arabic world is influenced by tradition linked with the Prophet. His *sunnah* and *hadiths* are a basis for trade and business behavior in particular situations, as well as the prestige they are granted till the present day (Misiak 2004, 130). According to Islamic rules, the worshippers are to follow the path laid down by the Qur'an and tradition, recognizing the principle of authority as the main guide post in the selection and realization of lifestyle. This path is demonstrated by the prophet's words: "Avoid what I have forbidden, and do what I ordered to the best of your ability. The people who lived before you were lost because of their question and disagreement with their Prophet" (an-Nawawi's tradition), (Mrozek 1967, 141).

The Prophet himself is the highest authority and transcendent role model for a Muslim. As he was a merchant himself and his whole life was linked with trade, many traditions referring to this issue are visible today. General respect for authority, commitment to the continuity of social standards of conduct, understanding knowledge as a source of information about the past, as a closed and ultimate field, "constituting a kind of museum," went hand in hand with the conviction of the imminent collapse of man with mistrust in his cognitive capabilities and would lead to religiosity.

The interest was not targeted at the essence of internal life of an individual, but to the revival of perfect and improved standards of behavior. The subject of interest for Islamic moralists is not the human personality and various forms of its manifestation, but common characteristics, being of particular value for the proper functioning of the groups of the faithful, the characteristics acting as a paragon, as an illustration of the general concept that has served to create the "wisdom of life." The model for merchant or businessman was established in a similar fashion.

Haram or Halal—What an Arab Merchant is Allowed To Do

A Muslim can earn money even during his pilgrimage, only if it does not interfere with important religious obligations (Qur'an 1986, 850). The same priority is given to the merchants by the tradition, placing them on the same level as martyrs (Mrozek 1967, 183). Fernand Braudel recalls the words of Muhammad, who said "a merchant enjoy happiness both on this and the other world" and "God loves those who earn money" (Braudel 1985). The authors researching the relations between Islam and business, and trying to determine the place of merchants in the social structure, recall the words of the Prophet: "[the] righteous and trustworthy merchant is associated with the prophets, righteous and Martyrs." Muhammad should be a paragon for a Muslim in conducting business.

Each religion defines the issue of wealth very clearly. As a system, Islam is well integrated. Islam in Arab countries determines all aspects of the social life as well as economic life (Nomani and Rahnema 1994). The actions of people living in the western world rely on calculations of goal achievement. In Arab countries, however, the actions of the Muslim person rely on divine law. In this system, each economic rule must be analyzed to check if it is in compliance with Islamic axioms and *sharia.* Economic goals such as optimalisation and maximalisation cannot be a criteria of judgment but they can be useful if they help to realize the goals of Islam.

Islam forbids the waste or misuse of wealth (Klöcker 2002, 142). The Qur'an warns against wealth related dangers, the main of which is abandoning God and the practices of Islam. Trade should not have any influences on fulfilling the basic duties of a Muslim person, such as prayer, fast and charity. Wealth in itself is a positive category in Islam because the profits of a company serve the whole of society.

Islamic trade traditions resemble free market rules, the rule of competition among businesses the same. Islam supports competition in many areas of life such as gaining wealth, customers and friends. Islam promotes success because it contributes to the development of the individual and the society (Kietliński 2005, 57).

Work is valued as confirmation of a person's worth and dignity, each aspect of human activity being perceived as service to God (Klöcker 2002, 93). The ultimate aim of economic activity is obtaining God's blessing, hence consumption is limited by the Qur'an, and idleness is considered a sin. The Qur'an forbids exploitation and child labor. In most Arab countries a work-free day had not been determined for a long time, with work stopping on Fridays for prayer only. At present, Friday is the only officially determined work-free day of the week.

There is a clear division of actions in Islam. These can be halal, which means allowed, and haram, which is forbidden or neutral. Similarly, commercial transactions are divided into acceptable and unacceptable. An example of an allowable way of earning is work, and a forbidden one is gambling (Tripp 2006). Generally, the Qur'an has introduced three essential norms: the prohibition of usury, gambling and the rule of shared responsibility for all parties of financial relation.

The basic issue originating from the religious system and connected with all economic actions is the statement that a Muslim rents property from God (Kietliński 2005, 55). Thus, they bear the responsibility of using it in the proper way in front of God. Opulence appears in numerous verses of the Qur'an as a danger, diverting the human being from God. However, neither wealth nor poverty are treated in Islam as a personal merit or punishment, as God himself is responsible for these differences (Kietliński 2005,142). There are three types of property in Islamic law: personal, common and the so-called "dead hand" property, mainly in religious foundations (Danecki 1997, 250). The most important rule of Muslim law connected with economic issues is *zakat*. Some consider *zakat* to be alms, whereas some think it is a kind of a tax. Regardless of the name, its role in the Islamic system is fundamental. The Qur'an and *sunnah* regulate *zakat* strictly. It is taken from all Muslims and unlike a typical tax, it is calculated from the whole of wealth possessed and not from the annual income (Danecki 2002, 144). In every school of law, minimum assets on the basis of which this tax was calculated were different, and discussion about it lasted several centuries. As a result, a complex system of calculating, collecting and dividing the tax was created. Property, possessions and income are divided into several categories (crop and fruit yield, farm animals, gold and silver, and personal property), and the tax is from 2.5% to 10% within each category. There is a minimal level of income called *nisab,* below which the property is not charged with *zakat* (Choudhury 1986, 51). *Zakat* can be directly given to the poor, or to social welfare funds. In certain countries, *zakat* is officially collected by the state e.g. in Pakistan or Saudi Arabia (Danecki 2002, 145). Moreover, the Shiites are obliged to pay *khums*, 1/5th of annual income, which in the past was given directly to the imam. In contemporary Iran, *khums* is only in the hands of the Shiite clergy. *Zakat* retained such a function up to the present day. It is contrasted with voluntary alms called *sadata* (Dziekan 2001, 363). Taxes such as *khums*, mandatory for a Muslim, are not all— Islam suggests each person should also participate in various charitable actions referring to his family and the poor.

The Spirit of Entrepreneurship

In running one's own business, the individualist approach as well as innovation and predisposition to take risks is extremely important. Therefore, when looking at Arabic culture, one should take into account these characteristics. Islam presupposes predestination (Mrozek 1967, 139). The formalism of Muslim religious practices in principle excludes the individual contribution of the human being, theoretically ruling out any individual human contribution. The most important duty of a Muslim is a prayer performed five times a day. When saying prayer, the Muslim sticks to the rules and does not add anything so as not to make any personal contact with God, instead reciting verses from the Qur'an. There are also additional ritual actions e.g. ablution, facing the direction of Mecca, spreading the mat and a series of body movements. These activities are also defined and have their origins in the Qur'an, and their comprehensive practice is as important as the prayer. The introduction of additional movements, which are not discussed in the Qur'an, invalidates the prayer. The formal, external nature of prayer can be exemplified by the fact that the Muslim praying with rosary beads can do this wherever they are, without even breaking from conversation. The sources of such passiveness can be found in the Qur'an containing precise formulas referring to such aspects as fasting, pilgrimage, prayer, specified food, all without addressing the responsibility for one's own life. According to researchers of Islam, such a formalized form of religious practice is at the heart of Muslim passiveness. Muslims are to follow the predetermined path; The Prophet is the highest role model to be followed; and the same applies to conducting business activities.

Another significant issue is accumulating wealth and the attitude of the respondents towards it. Involving religious precepts, the respondents pointed out that a person has a right to possess a business and wealth, but they must pay for this; in another words, they must share with others. The freezing of wealth is forbidden–a Muslim entrepreneur must incessantly accumulate and amass their wealth, and the money must bring profit. A host of respondents invoked the following verse from the Qur'an: "People who hide their money will burn at the stake built by Allah out of the very some money!" Therefore, an entrepreneur must continuously create something new and share their money.

A form of forcing people to economic activity is *zakat*. Everyone is obliged to give away the minimum 2.5 % of their possessed wealth every year, so if it's not amassed, it can be easily spent on *zakat*. *Zakat* also forces people to invest as it is not required to be paid from investments, as opposed to luxury. *Zakat* is not regulated by law but no incidents of disobeying have been noted. The legal norms are evaded while the religious ones are commonly accepted and obeyed. *Zakat* can therefore be considered the legally sanctioned element of building the spirit of the entrepreneurship.

Available data suggests that, at least in a few indicators of what entrepreneurship is, or in behaviors an entrepreneur should exhibit, there is a deficit of so-called spirit of entrepreneurship in the Arab society. It is visible first of all in the attitude towards risk, which is rejected particularly strongly in Muslim countries for religious reasons. It is demonstrated in the lack of an enterprising attitude at the very start, e.g. in the method of gathering the capital necessary to start a company. The entrepreneurs in the Middle East don`t take risks, for example borrowing money from the bank; instead they wait as long as necessary until they have collected enough money with the help of their family, or of their community.

Similarly, an Arab entrepreneur does not prepare for competition with his rivals, considering ignoring them to be the best strategy, in the belief that the market is big enough for everybody. It relates to Arab fatalism and the constant use of the term *insha`Allah,* which assumes that everything depends on God`s will, whereas human activity is not necessary at all. The competitive tactic adopted by an Arab entrepreneur is to compromise with his rivals, therefore we can state that the dominant ways of determining their own position on the market are indicative of a lack of enterprising attitude among Arab merchants.

Arab entrepreneurs usually act spontaneously, without determining any time perspective. The effects of this are that the plan of action includes the most immediate tasks, but there is no overall aim the respondents would like to achieve. The changes they allow are limited in their extent and are gradually introduced, the aims determined involving little risk. An Arab entrepreneur does not follow novelties, tending to be wary of them. Each change is perceived as a danger, and additionally rooted in the religious disinclination to change means the Arab entrepreneurs remain traditionalists.

Education and training do not play an important part in Arab entrepreneurship. They are not a basis for setting up one`s own shop nor contribute in any way to its functioning. The dominant role is of customs and tradition, as well as so-called "good trader`s stories," stories in the oral tradition of success and failure of other entrepreneurs, especially those significant in the local community. As education is not an important factor we can assume that this is the same among Syrian entrepreneurs. Although more educated, they remain faithful to tradition and believe in its strength and significance in running one`s own economic activity. Things such as economic reports, expert appraisal or a business plan seem to be unimportant for an Arab trader, focus on the present day having a dominant position in their way of thinking.

The dominant motivation for his actions is concentrated on public opinion and it`s connection with prestige, power and profit, and one of the most important indicators of success is maintaining the continuity of the company, especially when it has been run for generations. To open their own enterprise, Arab merchants usually borrow money from their close friends, avoiding any risks, such as borrowing from the bank. The negative attitude towards risk is also visible in the tactics of competition which they adopt. The most common strategy is ignoring competition, and not actively engaging with it. When assessing their own role in the company, the Arab entrepreneurs stressed that it`s them who increase the capital; they are seldom related to formalized roles in the company`s structure. A low percentage of the respondents identified with the role of an innovator, instead, the ordinary tasks of a merchant were pointed out. It is also worth stressing that an Arab entrepreneur is clearly dependent on God`s will: it is this and not his actions that are responsible for his success, or lack of it.

Arab Organizational Culture

When characterizing Arabic organizational culture, one could call it chaotic (Bjerke 2000). Several elements of this culture, so amazingly different and distinct, are worth mentioning in detail. One of the fundamental management problems in Arab society referred to by many authors is the way in which time is valued. Added to external pressures, its effective use is made even more difficult due to various factors: the weaknesses of the economic and organizational infrastructure (technological, transport and communication problems etc); restrictions arising from the sphere of professional and private life; the role of a director of the company and the community, linked with the commitments to the extended family; reluctance to transfer authority and duties; the style of contacts focused on one person; or the immense amount of rituals and customs involved in conducting business (Muna 1980, 90–91). Another element characterizing the mechanism of Arab company management mentioned by the interviewed businessmen is the lack of discipline and industrial mentality, which manifests itself in the aversion to systems and procedures, a lack of organization, and particularly the lack of skills and willingness to delegate, or any professional attitude in business practice. All these elements, strongly rooted in culture, require a lot of additional time from a person managing an Arab company, thus contributing to a lower efficiency of work.

The Role of the Family in Arab Business

When trying to define an Arab merchant we should pay attention to several elements. Firstly, whether there is a tradition of business in his family. A variety of analyses shows that Arab society is directed by the past and tradition plays an important role. Hence, we can assume that customs carefully cultivated by generations will be significant for Arab businessman. Not only is recruitment to this job category defined in this way, but also realization of the role. Customs kept throughout generations play a vital part in the model of an Arab entrepreneur, as the intergenerational professional message is particularly strong. Quite often entrepreneurs, like their ancestors, run a commercial enterprise and deal in a similar or the same type of goods. The position of the individual in the family structure is to a great extent defined by their potential participation in the process of taking over the company or the profession; it is not connected with the inheritance system but with the socially conditioned reliance on particular roles in the family, e.g. the role of the eldest son. The large influx of new individuals to this social category could lead to a change in the behavioral pattern. Men within the immediate family were most frequently indicated among the family members involved in their own commercial activity. The motivation for choosing the life path is still in respect of tradition, and the influence of the elders of the highest position within the family structure. Arab merchants give in to the encouragement of their elders and continue their ancestors` career, even more so because they start their professional career very early, quite often as children. Hence the attitude towards the basic elements of trade is formed at the early stages of life, as are the motives driving people engaged in trade. Each child who learns the story of Mahomet acquires at the same time the value system characteristic of this employment group. The Prophet was a merchant which is why many *hadith* concern this sphere of human activity. In the community of entrepreneurs the Prophet tradition is particularly visible, shaping the attitude towards entrepreneurship typical of Arab culture. One element of this attitude is the motive behind the actions of the community members. Among Arab entrepreneurs, the dominant motivation is prestige and status, and not, as among merchants of the western civilization, the willingness to profit or the satisfaction derived from expansion–it is conditioned by the particularities of Arab culture where the ascribed status dominates, and merchants and businessmen are socially and positively assessed.

Several of those interviewed who had adult children stressed that their sons also chose a similar professional career. From this perspective, the answers to the questions about the motivation to choose one's own business activities as a professional career should not be surprising. There were characteristic responses from men, who were the eldest of the siblings, and whose fathers ran their own businesses. They all emphasized that there was no choice as the pressure from the family was exceptionally strong–"tradition bonds." Family honor would be significantly affected if the men interviewed abandoned a "tradition continued by the ancestors." In addition, if they rejected the path of life indicated by their family, it could result in conflict, ostracism and often dissociation from the family.

One of the issues raised by businessmen was the domination of family links in all spheres of social life, including the professional. The use of family bonds and ties and friendship is not only widespread, but also an important and necessary means of performing business in the Arab world. Such an approach remains in clear contrast with a basis on the official, institutional and formal business channels in trade, typical examples provided by those surveyed being the acceleration of official paperwork and bureaucratic requirements. An explanation of this phenomenon can be found in the nature of primal bonds. For an Arab businessman it is far more convenient to use a network of personal ties rather than formal and institutional channels in the execution of specific tasks. This is partly due to the absence or failure of systems and procedures. Such a combination of institutional failure on one side, and the strength of family ties on the other, leaves no reasonable alternative. The outlay of time and effort will be minimized if personal contacts and links are used instead of formal channels. It is believed that thanks to his high position both in the organization and the community, the businessman will use his power to influence the course of events in a way that is beneficial for family and friends. This intermediary role, however, is characterized by its bilateral nature. Hence, according to the businessmen interviewed, it significantly affects the efficiency of their business activities, as they are forced to perform actions which are barely connected with their professional work, and are extremely time consuming. It is impossible for Arabs to separate issues related to running a business from social and personal ones—these three spheres of life known from the Western culture are all one dimension for an Arab. Both workers and clients, or people in managing positions, give little thought to calling someone at home during the weekend or late evening to discuss and resolve a business issue—many social cases are treated as elements supporting the running of business. Only a few businessmen explicitly inform their employees and customers that time off from work belongs exclusively to them and their families, and even these few admitted that it took a very long time before their employees took the idea seriously.

One of the characteristics of the Arab entrepreneurship culture is its peculiar attitude to time. In the respondents' answers there are many phrases conveying the idea that speed is not advisable, and that meeting strict deadlines isn't of a high value. Such phrases are, for instance:

- time solves problems
- rush is the devil's work

- time is a two-sided dagger which sometimes brings profit and sometimes a loss.

Some of the respondents cited that "time is gold" and "time is money," and Farid Muna has come to similar conclusions. However the last statement should be treated as the influence of western culture and globalization, as the author of the phrase "time is money" is Benjamin Franklin, and such statements cannot be treated as a part of Arab culture. Despite the fact that the sayings depicting time negatively were in the majorty, there were also sayings attributing a great significance to time, which is more of a declarative version than an actual way of behaving. The understanding of these sayings which attribute a great significance to time must be appropriately identified—they are just a reaction to the common indifference to time. Time is perceived in Arab societies in a totally different way to Western concepts. The Arab entrepreneurs may declare a great significance for time, yet other factors tend to be more important. One of the respondents stressed that "it's not ethical to say to an unexpected guest: I'm sorry but I'm otherwise engaged." Shortening the guest's visit is also problematical, even if it is justified by a heavy workload. In such situations other factors tend to dominate e.g. the precept of hospitality and respect for others. Although the Arab entrepreneurs who mentioned these factors were at the same time aware that in the situations mentioned above their time is wasted, they also pointed out that it's a kind of investment in friendship and personal bonds.

Arab culture is collectivist, visible in the decision making process. Collective decisions are valued more than individual ones, which has nothing to do with democracy in the Western meaning of the term. Individual responsibility is not important, and therefore a characteristic element of Arab trade culture is a very narrow range of delegating responsibilities. The entrepreneurs are not in the habit of delegating their entitlements or responsibilities to their subordinates, thus the full weight of work and decision process is on the entrepreneur and not his workers.

Moreover, while analysing Arab entrepreneurship, it's worth nothing that efficiency is quite often lower due to the interpersonal management style, a concern for rituals and the "tradition of open doors." At the declarative level, Arab entrepreneurs seem to prefer the consultative style of making decisions, however they often stress that such consultations have no binding power and sometimes no influence on the final decision. They are also a kind of a ritual, a ritual conducted in such a way so as to leave the workers feeling that they are participants in the life of the company. Actually, the influence on the decisions, if there is any, is usually connected with people from outside the company, but related to the entrepreneur. This is therefore a purely ritual element; the consultations are being conducted but do not influence the decision making. Behaving in this way, according to the respondents, is quite functional as it helps to reduce conflicts within the firm—the consultations are face to face while group meetings are avoided. It must also be stated that the list of people consulted is rather short. When asked to name the people most often consulted, the respondents stated that these were those they trusted—people of a higher position in the clan hierarchy, family members, friends and, finally, the workers. Among the workers most often consulted are the elders, the respected, the significant and those competent in the issue in question.

An Arab company works by a completely different set of rules than those which determine the functioning of western companies. An Arab entrepreneur focuses mainly on control, although in the declaratory version, the presence of superiors is essential to him in the issuing orders, maintaining discipline and supervision, he does not always admit the necessity of employing any additional workers for this, nor relaying powers to employees assuming that they are able to do the kind of job in question. An entrepreneur in this cultural zone tends to "steer manually," that is to concentrate on all the most important activities. Also, an important position in an Arab entrepreneur`s schedule is socializing, which is hardly surprising as its role as a factor influencing traders' actions is deeply rooted in Arab culture. Firstly, it is connected with the open door tradition, and secondly the entrepreneur is often a community leader so the social contacts take place at work too. Thirdly, running one`s own economic activity is connected with the network of informal contacts, which must be maintained if the activity is to be successful. In addition, Arab culture is highly ritualized and requires of its participants to perform such rituals as social observances, e.g. at the *ramadan brakfast.*

With no exceptions, all respondents pointed out that the religious precepts are much more important for them than any legal rule. When they converge, the element deriving from religion is of greater importance to them. Islam very clearly defines they way the enterprise should be run, and the norms specifying how to be a trader. In Islam, the respondents said, there are some forbidden goods which they would never trade in, despite the likely demand. It's particularly important to behave in compliance with the precepts of the *sunnas* of the Prophet; behaving in given situations in the same way as he did, thus many essential elements of running the economic activity reflect the Prophets actions. The operating of entrepreneurship in Arab countries is strongly based on Islam.

The Relationship Between Employer And Worker

The elements of professional life are culturally determined which can also be seen in the societies of the Middle East. For an Arab person, somebody who does not work is inferior. But the understanding of the term "work" is different from that agreed upon in western societies. Arabs don`t define work in the categories of effort or self-realisation—for them a working person is somebody belonging to an organisation. Similarly, when talking about entrepreneurship, Arab businessmen used completely different language then western businessmen do. Questions such as innovation, modernisation or effectiveness were not mentioned at all. Arabs usually have a negative attitude towards innovation as they perceive it as an element conflicting with Islam—an Arab entrepreneur defines entrepreneurship as running a company according to the rules and practices of Islam. The question of whether an entrepreneur is, or should be, an enterprising person is absent in the Arab merchants' self-identification. An individualistic attitude, innovation and a tendency to take risks are crucial in economic activity, and it is necessary to look at Arab culture from this perspective.

When analyzing the process of the functioning of Arab enterprises, it's important to take into consideration their organizational culture—in short, it could be described as "'organized chaos." There are 2 kinds of motivation in social systems: financial rewards and acceptance among other members of the organization. In Arab societies the last factor is dominant. The employees are generally members of the family. They gain satisfaction from social relations and should be motivated by praise rather than money. For an Arab person the most important motivating factor is pride and being on good terms with the leader. The employers' relations with the employee are usually close and long-term.

What is important in an Arab society is the context of the situation which determines its interpretation. Moral relativism is high; what counts is the person and the context. The perception of the organization is also important in Arab countries—it is generally expected that the organization will take responsibility, making sure the workers have specialist knowledge, duties, order and safety. Organizations often interfere in the private lives of their members. Planning, supervision and control have more of symbolic than actual significance in Arab companies. Employers have the tendency to use personal relations instead of formal contacts. The management style is informal and personal. The individual is emotionally dependent on the organization.

Communication is based on implicit signals whose source is non-verbal behavior and social context. Moreover, depending only on verbal communication is considered improper. Using titles is important in all spheres of life, and they are used also in situations which have nothing to do with work. Social position is transferred among different aspects of social life—the status of a person depends on their family's position and the network of social relations and not so much on the individual achievement. The status is therefore independent from the task or function.

Arab culture, according to various typologies, is a family type of culture. It is the sort of enterprise culture which is power oriented with the leader being considered a careful father. This type of power is not based on fear but on closeness and kindness. The atmosphere at work is family-like, with typical respect for the elderly, strict compliance and forbearance for the young.

The Place of a Businessman in Arab Community

The role an Arab businessman plays in his community is significantly different from that which we know from western societies. The expectations towards him are vast, and their extent grows with his enrichment. First of all, he is expected to give advice, not only concerning the economic sphere of life but also the private one; it is also expected that he should be an active member of the community, and a leader. The families, including the distant ones, expect financial support and the playing of an intermediate role—using the family ties and the entrepreneur`s position to enhance, develop or change the course of action which directly influences the family members or friends. Such expectations also define to a great extent the way the entrepreneur functions in the community and also the way his company functions. What is particularly important in the Arab society is having the contacts and connections necessary to settle and obtain things without using law ascribed procedures. An Arab entrepreneur is situated at both ends of this mutual exchange continuum; he uses his position and connections but at the same time he is being used in the process. An important facility in arranging some particular matters is for an Arab businessman using his own network of personal contacts instead of formal and institutional ones, partly connected with the absence or indolence of systems and procedures. This combination of institutional indolence and the strength of family ties does not leave any reasonable alternative. The input of time and effort will be minimalized if personal contacts are used instead of formal ones, and that makes it the basic element increasing the effectiveness of Arab entrepreneurs' actions.

Conclusions

The image of an Arab entrepreneur which emerges from the research conducted is different from the one dominant in the western culture. Despite the fact that the categories of the analysis are the same, the entrepreneurship in the Middle East works by different rules. The terms of effectiveness, efficiency or the entrepreneurship itself are perceived in a different way, which makes the businessmen working in this business zone base their actions on totally different premises.

Differences in the image of an Arab businessman and a businessman from the western culture concern every aspect of their activity. They define the basic categories in a different way and attach a different meaning to them. Tradition and cultivation of the customs of previous generations are particularly important in enacting this pattern. Today, in the globalization era, it will be very difficult for Arab entrepreneurs to keep this pattern unchanged, but at the moment, it seems firm enough to resist change. Yet, Arab societies undergo changes of socio-economic nature which will probably influence small-scale entrepreneurship. The analysis of these changes will be very interesting in the future, considering that trade has a strong cultural rooting in an Arab society, and therefore any changes in this sphere will be indicative of more general changes in the society.

References

Babbie, Earl. *The Practice of Social Research*. Belmont CA: Wadrsworht Publication, 2006.

Bjerke Björn, *Business Leadership and Culture. National Management Styles in the Global economy*. London: Edward Elgar, 2000.

Braudel, Fernand. *Civilization and Capitalism 15th-18th Century*. New York: HarperCollins, 1985.

Choudhury, Masudul Alam. *Contributions to Islamic Economic Theory*. Hong Kong: The Macmillan Press LTD., 1986.

Danecki, Janusz. *Podstawowe wiadomości o islamie* [*Basic information of islam*]. Warszawa: Dialog, 2002.

—. *Kultura islamu—Slownik* [*Culture of islam—dictionary*]. Warszawa: Wydawnictwa szkolne i pedagogiczne, 1997.

Dziekan, Marek M. *Arabowie slownik encyklopedyczny* [*Arabic dictionary*]. Warszawa: Wydawnictwo Naukowe PWN, 2001.

Greenwood, Scott. "Bad for business? Entrepreneurs and Democracy in the Arab World." *Comparative Political Studies* 20 (10) (2007). http://www.minaret.org/islamcommercebusinessethics.pdf (accessed April 3, 2009)

Klöcker, Michael, Monika Tworuschka, and Udo Tworuschka. *Etyka wielkich religii* [*The ethics of great religions*]. Warszawa: Verbinum, 2002.

Koran [Qur'an]. Warszawa: Państwowy Instytut Wydawniczy, 1986.

Krzysztof, Kietliński. "Religijne, historyczne i kulturowe uwarunkowania etyki biznesu" ["Religious, historical, cultural conditions of business ethic"]. In *Etyka w biznesie i zarządzaniu* [*Ethics in business and management*]. Edited by Krzysztof Kietlinski, Victor Martinez Reyes, and Tadeusz Oleksyn. Kraków: Oficyna Ekonomiczna, 2005.

Kuran, Timur. *Islam and Mammon, The economic predicaments of Islamism*. Princeton: Princeton University Press, 2004.

Misiak, Waldemar. *Narodowe cechy kultury organizacyjnej w biznesie* [*National characteristics of organizational culture in business*]. Warszawa: Wydawnictwo Uniwersytetu Warszawskiego, 2004.

Mrozek, Anna. *Qur'an a kultura arabska* [*Qur'an and Arab culture*]. Warszawa: Książka i wiedza, 1967.

Muna, Farid. *The Arab executive*. New York: St. Martin's Press, 1980.

Nanji, Azim. "Etyka islamska" ["Islam's ethics"] In *Przewodnik po etyce* [*Guide to ethics*]. Edited by Peter Singer. Warszawa: Książka i Wiedza, 2002.

Nomani, Farad and Ali Rahnema. *Islamic Economic Systems*. London: Zed Books, 1994.

Nydell, Margaret Omar. *Zrozumieć Arabów* [*Understanding Arabs*]. Warszawa: Wydawnictwo Studio Emka, 2001.

Sadr, Baqir. *Our Philosophy*. London: The Muhammadi Trust, 1987.

Sloane, Patricia. *Islam, Modernity and Entrepreneurship among the Malays*. Oxford: St Anthony's College, 1999.

Tripp, Charles. *Islam and the Moral Economy. The challenge of Capitalism*. Cambridge: Cambridge University Press, 2006.

PART IV

CHANGING ECONOMIES AND SOCIAL POLICIES

CHAPTER FOURTEEN

EARLY RETIREMENT AND FIRM SIZE IN SPAIN

ALBERTO VEIRA RAMOS
AND JESÚS SÁNCHEZ BARRICARTE[1]

Introduction: Definition of the Problem

Vast amounts of research has been carried out in developed societies on the socio-economic consequences of demographic ageing, which will be particularly dramatic in European countries. One major cause for concern in academic literature is the fact that as our lifespan is lengthening, our working lives are becoming shorter, as early exits[2] from the labor markets have become more common.[3] Thus, the causes of early retirement has been one of the fields of study that has received considerable attention from social scientists in various disciplines, including demographers, sociologists and economists.[4]

The list of potential explanatory variables which have been found to determine early exits from the labor market is quite long, and these can vary significantly depending on the theoretical and methodological approach chosen by any given social scientist. Some researchers emphasize the role played by the preferences of each individual worker

---

[1] Department of Sociology and Political Science, Carlos III University of Madrid.

[2] Those which take place before age 65.

[3] Clark, Burkhauser, Moon, Quinn and Smeeding 2004; Spiezia 2002; and Blanchet and Marioni 1996.

[4] Farr, Tesluk and Klein 1998; Barea, González-Páramo, Alonso Olea, Fernández Cordón, Pérez-Agote and Velarde 1996; Gustman and Steinmeier 1993; Barr 1990; Garber 1989; Treas 1986; Copperman and Keast 1983; Garrido and Chuliá 2005; Boldrin, Jiménez-Martín and Peracchi 2001; Ahn and Mira 2000; Ahn, Meseguer and García 2005; Sánchez Sánchez 2002; Herce, Meseguer and Fernández Cordón 2000.

concerning work for pay and leisure.[5] On the other hand, others pay special attention to the role played by institutions and social actors which operate at the "meso" and "macro" level. The former tend to conclude that most early retirement is truly voluntary, while the latter are more inclined to believe that most workers are actually forced out of the labor market.

Those researchers who support the idea that most workers cease their activities voluntarily consider that early retirement is mainly caused by so-called "pull factors,"[6] those which lure workers into retirement as described by the income–leisure preference models: people accumulate enough wealth and assets and are entitled to pension–rights. These scholars believe that the utility of postponing one's exit from the labor market has decreased over past decades, as a result of economic growth and prosperity.[7]

The opposite line of thought supports the idea that firms and employers force senior workers out of the labor market because they are found to be more expensive than younger ones and more reluctant to change. Moreover, early retirement schemes have been found to be a very useful instrument when, as a result of mergers and processes of downsizing, firms need to reduce the number of employees. Social scientists usually refer to this set of determinants as "push factors," because their effect is to push workers out of their jobs.[8]

A third course of research considers that the institutions which participate in the regulation of the labor market are the actors that determine the exit pathways. According to this institutional approach, social institutions respond to fluctuations in labor supply and demand.[9] One example of this would be the implementation of early retirement plans designed in cooperation with firms, unions and governments as a strategy to alleviate the pressure of youth unemployment.[10]

---

[5] Income–leisure preference models are described in Levine 1993 and Mallier and Shafto 1992.

[6] Also referred to as "jump factors" by Blekesaune and Solen 2005.

[7] Clark, Burkhauser, Moon, Quinn and Smeeding 2004; Short 2002; Levine 1993; Leonesio 1993; Owen 1990; Parnes and Nestel 1981; Sørensen 1998, Rhum 1990a.

[8] Sandel and Baldwin, 1990; Schooler, Caplan and Oates, 1998; Rosow, 1990; Lynch, 1990 and Hutchens, 1993; Stewman, 1990 and 1986.

[9] Hofäcker and Pollnerova, 2004; Buchholz and Hofäcker, 2004; Maltby, de Vroom, Mirabile and Overbye, 2004; Guillemard, 2004; 1992 and 1991 and Kohli, Rein, Guillemard and Van Gusteren, 1991.

[10] As described by Clark, 1990; Stepp, 1990; Sheppard, 1990 and Stewman, 1990.

Of course, the role played by the health status of the work force must also be mentioned.[11] Poor health can be a powerful reason to retire, but quite often is also a function of how rigorous welfare systems are when it comes to granting someone the right to early retirement on grounds of poor health.[12]

Whatever the relative importance of each set of causes (demand driven or supply driven), the unquestionable fact is that the employment rates of males in most OECD countries are much lower now than they were in the 1970s, before the first oil crisis began, as can be seen in figs. 14.1 and 14.2 below.[13] The increase in heterogeneity that has occurred over time must be noted. It seems that, regarding early retirement, the trend is toward increasing divergence rather than convergence. At first glance, it is hard to believe that this increasing divergence can be explained by the different preferences and attitudes toward work and leisure in different countries. Despite existing local cultural peculiarities, most workers in the countries analyzed do share basic living constraints and circumstances which by themselves should be enough to have prevented the increasing divergence observed. The occupations and branches of industry where workers find their jobs, as well as the education systems they go through, may differ significantly across the wealthiest OECD societies, but probably not enough to explain all the existing variability in employment rates of people aged 55–64 observed across countries like Austria and Denmark, England and the Netherlands or Switzerland and Germany or France.

Figs. 14.3 and 14.4 below provide information about female employment rates. All countries have experienced increases in employment of women. But that has been basically due to generational replacement, as cohorts of younger women, more attached to paid work, replace older ones. However, heterogeneity is not decreasing, as in some societies, women have access to employment at much higher rates than others. Early retirement is more complicated to explain among women, because the evolution of female employment rates is determined by a confluence of two different social changes, the trend towards early retirement and the trend towards an increasing participation of women in the workforce. As a

[11] Saurel, Bardot, Berneron et al. 1999 and Buisset, Lavilla and Volkoff, 1999.

[12] In Spain, since 1984 early exits due to poor health decreased due to changes in the legislation that made it more difficult to apply for (Suso Araico 2004, 270; Alba Ramírez 1997, 9).

[13] This trend is more extensively described in academic literature: Maltby, De Vroom, Mirabile,and Overbye 2004; Boldrin, Jiménez-Martín and Peracchi 2001; OCDE 1995; Guillemard 1991 and Kohli, Rein, Guillemard and Van Gusteren 1991.

result, the effect of age is mixed with the cohort effect. Older women belong to generations which showed lower levels of employment than younger ones even at younger ages. Thus, it should not come as a surprise to see that in most countries, the employment rates among women have gone up, and not fallen, as has been the case for men. Other variables must also be taken into account, such as years spent out of the labor force due to childbearing or whether the timing of their exit depends to some extent on the husband's health status and retirement plans. This is particularly complex when the age gap between couples is relatively large.

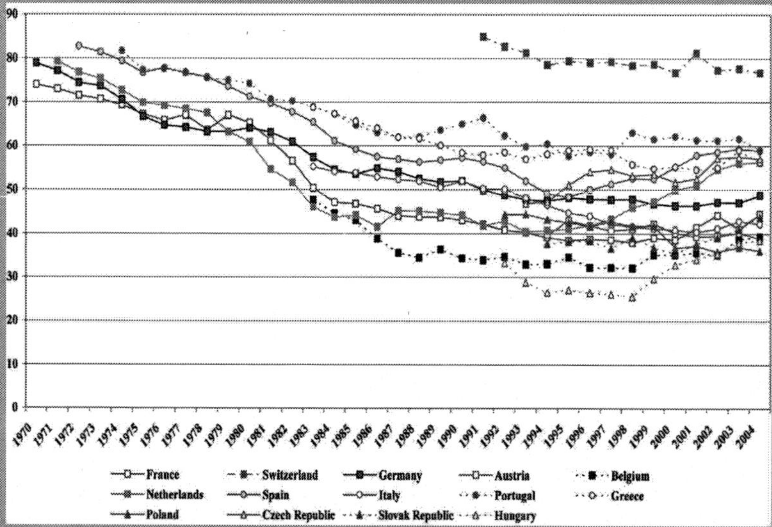

Fig. 14.1
Male employment rates in continental Europe.
Source: OECD labor force statistics.

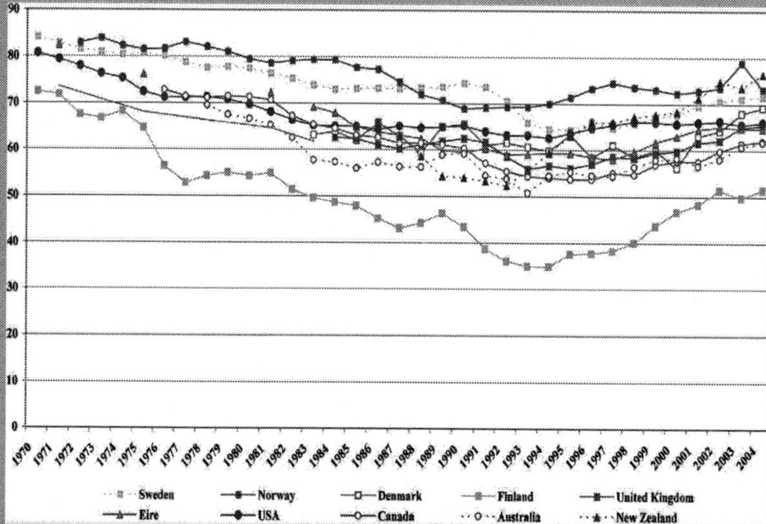

Fig. 14.2
Male employment rates in Scandinavian and English speaking countries.
Source: OECD labor force statistics.

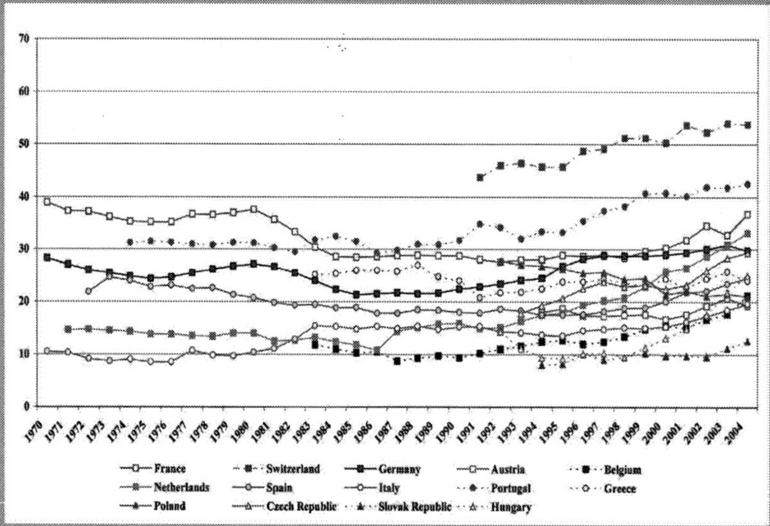

Fig. 14.3
Female employment rates in continental Europe.
Source: OECD labor force statistics.

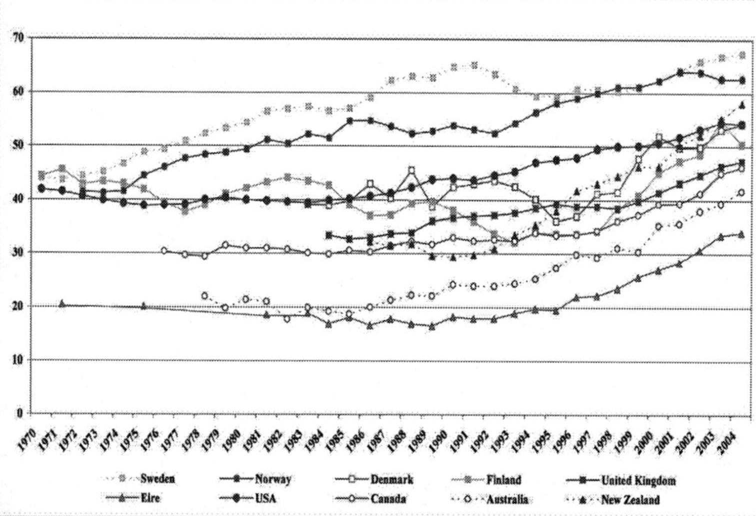

Fig. 14.4
Female employment rates in Scandinavian and English speaking countries.
Source: OECD labor force statistics.

Trends toward increasing diversity make it reasonable to think that institutional actors must be taken into account, as well as individual preferences, in order to explain the prevalence of early retirement. Legal systems and established patterns of interaction between social partners, specific to each country, operating at national and company level, are therefore major forces which have a great impact on retirement practices and are currently playing a decisive role in favor of greater divergence. Thus, collective agreements regarding early retirement between workers, governments and firms do not lead to the same outcomes in each country.[14] This complicates enormously the task of carrying out research on retirement at cross-national level, because it would be necessary to control for the effect of specific national legislation and institutionalized patterns of bargaining and conflict solving between social partners, as well as regulations concerning private pension schemes. For this reason, this chapter focuses exclusively on one country; Spain.

[14] Sánchez Sánchez 2002, 150–153; Guillemard 2004 and 1991.

Early Retirement and Size of Firms in Spain

Compared to Scandinavian and English speaking countries, Spain is in a very disadvantageous position. As it can be seen in table 14.1 below, the percentage of Spanish men and women from 55–64 years of age remaining employed is significantly lower than in those countries. However, compared to others like Italy, Poland or Austria, Spain can be seen to have higher percentages of employed men. With respect to France and Germany, Spain has higher employment rates among men but lower among women. Countries like Finland, Portugal and the Netherlands have similar levels of male employment, but much higher employment rates among females than Spain.

Table 14.1. Employed population between 55 and 64 years of age in 2004

	Less than 50% among males	**Between 50 and 60% among males**	**Between 60 and 70% among males**	**More than 70% among males**
More than 50% among females		Finland	Denmark United States	Iceland New Zealand Norway Sweden Switzerland
Between 40 and 50% among females		Portugal	Australia Canada United Kingdom	Japan South Korea
Between 30 and 40% among females	France Germany	Netherlands	Ireland	
Less than 30% among females	Poland Belgium Austria Hungary Italy Slovak Republic	Greece Spain Czech Republic		

Source: OECD Labor Force Statistics

In summary, it can be said that in an international context, Spain finds itself among those countries where employment rates are among the lowest. This situation is expected to improve in the future, as younger generations of Spanish women with higher activity rates replace older ones who have worked only in the home for most of their lives. This prognosis becomes clearer when we look at fig. 14.5 below. It can also be seen, though, that the desire of younger women to enter the labor market meets with major obstacles, reflected in the high rates of female unemployment.

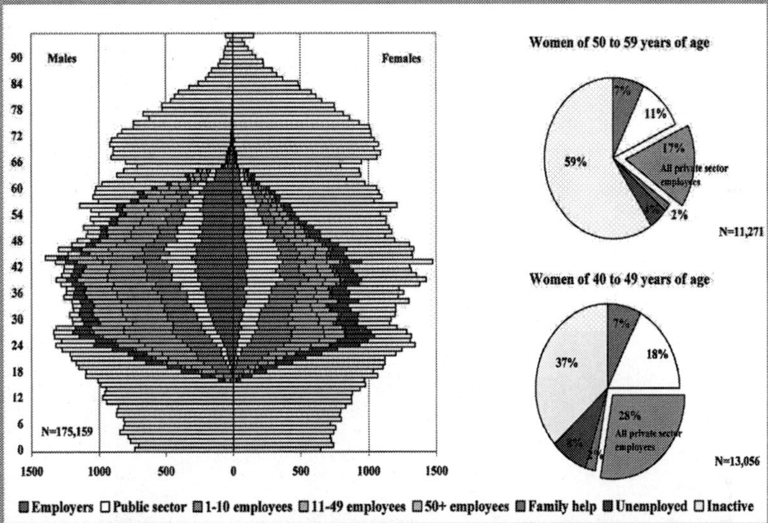

Fig. 14.5
Spanish population in 2004 by employment status and firm size of the employees of the private sector.
Source: EAPS micro data from 2nd quarter 2004; author's own calculations.

How employment rates among males will evolve in the future is rather uncertain. They have begun to increase since 1995, but the Spanish economy has shown in the past that in contexts of crisis, early retirement increases.[15] The most significant difference between the present situation in 2008 and the crisis of the mid 1990s is that now there is much less youth unemployment, and it is therefore very unlikely that the government and unions will endorse any early retirement policy for the sake of

[15] Alba Ramírez 1997, 2; Boldrin, Jiménez-Martín and Peracchi 2001, 41.

reducing unemployment among younger people.[16] However, it is less clear that firms will keep themselves from turning again[17] to early retirement schemes as their preferred instrument to reduce the number of employees.

According to the data shown in fig. 14.6 below[18], Spain is a country where 51% of firms are run by self-employed workers with no employees, and smaller firms of up to 10 employees make up about 43% of all firms. This leaves only the remaining 5% for those with more than 10, plus 1% for those with 50 and more employees. This predominance of rather small firms has not changed during the past decade, and the type of firm that has experienced the greatest growth has been those with 1 to 9 employees. Leaving aside firms with no employees, in 2004 those with 1 to 9 workers represented up to 87% of the total.

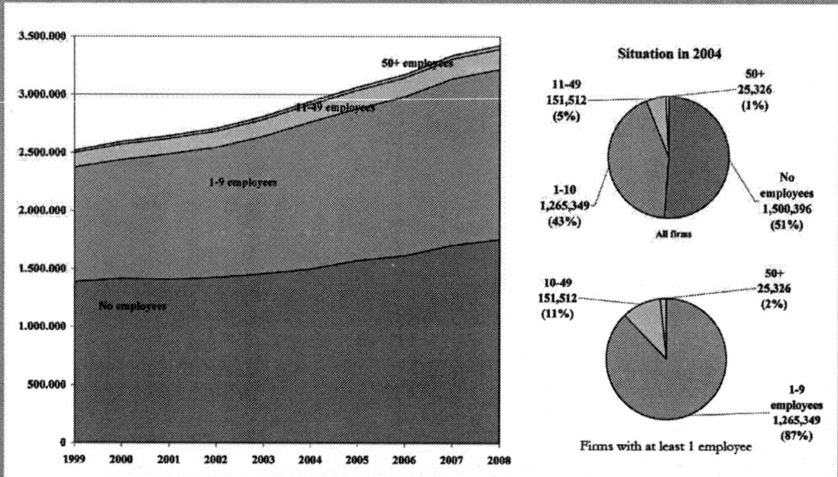

Fig. 14.6
Spanish firms by number of employees.
Source: central companies directory.

[16] Particularly in Spain, where very few young unemployed workers have actually found a job by replacing workers who had taken early retirement (Bazo 2001, 36).

[17] Previous episodes have been described by Farr, Tesluk and Klein 1998; Riera 1999; Castells and Ortíz 1992; Savoie 1990 and Farr, Tesluk and Klein 1998.

[18] The Central Companies Directory (CCD) joins together in just one information system all Spanish companies and their local units located in the country. It is updated once a year and generates a new information system to 1 January for each period. It is accessible at http://www.ine.es/en/inebmenu/mnu_empresas_en.htm

Despite this overwhelming dominance of small firms, it should be noted that the number of larger firms increased from about 20,000 to almost 31,000 between 1999 and 2008. Also, according to EAPS micro data from 2000 to 2004, the percentage of employees who are working for firms with over 50 employees constitutes 32.8% of the entire workforce in the private sector.[19] It could therefore be very useful to assess which types of firms are normally[20] more reluctant to keep senior workers on the payroll, larger or smaller ones, as is could be these that might be expected to begin implementing early retirement plans in the oncoming, somewhat economically disadvantageous circumstances.

Formulation of Hypothesis

Large companies, as is emphasized in the bibliography,[21] tend to hasten the exit of their senior workers at a higher rate than smaller ones. For such firms, this is a means of reducing costs and managing a generally younger age structure in their workforce. As a result, employees of larger firms are more likely to experience pressure to retire early from managers and supervisors. All this combines with the fact that employees in larger companies are more likely to have alienating jobs, subjected to a "taylorist" style of control of their activities, that is, with little self-control and autonomy over the management of their own workload.[22]

On the other hand, in smaller firms, the relationship between the employer and his or her employees allows for a greater degree of mutual confidence and respect. A long lasting relationship between an employer and his or her few employees constitutes an investment, and replacing a worker might therefore entail fewer advantages. Better interpersonal relationships also make it easier for the employees to remain attached to the workplace and it is less likely that they will become alienated by daily tasks.

---

[19] Excluding employers and self-employed. See table 3 for more detailed information.

[20] This research has used data from 2000 to 2004, a period of stable economic growth in Spain.

[21] Sandel and Baldwin 1990; Schooler, Caplan and Oates 1998; Rosow 1990; Lynch 1990 and Hutchens 1993; Stewman 1990 and 1986.

[22] Handel 2005; Blekesaune and Solem 2005; Benmore 2002; Rosse and Millar 2000; Solem and Mykletum 1997 and Natale, Sora and O'Neill 1995.

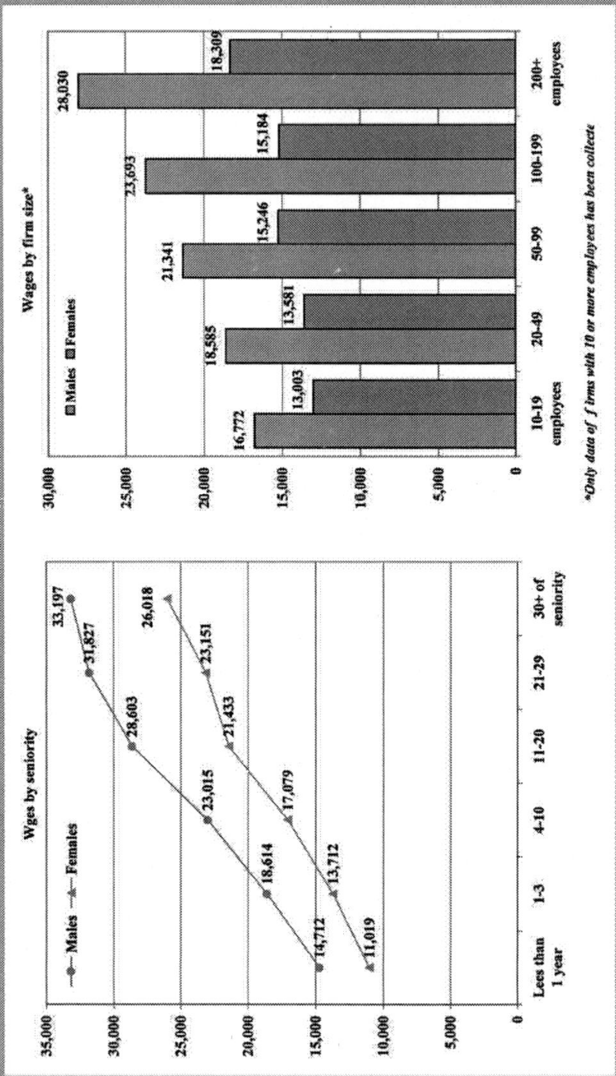

Fig. 14.7
Average yearly wage in Euros of Spanish workers by seniority and firm size.
Source: wage structure survey.

One disadvantage of being employed in a small firm is the fact that the salaries are lower on average, and this can become a factor in favor of late retirement. In large firms, where wage differentials between senior workers and newcomers is higher than in smaller ones (as can be deduced from fig. 14.7[23]) the substitution of a number of senior workers by younger ones with lower pay might save the firm a substantial amount of money. Thus, managers in larger firms might feel far more tempted to implement certain managerial practices specifically designed to alienate their employees and make them more likely to accept early retirement.

As a result of all the considerations mentioned above, it is expected that we may find that senior workers in Spain tend to enjoy a longer time in the labor market if they work for smaller firms than if they work in larger ones.[24]

Overview of the Sample

The sample has been taken from micro data files from the Spanish Economically Active Population Survey (EAPS).[25] A combined single data set was created using files from the four second quarters of the years 2000 to 2004[26] in order to increase the number of cases. Because the research was restricted to people aged 50–64 working for pay, the final sample consisted of 69,053 people. Up to 28,375 individuals had to be

---

[23] The Wage Structure Survey is a four yearly statistical operation (based on 2002 survey results) carried out in the framework of the European Union with common methodology and content criteria, with the objective of obtaining comparable results about the structure and distribution of wages among member states. This survey investigates the distribution of wages based on a large range of variables such as sex, occupation, activity branch, age or size of the company. It is accessible at: http://www.ine.es/

[24] The intermediate category of firms with 11–49 employees is expected to have higher proportions of older senior workers than larger firms but fewer than smaller ones.

[25] The Economically Active Population Survey (EAPS) is a continuous quarterly survey that targets households. Its main objective is to obtain data on the labor force (which is subcategorized by employed and unemployed), and on the people outside the labor market. The theoretical sample varies from 65,000 households per quarter, to approx. 60,000 households actually interviewed, which means approximately 180,000 people. Access to aggregate data and published reports is possible on the Spanish National Statistical Institute (INE) website: http://www.ine.es/en/welcome_en.htm

[26] More recent data is not available because since 2005 questionnaires no longer collect information about the size of the firm the person interviewed works for.

dropped because they were no longer working for pay at the time they were interviewed.[27]

The sample was also divided by professional status, since there are variables which can only affect employees but not employers and vice-versa. Also, private sector employees are more likely to suffer from downsizing and restructuring policies than civil servants. They are also more likely to have rather alienating jobs or jobs which demand great physical effort. As for employers and the self-employed, they enjoy more autonomy in their workplace, and can reduce their own workload according to their working capacity. It should also be mentioned that the self-employed tend to contribute with the minimum yearly amount to their public pension fund schemes throughout their working life, thereby clearly opting for retirement later in life. We therefore cannot afford to ignore the many major differences between the pathways towards retirement of employers, the self-employed, civil servants and private sector employees.

Table 14.2. Sample size I People of ages 50 to 64 interviewed between 2000 and 2004

Firm size	N	%	Valid %	Cum. %
No employees	11,441	11.7	16.6	16.6
1-10 employees	19,667	20.2	28.5	45.0
11-49 employees	17,329	17.8	25.1	70.1
50+ employees	20,616	21.2	29.9	100
Total	69,053	70.9	100	
Not working for pay	28,375	29.1		
Total	97,428	100		

Source: EAPS micro data from the 2nd quarters of the years 2000 to 2004. Authors' own calculations.

Fig. 14.8 below shows evidence that in Spain, the likelihood of early retirement varies greatly depending on professional status. It can be seen that among older workers, the percentages of employers and self-employed who remain active tend to be significantly higher than among employees. If we compare employees in the private and public sectors, it is clear that civil servants tend to retire later than employees in the private sector.

[27] Although retired people were asked a series of questions about their former jobs, information about the size of the firm they used to work for was not collected.

Another reason why the sample has been divided according to professional status is that the proportion of those who are employers or self-employed among the category of workers in smaller firms is much higher than among workers in larger firms. This can greatly affect the results, making differences due to composition look as if they are attributable to actual differences between workers in larger and smaller firms. Thus, in order to ensure that this variable does not distort the results, further analyses have always divided the working population into four groups; employers, the self-employed, civil servants, and employees in the private sector.

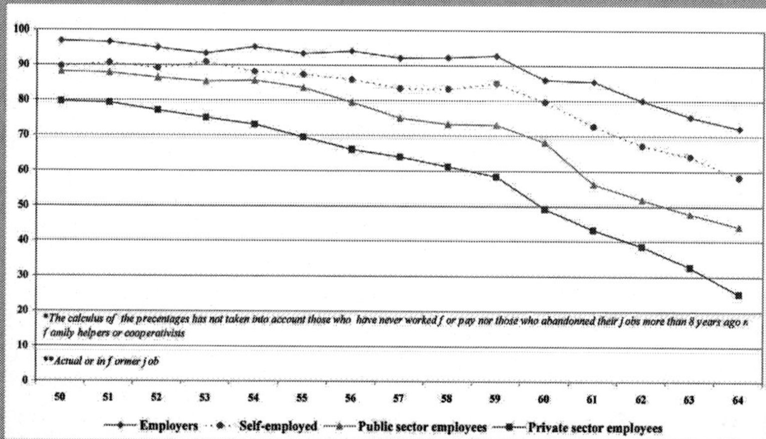

Fig. 14.8
Percentages of people still working for pay* by age and professional status.**
Source: EAPS micro data from the 2nd quarters of the years 2000 to 2004; author's own calculations.

Table 14.3. Sample size II
Working people aged 50 to 64 interviewed between 2000 and 2004

Professional status	Firm size				
	No. employees	1-10	11-49	50+	Total
Self-employed (20.4%)	11,441 (81.2%)	2,559 (18.2%)	63 (0.5%)	20 (0.1%)	14,083 (100%)
Employers (9.4%)	0	5,476 (84.6%)	872 (13.5%)	127 (1.9%)	6,475 (100%)
Public sector employees (20.6%)	0	719 (5.1%)	4,272 (30.1%)	9,205 (64.8%)	14,196 (100%)
Private sector employees (49.6%)	0	10,913 (31.8%)	12,122 (35.4%)	11,264 (32.8%)	34,299 (100%)
Total (100%)	11,441 (16.5%)	19,667 (28.5%)	17,329 (25.1%)	20,616 (29.9%)	69,053 (100%)

Source: EAPS micro data from the 2nd quarters of the years 2000 to 2004. Author's own calculations.

As table 14.3 above shows, almost 30% of the sample are employers (9.4%) and self-employed (20.4%), about 20% are employed in the public sector and the remaining 50% are private sector employees. The large number of firms without employees is the reason that explains why the proportion of self-employed with no employees among all self-employed[28] is as high as 81.2%. Also, the overwhelming majority of employers, 84.6%, run firms with fewer than 11 employees. Concerning public sector employees, it should not be surprising that most of them work in rather large firms and institutions, although some 5.1% do work in small town halls with fewer than 11 workers. As for private sector employees, they are found to be rather evenly distributed between the three established categories of firm size. About one third work in firms of 1–10 employees, another third for firms of 11–49 and the remaining third in firms of 50 and more employees.

Method of Analysis

To show differences in the likelihood of retiring between workers in larger and smaller firms, a slightly different strategy must be adopted than the one used to highlight differences between workers depending on their

[28] Some of the self-employed can actually hire workers while keeping their status as self-employed.

professional status (see fig. 14.8 above). This is because the data set contains information about professional status but not about the size of the firm where those already retired had worked. It is therefore not possible to make a contrast between those already retired and those remaining active as far as firm size is concerned, comparing, at each given age, the differences in the respective probabilities of already being retired, for people who work or worked in larger firms with those who work or worked in smaller firms. Concerning firm size, only the "survivors" that remain active and do not retire can be observed. This should be enough information to test the hypotheses, assuming that the distribution of people working for firms of different sizes do not vary significantly depending on cohorts.[29] Under such an assumption, an observed increase in the proportion of workers employed in smaller firms at older ages is assumed to be due to an equivalent decrease in the percentages of workers employed in larger firms. Therefore, if such an observation is made, it will be concluded that the likelihood of retirement increases faster with age among workers in larger firms than among workers in smaller ones. Pearson Chi2 tests have been conducted to test whether the observed differences between age groups are statistically significant or not.

Another method of analysis is the comparison of mean ranks (instead of mean ages) of senior employers in different types of firm. That is to say, we compare the mean rank of senior workers working in smaller firms with the mean rank of senior workers working in larger firms, using the Kruskal-Wallis H Tests to check for significance.[30]

Results and Findings

All results presented are controlled by professional status. For employees in the private sector, further refined analyses were carried out, in order to rule out the influence of other variables such as education, occupation and branch of industry.

[29] Looking at graph 10, it becomes clear that differences between generations regarding the distribution of employed population in different firm types in the private sector do not vary significantly until the age of 59.

[30] The Kruskal-Wallis H Test is the non-parametric alternative to a one-way, between-groups analysis of variance. It allows us to compare the scores on one continuous variable (age) for three or more groups (types of firms depending on their size). This test does not compare means but mean ranks. Scores are converted to ranks and then the mean rank of each group is compared.

Table 14.4. Workers from 50 to 64 years of age by profesional status.

Table 14.4a: Self-employed				
Firm Size	**Mean Ages**	**Mean Ranks**	**N**	**Std. Dev.**
No employees	56.3	7042.7	11,441	4.139
1-10 employees	56.4	7067.0	2,559	4.143
11-49 employees	55.3	6049.2	63	3.930
50+ employees	55.9	6590.7	20	4.158
Total	**56.3**	-	**14,083**	**4.139**
Kruskal-Wallis	Chi2		df	Asymp. Sig.
	4.119612959		3	**0.2488344**
Table 14.4b: Employers				
Firm Size	**Mean Ages**	**Mean Ranks**	**N**	**Std. Dev.**
1-10 employees	55.9	3259.4	5,476	4.060
11-49 employees	55.6	3089.8	872	3.994
50+ employees	56.1	3331.9	127	3.931
Total	**55.9**	-	**6,475**	**4.050**
Kruskal-Wallis	Chi2		df	Asymp. Sig.
	6.552874706		2	**0.0377626**
Table 14.4c: Employees of the Public Sector				
Firm Size	**Mean Ages**	**Mean Ranks**	**N**	**Std. Dev.**
1-10 employees	55.5	7438.2	719	3.954
11-49 employees	55.2	7192.2	4,272	3.845
50+ employees	55.1	7028.5	9,205	3.921
Total	**55.2**	-	**14,196**	**3.901**
Kruskal-Wallis	Chi2		df	Asymp. Sig.
	9.923992394		2	**0.0069989**
Table 14.4d: Employees of the Private Sector				
Firm Size	**Mean Ages**	**Mean Ranks**	**N**	**Std. Dev.**
1-10 employees	55.3	17756.6	10,913	3.972
11-49 employees	55.0	17126.6	12,122	3.794
50+ employees	54.8	16587.5	11,264	3.569
Total	**55.0**	-	**34,299**	**3.786**
Kruskal-Wallis	Chi2		df	Asymp. Sig.
	77.92682442		2	**1.198E-17**

Mean ages and ranks by firm size and results of Kruskal-Wallis H tests.

Table 14.5. Workers from 50 to 64 years of age by profesional status.

Table 14.5a: Self-employed					
Age group	Firm size: No employees	1-10	11-49	50+	Total
50-54	38.4	37.7	49.2	30.0	38.3
55-59	35.4	35.6	30.2	50.0	35.4
60-64	26.2	26.8	20.6	20.0	26.3
Total	**11,441**	**2,559**	**63**	**20**	**14,083**
Pearson Chi2 test		Value=5,632	df=6	Sig.=0,466	

Table 14.5b: Employers				
Age group	Firm size: 1-10	11-49	50+	Total
50-54	41.3	46.0	41.7	41.9
55-59	36.5	34.4	32.3	36.1
60-64	22.2	19.6	26.0	21.9
Total	**5,476**	**872**	**127**	**6,475**
Pearson Chi2 test	Value=8,645	df=4		Sig.=0,071

Table 14.5c: Employees of the Public Sector				
Age group	Firm size: 1-10	11-49	50+	Total
50-54	46.5	48.4	50.3	49.5
55-59	35.6	35.3	33.4	34.1
60-64	17.9	16.3	16.3	16.4
Total	**719**	**4,272**	**9,205**	**14,196**
Pearson Chi2 test	Value=8.512		df=4	Sig.=0,075

Table 14.5d: Employees of the Private Sector				
Age group	Firm size: 1-10	11-49	50+	Total
50-54	48.3	50.3	52.1	50.3
55-59	34.0	34.7	36.1	34.9
60-64	17.7	15.0	11.8	14.8
Total	**10,913**	**12,122**	**11,264**	**34,299**
Pearson Chi2 test	Value=155,929		df=4	Sig.=0

Percentages by age group and firm size and results of Pearson Chi2 tests.

Self-employed

The results shown in tables 14.4a and 14.5a suggest that there is no relationship between age or age group and firm size among the self-employed. The result of the non-parametric Kruskal-Wallis H Test indicates that observed differences in the mean ranks of self-employed workers, classified according to the size of their firms, are not statistically significant (Sig. = 0.248 > 0.05). The result of the Pearson Chi2 Test (Sig. = 0.466 > 0.05) also leads to the conclusion that observed differences in the distribution of percentages of senior workers (those of 50 to 64 years of age) of different age groups between different types of firms are not significant, and therefore it cannot be stated that if we look at smaller firms the likelihood of finding older senior workers (e.g. workers of 60–64) is higher than if we look at larger ones. These findings are consistent with the idea that managing a firm with no employees allows one to reduce the workload without having to pay fixed costs such as the salaries of employees. The activity of such firms can, therefore, be more flexible and adapt more easily to the changing needs and preferences of the owner. It could also be argued, however, that these results are a consequence of the peculiarities of the public pension schemes that the self-employed have in Spain. Unlike other workers, the self-employed are allowed every year to decide how much money they want to put into their retirement plan. Virtually all the self-employed choose to submit the minimum amount all their working life, discarding the possibility of retiring earlier by making greater contributions to the system.

Employers

The relationship between age and firm size is more complicated to assess among employers (tables 14.4b and 14.5b above). While the result of the Pearson Chi2 Test (Sig. = 0.07 > 0.05) indicates that the relationship between age group and firm size is not statistically significant, the Kruskal-Wallis H Test (Sig. = 0.037 < 0.05) shows that the relationship between age and firm size is statistically significant at 0.05 level, although not at a more rigorous 0.01 level. The fact that both tests show results very close to the tolerance level should make us very cautious when interpreting the relationship between age and firm size. There might actually be a very weak relationship between age and firm size among employers due to the fact that as some of them grow older, they see the size of their firm increase. This would explain why the average age of employers in firms of 50 and more employees is slightly higher.

Public Sector Employees

The analysis of the results shown in table 14.4c above reveals that there is a statistically significant relationship between age and firm size

(Sig. = 0.0069 < 0.05). It seems that in the public sector the average age of workers is higher among those who work for small local administrative units and institutions. However, the results displayed in table 14.5c above indicate otherwise. According to the level of significance of the Pearson Chi2 Test (Sig. = 0.075 > 0.05), the relationship between firm size and age group is not statistically significant. One interpretation of these results is that employees in the public administration at a local level do not have preferences different to those of their regional or national counterparts regarding retirement age. Another way of interpreting this result is that national, regional and local governments do not have different policies concerning the age composition of their employed populations. The significance of the relationship between age and firm size showed by the Kruskal-Wallis Test could be a result of the fact that the average age of inhabitants of smaller municipalities tends to be higher than that of those living in larger urban areas, which would make the local pool of eligible civil servants slightly older.

Private Sector Employees

For the employees of the private sector, the results of the two parametric tests are again consistent with each other (see tables 14.4d and 14.5d above). However, unlike the self-employed, the results for this type of worker reveal that there is a very strong statistical relationship between age and firm size. We can see in table 14.5d above that the proportion of workers of 60–64 years of age is significantly smaller among those employed in firms of 50 and more employees than for those employed in smaller firms.

A more detailed view of this is provided by fig. 14.9 below, where the proportion of employed people by firm size is shown age by age, and not by 3 age groups. Again, a Pearson Chi2 Test denotes a statistically significant relationship between age and firm size. It shows that this relationship becomes clearer from the age of 60: between employees of 50–59 years of age there is a drop from 33.8% to 31.3% (-2.5 points in a ten year span) in the proportion of senior workers employed in larger firms, while between employees of 59–60 years of age the drop is from 31.3% to 28.3% (-3 points in just one year). Among workers aged 64, the proportion of those who remain employed that are working for larger firms is already 21.1%. This finding is consistent with the hypothesis which states that conditions inside large firms increase the likelihood of early retirement.

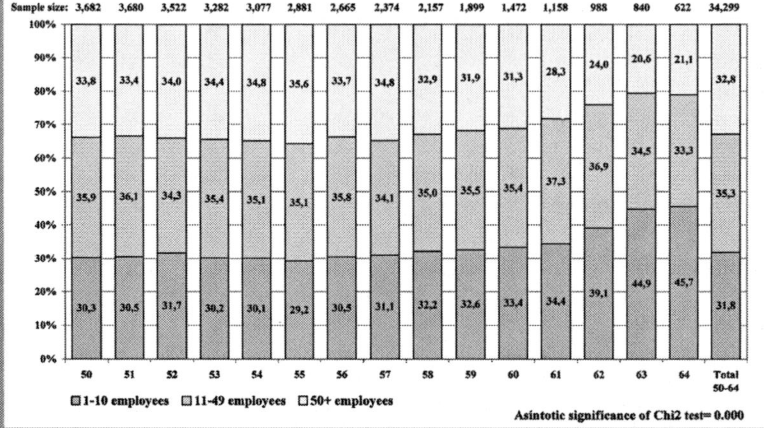

Fig. 14.9
Employees of the private sector in Spain by age and firm size.
Source: EAPS micro data from the 2nd quarters of the years 2000 to 2004; author's own calculations.

It is possible, however, that the relationship between the age of private sector employees and firm size is a spurious one, and that other variables which are also related to the likelihood of remaining active such as education, occupation and branch of industry play an intervening role in the relationship observed. In order to control for the effect of those variables, more analyses were carried out. However, the sample was restricted to 5,080 employees of 60–64 years of age, for it is among these that differences are more likely to be observed.[31] Kruskal-Wallis H Tests were therefore conducted to test the relationship between firm size and age among employees of the private sector, taking into consideration education, occupation and branch of industry. Thus, one test was performed for each category of those three variables, providing valuable information about among which social groups the relationship between firm size and age is found to be statistically significant.

[31] As shown in graph 9, significant differences between the distributions of employees in the private sector regarding firm size do not begin to appear until ages 60–64.

Private Sector Employees by Education

Educational attainment plays an intervening role in the relationship between firm size and age, as can be deduced from the results of the Kruskal-Wallis H Tests shown in table 14.6 below. They indicate that employees with a high school certificate or university degree are not exposed to a greater risk of earlier retirement if they work for a larger firm. In other words, the relationship between firm size and age is statistically significant only for employees with no formal education, or who have only completed primary or secondary education.

Table 14.6. Employees from 60 to 64 years old of the private sector by level of education

Table 14.6a: No formal education				
Firm Size	**Mean Ages**	**Mean Ranks**	**N**	**Std. Dev.**
1-10 employees	62.0	601.772	523	1.42
11-49 employees	61.7	550.231	411	1.36
50+ employees	61.6	519.527	202	1.45
Total	61.8	-	1,136	1.41
Kruskal-Wallis	Chi2		df	**Asymp. Sig.**
	11.65040808		2	**0.0029522**

Table 14.6b: Completed primary education				
Firm Size	**Mean Ages**	**Mean Ranks**	**N**	**Std. Dev.**
1-10 employees	61.7	1330.229	992	1.39
11-49 employees	61.6	1257.205	933	1.37
50+ employees	61.4	1174.399	606	1.32
Total	61.6	-	2,531	1.37
Kruskal-Wallis	Chi2		df	**Asymp. Sig.**
	18.2074816		2	**0.00011125**

Table 14.6c: Secondary education				
Firm Size	**Mean Ages**	**Mean Ranks**	**N**	**Std. Dev.**
1-10 employees	61.7	373.399	233	1.40
11-49 employees	61.4	336.154	214	1.25
50+ employees	61.2	305.183	229	1.28
Total	61.4	-	676	1.33
Kruskal-Wallis	Chi2		df	**Asymp. Sig.**
	15.10455093		2	**0.00052491**

Table 14.6d: High school degree				
Firm Size	**Mean Ages**	**Mean Ranks**	**N**	**Std. Dev.**
1-10 employees	61.4	180.708	106	1.20
11-49 employees	61.1	163.685	108	1.17
50+ employees	61.1	156.314	118	1.24
Total	61.2	-	332	1.20
Kruskal-Wallis	Chi2		df	**Asymp. Sig.**
	4.07397069		2	**0.13042129**

Table 14.6e: University degree				
Firm Size	**Mean Ages**	**Mean Ranks**	**N**	**Std. Dev.**
1-10 employees	61.7	217.317	82	1.43
11-49 employees	61.6	205.205	149	1.38
50+ employees	61.4	194.365	174	1.34
Total	61.5	-	405	1.37
Kruskal-Wallis	Chi2		df	**Asymp. Sig.**
	2.355519165		2	**0.30796794**

Mean ages and ranks by firm size and results of Kruskal-Wallis H tests

This finding is consistent with existing literature on early retirement. Workers with lower education also tend to begin their working lives early, so they became entitled to basic pension rights at younger ages than those who spent more time in the education system. Furthermore, because they are also more likely to be employed in rather alienating or physically demanding jobs, they often retire as soon as they are entitled to do so. Thus, few highly educated people retire earlier because they actually prefer to do so. However, from another point of view, it could be argued that workers with a lower educational level have fewer resources to avoid professional redundancy during their late careers, and are more vulnerable to managerial policies aimed at reducing the proportion of workers with more years of accumulated seniority, which often entitles workers to higher wages.

Private Sector Employees by Occupation

Results from the tests indicate quite clearly that workers in certain occupations are not affected by firm size when it comes to retirement age. These are managers, technicians, professionals, administrative workers, farmers and fishermen. On the other hand, unskilled employees and skilled blue collar workers are believed to have greater chances of remaining active for a longer time in their lives if they work for smaller firms. It can be seen in tables 14.7e, 14.7f and 14.7g below that the mean ages and mean ranks of such workers are always higher among those employed in smaller firms, and the Kruskal-Wallis Test indicates that these differences are statistically significant at a 0.01 level.

Some social scientists would argue that these findings show that managerial and professional classes enjoy a privileged situation inside larger firms and the broader labor market compared to blue collar workers, as a result of which they are less likely to be "asked" to retire early. However, from another perspective, it could be stated that senior blue collar workers have in general a greater preference for leisure than white collar employees because their jobs are more alienating and physically demanding, and also because they normally begin their working lives at earlier ages. Thus, many of them are looking forward to retiring as soon as they can, and since collective agreements between unions and employers concerning retirement plans are more typical in larger firms, it should not come as a great surprise that such workers (unskilled and skilled blue collar employees) in larger firms are more likely to have greater chances of early retirement.

Table 14.7. Employees from 60 to 64 years old of the private sector by occupation.

Table 14.7a: Managers				
Firm Size	**Mean Ages**	**Mean Ranks**	**N**	**Std. Dev.**
1-10 employees	61.5	87.167	33	1.12
11-49 employees	61.9	101.210	62	1.33
50+ employees	61.4	82.839	84	1.24
Total	61.6	-	179	1.26
Kruskal-Wallis	Chi2		df	**Asymp. Sig.**
	4.887762288		2	**0.08682322**

Table 14.7b: Technicians and professionals				
Firm Size	**Mean Ages**	**Mean Ranks**	**N**	**Std. Dev.**
1-10 employees	61.6	340.131	187	1.39
11-49 employees	61.4	316.672	227	1.39
50+ employees	61.3	302.149	222	1.32
Total	61.4	-	636	1.37
Kruskal-Wallis	Chi2		df	**Asymp. Sig.**
	4.678456521		2	**0.09640201**

Table 14.7c: Administratives and other services				
Firm Size	**Mean Ages**	**Mean Ranks**	**N**	**Std. Dev.**
1-10 employees	61.7	442.511	444	1.38
11-49 employees	61.6	417.343	229	1.34
50+ employees	61.4	395.952	178	1.37
Total	61.6	-	851	1.37
Kruskal-Wallis	Chi2		df	Asymp. Sig.
	5.205041464		2	**0.07408659**

Table 14.7d: Workers of primary sector				
Firm Size	**Mean Ages**	**Mean Ranks**	**N**	**Std. Dev.**
1-10 employees	61.8	98.208	125	1.43
11-49 employees	62.0	106.240	52	1.43
50+ employees	62.0	108.100	25	1.14
Total	61.9	-	202	1.39
Kruskal-Wallis	Chi2		df	Asymp. Sig.
	1.106138959		2	**0.57518159**

Table 14.7e: Workers of industry and construction				
Firm Size	**Mean Ages**	**Mean Ranks**	**N**	**Std. Dev.**
1-10 employees	61.6	575.173	286	1.34
11-49 employees	61.6	561.849	535	1.33
50+ employees	61.3	490.390	273	1.32
Total	61.5	-	1,094	1.34
Kruskal-Wallis	Chi2		df	Asymp. Sig.
	12.90293905		2	**0.0015782**

Table 14.7f: Machinery operators and drivers				
Firm Size	**Mean Ages**	**Mean Ranks**	**N**	**Std. Dev.**
1-10 employees	61.9	452.971	175	1.36
11-49 employees	61.5	391.439	330	1.32
50+ employees	61.3	357.357	280	1.30
Total	61.5	-	785	1.34
Kruskal-Wallis	Chi2		df	Asymp. Sig.
	20.29260694		2	**3.9221E-05**

Table 14.7g: Unskilled workers				
Firm Size	**Mean Ages**	**Mean Ranks**	**N**	**Std. Dev.**
1-10 employees	61.9	707.630	686	1.44
11-49 employees	61.6	633.853	380	1.35
50+ employees	61.5	609.787	267	1.40
Total	61.8	-	1,333	1.42
Kruskal-Wallis	Chi2		df	**Asymp. Sig.**
	17.11140911		2	**0.00019244**

Mean ages and ranks by firm size and results of Kruskal-Wallis H tests.

Regarding workers in the primary sector, it should be mentioned that the size of the sub-sample was quite small for those working for firms of more than 10 employees, so the interpretation of these results should be undertaken with great caution. It can be said, though, that in the agricultural and fishing sectors in Spain there is an important labor shortage, so few employers in larger firms would want to push their senior employees towards early retirement. This scarcity of labor made it possible for numerous immigrants to arrive in Spain in the past decade in order to do jobs that the Spanish refused to do. As a result, many Spaniards remaining in work in this sector tend to do so in the best jobs, often as middle-men between managers and immigrants.

Private Sector Employees by Branch Of Industry

The branch of industry does not seem to be a variable that greatly influences the relationship between firm size and age. Only senior workers in the manufacturing and mining sector are clearly found to experience higher odds of remaining employed if they work for smaller firms. This finding is consistent with the one made above regarding certain occupations. It is also true that among workers employed in commerce, sales and finances services there is a statistically significant relationship between firm size and age, but only at a 0.05 level (Sig. = 0.022 > 0.01).

Table 14.8. Employees from 60 to 64 years old of the private sector by branch of industry.

Table 14.8a: Agriculture and fishery				
Firm Size	**Mean Ages**	**Mean Ranks**	**N**	**Std. Dev.**
1-10 employees	61.9	217.063	247	1.44
11-49 employees	61.9	210.557	140	1.37
50+ employees	61.6	189.392	37	1.21
Total	61.9	-	424	1.40
Kruskal-Wallis	Chi2		df	**Asymp. Sig.**
	1.76700483		2	**0.41333271**

Table 14.8b: Manufacturing and mining				
Firm Size	**Mean Ages**	**Mean Ranks**	**N**	**Std. Dev.**
1-10 employees	61.6	660.315	181	1.36
11-49 employees	61.5	640.391	482	1.33
50+ employees	61.3	581.180	568	1.29
Total	61.4	-	1,231	1.32
Kruskal-Wallis	Chi2		df	**Asymp. Sig.**
	11.2567171		2	**0.00359447**

Table 14.8c: Construction				
Firm Size	**Mean Ages**	**Mean Ranks**	**N**	**Std. Dev.**
1-10 employees	61.7	395.157	201	1.29
11-49 employees	61.6	387.284	392	1.34
50+ employees	61.4	346.934	167	1.38
Total	61.6	-	760	1.34
Kruskal-Wallis	Chi2		df	**Asymp. Sig.**
	5.44754541		2	**0.0656267**

Table 14.8d: Commerce, sales and financial services				
Firm Size	**Mean Ages**	**Mean Ranks**	**N**	**Std. Dev.**
1-10 employees	61.7	568.689	473	1.35
11-49 employees	61.5	527.193	370	1.36
50+ employees	61.4	507.435	238	1.31
Total	61.6	-	1,081	1.35
Kruskal-Wallis	Chi2		df	**Asymp. Sig.**
	7.591870862		2	**0.02246188**

Table 14.8e: Hotels and restaurants				
Firm Size	**Mean Ages**	**Mean Ranks**	**N**	**Std. Dev.**
1-10 employees	61.6	152.637	131	1.42
11-49 employees	61.4	142.186	102	1.37
50+ employees	61.3	137.716	58	1.26
Total	61.5	-	291	1.37
Kruskal-Wallis	Chi2		df	**Asymp. Sig.**
	1.682019247		2	**0.43127488**

Table 14.8f: Transportation				
Firm Size	**Mean Ages**	**Mean Ranks**	**N**	**Std. Dev.**
1-10 employees	61.7	181.638	98	1.36
11-49 employees	61.6	171.604	135	1.24
50+ employees	61.6	167.125	112	1.45
Total	61.6	-	345	1.35
Kruskal-Wallis	Chi2		df	**Asymp. Sig.**
	1.210091282		2	**0.5460495**

Table 14.8g: Health and education				
Firm Size	**Mean Ages**	**Mean Ranks**	**N**	**Std. Dev.**
1-10 employees	61.9	140.741	54	1.25
11-49 employees	61.6	124.659	123	1.39
50+ employees	61.7	132.494	83	1.37
Total	61.7	-	260	1.35
Kruskal-Wallis	Chi2		df	**Asymp. Sig.**
	1.888548354		2	**0.38896179**

Table 14.8h: Cleaning and others				
Firm Size	**Mean Ages**	**Mean Ranks**	**N**	**Std. Dev.**
1-10 employees	61.9	348.217	551	1.46
11-49 employees	61.9	348.901	71	1.42
50+ employees	61.6	308.735	66	1.48
Total	61.9	-	688	1.46
Kruskal-Wallis	Chi2		df	**Asymp. Sig.**
	2.469143106		2	**0.2909594**

Mean ages and ranks by firm size and results of Kruskal-Wallis H tests.

Within each branch of economic activity there are workers with different occupations and educational attainments. As we have previously seen, occupation and education are variables which greatly affect the relationship between firm size and average age of employees. This heterogeneity within each branch might be contributing to hide the real effect of this variable. However, there are other reasons which could also explain the absence of a clear relationship between firm size and retirement age among workers in branches such as the construction, cleaning and transport sectors.

Concerning the construction sector, it is widely acknowledged that, as in the agricultural sector, there has been a great shortage of native labor in what is a boom sector in Spain. As a result of this, senior Spanish workers have been enjoying an environment which is too favorable to opt for retirement and thereby renounce the many opportunities of increasing their income level. In larger firms, they found numerous possibilities of promotion, becoming chiefs of immigrant workers who would be given the most physically demanding tasks. As for senior workers in the transportation sector, they are probably more highly valued by their employers because of their experience than are employees in other sectors. In addition, those who work for larger firms are likely to have their working hours limited by collective agreements and legislation, which makes their job more manageable. With regard to senior workers in the cleaning sector, it must be said that the risk of professional redundancy is minimal and the demand for cleaning services has been increasing over the last decade, which also applies in the case of hotel and restaurant workers. Last, senior workers in the health and education sectors employed in larger firms are not exposed to a greater risk of early retirement, probably because of their rather high average level of education and favorable working conditions.

Conclusions

Smaller firms tend to employ higher percentages of older senior workers[32] than larger ones, especially those aged 60–64. As a result, when we compare the mean age of the senior employees in larger and smaller firms, the latter tend to show higher values. This is believed to be caused by the fact that senior workers tend to retire earlier if they work in a larger firm than if they do so in a smaller one. Whether this is due to managerial policies aimed at reducing the proportion of older workers or due to a stronger preference for leisure among employees in larger firms cannot be assessed from this data, and further analysis would be necessary to answer that question. However, from the statistical analysis conducted it could be concluded that for a certain type of worker, the processes of negotiating

[32] Workers of 50–64 years of age.

the pathways to retirement with the managers of their firms are greatly affected by the number of employees the firm has.

Firm size has been found not to have the same effect on the likelihood of early retirement among all types of workers. According to the results of statistical tests, it can be concluded that workers with higher education, employed as managers, professionals or technicians are very unlikely to experience great differences in their exposure to early retirement depending on the size of the firm they work for. On the other hand, less highly educated workers, employed in the manufacturing or mining industry as skilled or unskilled labor, are very much more likely to retire earlier if they work in larger firms. Senior workers in larger firms in the agricultural, cleaning, tourist and construction sectors have not been found to have higher probabilities of early retirement than those employed in smaller ones. However, this situation may change during the oncoming crisis, especially among those with lower levels of education.

References

Ahn, Namkee, Javier A. Meseguer and Juan R. García. *A Projection of Spanish Pension System under Demographic Uncertainty.* Working paper Nº 2005-20: FEDEA, Madrid, 2005.

Ahn, Namkee and Juan Ramón García. *Job Satisfaction in Europe.* Working paper Nº 2004-16: FEDEA, Madrid, 2004.

Ahn, Namkee and Pedro Mira. *Labor Force Participation and Retirement of Spanish Older Men: Trends and Prospects.* Working paper Nº 2000-25: FEDEA, Madrid, 2000.

Alba Ramírez, *Labor Force Participation and Transitions of Older Workers in Spain*: Working paper Universidad Carlos III, Madrid, 1997.

Barea, José, José Manuel González-Páramo, Manuel Alonso Olea, Juan Antonio Fernández Cordón, Alfonso Pérez-Agote, and Juan Velarde. *Pensiones y Prestaciones por Desempleo* [*Pensions and Unemployment Subsidies*]. Bilbao, Spain: Fundación BBV, 1996.

Barr, Judith K. Health Care Costs for Older Workers and Retirees: "Social Needs in a Changing Benefit Structure." In *The Aging of the American Workforce*. Edited by Irving Bluestone, Rhonda Montgomery and John D. Owen. Detroit: Wayne State University Press, 1990.

Bazo, Teresa. *La Institución Social de la Jubilación de la Sociedad Industrial a la Posmodernidad* [*The Social Institution of Early Retirement from Industrial Society to Posmodernity*]. Valencia, Spain: Nau Llibres, 2001.

Benmore, Graham. Perceptions of the Contemporary Academic Employment Relationship. *International Studies in Sociology of Education* 1 (12) (2002): 43–58

Blanchet, Didier and Pierre Marioni. "L´Activité Après 55 ans : Évolutions Récentes et Élements de Prospective" ["Economic Activity after 55 years old : Recent Evolutions and Elements for Prognosis"]. *Économie et Statistique* 300 (1996): 105–119.

Blekesaune, Morten and Erik Solen. "Working Conditions and Early Retirement: A Prospective study of Retirement Behavior." *Research on Aging* 1 (27) (2005): 3–30.

Boldrin, Michele, Sergi Jiménez-Martín, and Franco Peracchi. *Sistema de Pensiones y Mercado de Trabajo en España* [*Pension and Market Systems in Spain*]. Bilbao, Spain: Fundación BBVA, 2001.

Buchholz, Sandra and Dirk Hofäcker. *Late Careers and Career Exits in Times of Accelerating Social Change: Globalization and its Impact on Late-midlife Workers*. Working paper Nº 62, Globalife, 2004. http://web.uni-bamberg.de/sowi/soziologie-i/globalife/workingpapers/ index.html (accessed October 15, 2005).

Buisset, Claude, Antoine Laville and Serge Volkoff. "Enquêtes Épidémiologiques et Pratiques Professionnelles dans le Domaine du Vieillissement au Travail" ["Epidemiological Surveys and Professional Practices on the Domain of Ageing and Employment"]. *Travail, Santé, Vieillissement. Relations et Évolutions. Colloque des 18 et 19 novembre à Paris.* Toulouse, Francia : OCTARÈS, 1999.

Burkhauser, Richard V. and Joseph F. Quinn. "Retirement Wealth Accrual and the Patterns of Post-Career Employment." In *The Aging of the American Workforce*. Edited by Irving Bluestone, Rhonda Montgomery and John D. Owen. Detroit: Wayne State University Press, 1990.

Burtless, Gary. "The Fiscal Challenge of an Aging Education." In *As the Workforce Ages*. Edited by Olivia Mitchell. Ithaca, New York: ILR Press, 1993.

Calot, Gérard and Jean-Paul Sardon. Vieillissement Démographique et Protection Sociale [Demographic ageing and Social Protection]. *Futuribles* 244 (1999): 19–45.

Casey, Bernard and Gert Bruche. *Work or Retirement? Labour Market and Social Policy for Older Workers in France, Great Britain, the Netherlands, Sweden and the USA*. Aldershot, England: Gower Publishing Company Limited, 1983.

Castells, Manuel and Lourdes Pérez Ortiz. *Análisis de las Políticas de Vejez en España en el Contexto Europeo* [*Analysis of Ageing Policies in Spain within the European Context*]. Madrid, Spain: INSERSO, 1992.

Clark, Robert L., Richard V. Burkhauser, Marylin Moon, Joseph F. Quinn, and Timothy M. Smeeding. *The Economics of an Aging Society.* Oxford, England Blackwell Publishing, 2004.

—. "Population Aging and Work Rates of Older Persons: An International Comparison." In *As the Workforce Ages* Edited by Olivia Mitchell. Ithaca, New York: ILR Press, 1993.

—. "Pensions in an Aging Society." In *The Aging of the American Workforce*. Edited by Irving Bluestone, Rhonda Montgomery and John D. Owen. Detroit: Wayne State University Press, 1990.

Copperman, Louis Farrer and Frederick D. Keast. *Adjusting to an Older Work Force.* New York: Van Nostrand Reinhold Company Inc., 1983.

Farr, James L., Paul E. Tesluk, and Stephanie R. Klein. "Organizational Structure of the Workplace and the Older Workplace." In *Impact of Work on Older Adults.* Edited by K. Warner Schaie and Carmi Schooler. New York: Springer Publishing Company, 1998.

Garber, Alan M. Long-Term Care, "Wealth, and Health of the Disabled Elderly Living in the Community." In *The Economics of Aging.* Edited by David A. Wise. Chicago: The University of Chicago Press, 1989.

Garrido Medina, Luis and Elisa Chuliá Rodrigo. *Ocupación, Formación y el Futuro de la Jubilación en España* [*Employment, Training and the Future of Retirement in Spain*] Madrid: CES, 2005.

Guillemard, Anne-Marie. "Les Sociétés à l'Épreuve du Vieillissement" ["Societies Facing the Challenge of Ageing"] *Futuribles* 299 (2004): 45–67.

—. *Análisis de las Políticas de Vejez en Europa.* [*Analysis of Ageing Policies in Europe*]. Madrid, Spain: INSERSO, 1992.

—. *Envejecimiento, Edad y Empleo en Europa. Situación Actual y Perspectivas* [*Ageing, Age and Employment in Europe. Situation and Perspectives*] Madrid, Spain: Instituto de Estudios de Prospectiva, 1991.

Gustman, Alan L. and Thomas L. Steinmeier. "Cost-of-Living Adjustments in Pensions." In *As the Workforce Ages.* Edited by Olivia Mitchell. Ithaca, New York: ILR Press, 1993.

Handel, Michael J. "Trends in Perceived Job Quality, 1989 to 1998." *Work and Occupations* 1 (32) (2005): 66–94.

Herce, José Antonio, Javier Alonso Meseguer, and Juan Antonio Fernández Cordón. *La Reforma de las Pensiones ante la Revisión del Pacto de Toledo* [*The Reform of Pension Systems and the revision of*

Toledo Agreement]. Barcelona, Spain: Servicio de Estudios de La Caixa, 2000.

Herce, José Antonio and Víctor Pérez Díaz. *La Reforma del Sistema Público de Pensiones en España* [*The Reform of the Public Pension System in Spain*]. Barcelona, Spain: Servicio de Estudios La Caixa, 1995.

Hofäcker, Dirk. and Stepanka Pollnerova. *Late Careers and Career Exits: an International Comparison of Trends and Institutional Background Patterns*. Working paper No. 70 Globalife, 2005. http://web.uni-bamberg.de/sowi/soziologie-i/globalife/workingpapers/ index.html (accessed October 15, 2005).

Hurd, Michael D. "The Effect of Labor Market Rigidities on the Labor Force Behavior of Older Workers." In *Advancements in the Economics of Aging*. Edited by David A. Wise. Chicago: The University of Chicago Press, 1996.

Hurd, Michael D. and Kathleen McGarry. "The Relatinship Between Job Characteristics and Retirement." *NBER Working Paper Series* No. 4558. National Bureau of Economic Research, Cambridge, Massachusetts, 1993.

Hutchens, Robert M. "Restricted Job Opportunities and the Older Worker." In *As the Workforce Ages*. Edited by Olivia Mitchell. Ithaca, New York: ILR Press, 1993.

Kohli, Martin, Martin Rein, Anne-Marie Guillemard, and HermanVan Gusteren. *Time for Retirement: Comparative Studies of Early Exit From the Labor Force*. Cambridge: Cambridge University Press, 1991.

Leonesio, Michael V. "Social Security and Older Workers." In *As the Workforce Ages*. Edited by Olivia Mitchell. Ithaca, New York: ILR Press, 1993.

Levine, Philip B. "Examining Labour Force Projections for the Twenty-First Century." In *As the Workforce Ages* Edited by Olivia Mitchell. Ithaca, New York ILR Press, 1993.

Lynch, Leon. "The Older Worker in a Fast-Shrinking Industry." In *The Aging of the American Workforce*. Edited by Irving Bluestone, Rhonda Montgomery and John D. Owen. Detroit: Wayne State University Press, 1990.

Mallier, A. Tony and Thomas A. C. Shafto. *The Economics of Flexible Retirement*. San Diego: Academic Press, 1992.

Maltby, Tony, Bert De Vroom, Maria Luisa Mirabile, and Einar Øverbye. *Ageing and the Transition to Retirement: A Comparative Analysis of European Welfare States*. Aldershot, England: Ashgate Publishing Limited, 2004.

Natale, Samuel M., Joseph W. Sora, and William O´Neill. "The Meanings of Work." In *Values, Work, Education: The Meanings of Work.* Edited by Samuel M. Natale and Brian M. Rothchild. Amsterdam, The Netherlands Ed. Rodopi, 1995.

OCDE *The Labour Market and Older Workers* Paris: OCDE Publications, 1995.

Owen, John D. "An Aging Work Force? The Dog That Didn´t Bark." *The Aging of the American Workforce.* Edited by Irving Bluestone, Rhonda Montgomery and John D. Owen. Detroit: Wayne State University Press, 1990.

Parnes, Herbert S. and Gilbert Nestel. "The Retirement Experience." In *Work and Retirement.* Edited by Herbert S. Parnes. Cambridge: The MIT Press, 1981.

Riera, Josep María. *Jubilarse a los 50. Viejos para Trabajar, Jóvenes para Jubilarse* [*Too Old to Work, too Young to Retire*]. Madrid, Spain: Pirámide, 1999.

Rosow, Jerome M. "Extending Working Life." In *The Aging of the American Workforce.* Edited by Irving Bluestone, Rhonda Montgomery and John D. Owen. Detroit: Wayne State University Press, 1990.

Rosse, Joseph G. and Howard E. Miller. *Toward a Comprehensive Model of the Employee Adaptation Decision Process*: Paper presented at annual meeting of the Western Decision Sciences Institute, Maui, Hawaii, Estados Unidos, April 18 2000.

Ruhm, Christopher J. "Determinants of the Timing of Retirement." In *Bridges to Retirement: Older Workers in a Changing Labor Market*: Edited by Peter B. Doeringer. Cornell University, Ithaca, New York: ILR Press, 1990a.

—. "Career Jobs, Bridge Employment, and Retirement." In *Bridges to Retirement: Older Workers in a Changing Labor Market.* Edited by Peter B. Doeringer. Cornell University, Ithaca, New York: ILR Press, 1990b.

Sánchez Sánchez. "Antonio Pensiones de la Seguridad Social: Reforma de la Pensión de Jubilación" ["Social Security Pensions: The Reform of the Retirement Pension"]. In *Las Estructuras del Bienestar. Propuestas de Reforma y Nnuevos horizontes.* Edited by Muñoz Machado, S. García Delgado, J.L. and González Seara, L. Madrid, Spain: Civitas, 2002.

Sandell, Steven H. and Stephen E. Baldwin. "Older Workers and Employment Shifts: Policy Responses to Displacement." In *The Aging of the American Workforce.* Edited by Irving Bluestone, Rhonda

Montgomery and John D. Owen. Detroit: Wayne State University Press.

Saurel, Bardot, Berneron et al. "Etat de Santé Perçu et Perte d'Emploi" ["Perceived Health Status and Job Loss"]. In *Travail, Santé, Vieillissement. Relations et Évolutions. Colloque des 18 et 19 novembre à Paris*. Toulouse, France: OCTARÈS, 1999.

Savoie, Ernest J. "The Aging of Organizations: Strategic Issues." In *The Aging of the American Workforce.* Edited by Irving Bluestone, Rhonda Montgomery and John D. Owen. Detroit: Wayne State University Press, 1990.

Schooler, Carmi, Leslie Caplan, and Gary Oates. "Aging and Work: An Overview." In *Impact of Work on Older Adults.* Edited by K. Warner Schaie and Carmi Schooler. New York: Springer Publishing Company, 1998.

Sheppard, Harold, L. "The New Early Retirement: Europe and the United States." In *The Aging of the American Workforce.* Edited by Irving Bluestone. Rhonda Montgomery and John D. Owen. Detroit: Wayne State University Press, 1990.

Short, Johana. *Economic History of Retirement in the United States* in EH.Net Encyclopedia. Edited by Robert Whaples, 1st October 2002. http://www.eh.net/encyclopedia/contents/short-retirement.history.us.php (accessed March 15, 2006).

Solem, Per Erik and Reidar J. Mykletum. "Work Environment and Early Exit from Work." In *Work after 45?* Edited by Kilbom; Westerholm; Hallsten and Furaker. Solna, Sweden: National Institute of Working Life, 1997.

Sørensen, Aage B. "Career Trajectories and the Older Worker." In *Impact of Work on Older Adults.* Edited by K. Warner Schaie and Carmi Schooler. New York: Springer Publishing Company, 1998.

Spiezia, Vincenzo La población que Encanece, "Es una Carga para la Sociedad o un Capital Humano Desperdiciado" ["Ageing Population. Is it a Burden for Society or Underused Human Capital?"]. *Revista Internacional del Trabajo* 1–2(121) (2002): 77–122.

Stewman, Shelby. Labour Market Opportunities for Middle-Aged and Older Workers. In *The Aging of the American Workforce.* Edited by Irving Bluestone, Rhonda Montgomery and John D. Owen. Detroit: Wayne State University Press, 1990.

—. Labour Markets, Aging, and Health. In *Age Health and Employment* Edited by James E. Birren, Pauline K. Robinson, and Judy E. Livingston. Englewood Cliffs, New Jersey: Prentice-Hall inc., 1986.

Suso Araico, Anabel. "Ageing and Work in Spain: The End of Working Life?" In *Ageing and Transition to Retirement.* Edited by Maltby De Vroom and Mirabile Overbye. Aldershot, England: Ashgate, 2004.

Tamburi, Giovanni. "L´Avenir des Retraites en Europe" ["The Future of Retirement in Europe"] *Futuribles* 244 (1999): 61–81.

Treas, Judith. "The Historical Decline in Late-Life Labor Force Participation in the United States." In *Age Health and Employment.* Edited by James E. Birren, Pauline K. Robinson, and Judy E. Livingston. Englewood Cliffs, New Jersey: Prentice-Hall Inc., 1986.

CHAPTER FIFTEEN

ATTITUDES TOWARDS RETIREMENT WITH PREFERENCES ABOUT SAVING FOR OLD AGE– THE CASE OF POLAND

JOLANTA PEREK-BIAŁAS AND MAŁGORZATA RÓSZKIEWICZ[1]

Introduction

Simply put, the lives of almost all people are usually related to the behaviour of different institutions. The institutions usually initiate and then propose, organize and introduce changes in different systems which then affect the situation of the society and their members. In this chapter, people play a key role as we are interested in their opinions, preferences and attitudes towards retirement in the society of one particular country—Poland. In Poland, the pension reform in 1999 is the main cause for analysis of the topic, not only from an economic point of view, but also via a combination of economic and sociological aspects.

Why the Attitudes of Poles to Retirement and their Saving Preferences for Old Age Should be Analyzed

The reform of the Polish pension system introduced in 1999 (Chłoń, Góra, and Rutkowski 1998; Góra and Rutkowski 1999, Holzmann 2000) should change the individual way of thinking about retirement. The pre-reform system in Poland was based on two main pension systems: (1) employees and the self-employed system; (2) the pension system for

[1] Institute of Statistics and Demography, Warsaw School of Economics.

farmers. The regular retirement age for women was 60 years old and for men 65 years old, but in fact most retired earlier than eligible age due to many early retirement possibilities. What is important is that this system in general is based on a pay-as-you-go philosophy and defined benefit concept. The pension systems for employees and the self-employed were substantially reformed in 1999, but for farmers it was not. The reforms allowed those paying old-age pension to split contributions between two mandatory tiers: (1) defined contribution PAYG (pay-as-you-go) with notional accounts (NDC—"Notional Defined Contribution," contribution rate 12.22%); (2) defined contribution advance funded (FDC—"Funded Defined Contribution," contribution rate 7.3%). The future pensions benefits will therefore depend on how much we could save for old age (in different forms of savings, not only in the 1st and 2nd tier, but also including our individual willingness and action for additional saving for old age), and if we work longer (beyond the retirement eligible age) this also creates an additional surplus which increases pension benefits. The insured were obligatory or voluntarily covered depending on their age on 1st Jan 1999, as not everyone was obliged to enter into the new system. Those under 30 have to enter into the new system, whereas those between 30 and 50 have an option to choose between entering into both tiers or staying in the old one, with those above 50 not able to enter new system. Additionally, the idea was that the regular retirement age remain the same as the old one but with a need for slowly increasing it (or at least making it equal for men and women), and importantly with no early retirement options available. Therefore, the age at which Poles would like to retire is important in addition to whether they have enough savings for this period of life.

Besides the reasons mentioned above, making the decision to continue working or to retire is crucial in the recent socio-economic discussion as not only economic but sociological consequences are related to it. Economists are mostly concerned as to whether or not the retirement age could be increased, however the problem of early retirement exists in many countries and is therefore widely discussed and analyzed (Contini and Leombruni 2006; Eilers, Kim and Newman 2006; Van Tilburg 2003; Calasanti 2002; Dahl, Nilsen and Vaagej 2000; Kee-Lee and Chow 2009). On the other hand, sociologists dealing with the retirement issue have focused mainly on the social structure and the institutional aspects that shape the retirement process, on structural dependency, societal marginalization and most recently welfare and life-course regimes (Naegele and Walker 2007). The sociological explanation for the early exit phenomenon mainly focuses on "push" factors of labor markets and firms, and on the coalition of interests between firms, older workers, and the state. For companies, early exit is an effective way of reducing the workforce or of adjusting the age structure to better suit the market situation. Many studies show that an early exit is highly attractive for older workers as long as it is financially acceptable, and could also lead to an improvement in the general quality of life (the argument of trade unions). For the state, creating specific pathways for early exit, or letting other people use existing institutions such as disability or unemployment insurance, seems attractive not only in order to fit into the interest coalition of firms, older workers and unions; it has also been a widely accepted measure to reduce unemployment rates and promote employment of younger age groups. Such a situation happened in Poland in the mid 1990s, where in order to decrease unemployment rates the solution was to allow older workers to retire earlier. The state, however, did not force a decision without the acceptance of public opinion. Society was convinced, as shown in the public opinion surveys of the time (see fig. 15.1 below), that when there are not enough jobs on the labor market, older workers should retire earlier.

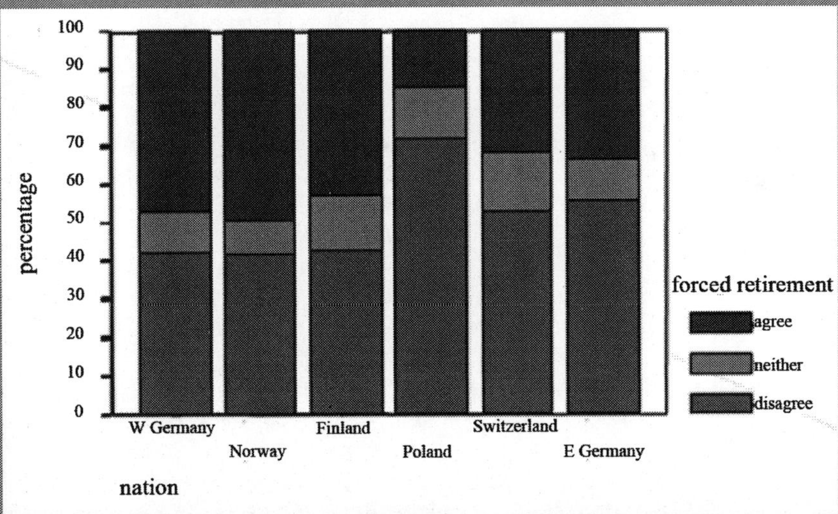

Fig. 15.1
Agreement/Disagreement on the statement: "When jobs are scarce, older people should be forced to take early retirement."
Source: author's own calculations based on World Value Survey, 1995 to 1997.

Additionally, looking at the employment rate of the working population around retirement age from 1999 to the present, we can observe that in this period of almost ten years in Poland, this indicator still is at a very low level (table 15.1 below).

Table 15.1. Employment rate of the population in age 55-64 in %

M – men, F - female

	1999			2002			2005			2006			2007		
	Total	M	F	Total	M	F	Total	M	F	Total	M	F	Total	M	F
UE-27	36.5	46.9	26.7	38.5	48.4	29.1	42.4	51.6	33.6	43.5	52.7	34.9	44.7	53.9	36.0
PL	31.9	40.6	24.5	26.1	34.5	18.9	27.2	35.9	19.7	28.1	38.4	19.0	29.7	41.4	19.4

Source: Eurostat, indicators database.

In the economic literature, incentives for early retirement are identified in the institutional and legislative rules of the pension systems which have to be changed in order to adjust the retirement age (Gruber and Wise 2002)—in this regard "pull" factors are underlined. This is why the increase of retirement age and so reduction in the level of pension for every year of pre-retirement is suggested. Now, the promotion of life-long learning and better health by means of improvement in working conditions, and to combat common stereotypes about older workers, should also help to promote labor force participation. These factors are helpful but we should not forget that it also depends on the general economic development of other factors, such as: cultural norms; prejudices; expectations; individual factors like meaning of work and leisure; family responsibilities; interaction of choices within couples; available income. Seeing the problem in this way, it was obvious that the reasons making Poles more or less willing to retire at an earlier age are of great interest. Before we present the results of our survey on this topic, it is important to mention that in Poland there are frequently surveys in which workers are asked about retirement plans (CBOS, 2005). In 2005, about

70% of respondents considered that men should retire in the age of 60 or less (compared to 85% in 1999) and about 95% of them considered that women should retire in the age of 60 or less in 2005 (97% in 1999). Additionally, in a survey by CBOS from 2007, almost 63% of respondents considered that people who retired at their eligible retirement age should have the right to a full pension and salary if they work (in 2002 only 42%). However, except for some ad hoc surveys[2] related to this topic (besides some national surveys, also a PPA-Study[3]) there remains little understanding as to why Poles demonstrate such preferences and attitudes to earlier retirement. Therefore, the intention of this chapter is to present a more detailed analysis of the preferences and attitudes/expectations of Poles regarding retirement, and combine this with information on whether they need to save for old age and if so, how they are preparing for this (i.e. by additional/voluntarily[4] saving).

Methodology

Studies were conducted for Poland from the beginning of the pension reform to identify some economic, social and demographic determinants in shaping economic behaviour such as obtaining material security (including saving behavior) of Poles (Perek-Białas and Rószkiewicz 1999), also taking account of provisions for security in old age (Perek-Białas 2001; Rószkiewicz 2003, 2004). There were already four surveys in existence: one from the end of 1998 (just before the introduction of the pension reform); then in 2001, 2004 and the last in 2006. In this last survey the national representative sample (stratified sampling strategy) of 1,320 adults with 430 Poles who had already retired (including disability pension) were interviewed about: (1) perception of saving for retirement; (2) retirement plans with expectations about their consumption during retirement. Questions used in this second part of the questionnaire regarding retirement plans were based on the US Health and Retirement

[2] In recent years, the Ministry of Labour and Social Policy, thanks to European funds via projects, analyzed these aspects (more on the web page: http://www.mpips.gov.pl/)

[3] See also results of the DIALOG project: http://www.bib-demographie.de/

[4] We only analyze if a person additionally would like to save and is saving already/can save for future consumption during old age, independently from the system organized by the state (1st and 2nd tier).

Survey.[5] Analysis about savings are extensively presented in other studies (Rószkiewicz 2008). All analysis presented here is weighted by: the probability of selection, non-response and calibration (adjusted the structure of sample by sex, age and place of living to population) in order to make conclusions about the whole population.

Main results

Characteristics of Sample

As mentioned, the whole sample consists of 1320 respondents, and 430 of the sample were pensioners (including disability pensioners and those who retired early). In the sample there were more men (60.1%) than women (39.9%) interviewed. The sample includes respondents of following age: up to 34, 18.2%; from 35 to 44, 19.7%; from 45 to 64, 39.1% and more than 65 years old, 23%. Regarding level of education, 21.5% of the sample had at least primary, secondary 61.8% and tertiary 16.9%. 32.8% of the sample lived in the countryside, while 14.8% lived in big cities, the rest living in smaller cities. Regarding employment, 8% were disability pensioners, 26.4% pensioners, about 1% of students/pupils, about 1% were responsible for taking care of their home (e.g. housewives), and 3.3% were unemployed. So in total 32.6% of the sample was not working and about 67.4% could be classified as those in work. 61.9% were married and 16.3% were widowed, 13.1% were single and 8.7% divorced. Finally, regarding saving, about 31% considered the present situation of their living conditions as bad or quite bad, while 7.9% of the sample termed it good, with 16.1% stating it quite good.

Preferences Regarding Retirement Age

One of the questions in this survey was about individual opinions regarding retirement age, but in asking this question we phrased it, not as in other studies, i.e. "What age do you think women or men should retire at?", but as the following: "What age do YOU think you should retire at?" First, it has to be said that 23.3% of respondents who answered this question at the time of survey admitted that they do not know at what age they will leave the labor market to claim a pension. This question was

[5] The research was coordinated by the Institute of Statistics and Demography, Warsaw School of Economics within collaboration of the Centre for Social Opinion Research (CBOS) in Warsaw, Poland.

asked only to those who were considered as not pensionable age. Those who gave answers differed in their opinions and it is best to see these differences (taking into account different retirement age by gender in Poland) in these perceptions by gender (fig. 15.2 below).

It is evident that women think that they retire much earlier than men. The peaks for women are around 60 and 65 for men. It is also the case that the majority accept working until eligible retirement age even though they know that they retire, or could retire, earlier than this.

Important Reasons to Retire

To identify the reasons for retirement we asked the following question: "I'm going to read you a list of reasons why some people retire. Please tell me whether, for you, these were very important reasons for retirement, moderately important, somewhat important, or not important at all." In table 15.2 below, the answers show how many respondents by gender consider what are very important reasons for retirement. It is important to stress that poor health (and the poor health of other family members) are significant causes. So, in considering ranking these responses, it is obvious that these reasons are quite easy to explain from the cultural perspective of the norms and values of the Polish. And these answers do not prove that Poles have an individualistic approach with the aim of just leaving the labor market because they prefer to do other (more exciting) things. Also, it is important to state that if the husband/wife/partner is going to retire, it is not enough reason to take such a decision. In almost all responses (excepting those concerning poor health) there are no statistically significant differences between men and women. Of course, the differences could be noted for persons who are still working and those who have already retired, but surprisingly we do not find statistically significant differences in their opinions.

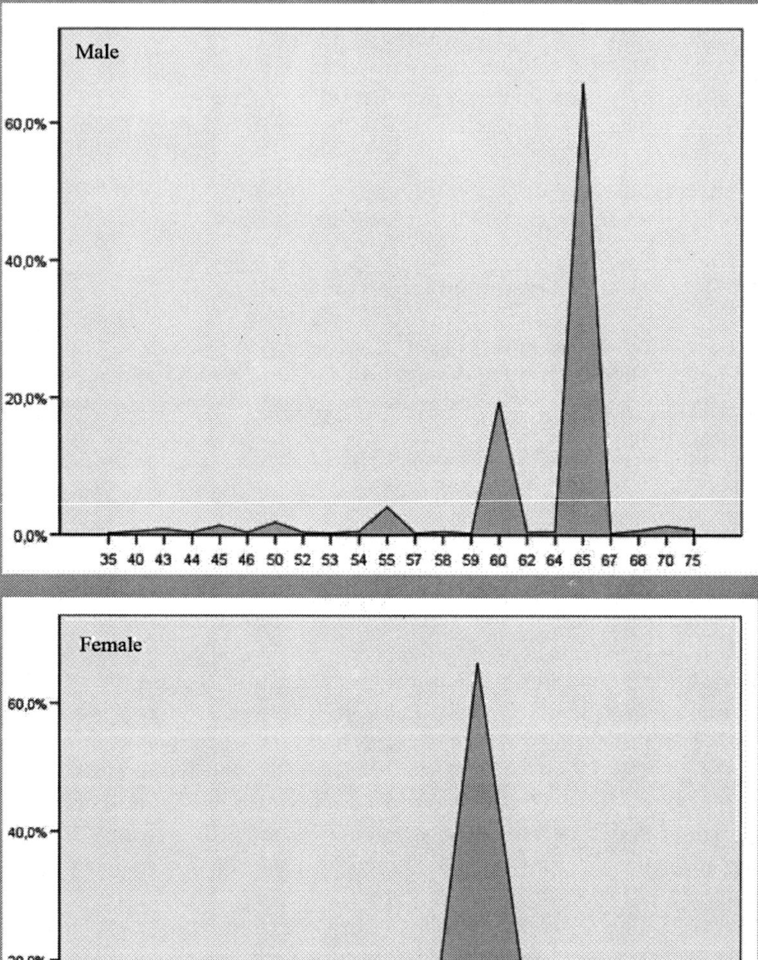

Fig. 15.2
Comparison of opinions on the age at which men and women think they retire.
Source: author's own calculations.

Table 15.2. Important reasons to retire (answers: very important).

	Male	Female
Poor health.	63.8	58.1
The health of other family members	43.8	44.9
Possibility to have a pension and additional job	30.4	29.0
Couldn't find any work.	32.2	31.7
Employer policy toward older workers	23.5	26.4
Didn't like the work.	23.2	22.0
Didn't get along with the boss	23.9	25.1
My work was not appreciated	20.9	24.0
Didn't need to work — had enough income	22.8	20.7
Wanted to do other things.	17.7	15.7
[IF MARRIED:] My (husband/wife/partner) was about to retire.	10.9	7.4

Source: authors' own calculations.

Good Reasons to Retire

On the other hand, to identify good reasons for why it is worth retiring we asked the following question: "I'm going to read you a list of reasons given by some for retiring. Please tell me whether, for you, these are very important reasons for retirement, moderately important, somewhat important, or not important at all." Similarly, as above, in table 15.3 below only very important reasons are indicated and what is not surprising is that spending more time with children and grandchildren is a strong advantage to being on retirement, as Poles place a high value on family life, as well as the lack of pressure and being able to take life easier. Usually, it is supposed that in retirement people can participate in different social activities; here it is presented as the least important reason for being on retirement in Poland.

We also looked for differences in preferences and attitudes about retirement of people who are still working and those who are on a pension. We could not find statistically significant differences, except for three reasons: spending more time with partner (30.5% of working and only 19.5% of pensioners), having time for hobbies (30% of working and only 22.2% of non-working respondents) and having time for travel (almost again 30% of working group and only 17% of pensioners).

Table 15.3. Good reasons to retire (answers: very important).

	Male	Female
Spending more time with children and grandchildren	48.3	51.8
Lack of pressure.	43.9	44.6
[IF MARRIED] Having more time with (husband/wife/partner).	31.8	19.1
Being able to take it easy	37.2	36.3
Being your own boss.	37.0	38.2
Spending more time on hobbies or sports	29.7	23.2
Having the chance to travel	24.8	25.1
Having more time for volunteer work (church, civic organizations, etc.)	7.1	11.8

Source: authors' own research.

Retirement and Saving

In 2006 about 24% of respondents could be considered as those who were saving anything at all. In our analysis we used Schrab's classification of needs in which, among others, one is of interest for this discussion: the need to provide for security in old age (Schrab 1943). This need was, in 2006, more frequently rated as more important than others listed in Schrab's classification.[6] Only 1.5% of respondents rated it as more and 0.3% as less important than all the other needs defined by Schrab. The structure of respondents according to their opinion on the importance of the need to provide for security in old age versus particular needs listed in Schrab's classification is presented in table 15.4 below.

[6] In this scale -5 means that providing for security in old age is considerably less important compared to other needs, +5 means that providing for security in old age is considerably more important, and 0 means that providing for security in old age is as important as other needs.

Table 15.4. Structure of respondents according to their opinion on the importance of the need to provide for an old-age security versus particular needs listed in the Schrab's classification.

Category of needs	Percentage of respondents stating that the need to provide for an old-age security is in relation to listed category of needs:										
	less important					*equally import–ant*	*more important*				
ranks	*-1*	*-2*	*-3*	*-4*	*-5*	*0*	*1*	*2*	*3*	*4*	*5*
obtaining money and a steadily higher income	3.3	1.1	2.9	2.7	3.5	40.3	5.8	9.4	6.6	8.3	16.1
	13.4						46.2				
earning popularity and friendship	20.7	8.8	9.6	6.0	5.3	18.2	4.9	4.6	5.0	4.8	12.0
	50.4						31.4				
obtaining general respect and esteem of others	9.0	2.6	4.5	3.8	6.7	33.3	7.8	8.4	5.8	7.3	10.7
	26.7						40.0				
providing for a comfortable lifestyle	3.2	1.8	3.6	3.5	4.4	33.1	10.4	11.3	8.1	9.2	11.4
	16.4						50.5				
advancement in social status	9.2	3.4	6.4	5.6	6.9	31.9	8.6	10.3	5.8	5.3	6.5
	31.6						36.5				
improving one's individual appearance	9.6	6.5	7.1	6.8	7.7	22.8	7.7	8.6	4.8	7.7	10.7
	37.8						39.5				
personal happiness	7.5	4.5	5.7	8.0	7.2	31.8	7.5	7.7	6.2	6.9	7.0
	33.0						35.2				
achieving and preserving good physical fitness	5.1	2.5	4.8	3.7	6.6	30.4	8.7	11.0	6.9	8.3	12.0
	22.6						47.0				
entertainment and pleasure	6.2	4.3	8.0	5.5	6.7	27.8	8.9	9.8	6.1	5.9	10.7
	30.7						41.5				

Source: authors' own calculations.

The prominent feature of the results is the considerable diversity of responses, indicating several separate sets of preferences. The differentiating factor in these sets is the ranking of provision for security in old age among listed needs, as well as the categories of needs against which it proved more or less important. Within the extracted groups of individuals with regard to diversified sets of preferences, one can observe three characteristic types when it comes to ranking the need for provision of security in old age. These are: a type dominated by the need to provide for security in old age, within which this need is more important than all other needs; a type of moderate importance, within which the need is located at medium level rank; and a type of marginal value, within which the need is rated as less important than all other needs. Within these three main groups one can extract more detailed divisions. Finally, five groups with different perceptions of the need to provide for security in old age as opposed to other needs in Schrab's classification were extracted.[7] The relative importance of the need to provide for security in old age versus other needs in each of five extracted clusters is presented in fig. 15.3 below.

The first cluster comprised 15.3% of all respondents. Respondents in this cluster ranked the need to provide for security in old age in first place compared with all other needs. Moreover, the characteristic feature of this set of preferences is the considerable distance between the need to provide for security in old age and other needs, as well as the relatively equal importance of all other needs. The latter is reflected in low differentiation of their relative importance compared to the need to provide for security in old age. This cluster represents the type of preferences dominated by the need to provide for security in old age. The preference ranking characteristics of this group are presented in table 15.5 below.

[7] The respondents using the 11-level scale evaluated the importance of providing for security in old age versus other needs listed in Schrab's classification. A paired comparison test was used as earlier surveys referring to saving motives and using monadic scales did not show such significant differences as had been expected. Such a testing method allowed on the one hand to determine the ranking of provision for security in old age among all other needs, and on the other made it possible to build a preference structure as opposed to all listed needs. Extracting homogenous groups with regard to the set of preferences versus the importance of particular needs was conducted by applying the *k-means* method. Five clusters were differentiated, as this number was the highest possible to guarantee sufficient frequency of extracted groups with a satisfied level of their homogeneity. For each of the extracted clusters of respondents, the average level of importance of need for providing for security in old age, as well as the structure of preferences bearing in mind all listed needs, were extracted. Relative importance of the distinguish needs was estimated by comparing average level of importance with extreme limits. Results of the comparison were presented in percentages.

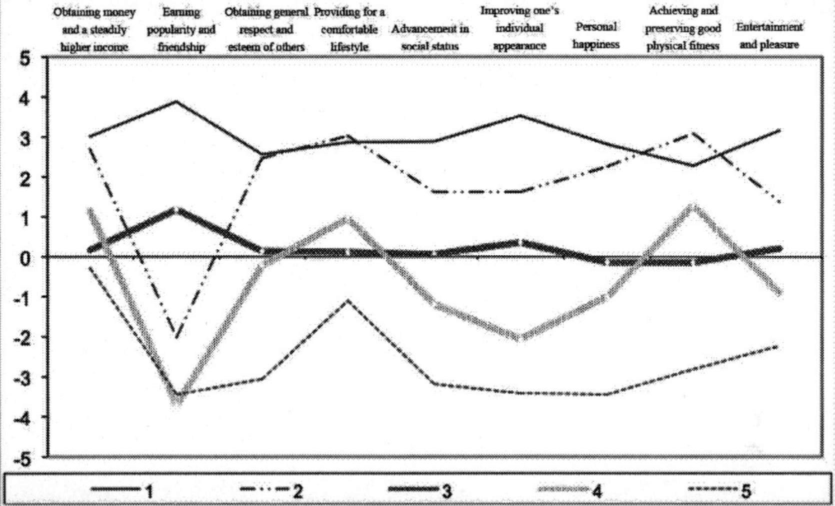

Fig. 15.3
The relative importance of the need to provide for security in old age versus other needs.
Source: author's own calculations.

Table 15.5. Preference ranking in the first cluster of respondents.

Category of needs	Relative importance of the need (providing for security in old-age = 100)
Security in old age	**100**
Achieving and preserving good physical fitness.	**54.5**
Obtaining general respect and esteem of others.	48.8
Personal prestige and happiness.	43.8
Providing for a comfortable lifestyle.	42.7
Advancement in social status.	42.3
Obtaining money and a steadily higher income.	39.8
Entertainment and pleasure.	36.8
Improving one's individual appearance.	29.4
Earning popularity and friendship.	22.3

Source: authors' own calculations.

The characteristic feature of all other clusters is the considerably lower ranking of the need to provide for security in old age than in the first two clusters. At the same time, these clusters differ in both the distance from the need to provide for security in old age and by the set of preferences. The second cluster comprised 18.5% of all respondents. Similarly, in this cluster the respondents ranked the need to provide for security in old age highly, in second place just under the need referring to earning popularity and friendship. However, unlike the set of preference characteristics of the first group, in the second cluster the need to provide for security in old age is not substantially distanced from other needs. This cluster represents the type of preference with only a distinct need to provide for security in old age. The preference ranking characteristics of this group are presented in table 15.6 below.

Table 15.6. Preference ranking in the second cluster of respondents.

Category of needs	Relative importance of the need (providing for security in old-age = 100)
Earning popularity and friendship.	140.2
Security in old age	**100**
Entertainment and pleasure.	72.3
Advancement in social status.	67.6
Improving one's individual appearance.	67.6
Personal prestige and happiness.	54.9
Obtaining general respect and esteem of others.	50.7
Obtaining money and a steadily higher income.	46.2
Providing for a comfortable lifestyle.	39.6
Achieving and preserving good physical fitness.	**38.3**

Source: authors own calculations.

The third cluster comprised 30.3% of all respondents and its prominent feature is in ranking the need to provide for security in old age at a medium level amongst listed needs. The need in question is considerably less important than the group of needs related to the social position of an individual but more important than the needs of a material character and those related to health and entertainment. This cluster represents the type of preferences in which the need to provide for security in old age has been dominated by needs related to social position. Table 15.7 below shows the preference ranking characteristics of this group.

Table 15.7. Preference ranking in the third cluster of respondents.

Category of needs	**Relative importance of the need (providing for security in old-age = 100)**
Personal prestige and happiness.	103.0
Achieving and preserving good physical fitness.	**102.9**
Security in old age	**100**
Advancement in social status.	98.8
Providing for a comfortable lifestyle.	97.8
Obtaining general respect and esteem of others.	97.2
Obtaining money and a steadily higher income.	96.6
Entertainment and pleasure.	95.8
Improving one's individual appearance.	92.8
Earning popularity and friendship.	76,4

Source: authors' own calculations.

The fourth cluster comprised 24.2% of all respondents and similarly its prominent feature is in ranking the need to provide for security in old age at a medium level amongst listed needs. The need in question is considerably less important than the group of needs related to the social position of an individual but more important than the needs of a material character and those related to health and entertainment. Unlike the set of preference characteristics of the third group, in this cluster the need to provide for security in old age is substantially distanced from other needs. This cluster represents the type of preferences in which the need to provide for security in old age has been strongly dominated by needs related to social position. Table 15.8 below shows the preference set characteristics of this group.

Table 15.8. Preference ranking in the forth cluster of respondents.

Category of needs	Relative importance of the need (providing for security in old-age = 100)
Earning popularity and friendship.	174.2
Improving one's individual appearance.	141.4
Advancement in social status.	123.9
Personal prestige and happiness.	120.0
Entertainment and pleasure.	117.9
Obtaining general respect and esteem of others.	104.5
Security in old age	**100**
Providing for a comfortable lifestyle.	80.7
Obtaining money and a steadily higher income.	77.2
Achieving and preserving good physical fitness.	**74.3**

Source: authors' own calculations.

The final cluster comprised 11.7% of all respondents and is characterised by ranking the need to provide for security in old age as the least important compared to all other needs. Moreover, the prominent feature of this group is the relatively lower ranking of those needs which are related to material conditions, and higher ranking of those which are related to social position. This cluster represents the type of preferences with a marginal need to provide for security in old age. Preference ranking characteristics of this cluster are presented in table 15.9 below.

Table 15.9. Preference ranking in the forth cluster of respondents.

Category of needs	Relative importance of the need (providing for security in old-age = 100)
Earning popularity and friendship.	168.9
Personal prestige and happiness.	168.8
Improving one's individual appearance.	168.3
Advancement in social status.	163.7
Obtaining general respect and esteem of others.	161.1
Achieving and preserving good physical fitness.	**156.2**
Entertainment and pleasure.	144.7
Providing for a comfortable lifestyle.	122.1
Obtaining money and a steadily higher income.	105.8
Security in old age	**100**

Source: authors own calculations.

The first structure of preferences, dominated by the need to provide for old age security, most frequently appeared among young people on the first phase of the family life cycle, who are childless, and whose monthly personal income was 330 USD and over; it least frequently appeared among people whose average monthly income did not exceed 330 USD. The second structure of preferences, with only a distinct need to provide for security in old age, most frequently appeared among young people on the first phase of the family life cycle, who are childless, with basic vocational education; and least frequently appeared among married people with adolescent children, with higher education. It is hard to discern apparent differences of socio-demographic features for the third structure of preferences, characterised by the equal position of listed needs. It appeared independently from level of education, family status and level of personal income.

The forth structure of preferences, in which the need to provide for old age security is dominated by the needs related to social position, most frequently appeared among either people whose monthly personal income is 500 USD and over, with an independent family status, age and social position or young people, on the first phase of family life cycle, who are childless, and whose monthly personal income is lower than 330 USD.

The fifth structure of preferences, in which the need to provide for old age security is ranked marginally, most frequently appeared either among young people, on the first phase of family life cycle, who are childless, and whose monthly personal income is 330 USD and over, or among married people with adolescent children, living from unearned sources. This structure of preferences appeared least frequently either among people with basic vocational education and whose monthly personal income is about 330–500 USD.

While socio-demographic profiles of extracted clusters do not show characteristic unambiguous differences, the apparent differences relate to their economic situation and attitudes towards saving. The economic regularities (the shift to higher saving capabilities with an increase in average monthly income) are connected with a position of the need to provide for security in old age in hierarchy of needs. The ANOVA procedure confirmed a significant (p = 0.016) relation between the level of monthly income and position of this need in the structure of preferences. The highest differences are observed between the forth cluster, in which the need to provide for old age security is dominated by the needs related to social position, and the fifth cluster, in which the need to provide for old age security is ranked marginally. The relationships discussed are illustrated in table 15.10 below.

Table 15.10. Average monthly income per one person in a household, and percentage of people who in 2006 saved part of their income along extracted clusters.

Cluster	Average monthly income (in USD)	Percentage of people who in 2006 saved regular part of their income
1. Dominated by the need to provide for an old-age security	492.0	16.5
2. With only a distinct need to provide for security in old age	444.0	13.5
3. Characterised by the equal position of listed needs	465.0	15.8
4. In which the need to provide for an old-age security is strong dominated by the needs related to social position	519.5	21.9
5. In which the need to provide for an old-age security is ranked marginally	370.1	12.6

Source: authors' own calculations.

Conclusions

Economic incentives, sociological and psychological factors and health and work conditions are all important in making people work longer, so neither solely push nor pull factors, but rather a combination of "push-pull" (Phillipson 2002) factors, could be a recommendation for those who are responsible for policy in this field to obtain financial stability of the pension system and high employment rates. On the one hand, these preferences and attitudes (like these about retirement age) are changing over time and are quite difficult to explain but still—even today—show that in Poland, even after more than ten years after introducing the pension reform, people prefer to retire earlier. Some could say that the institutional impact of the media could influence those opinions that quite a lot Poles prefer, in fact, a lower retirement age than official. But nevertheless the hope is that with time, the awareness that early retirement creates more negative consequences than positive will increase, as it is not only the cause of lower pension benefit, but also a lot of studies underline that non-workers are more frequently at risk to be socially excluded than those who are still at work. Additionally, we have presented a perception about retirement age in which people express that they would like to leave the labor market and are looking forward to retirement. In addition, we have shown a short presentation of results about saving rates and saving motives for retirement, combining these issues with results on thinking about consumption and the change of its level. So, without doubt, consumption is important in relation to saving and poverty and it should be as well presented. The last point of this discussion is that these different cultural implications of preferences towards retirement are not the same across Europe. There are already additional analyses and surveys which compare Poles to other nations based on recent surveys which fortunately show a very comprehensive picture including sociological and economics aspects of this field. The last part of the chapter was about the identification attitude amongst workers towards retirement regarding saving for old age and their relevant position among others needs. It seems that this need does not yet play a significant role with relation to attitude and decision about (early) retirement. There is then still an unanswered question about how workers in Poland could be convinced that early retirement with not enough savings for old age will not allow them to maintain their optimistic expectations of life on retirement expressed in this survey and presented here.

References

Calasanti, Toni. "Work and Retirement in the 21st century: Integrating Issues of Diversity and Globalization." *Ageing International* Vol. 27 (3) (2002): 3–20.

Chou, Kee-Lee and Nelson W. S. Chow. "To Retire or Not to Retire: Is There an Option for Older Workers in Hong Kong?" *Social Policy and Administration* Vol. 39 (3) (2009): 233–246.

Chłoń, Agnieszka, Marek Góra and Michał Rutkowski. *Shaping Pension Reform in Poland: Security through Diversity*. World Bank Pension Primer, No. 9923, 1999.

Contini, Bruno and Roberto Leombruni. "From Work to Retirement: a Tale of Bumpy Routes." *Review of Political Economy* Vol. 18 (3) (2006): 359–378.

Dahl, Svenn-Age, Oivind Anti Nilsen and Kjell Vaagej. "Work or retirement? Exit Routes for Norwegian Elderly." *Foundation for Research in Applied Economics* 32 (2000): 1865–1876.

Góra, Marek and Michał Rutkowski. *The Quest for Pension Reform: Poland's Security through Diversity*. World Bank Pension Primer, No. 9815, 1998.

Gruber, Jonathan and David A. Wise. *Social Security Programs and Retirement Around the world: Micro Estimation*. NBER working paper No. 9407, Cambridge M.A., National Bureau of Economic Research, 2002.

Holzmann, Robert. "The World Bank Approach to Pension Reform." *International Social Security Review* 53 (1) (2000): 11–34.

James, Jacquelyn Boone, Paul Wink and Warner K. Schaie. "The Crown of life: Dynamics of the Early Post-Retirement Period." *Annual Review of Gerontology* 26 (2006).

Lahey, Karen Eilers, Kim Doseong and Melinda L. Newman. "Full Retirement? An Examination of Factors that Influence the Decision to Return to Work." *Financial Services Review* 15 (2006): 1–19.

Naegele Gerhard and Alan Walker. "Social Protection: Incomes, Poverty and the Reform of Pensions Systems." In *Ageing in Society. European Perspectives on Gerontology*, 3rd Edition. Edited by John Bond, Sheila Peace, Freya Dittman-Kohli, Gerben J. Westerhof. London: SAGE Publications, 2007.

O wieku emerytalnym kobiet i mężczyzn, [*About the retirement age of women and men*], Warszawa: CBOS, No. BS/205/2005, 2005.

Phillipson, Chris. *Transition from Work to Retirement. Developing a New Social Contract*. Bristol: Policy Press, 2002.

Perek-Białas, Jolanta and Małgorzata Rószkiewicz. *Sklonność do oszczędzania polskich gospodarstw domowych* [*Propenstity to Save of Polish Households*]. Warszawa, PONT INFO, 1999.

—. *Attitudes Towards Saving in Polish Society During Transformation.* Conference paper at European Sociological Ass., Glasgow, 2007, RN on Economic Sociology.

Perek-Białas, Jolanta. "Retire or not Reiter? Different Preferences of Ageing Workers." In *Advances in Gerontology, abstract* 3 (20) (2007): 287; conference paper at Gerontological Society of the Russian Academy of Science, International Association of Gerontology and Geriatrics.

Rószkiewicz, Małgorzata. "Uwarunkowania gromadzenia zasobów w polskich gospodarstwach domowych w okresie reformowania systemu ubezpieczeń spolecznych" ["The determinants of saving behaviour among Polish households in the period of Social security reform"]. *Gospodarka Narodowa* (3) (2003): 31–54.

—. "The Need to Provide for Security in Old Age in Hierarchy of Needs—An Estimation of its Ranking Within the Polish Population." *Social Indicators Research* 69 (2) (2004): 199–218.

—. *Oszczędzanie. Postawy i zachowania polskich gospodarstw domowych wobec oszczędzania* [*Saving. The attitude and behaviour of Polish households towards saving*]. Kraków: Wyd. Aureus, 2008.

Schrab, Victor. *Ten Copy Appeals*, Printers Ink, 1943.

Taylor, Paul. *New Policies for Older Workers.* Bristol: Policy Press, 2002.

Van Tilburg, Theo. "Consequences of Men's Retirement for the Continuation of Work-related Personal Relationships." *Ageing International* 28 (4) (2003): 345–358.

CHAPTER SIXTEEN

FACTORS OF PRICING IN MEDICINE: OUT-OF-POCKET PAYMENTS IN MOSCOW PUBLIC DENTISTRY

ELENA BERDYSHEVA[1]

Introduction

Where do market prices for goods and services come from? This question seems to have been settled long ago, and one can find the answer in any textbook on economics. There, one will read that price results from the proportion between supply and demand on the market. Unfortunately, the textbooks do not tell us that supply and demand are only "overarching categories useful for analysis of multiple forces, causes and factors exerting influence on price" (Samuelson 2004, 14), and only rarely will textbooks reveal the secret of whether abstract principles of price formation described in theory correlate with real practices of pricing on consumer markets. In order to experience these practices one should step back from the banal explanation of price in terms of supply and demand and return to "the multiple forces which determine these demand and supply or being expressed through them" (Samuelson 2004, 13). It may help one to find principles which are observed by market actors when they set prices for goods and services, for example for informal dental services in Russian public dentistry.

Plenty of recent studies show that out-of-pocket payments are widely distributed in medical systems in the countries of Eastern Europe, modern Russia not being an exception, a doctor being to great extent free in setting prices. Thus the case of informal commercial services in public dentistry seems to be a relevant example for studying principles observed by price

[1] Department of Economic Sociology, State University—the Higher School of Economics, Moscow.

makers. Therefore our study is focused on the pricing behavior of actors in the informal segment of the Moscow dental market. Due to the special position of the Moscow region in relation to other regions of Russia it is better to look at our investigation as a case study.

Towards the Social Nature of Market Price

There is barely much to speak of regarding the sociological tradition of investigating market pricing. Having advanced to the study of economic life later than economics, sociology confronted the list of terms being used in economic research of economy and adopted them according to its aims. There are still only a few sociologists working on the problem of market pricing, the question of price and pricing usually mentioned only in passing, often when discussing consumer markets. Therefore the conceptualizing of price usually depends on the way one takes the interplay between social and economical parts of life. Sometimes pricing is seen as a consequence of commensuration and rationalization, price being accepted as an indicator of market in its negative sense. Pricing seems to dry up social relations and values and lack any social meanings.

This chapter takes such an approach to be reductive. Contrary to this, the interplay between economic and social items (between price and value) on the market is not as direct and destructive as one may think. "Value is the epigone of price" assumed Georg Simmel and showed that illusive unbalance between price and value is being overcome during the process of exchange (Simmel 1990, 95). Indeed, people pay the price by sacrificing some amount of goods in getting others. However, when we speak about market exchange we can see that people benefit from market transactions i.e. required goods compensate money sacrifices: "If the robber forces someone at pistol point to sell his watch and rings for three pennies, what he receives under these conditions is worth the price, since it is the only way to save his life" (Simmel 1990, 95). Price and value differ by appearance but have a lot in common through their social sense, society approving prices that contain and convey the value of things. Pricing provides standards and as a consequence simplifies the process of commensuration widely used in society (Simmel 1990).

One should recognize that pricing is a dynamic process. Price is both a condition of exchange and a tangible representative of market choice, its circumstances and consequences, a numerical mark of the ratio among different goods that resulted from bargaining. It plays a part of "equivalent inherent in economies integrated on the base of exchange" (Polanyi 1957). However, this "equivalent" does not point at the amount one should sacrifice for the good but at amount one can require instead of it (Polanyi 1957). The price is an institutionalized cause for beginning a discussion about the exchange—some fixed quantity being required for a deal is begun (Polanyi 1957). One is wrong if they think that prices are set artificially. Following Polanyi, the notion of fixed price points at the previous volatility of price (Polanyi 1957). In simple economies, prices originate from bargaining and if we look this analytically we may discover many factors exerted influence on price in simple economies and continue to do so in contemporary ones. Some of these factors deserve to be noted by sociology.

From the sociological prospective any economic action is a social action being pursued in the sphere of economy, both types of action undergoing the influence of absolute social values (Weber 1978). Traditions, superstitions, relationships between individuals, status privileges, social policy and political interests are considered to determine market life. Therefore price is not only an economic feature but also a cultural and social entity. It accounts for some empirical evidence confirming, for instance, that rational market actors try to set fair rather than profitable prices. They follow some social conventions and use prices of different types and social meanings; prices carry both economic and moral symbolic meanings, and their meanings are always relative and multiple (Velthuis 2005). For example, art dealers regard high prices for contemporary art to be the proof of value of masterpieces while regular people view such prices as fraudulent. (Velthuis 2005). At the same time prices for fashionable photography turn out to be an "epiphenomenon of status hierarchy" and reflect how photographers combine logic of art, creation and uniqueness with economic approach to photographing as a source of earnings (Aspers 2005).

One should remember that price is an instrument of quantitative estimation of relative chances in the struggle of interests (Weber 1978). First of all we should focus on the opposition between a seller and a buyer. According to sociological studies, economic exchange is more or less standardized: "Exchange is simply a subjective action between two persons, the result of which depends only upon the shrewdness, the eagerness and the persistence of the two parties, not upon the object and its supra-individually determined relation to price" (Simmel 1990, 92). Thus pricing is closely related to the character of social interaction between the participants of exchange—their sex, age, reputation, social ties and status may matter. For instance, prices may vary according to the extent of personification of relationships between the provider and consumer, and market relationships between individuals may be ranged along the scale.

On the one hand there are interactions at arm's length and on the other there are socially embedded interactions. When a deal takes place between socially related partners, a seller may reduce the final price (Velthuis 2005). Thus price often contains information both about goods and about people who produce, sell or buy these goods. Being the initial point of economic exchange, price encourages bargaining and undergoes changes due to it. To a great extent the results of bargaining are determined by the social features of the individuals involved, and consequently the structure of fixed prices may carry traces of previous social situations of bargaining.

However the seller–buyer relationship is only one type of possible market ties. Following Max Weber we may look at the market as a fight for market power between competitors, price depending on the power arrangements of the market (Weber 1978). The mutual orientations of producers or buyers towards each other also have an influence on market price (White 1981). Often, such orientations are much more important than sellers' orientations towards consumers or the characteristics of demand. Providers trace each other's prices and base their pricing strategies on the results of this price monitoring (White 1981). Sellers may either imitate close pricing practice or come to mutual agreements, and suffer from uncertainty in the market. Communication with each other helps them to overcome market uncertainty and to get an idea of possible market prices, social ties between sellers leading to differentiation of market prices. Insiders of such networks are inclined to coordinate their prices, to compete inside the niche that leads to prices becoming more or less similar. Each niche has its own level of prices which may be quite different from prices of other market niches (Baker 1984).

In discussing market price we cannot avoid marketing studies on pricing. Marketing research is shaped by customers and so marketologists dispose of practical information on pricing rules and laws useful for sociology. There is a long list of price determinants taken into consideration by marketologists including, for instance, consumers' perception of price and quality, price elasticity related with demand, existence of complimentary and substitutive goods, and so on. Basing this study on such arguments it is proposed that pricing undergoes the influence of social attitudes and social relationships of market actors. The overarching argument is that, like many other market processes, pricing may be regarded as a socially embedded phenomenon. To check this hypothesis, this chapter examines the pricing behavior of dentists who are engaged in public dentistry but also provide additional services to their basic duties and therefore face the necessity of defining the size of out-of-pocket payments for each patient.

The Design of the Research

The dental services market has been selected on purpose. Due to the ambivalence of marketization of medicine, the medical services market is a good example of a sphere in which the tangle of social and economical motivation of price makers may be revealed and observed. Some time ago, sociologists led by Talkott Parsons considered the relations between a doctor and a patient to be a social system with an uneven distribution of power. Thanks to the position of the expert, a doctor is allowed much more power and freedom to make decisions while a patient has to occupy a subordinate position and follow the rules set by the doctor. Since medicine has become more market oriented, the doctor–patient relationship has gained some new features. Doctors have lost some power as their profit now depends on money paid by the patient. Patients, by contrast, have obtained the advantage to act as consumers of medical services, meaning that now they are free to choose a doctor based on the quality of provided treatment. The mutual positions of doctor and patient have become much more equal than they were before.

At the same time, despite the marketization of medicine, the doctor and patient deal with health which is a socially entangled good (Callon 1998). Required by each person, health cannot be marketed directly, and is an absolute value, medicine carrying responsibility for it. Being incorporated into the medical norms these obligations may restrict the marketization of the doctor–patient relationship. As a consequence some economic phenomenon may gain social features and undergo the influence of social factors, and pricing in medicine is not an exception. The level of freedom in the market situation of public dentistry in defining prices is much higher when compared with legal segments of the medical market.

One can distinguish five segments of dentistry market in Moscow:

(1) A segment of dentistry chains. At present in Moscow, dentistry chains tend to work with corporate clients according to their insurance programs, prices also being indicated here. Doctors conform to stable price lists (various prices for different insurance programs) and have few opportunities to manage the price (among the main players in this segment there are Masterdent, Denta-L and Denta-Vita).

(2) A segment of single dental clinics, from the cheapest on the outskirts of Moscow to the high class dentistry in the centre of the city. Pricing is supervised by managers working for the owners, with doctors following rigid price lists.

(3) A segment of private dentists who rent dental surgeries and work as entrepreneurs. Unfortunately, at present researchers lack of any clear description of this part of the Moscow dental services market.
(4) A segment of commercial departments in public dentistry. The level of prices here is defined according to instructions imposed by the Health Ministry. As prices are standardized by health authorities, doctors are obliged to keep to them.
(5) An informal segment of commercial dental services provided by doctors for additional fee in public clinics without commercial departments. Due to its illegal nature this segment is a sphere where doctors may define prices by themselves.

This study focuses primarily on price makers—though the participation of patients in market price formation is acnowledged, "client effects" have been placed to one side in order to simplify the tasks of the study. The aim was not to provide a complete account for pricing in dentistry, instead to attempt to raise the awareness of pricing among sociologists. The main purpose was to identify and to explore principles observed by dentists while defining the size of out-of pocket payments for each patient, and to understand whether doctors manage prices in order to compensate for their costs and to increase their profit, or whether pricing is driven by values, norms, traditions, social attitudes or affects significant for them. The pricing strategies of dentists providing informal commercial services in Moscow public dentistry were therefore questioned, the study encompassing 9 female dentists aged from 34–52, being employed in different public clinics in Moscow, respondents being recruited by the snow-ball method. All of them considered out-of-pocket payments an important source of their monthly income. The analysis is based on qualitative data obtained from in-depth interviews, while quantitative information was gathered from 3 dentists who agreed to keep diaries of observation. Thanks to such self-observation there was a database of 139 patients: their social, demographic, clinical features and prices paid for informal dental treatment.

Socio-Economical Peculiarities of Medical Services Market: Prerequisites of Doctors' Pricing Behavior

Medical services is a specialist market, economists often calling it "a market with flaws." We argue that such "flaws" result from the nature of medical service as a subject of market transaction and the position of a doctor as a member of a professional community. So these are not "flaws," but natural features typical for the medical services market.

This study builds on the theoretical concept of medical service as a credence elaborated in institutional economics (Fridolin 1999), which supposes that due to the patient's lack of medical knowledge they have to rely upon the word of the doctor, and as a result there is a danger of opportunism on the doctor's part. Following their pecuniary interests the latter may use their beneficial position in order to induce an additional demand and to gain additional profit (Anderson, House and Ormiston 1981). Actors of confiding commodities markets face the problems of uncertainty and asymmetric distribution of information. In the medical services market these problems are caused by the illusiveness of medical treatment quality. A patient can hardly estimate whether a doctor has done his best to improve his health and that is why patients often regard the price of a service as the main indicator of quality. In addition they are inclined to build their impressions about a doctor on their skills of communication, the décor and equipment of the clinic and so on. Patients have to look for some tangible indicators to estimate the quality of a doctors' work. Sometimes they suffer from the consequences of their impression as it is frequently based on factors which do not necessarily correlate with the professionalism of the doctor. Despite this, a positive impression is a strong stimulus for a patient to visit the particular doctor next time when they fall ill—patients will avoid changing from a doctor who has gained their confidence. So the price elasticity of demand for goods such as medical services turns out to be lower than in case with normal goods, and thus a doctor obtains the opportunity to act as if he is a local monopolist with loyal patients. Monopoly implies freedom in managing prices, and such monopolists have the opportunity to pursue pricing discrimination, to vary prices according to the characteristics of their clients. Empirical studies have rejected the hypothesis of doctor's affective neutrality—in other words doctors have various attitudes towards patients with different features. They like and dislike patients and may take these likes and dislikes into consideration when setting their prices, thus the interaction with an unpleasant patient may be compensated by means of increasing the price.

There is empirical evidence to support the idea that doctors observe the norms of professional community in their daily practice (Freidson 1988, Rhee Sang 1977). Sometimes such norms may prevail over doctor's personal intentions as preservation of professional status is the target for doctors (Rhee Sang 1977). Therefore during the market transaction a doctor has to take into consideration both market laws and principals of medical community.

Principles of Pricing in Medicine: Empirical Evidences from Informal Public Dentistry

The data obtained from the interviews may be packed into a simple analytical model of price, showing price for a dental service as consisting of two parts—a core and a covering (see Fig. 16.1 below).

The core is a stable part of price which cannot vary with the inspiration of a single seller. The covering includes two layers—constant and flexible—based on different factors. The constant layer of price covering is shaped by "social traditions, habitual experiences and apparently logical necessities," while the flexible part of price covering carries the influences of individual situations, momentary needs and the force of circumstances (Simmel 1990, 95). If a seller has the opportunity to define price for each buyer, a price covering varies according to the cognitive map by means of which a seller perceives market transactions.

It is necessary to state that at the current stage of the study this model of price can be used only as an analytical frame helpful for exploring the dependence of price on social attitudes of price makers—an attempt to look at price structure from the sociological point of view has only begun. Nevertheless the task of structuring price and finding its multiple determinants seems to be prospective for several reasons. First of all, because in the light of this task, researchers are forced to take into consideration the variety of processes laid behind the observed market prices. Usually, price is explored when it has already been set, researchers being interested primarily in the market consequences of existing prices, and in market actors' reactions to them, the process of price formation staying to one side. This is fine until we put aside the models of market and address real consumer markets wherein we may discover multiple practices being pursued by regular people—sellers or price makers. As price and pricing are rooted in the market, getting information about the ways in which real prices are formed will advance our understanding of the consumer markets themselves. Therefore the task of structuring price and finding its multiple determinants is worth accomplishing. This chapter can now make the first step in this direction and illustrate the model of price with information gathered from the interviews with our respondents who are experienced in "autographic" setting of price for informal medical services.

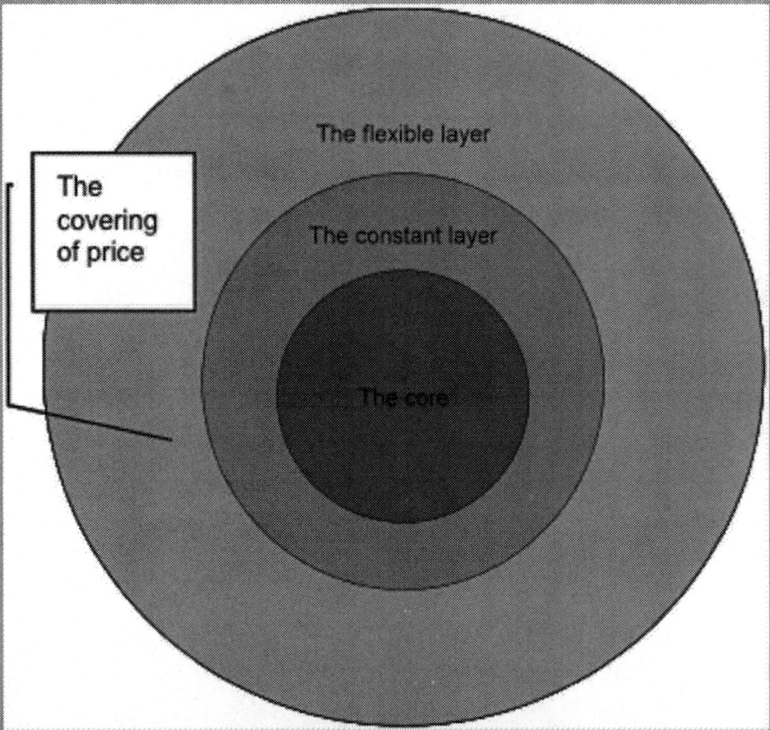

Fig. 16.1
Mean of respondents that bought or boycotted products in the last 12 months (% yes answers).
Source: ESS 2002/2003; author's own calculations.

The results of the study show that the core of informal prices for dental services is shaped by the costs and expenses of providing treatment, expenses for materials and rent the main among them, although when we speak about informal business activity of public dentists one should remember that to some extent their costs may be shifted to the state as they use space, equipment and often materials of the public clinic where they are engaged. Nevertheless, dentists have to legitimate their commercial activity in the eyes of their managers and colleagues. It was assumed that such legitimacy was based on the systematic payments in managers' favor, however our respondents argued that none of them had faced the necessity to share their informal profit with administration. Instead, they compensate their commercial activity by providing qualified treatment for the relatives and acquaintances of the administration free of charge: "Though the head doctor does not approve of such practices, she ignores them as she also has relatives interested in treament here." At the same time doctors assume informal payments in favor of administration may exist in other clinics, and some of them have even heard about such practices from their friends. According to the doctors interviewed, the necessity to treat relatives of the administration does not exert influence on the size of the out of-pocket payments they get from each patient. The price core may also vary in regard to materials of different quality and different costs being used by a doctor. The amount of time a doctor spends on a treatment is also taken into account. Furthermore the price core may increase if a doctor has to share informal profit with his assistants.

What Factors Lay Behind the Size of Price Covering?

The lowest level of price covering is determined by a doctor's expectations concerning profit from informal medical activity, with these expectations in turn modelled by an ideal of personal income. Yet there is a gap between expectations in desire and in practice. Very often the respondents insisted on the principle of achieving a definite level of income. Dentists rarely maximize their profit from informal activity. They are income satisfiers rather than profit maximizators. The level of desired income depends on the doctor's ideas about merited wage which includes the doctor's esteem of their human capital value, costs of obtaining this capital in the past and expenses for supporting its level in the present.

Besides money and self-actualization doctors are willing to get recognition from their work. The value of doctor's human capital is a base for institutionalized trust towards them, and the price of their service should reflect this meaning. "Will the oligarch visit me if the price of my work is three pence? He will say: a well qualified professional cannot estimate himself so low." However, doctors are able to accept the fact that the price of their work in Russia neither reflects the social value of their profession nor compensates for their efforts of gaining a medical education. Real estimations of everyday life help them with this: "All people in our country have low wages. How can doctors earn as much as they need?"

Doctors' knowledge about the cost of living also contributes to the level of price covering. "First of all one should account that a doctor needs a merited wage." They also have to coordinate their prices according to changes in economy—inflation, weakening of currency and everything of this kind. Our respondents confirm that there are situations when medical ethics may prevail over the business aims of a doctor. However, one can hardly face such situations in dentistry since the latter never meets matters of live or death. Thus in dentistry a doctor's market motivations are much clearer in comparison with other medical spheres: "If a patient comes to me he is ready to pay. But I am a dentist. If I were a surgeon I would not be able to deny a patient with acute appendicitis."

Prices in dentistry depend on a doctor's self esteem. They are the only person who can honestly estimate their own qualification. In medical services market professional qualification is a key to competitiveness. The doctor's opinion about competition in the market, information about supply, and market stability also influence their decisions on price: "If I worked in the field I would act as monopolist … But today there are many public and private clinics around me…" When setting a price a doctor takes into account his own reputation through their patients' social networks and the quantity of loyal patients: "There are patients who have been visiting me for many years and they accept my prices. And their friends who come to me on their advice also do." It is also important to foresee the level of demand.

Besides market parameters, doctors take into consideration technological progress in medicine: a treatment with modern materials or modern equipment costs more. Doctors may exploit the symbolic meaning of "new and more progressive" in their interests, though in public dentistry the opportunities for it are not very wide. The equipment of dental surgeries in public dentistry leaves much to be desired. Poor equipment prevents the price level in public dentistry from being increased since the arrangements of treatment are not able to vindicate high prices. So high class facilities lead to a price increase while bad facilities are forced to decrease: "Can I ask for high prices if our interior is so poor?"

Dental prices must be fair, and when pricing dental services doctors follow the principle of fair price. Though they regret the attitude of the state towards healthcare and health of the nation they try to set prices available for regular people.

The size of out-of-pocket payments or informal prices in dentistry may vary in relation with the normative atmosphere in the collective where a doctor works. Public dentists have to reckon with colleagues' attitudes to the practice of getting out-of-pocket payments: whether these practices are accepted or criticized; whether they are approved or disapproved of; whether they coincide with the conception of professionalism or not. Since doctors have to support the stability of their local market in public dentistry they form conventions about prices. If a doctor breaks the rules he may face problems with colleagues as they perceive such practices as damaging.

The data from interviews emphasize that although doctors regard out-of-pocket payments to be a significant source of their income they do not perceive the informal services as their own private business on the base of public dentistry. It is well known that medical wages in Moscow exceed doctors' wages in other regions, and such wages are likely to encourage public dentists to accomplish their main duties. They also explain why doctors accept out-of -pocket payments as an exception rather than a rule, despite their frequency. One important consequence of such a view of informal payments is the inclination of doctors to save their efforts in defining prices. In order to avoid the process of commensuration with each patient, doctors develop schemes of pricing behavior and apply them to their daily practice.

How Do Doctors Find the Information about Possible Market Prices for Dental Services?

Some dentists have confessed that they acquire data about prices from speaking with colleagues. Others have said they explored the Moscow market of dental services, the internet, and similar dentists working in different clinics, while friends who visit other dentists, speaking with new patients who come from other dentists and their own experience as a patient may also supply information about market prices. Official tariffs developed by the national health authorities are also used by doctors as a flash-light in the atmosphere of market uncertainty. Having obtained the idea of a possible price on the market a doctor adopts this line according to the market segment he works in.

While a constant layer of price covering is strong, a flexible layer may fluctuate under the influence of local circumstances, the interval for such fluctuation being limited. Its borders are assigned by the payment capacity of patients or more precisely by doctors' thoughts about it. How does a doctor recognize the level of payment capacity? According to our interviews they directs attention to the external signs of a patient's social status, payment capacity being a socially constructed item. Therefore, to identify it a doctor should have social, rather than professional or market, competence. "I see people visiting me and I may understand how much they will be able to pay … I look at a patient's appearance, his watch, shoes, mobile phone … I notice what he talks about, what questions he asks …"

The payment capacity of patients may provoke a doctor to price discrimination. Price discrimination is usually based on a doctor's prejudices or thoughts about interplay between some patient's characteristics and the opportunity to earn some additional money for the treatment. In the first case it is necessary to explore which patient characteristics may cause price discrimination, and in the second case one should question norms regulating practices of price discrimination. Unfortunately, the interviews did not allow us to discover which characteristics may cause variations of price. According to the dentists, payment capacity is the main base for price formation. Other social features of patients and interaction with them are said to be unimportant from the point of view of price. As one dentist argued, even when a doctor holds kind feelings towards a patient he won't decrease the price of treatment. As to whether doctors' pricing behavior varies in regards with patients' features has been tested using quantitative data.

Social, Demographic, Clinical Features of Patients: Sources of Price Variability

As was mentioned, three female dentists had agreed to participate in our experiment by keeping diaries of self-observation. They are employed in three different public clinics but the conditions of their work can be viewed as comparable: they work in public clinics without commercial departments, are working full time from Monday through to Friday, and they work in the same dental surgery with their colleagues.

According to the results of previous studies, doctor's attitudes towards the patient may influence the doctor–patient interaction. Contrary to the medical sociology of Talkott Parsons, in practice doctors often fail to follow the principle of affective neutrality (Hornung, Massgli 1979). They perceive patients differently, paying attention to their social and behavioral features (Richman, Goldthorp 1977, Staudenmayer, Lefkowitz 1981), therefore we tested whether the differentiation of patients' characteristics contributes to the level of heterogeneity of informal prices for dental services.

We came to an agreement that these dentists would record the information about informal treatment provided in the diaries of observation we had agreed on. In the end, we attained information regarding 139 patients. Furthermore the doctors agreed to discuss our conclusions when the data was analyzed.

Which of Our Expectations Have Been Proved by Empirical Data?

We have discovered that customers pay lower prices in comparison with patients who come to the dentist for the first time. The dentists accounted for this statistical result in the manner of marketologists: they said that a patient's loyalty is a source of stability for a doctor, and that a doctor is ready to pay for such stability, and so he tries to retain customers. Furthermore, a customer may recommend the doctor to his friends and acquaintances. Such recommendations are viewed by doctors as a method of advertisement: "The customer who has been visiting me for a long time has already paid very much. And I know that he will come back the next time when he needs any dental help. And maybe he will bring his family or friends for treatment."

At the same time, a patient's experience of previous payments sets the conditions of transaction, and restrains the freedom of doctors' pricing behavior—prices for customers are not increased since the last visit. It is quite difficult for a doctor to increase a price for a customer and to therefore lose his confidence. A doctor must explain price changes to a patient: "In case of raising the cost of living a patient is ready to see rises in prices. But if there were no changes, how may I tell him that prices have become more expensive?"

Our quantitative data showed the interplay between prices and the level of personalization of doctor–patient relations. The level of personalization implies how a patient comes to know about this doctor, whether they do so by accident, on the referrals of other patients, on referrals of doctor's acquaintances or if they are a doctor's acquaintance themselves. We asked doctors to comment on this result and offer some explanations, and it appears that when a patient comes by way of referral from another patient they usually disclose the information regarding a possible price. When this patient has the same diagnosis as the person upon whose recommendation they chose this dentist, it is very difficult for a dentist to then show the ground of price discrepancy. One way to do it is to address the time factor, however patients often insure themselves against such actions by mentioning the time when their adviser was treated: "What can I do if she sits down and says that her friend visited me last month and was really satisfied with provided treatment and with 'such a good price'."

For patients who come by way of referral from a doctor's acquaintance, the context of informal transaction is different. In this case the character of the doctor–acquaintance relation plays the most important part. What level of personalization exists between them? What is the reason for protection being provided by the doctor's acquaintance? Everything of this kind matters. Nevertheless, with few exceptions, patients who come informally pay money for treatment, though prices for them may be discounted. As for the doctor's acquaintances themselves, they usually receive dental treatment free of charge. It is interesting to note that the doctors themselves state that they would offer free healthcare if they had their own private dental clinics, discounts being the only advantage doctors' acquaintances might account for. The possibility and willingness to treat relatives and acquaintances for free happens only in the case of informal services in public dentistry: "The wage is dropping ... And I may allow to treat some people for free."

A very similar picture may be found in regards to pricing reactions to the situations when a patient breaks the rules of the clinic. When dentists consider the opportunity of founding their own business they declare their intention to compensate for a patient missing an appointment by raising the price. However, in public dentistry doctors do not punish patients for "truancy"—if an informal patient misses an appointment, a doctor uses the unexpected "free" time to accomplish basic charges. Doctors are not willing to punish patients who are late by price changes. According to the interviews, lateness affects the quality of treatment as a doctor has less time. However, such an approach is typical of informal treatment in public dentistry—according to the interviews, doctors consider this pricing strategy inappropriate for interactions with patients in the commercial sector.

Being acquainted with local standards of living a doctor is able to arrange patients according to their paying capacity. The data in this study has confirmed that the level of price capacity in a doctor's opinion and the price itself directly correlate, and thus we can note the traces of price discrimination. However one should not jump to the conclusion that a doctor exploits the payment capacity of patients—in our sample the well-to-do patients were often treated with more qualitative and therefore more expensive materials. And according to doctors, the price of treatment is discussed beforehand, the choice of materials of different quality a voluntary choice of the patient. If the choice is made by a patient at this stage of our study we cannot identify price discrimination on the part of the doctor—the hypothesis that high income patients get a treatment of higher quality therefore looks to be more relevant (Newhouse 1970, 176).

There are also factors which have proved to be insignificant from the point of view of pricing in dentistry. Thus, according to the results of statistical analysis, doctors do not pay attention to the level of patients' education when they set prices. Patients' age also exerts little influence on the prices for informal dental services.

On the whole it is possible to say that the attitudes of dentists involved in this analysis reflect both traditional determinants of prices such as pecuniary and time costs, or level of demand and social determinants of prices such as principle of fair price, absolute values, social stratification and doctor–patient or doctor–colleague relationships.

Conclusions

In order to set an acceptable price a doctor must consider the opinions of their colleagues and rely on information gathered with the help of their social network, and so their pricing behavior may be qualified as a socially embedded phenomenon.

Although our results do not allow us to prove the social embeddedness of price, they seem to be quite reliable in order to show that social and economical determinants of price work at least in parallel. The level of personalization of doctor–patient relationships, the previous experience of treatment provided by this doctor, or the social status of a patient may cause variations in prices for informal dental services. Behind these prices one may find both pecuniary interests of a doctor and his willingness to help a patient. Thus the process of coordination between supply and demand is realized by the individual who has to make a decision on price. Theoretically possible price determinants are learned by a doctor during the process of socialization, the bridge between practice and theory running through their attitudes. Objective conditions of price formation are transformed into arguments in favor of the acceptability of prices being set.

The paradox of the coexistence of rational and value motives in commercial medicine is settled by means of the doctor's orientations at selling their work time rather than human health—work time of professionals turns out to be a commensurable commodity. As for the moral value of health it remains beyond the market context. It is built into the professional principles being observed by doctors in their daily medical practice.

Doctors say that their intentions to reduce prices for relatives and acquaintances are a way to maintain social relations external to the job. According to the interviews, such cases stay beyond the commercial activities of doctors. At the same time relationships with patients who pay are built into the market context. Kind feelings here are pleasant attributes of work in medicine rather than the cause of price changes. On the one hand, this conclusion fits Biggart and Delbridge's concept about different systems of exchange which are differentiated on the basis of an individual's logic of action and the structure of social relations between actors. According to this concept actors may have different understandings of "rationality" at different times depending on their situation, the social structures of the exchange settings and the social structure's cultural context (Biggart and Delbridge 2004). On the other hand the finding about discounts for relatives and acquaintances may contribute to the hypothesis that social factors restrict selfish motivation which is possible on the market.

The fact that doctors are inclined to set prices according to the payment capacity of their patients also seems to be controversial. It may be explained from a sociological point of view as well as by the economical concepts. In any case, this finding should attract the attention of sociologists to the social bases of market price. We do not claim that sociology should set its mind on disproving the economical explanations of pricing on the market, instead we assume that sociological theory allows for some complimentary findings which can help in shedding light on the question of market price. In our opinion this question has not yet been settled.

This study has made the first sociological step in the direction of pricing on the market, the results perhaps contributing to the accumulation of semantic meanings concerned with price. However we cannot aspire to the reliability and universality of our conclusions as they require checking in a more representative sample, and as such is prospective research for the future.

References

Abolafia, Mitchel. *Making markets: opportunism and restraint on Wall Street*. London: Harvard University Press, 1996.

Anderson, Richard, Donald House and Micheal Ormiston. "A theory of physician behavior with supplier-induced demand." *Southern Economic Journal* 48 (1981): 124–133.

Aspers, Patrik. *Markets in Fashion: A phenomenological approach*. London: Routledge, 2005.

Baker, Wayne. "The social structure of a national securities market." *The American Journal of Sociology* 89 (1984): 775–811.

Biggart, Nicole and Rick Delbridge. "Systems of exchange." *Academy of management review* 29 (2004): 28–49.

Browne, Katherine. "Work style and network management: gendered patterns and Economic consequences in Martinique." *Gender and Society* 14 (2000): 435–456.

Deneckere, Raymond, Dan Kovenock and Robert Lee. "A model of price leadership based on consumer loyalty." *The Journal of Industrial Economics* 40 (1992): 147–156.

Feldstein, Martin. "The rising price of physician services." *The Review of Economics and Statistics* 52 (1970): 121–133.

Freidson, Eliot. *Profession of medicine. a study of the sociology of applied knowledge*. Chicago and London: The University of Chicago Press, 1988.

Hornung, Carlton and Michael Massagli. "Primary-care physicians' affective orientation toward their patients." *Journal of Health and Social Behavior* 20 (1979): 61–76.

Newhouse, Joseph. "A model of physician pricing." *Southern Economic Journal* 37 (1970): 174–183.

Pauly, Mark and Mark Satterthwaite. "The pricing of primary care physician's services: a test of the role of consumer information." *The Bell Journal of Economics* 12 (1981): 488–506.

Polanyi, Karl. "The Economy as Instituted Process." In *Trade and Market.* Edited by Karl Polanyi, Conrad Arensberg and Harry W. Pearsom. Glencoe IL.: Free Press, 1957.

Rhee, Sang-O. "Relative importance of physician's personal and situational characteristics for the quality of patient care." *Journal of Health and Social Behavior* 18 (1977): 10–15.

Richman, Joel and W.O. Goldthorp. "Becoming special: gynecological ideology, gift exchange and hospital structure." *Social Science and Medicine* 11 (1977): 256–276.

Samuelson, Paul. *Economics*. New York: McGraw-Hill, 2004.

Staudenmayer, Herman and Martin Lefkowitz. "Physician–patient psychosocial characteristics influencing medical decision –making." *Social Science and Medicine* 15E (1981): 77–81.

Silberston, Aubrey. "Surveys of applied economics: price behavior of firms." *The Economic Journal* 80 (1970): 511–582.

Simmel, Georg. *The Philosophy of Money*. London: Routledge and Kegan Paul, 1990.

Uzzi, Brian and Ryon Lancaster. "Embeddedness and the price formation in the corporate law market." *American Sociological Review* 69 (2004): 319–344.

Velthuis, Olav. *Talking Prices: Symbolic Meanings of Prices on the Market for Contemporary Art*. Princeton: Princeton University Press, 2005.

Weber, Max. *Economy and Society*. Berkeley: University of California Press, 1978.

Zelizer, Viviana. "Human values and the market: the case of life insurance and death in 19th – century America." *The American Journal of Sociology* 84 (1978): 591–610.

CHAPTER SEVENTEEN

HOUSING IN TRANSITIONAL COUNTRIES: THE EMERGENCE OF LOW-COST HOMEOWNERSHIP AND ITS CONSEQUENCES

KATARZYNA KRÓLIKOWSKA[1]

Introduction

The fall of socialism in 1989–1990 led to the end of the Central Eastern European communist economies and to the emergence of transition economies where rapid economic institutional changes took place, one of such changes being the transition to private property. Sykora argues that "post-socialist transition does not proceed in a vacuum, involving the replacement of one reality with another. It is a highly complex process that reformulates existing and creates new structures" (Sykora 2007, 129). According to most common post-socialist theories (Musil 1993), transition can be described as a process that brings about changes of institutions, economics and political systems from the socialist stage to the democratic. Following this approach, everyday life, attitudes and behavior should be regarded as a consequence of institutional transitional reforms (Blazek 2008, 14).

This chapter discusses homeownership as an economic institution and its social perception within transitional societies. The ownership of a property, as the key phenomena, should be regarded not only in relation to its strict economic function, but in its broader social connotations (Barteczek 2000, 35). The main thesis of this chapter is that the current ongoing changes of ownership relations in various post-socialist transition countries led to an identical outcome—emergence of widespread low-cost homeownership and to the creation and preservation of specific attitudes to that ownership.

---

[1] Katarzyna Królikowska is a stipendee of the Foundation for Polish Science and a member of the institute for Civil Law at Warsaw University.

The scope of the analysis is international and includes changes in the housing market of the Central Eastern European countries during the time of transition.

Housing in Transition

The system of property rights is a crucial element influencing housing policy. Housing policy has been traditionally divided into three fields: (1) ensuring access to new housing construction; (2) resolving problems of exchange of existing stock; (3) social policy based on redistribution of housing units for vulnerable groups through the state. In socialist Central Eastern Europe, housing policy has been carried out within the framework of an economic command system and the communist state. The housing model was based on the limitation of property rights, extensive central planning and politically determined administrative allocation of subsidies. The socialist system of production and redistribution of dwellings by the state resulted in the field of housing policy in a massively planned and subsidized production of public housing. States also supported the creation of new housing cooperatives.

In centrally planned economies, the system of property rights was subject to tight state control. Under communist regimes in Central Eastern Europe, there were three basic types of housing:

- Units owned directly by the state or by state-owned enterprises
- Units owned by housing cooperatives
- Private housing, primarily single-family dwellings in rural areas

With the exception of family houses, the entire privately owned housing stock was usually nationalized. In some countries, such as Albania under the repressive communist regime of Enver Hoxha, the economic system was completely socialized. The 1976 Constitution of Albania imposed a complete ban on private property, including even private plots in rural areas.

The fall of socialism in 1989–1990 led to the end of the Central Eastern European housing model. Abandoning the communist system, many Eastern European countries transformed their public housing systems into market based systems. One of the major policy changes in the early 1990s was the swift implementation of housing reforms. Introduction of a market economy totally dismantled the previous system of housing production, financing and allocation. States in transition had to reinvent their whole housing policy. However, transition from a centralized system to one based on market competition and private ownership has been difficult.

The first step was the reduction and decentralization of public finance. Financial resources, which previously ensured availability of funds for the state owned construction companies or housing cooperatives (enabling them to undertake housing construction) were lifted and abolished by new laws. The immediate effect was that the number of new housing construction decreased.

The transitional period was characterized by decentralization of power from a central to local (regional) level of public administration. Decentralization of public finance led to the creation of new landlords: local governments. The decentralization in housing policy started in the early 1990s with a massive transfer of dwellings from state to municipal ownership. It was expected that the local authorities would become the major administrators of housing policy and, therefore, were given responsibility to act in the field.

However, the transfer of public properties was not accompanied by sufficient financial means. It has emerged that housing became a heavy financial burden for the municipal budgets regarding management and maintenance costs. Local governments were not able to generate resources without support from central governments and, in the majority of cases, seemed to be incapable of introducing efficient management of the communal housing stock they owned.[2]

On the other hand, the state has not assumed any responsibility for provision of housing. The abolition of the previous system of housing production and financing, and the shift in the government's role from direct provision of housing to policy director and regulator of housing activity implemented by others, meant that the state effectively relieved itself of its previous obligation to provide housing care and housing units for all. New housing policy, adopted by central governments, secures housing environment and supports the individual efforts of citizens. The role of governments is, therefore, only to provide assistance to satisfy the housing needs of citizens and their families, without making any legal

---

[2] As far as the management of public resources is concerned, good results have been recently reported in Poland in the area of institutional framework of cooperation between the public and private sectors. See Palinska. U, "Mieszkalnictwo jako obszar wspolpracy sektora publicznego i prywatnego na przykladzie miasta Wloclawek" ["Housing as an area of cooperation between the public and private sectors on the example of Wloclawek"], In *Uwarunkowania funkcjonowania sektora publicznego* [*Conditions for functioning of the public sector*], Ed. Olinski M., Olsztyn, 2006

obligations.[3] It must be stressed that the new role of the central government was misunderstood during the transitional period and after the fall of socialism people still allocated their expectations of common benefits and social protection towards the state (an attitude called "post-communist syndrome").

Since the first years of transition, Central Eastern European countries had also to solve the problem of restitution of property expropriated by the communist regimes after the Second World War. In some countries property has been returned to its previous owners or to their descendants in the first period of transition. For example, in Slovenia the Denationalization Act introduced in 1991 allowed for restitution of 13,000 dwellings to their rightful owners. In the Czech Republic, most of the transfers were accomplished by the end of 1993. It is estimated that 7% of dwelling stock was restituted to previous owners, mainly blocks of flats in the centers of the towns. In central Prague 70–75% of all houses were returned.[4] In other countries the restitution process started in the late 1990s and continues to the present day. Because there is no exact statistical data available as to the real size of stock already regained by previous owners, restitution problems will not be discussed in this chapter.

Mass Privatization of Public-Rented Housing Stock and Housing Units Owned by Housing Cooperatives

Since the early 1990s, sale of public rented dwellings and cooperative flats to individual households has become a significant phenomenon in Central Eastern European housing policies. The massive privatization of public housing stock was used as the main instrument of transformation resulting in an enormous increase of homeownership in Central and Eastern Europe. Mass privatization was carried out mostly through transfer to current tenants who obtained the right to purchase housing at substantial discounts or were given them for free. The most important aim of privatization of public housing was the willingness of the local governments and state enterprises to get rid of the large social housing stock that burdened their budgets with inherited debt and current maintenance costs. It was also said that private homeownership would lead to better management and efficiency of panel-block housing. It must be stressed

---

[3] More housing care is expected in the field of social housing.

[4] The process was the most important incentive for the development of market-based real estate market because re-privatized houses were immediately marketed (Sýkora and Šimoníčková 1994).

that privatization of the public dwellings was widely applauded by the societies, especially by the current tenants who had been directly offered the opportunity to purchase the ownership. In the social perception it was a just solution to redistribute in that way the wealth accumulated in housing units. This “public property” was financed and maintained by citizens during the socialist period through their monthly payments.

The selling was executed by the landlords (municipalities, state enterprises) and in the majority of cases the landlord was obliged to sell the dwelling primarily to the sitting tenant if he or she or family members expressed a willingness to purchase the property. Housing privatization strategies differed as far as the selling price was concerned: from voucher privatization in Bosnia and Herzegovina and privatization free of charge in Albania, to the low-price privatization in most countries. In this kind of transaction, the buyer was entitled to a large discount on the total value of the dwelling and additional discount equivalents to personal investments in the housing unit (improvements) and to payments that tenants were obliged to pay during the period of tenancy contributing to social housing funds. Taking into account all discounts, the average selling price was typically between 5–15% of the average real market value of the housing unit.

The extent and process of sales has varied considerably between countries (table 17.1 below). Privatization progressed rapidly in South Eastern Europe (Albania, Bulgaria, Romania). According to research findings (Tsenkova 2005), out of 3.5 million public housing units in South East Europe, 2.8 million were privatized to sitting tenants, most of them in multi-apartment housing (fig. 17.1 below).

Table 17.1. Evolution of the tenure structure, 1991–2005.

	Czech Republic	Hungary	Estonia
Ownership (including right of co-operative occupancy in co-operatives of home owners)	+ 24%	+ 24 %	+ 146 %
Private rental tenure	---	- 49 %	Not relevant
Public/social rental tenure	- 50%	- 81 %	- 95 %

Sources: CECODHAS-USH-Dexia Survey (2007), Eurostat (2007).

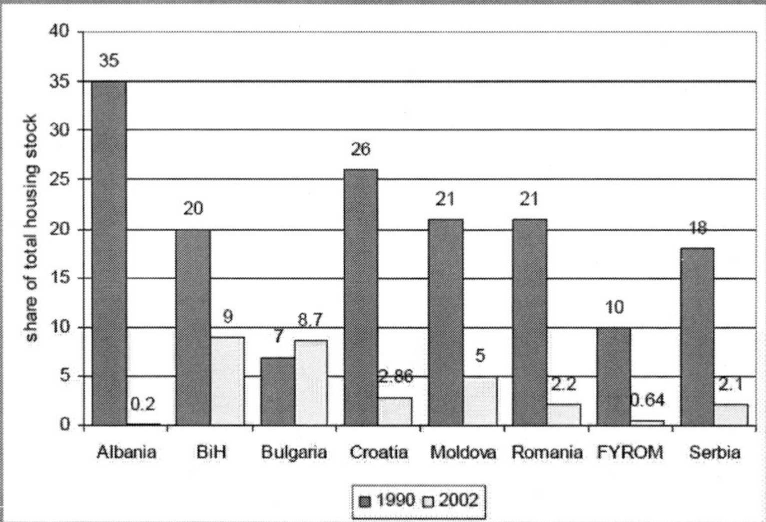

Fig. 17.1
The privatization of public housing in South East Europe, 1990 to 2002.
Source: S. Tsenkova, *Trends and Challenges in Housing Reforms in South East Europe*, (Paris: Council of Europe Development Bank 2005).

The privatization process in Central Eastern Europe has differed from other transition countries. In Poland and the Czech Republic (a limited version was also introduced in Slovakia) municipalities and state enterprises have not automatically passed the "right to buy" for tenants (unlike Hungary or Bulgaria). In the Czech Republic, tenants did not acquire an unlimited purchase right. The decision on whether or not to sell the dwelling stock was entirely left to the consideration of the municipalities. In addition, the determination and calculation of prices for offered flats was not set forth. Many municipal rental dwellings were not subject to privatization, which often appeared to be cumbersome and chaotic. The acceleration of housing privatization was observed after 2000 when privatization (popular among the tenants) was used as an argument in local elections. Nevertheless, rental housing formed a substantial part of the Czech Republic stock in 2005.

Furthermore, in Poland the ownership of the building usually remained with the original institutions rather than being passed over to the tenants living in the structure. Significant transfers were accelerated after 2000. From 1988 to 2002, the amount of public stock in Poland declined from

1.3 million to 250,000 dwellings (Cesarski 2007, 206). Privatization after 2005 leads to many political and legal problems. The Constitutional Tribunal of Poland has dealt with several fundamental cases regarding the process of transferring public housing stock still remaining in the ownership of large state enterprises and some public agencies (i.e. the Polish Railway Company, the Army, the Polish Forests). Legal provisions introduced after 2000 forcing municipalities to take over—without consent or compensation—the ownership and management of public stock, unsold and not transferred to tenants who refuse to purchase the offered dwellings even at great discount prices, were found unconstitutional in the late period of transition.

Changes in the Housing Tenure Structure

The above mentioned processes, especially the sale of public housing, considerably changed the housing tenure structure. The immediate effect was the sharp increase in the level of homeownership, enlarging the sector of owner occupied housing as well as the sector of cooperative housing.

Data for 2001–2003 presented in Fig. 17.2 below shows high levels of homeownership in Central Eastern European countries in comparison to Western Europe. The data presented proves the sharp increase in homeownership in all Central Eastern European countries. Privatization of public housing and purchasing ownership through the marketplace accelerated the expansion of home ownership, creating "nations of homeowners"[5] that register levels of homeownership higher than 80 percent. On the other hand, large scale privatization of public housing also resulted in the almost complete eradication of public housing. As public housing is often the only affordable housing available on the housing market, efforts by central or local governments to sell almost all the public housing stock has had considerable consequences for needy households. Rented housing is in a majority in Germany (57% of the total stock) and in Sweden (55% of the total stock). In Denmark, France, Holland and Austria it represents over 40%.

---

[5] Mandič and Clapham "The meaning of Home Ownership in the Transition from Socialism: The Example of Slovenia," *Urban Studies* vol. 33 (1996): 83; In Slovenia at the end of the privatization process, about 77,000 dwellings remained as public housing stock leading to a ratio of 89% private housing to 11 % public stock. Before privatization, the ratio of private to public stock had been 67 % to 33 % respectively. This means that 22 % of the present homeowners acquired ownership through the privatization process.

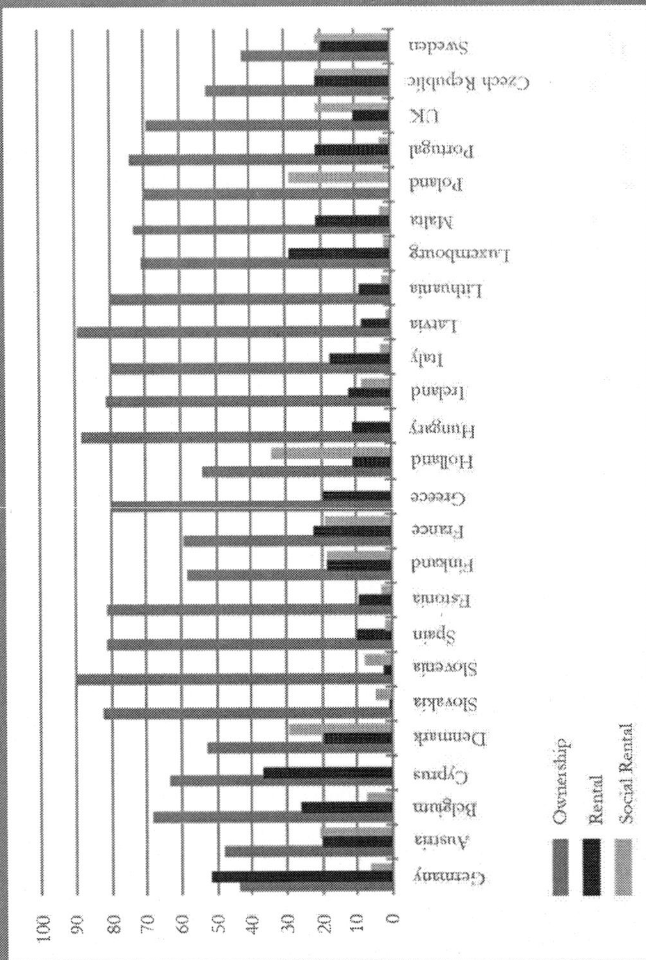

Fig. 17.2
EU housing stock distribution according to system of tenure, 2001 to 2003.
Source: Regular National Report on Housing Developments in European Countries (2005).

The real scope of changes differs from country to country depending on the tenure structure in the starting point of the year 1990 (Table 17.2 below).

Although the socialist system of government did not favor private ownership, individual housing construction and private ownership have traditionally been more widespread in some transitional countries. Taking this approach we must recognize that the biggest increase in the level of homeownership during the time of transition was registered in Albania. In

Albania, owner occupied housing nowadays forms more than 95% percent of the housing stock. In the early 1990s Albania was the last of the Central and Eastern European countries to establish democratic institutions and to introduce market mechanisms (Drisscoll Chuvalaand and Shutina 2007). Private property had more significance for people in Albania than in other socialist countries because of its total abolition in the communist period (Hashi and Xhillari 1999). The problem is that almost 70% of all buildings in Albania were constructed between 1991–1999. More than 80% of the dwelling users declare themselves as owners of the property, but 30% dispose of ownership evidence.[6]

Table 17.2. Dwellings by the type of stock tenure in 2005

	Czech Republic	Hungary	Estonia	Poland
Homeownership (including right of co-operative occupancy in co-operatives of home owners)	66 %	94 %	84 %	75 %
private rental social rental other	13% 20 % 1 %	2 % 4 % -----	9 % 7 % ----	13 % 12 % ----

Sources: CECODHAS-USH-Dexia Survey (2007), Eurostat (2007), Statistical Yearbook of the Republic of Poland (2007)

The above mentioned presentation of data seems problematic for certain reasons. International comparisons of data on tenure structure include also other tenure categories: the owner occupation, the private rented sector and the public rented sector (sometimes called social housing or non-profit housing[7]). It is also important to recognize that "homeownership" does not

---

[6] INSTAT 2002. Data cited by Mele, M., "The role of property in livelihood strategies of recent migrants to suburban areas of Tirana city-region, Albania," in *"New" Europe and Challenges of Sustainable Development*, Collection of Papers from the 2nd Forum of Social Sciences PhD Students, International Seminar, Bratislava, June 5-8, 2008.

[7] There is no one definition or common understanding of the term "social housing." For example, in some countries social housing usually refers to rental housing, while in others owner occupied housing also falls into the category of social housing.

always mean (is not equated with) owner occupation. Therefore, dwellings presented as homeownership may include a certain percentage used for private rental purposes and the exact scope of this housing sector may not be officially identified correctly. Research has shown that the private rental sector is playing an increasingly bigger role in housing provision, especially in the urban centers.[8]

A second remark must be made regarding cooperative rights. During communist regimes, cooperative ownership was viewed ideologically as superior towards individual property. In the market based economy cooperative property constitutes the private sector (along with private individuals and enterprises).[9] Usually, members of cooperatives using cooperative flats could acquire and sell the right to their flats (in fact their share in housing cooperative) for a market price. Housing cooperative members are not considered to be full homeowners by legislative framework. Cooperative housing formally remained a part of the rental sector. Nevertheless, for statistical purposes cooperative housing became a part of the homeownership sector (see fig. 17.1 above). The position of occupancy right in housing cooperatives emphasizes the disparity between ideology and practice and proves that the absence of private ownership in some economic fields did not signify the absence of ownership relations (Hann 2005). Since the early 1990s some countries increased the proprietary rights of cooperative members by introducing the possibility to purchase or even the free transfer of a cooperative flat to the full ownership in a cooperative building. When some dwellings in a cooperative building are transferred to the exclusive ownership of members, the homeowners association in cooperative building may be established.

---

[8] Sendi R., "Managing privatised housing: the case of Slovenia" (paper presented at the ENHR conference Housing in an expanding Europe: theory, policy, participation and implementation, Lubljana, Slovenia July 2–5, 2006, available at www.uirs.si); the Author stresses that it is commonly acknowledged that the private rented sector was tolerated during socialist regimes. The private rented sector was officially considered to be unnecessary in socialist economy but since the state could not provide cheap housing "for all" private rents allowed to operate for those who could not satisfy their housing needs otherwise.

[9] The public sector includes state and local governments and governmental bodies or non-profit private organizations providing low cost housing whose functions have public aspects.

Managerial Problems

The large privatization of the public stock constitutes serious management problems. First of all, the massive housing estates built in the communist time are of relatively poor quality. The results of socialist housing policies influence even now the situation on the housing markets: the stock of units is inconsistent with household preferences and needs, units are severely neglected and under maintained, and there is severe shortage of affordable units (Furman 2006). The rapidly aging housing stock constitutes a great burden for private households. Probably the most worrying consequence of widespread privatization in Central Eastern European countries is the growing inability of the new homeowners to meet the financial demands that ownership entails. There are limited financial resources for maintenance and renewal among private owners (Gruis Tsenkova and Nieboer 2006). Some households that purchased public housing stock at extremely low prices have great difficulties in paying not only the running costs, but also the management, maintenance and refurbishment costs.

Moreover, the research findings show that the new homeowners are not completely aware of the responsibilities and obligations that come with homeownership, concentrating only on acquired rights linked with the tenure. The situation was partly improved thanks to the introduction of housing management reforms. Legal reforms introduced in the mid 1990s have provided the legal framework for the organization of owners. The new laws have defined detailed rights and responsibilities of owners, as well as the procedures of sharing common costs. The Central and Eastern European countries have chosen different strategies to regulate the management of private and privatised housing (Lux 2003). In the 1990s, most countries in the region have introduced condominium ownership with the organization of homeowners typically defined as Homeowners' Associations as the institutional entities which manage multi apartment housing and help the owners to meet their financial obligations. From the legal point of view, Homeowners' Associations can be legal entities that enable the owners to initiate contracts with third parties or not registered as legal entities (behind every contract there are individual owners). They may be mandatory or the owners may only be given the possibility to create an association.

The functioning of Homeowners' Associations show that many homeowners are encountering great difficulties in getting to terms with the obligations and burdens that property ownership entails, the majority of newly privatized homeowners being individuals with no previous knowledge about the functioning of private property ownership. A lack of understanding on the part of homeowners of their obligations is expressed by their non-payment of maintenance and management costs, unwillingness to pay additional costs that are necessary for major repairs and insurance of the building and a lack of interest to execute their rights in the procedure prescribed by law, i.e. to attend meetings and discuss matters concerning maintenance and renewal.

One of the reasons for the lack of understanding of obligations is the privatization process itself as it was often executed too hurriedly and without due consideration of further potential implications such as conflicts concerning the relationships between the homeowners and the housing managers. Many problems of the ownership of the land within housing estates, especially in big cities, remain unsolved. The number of conflicts goes up as a consequence of privatization that resulted in many buildings having mixed ownership. Since not all tenants may decide to buy the flat and may continue to live in public rental structure as tenants together with individual homeowners, mixed ownership became common in many cities raising questions about the division of responsibilities and obligations between the private and public owners.

Social Effects of Increases of Homeownership

High levels of homeownership in transitional countries indicate a relatively large equity held in current housing wealth, but the social perception of homeownership constitutes new problems. Home represents the most important space for material culture research (Miller 2001, 239). In economic anthropology, the analysis of ownership relations contains not only the housing unit as material object but also other socially significant property relations of the subject. The ownership of a property presents not only a significant economic, but mainly emotional problem for many individuals (Hann 2005, 552).

The housing unit plays an important role in understanding sociological and social relations within the society. The organization of property relations in society can be classified through various layers: (1) Cultural tradition and norms in society; (2) Legal-institutional; (3) Social relations; (4) Practices of concrete agents (Benda-Beckmann and Benda-Beckmann 1999). Those layers do not have to be in line with each other. The clash between the cultural-normative and the legal-institutional level in ownership relations was observed during the communist regimes in housing cooperatives where the right of occupancy in the cooperative building was valued as a kind of ownership.

Material goods are usually valued by their ability to heighten the social prestige of their owners (Douglas and Isherwood 1996). The research findings for Central Eastern Europe revealed important weaknesses on the part of homeowners concerning their level of awareness of the value of their property. The great discount prices they paid for the ownership of their dwellings do not help them to appreciate the real value of the property they own. The dwellings were practically donated to them and that fact influences the attitude of homeowners towards their property: they put very little value on the maintenance of acquired dwellings. Most of the owners do not worry about the depreciation of the value of property resulting from negligence and poor maintenance of the stock. They consider acquired housing units as simply providing them with a place to live. People do not consider and treat their dwelling as a marketable commodity that may be exchanged on the housing market and, in the majority of cases, do not make considerations about the realization of capital gains in the future (Kemeny 1981).

One of the reasons why people do not consider and do not treat their dwelling as a marketable commodity may be down to the fact that existing owned stock cannot be so simply exchanged for other housing equity on the housing market. Deregulation of the housing markets in transitional economies resulted in a shortage of housing supply since the early 1990s. The main consequences of more restrictive public housing financing, housing privatization and liberalization of construction and utility prices were that the scale of new housing construction as well as housing affordability decreased during the transitional period. New housing production, concentrated mainly in the private sector, has not returned to the pre-transitional levels in all Central Eastern European countries (Figure 5 below). Moreover, housing needs in transitional countries are generated not only from inadequate availability of new construction, but also from physical degradation of existing stock and worsening affordability of social housing. The poor condition of the existing stock means high costs for its renovation, maintenance and demolition. 60% of the stock in Poland is in need of significant repair and 10% requires major renovation (Deniszczuk 2005).

As Cirman argues, a lack of available rental alternatives makes homeownership a preferential tenure *per se* (Cirman 2006). But increasing management costs and obligations related with homeownership may be more critical than ownership *per se*. People may reject increased managerial power over the property and free access to information (indicated by Hann 2005) and this fact should be reflected in research focusing on property relations. Some research findings for Eastern Europe

Table 17.3. Availability of housing in CEE countries

	Dwellings per 1000 inhabitants			
	1990	1995	1998	2002
Bulgaria	377	408	418	471
Croatia	---	336.4	355 (1997)	417.3 (2001)
Czech Republic	---	---	365	427 (2001)
Estonia	411	418	430	457.3
Hungary	372	390	401	406.7 (2000)
Latvia	358	381	391	411
Lithuania	310	336	353	374
Poland	289	298	302	307.7
Republic of Moldova	---	339	346	357.2
Romania	345	343	349	373
Slovakia	---	310	312	320.6
Slovenia	---	343.6	349.4 (1997)	393.2

Source: Eurostat 2003, Bulletin of Housing Statistics for Europe and North America 2000, United Nations Economic Commission for Europe, Bulletin of Housing Statistics for Europe and North America 2006, United Nations Economic Commission for Europe.

show that a great share of low income households would rather stay on as tenants or move to cheaper rental housing elsewhere than purchase ownership, even at a large discount.[10] According to Polish public reports on household budgets, in 2003 the expenditures on housing amounted (on average) for 21% of all consumer expenditure.[11] For many households it is

---

[10] Sendi R. "Housing Reform and Housing Conflict: The Privatisation and Denationalisation of Public Housing in the Republic of Slovenia in Practice," *International Journal of Urban and Regional Research*, vol. 19 (1995): 435–446. The previous sitting tenants opted to "sell off" (unlawfully of course) their right to buy to another person who then purchased the dwelling either for rental purposes or for the immediate or future use of their children.

[11] *Budżety gospodarstw domowych w 2003 r.* [*Polish households budgets in 2003*], Warszawa: GUS 2004, 32–56.

very hard to sustain their housing status even with that level of housing expenditure, which is rather low in comparison to Western Europe. Therefore it is understood that households are reluctant to upgrade their housing conditions and are unwilling to pay significantly more not only for new construction but also for purchasing of currently occupied dwellings (Kaltemberg-Kwiatkowska 2005, 56). The last reason for perception of ownership in transitional societies is in the comparison of acquired homeownership with the status of tenants having quasi-ownership tenure in rental housing.[12] Tenants and their families in most Central Eastern European countries enjoyed, until recently, extraordinary tenant protection, and were regarded as *de facto* homeowners due to unreformed tenant protection laws. Additionaly, they were granted a reduced rent due to state control in the public and private housing sector, often below costs.

Conclusions

The fall of socialism in 1989–1990 led to the end of the Central Eastern European housing model. Introduction of a market economy totally dismantled the previous system of housing production, financing and allocation. However, transition from a centralized system to one based on market competition and private ownership has been difficult. The massive privatization of public housing stock was used as the main instrument of transformation resulting in an enormous increase of homeownership in Central and Eastern Europe. The expansion of homeownership created "nations of homeowners" that register levels of homeownership in the tenure structure higher than 80 percent.

Mass privatization was carried out mostly through transfer to current tenants who obtained the right to purchase their dwellings at substantial discounts, or were given their dwellings for free. It was said that private homeownership would lead to better management of public stock. However, large privatization of the public stock raises serious management problems. Limited financial resources for maintenance and renewal of rapidly aging housing stock constitute a great burden for private households. Moreover, the research findings show that new homeowners are not completely aware of the responsibilities and obligations that come with homeownership. Their lack of awareness is expressed, above all, in their non-payment of maintenance and management costs.

[12] Once they occupied a flat, it was almost certainly theirs for life and it could be passed on to relatives.

Institutional and social changes in the transition period led to the emergence of cheap low cost homeownership, not only in economic terms. Research findings show that cheap ownership also influences social perception. The great discount prices paid for the ownership of the dwellings do not help occupants to appreciate the real value of the property. Therefore, people do not consider their dwelling as a marketable commodity and relative high levels of homeownership do not constitute real economic wealth. Moreover, the transition economies register low levels of new housing construction which influences the existing shortage of avoidable housing units on the market. This situation may, in the future, result in worsening of the living standards in the transitional economies due to the inability of new owners to fulfill their obligations and undertake the necessary stock improvements.

References

Angel, Shlomo. *Housing policy matters: A global analysis*. Oxford and New York, Oxford University Press, 2000.

Barteczek, Andrzej. "Infrastruktura społeczna" [Social infrastructure]. In *Polityka społeczna w okresie transformacji* [*Social Policy in the time of transition*]. Edited by Aldona Frąckiewicz-Wronka and Maria Zralek. Katowice: Akademia Ekonomiczna, 2000.

Blazek, Matej. "A cultural landscape of Petržalka: towards the place of simultaneous histories in a panel-block housing estate." In *"New" Europe and Challenges of Sustainable Development*. Collection of Papers from the 2nd Forum of Social Sciences PhD Students, International Seminar, Bratislava, June 5–8, 2008.

Benda-Beckmann, von Franz and Keebet von Benda-Beckmann. "A functional analysis of property rights, with special reference to Indonesia." In *Property rights and economic development: land and natural resources in southeast Asia and Oceania*. Edited by Toon van Meijl and Franz von Benda-Beckmann. London: Kegan Paul International, 1999.

Boelhouwer Peter J., John Doling and Marja Elsinga. *Home ownership. Getting in, getting from getting out*. Delft: DUP Science, 2005.

Budżety gospodarstw domowych w 2003 r. [*Polish households budgets in 2003*]. Warszawa: GUS 2004.

Cesarski, Maciej. *Sytuacja mieszkaniowa w Polsce w latach 1988-2005—dziedzictwo i przemiany* [*Housing problems in Poland 1988-2005—heritage and changes*]. Warszawa: Oficyna Wydawnicza SGH, 2007.

Cirman, Andreja. "Housing tenure preferences in the post-privatisation period: The case of Slovenia." *Housing Studies 2006* 21 (1) (2006): 113–134.

Czasny, Karl. *The Importance of Housing Systems in Safeguarding Social Cohesion in Europe, Final Report*. Vienna: SOCOHO, 2004.

Deniszczuk, Lucyna. "Warunki mieszkaniowe gospodarstw domowych. Podstawowe zjawiska i problem" ["Housing Conditions of Polish Households. Common Problems and Phenomena"]. *Kontrola Państwowa* [*Public Audit*] 6 (2005): 120–134.

Douglas Mary and Baron Isherwood. *The World of Goods*. London, New York: Routledge, 1996.

Hashi, Iraj and Lindita Xhillari. "Privatization and transition in Albania." *Post Communist Economies* 11 (1999): 99–125.

Dübel, Hans, Jan W. Brzeski and Ellen Hamilton. *Rental Choice and Housing Policy Realignment in Transition: Post-privatization Challenges in the Europe and Central Asia Region*. World Bank Policy Research Working Paper 3884, Washington D.C., April 2006.

Frąckiewicz, Lucyna. *Przeszłość i przyszłość polskiej polityki mieszkaniowej* [*Past and Future of Polish Housing Policy*], Warszawa: IPiSS, 2005.

Furman, Stanislaw. "Poland in European Space: the Urban Perspective." *Regional and Local Studies* Special Issue (2006): 85–97.

Goodman J.L., Ittner J.B. "The Accuracy of Home Owners' Estimates of House Value." *Journal of Housing Economics* 2 (4) (1992): 339–57.

Gruis, Vincent, Sasha Tsenkova and Nico Nieboer. *Managing privatized housing: An international overview of developments and challenges*. Paper presented at the ENHR conference "Housing in an expanding Europe: theory, policy, participation and implementation." Ljubljana, Slovenia, July 2–5, 2006.

Hann, Chris. "Property." In *A Handbook of Economic Anthropology*. Edited by James Carrier. Cheltenham: Edvard Elgar Publishing Limited, 2005.

Harsman, Bjorn and John M. Quigley. *Housing markets and housing institutions: An international comparison*. Massachusetts: Kluwer Academic Publishers, 1991.

Hegedüs, Jozsef, Ivan Tosics and Stephen K. Mayo. "Transition of the Housing Sector in the East-Central European Countries." *Review of Urban and Regional Development Studies* 8 (1996): 101–136.

Kaltenberg-Kwiatkowska, Ewa. "Warunki mieszkaniowe w świadomości społecznej" ["Housing conditions in social perception"]. In *Przeszlość i przyszłość polskiej polityki mieszkaniowej* [*Past and future development of Polish housing policy*]. Edited by Lucyna Frąckiewicz. Warszawa: IPiSS, 2005.

Kemeny, John. *The myth of homeownership.* London: Routledge and Keegan Paul, 1981.

Lux, Martin. *Housing Policy: An End or a New Beginning,* Budapest: Local Government Initiative, Open Society Institute, 2003.

Malpass, Peter. *Ownership, control and accountability: The new governance of housing.* Coventry: The Chartered Institute of Housing, 1997.

Mandič, Srna and David Clapham. "The meaning of Home Ownership in the Transition from Socialism: The Example of Slovenia." *Urban Studies* 33 (1996): 83–97.

Mele, Marcela. "The role of property in livelihood strategies of recent migrants to suburban areas of Tirana city-region, Albania." In: *"New" Europe and Challenges of Sustainable Development*, Collection of Papers from the 2nd Forum of Social Sciences PhD Students, International Seminar, Bratislava, June 5-8, 2008.

Miller, Daniel. "Consumption." In *The Material Culture Reader.* Edited by Victor Buchli. London: Berg Publishers, 2002.

—. "Behind closed doors." In *Home Possessions: Material Culture Behind Closed Doors.* Edited by Daniel Miller. Oxford; New York: Berg, 2003.

Musil, Jiri. "The transition to democracy." In *The New Political Geography of Eastern Europe* Edited by John O'Loughlin and Herman van der Wusten. London: John Wiley and Sons, 1993.

Nordvik, Viggo. *Homeownership and Selective Means—A Cross-market approach.* Paper presented at the ENHR-seminar on Housing Economics, Copenhagen, Denmark, February 2006.

Palińska, Urszula. "Mieszkalnictwo jako obszar współpracy sektora publicznego i prywatnego na przykładzie miasta Włocławek" ["Housing as an area of cooperation between the public and private sectors on the example of Włocławek"]. In *Uwarunkowania funkcjonowania sektora publicznego* [*Conditions for functioning of the public sector*]. Edited by Marian Oliński. Olsztyn: Uniwersytet Warmińsko-Mazurski, 2006.

Renaud, Bertrand M. *Housing finance in transition economies*, The World Bank, Policy Research Working Paper, No. 1565. 1996.

Saunders, Peter. *A Nation of Home Owners.* London: Unwin Hyman Ltd., 1990.

Schweinichen, von Christina. *Challenges in the housing sector: Experiences from Western and Eastern countries.* Paper presented at the ENHR conference "Housing in an expanding Europe: theory, policy, participation and implementation" Ljubljana, Slovenia, July 2–5, 2006

Sendi, Richard. "Housing Reform and Housing Conflict: The Privatisation and Denationalisation of Public Housing in the Republic of Slovenia in Practice." *International Journal of Urban and Regional Research* 19 (1995): 435–446.

—. *Managing privatised housing: the case of Slovenia*. Paper presented at the ENHR conference "Housing in an expanding Europe: theory, policy, participation and implementation", Lubljana, Slovenia, July 2–5, 2006.

Sýkora, Luděk. "Between the State and the Market: Local Government and Housing in the Czech Republic." In *Housing Policy: an End or a New Beginning*. Edited by Martin Lux. Budapest: LGI-OSI, 2003.

—. "Office development and post-socialist city formation." In *The Post Socialist City. Urban form and Space transformations in Central and Eastern Europe after Socialism*. Edited by Kiril Stanilov. Dordrecht: Springer, 2007.

Sýkora Luděk and Ivana Šimoníčková. "From totalitarian urban managerialism to a liberalized real estate market: Prague transformation in the early 1990s." In *Development and Administration of Prague*. Edited by Max Barlow, Petr Dostál and Martin Hampl. Amsterdam: University of Amsterdam, 1994.

Thalmann, Philipe. *The Determinants of Perceived Housing Shortage*. Paper presented at the ENHR-seminar on Housing Economics, Copenhagen, Denmark, February 2006

Tsenkova, Sasha. *Housing in Transition and the Transition in Housing: The Experience of Central and Eastern Europe.* Sofia: Kapital Reklama, 2000.

—. *Trends and Challenges in Housing Reforms in South East Europe.* Paris: Council of Europe Development Bank, 2005.